GHOST HUNT

6

MANGA BY SHIHO INADA

STORY BY FUYUMI ONO

TRANSLATED BY EGAN LOO

ADAPTED BY DAVID WALSH

LETTERED BY FOLTZ DESIGN

BALLANTINE BOOKS · NEW YORK

A Del Rey Trade Paperback Original

Ghost Hunt copyright © 2001 by Shiho Inada and Fuyumi Ono
English translation copyright © 2006 by Shiho Inada and Fuyumi Ono

Published in the United States by Del Rey Books, an imprint of The Random House Publishing Group, a division of Random House, Inc., New York.

DEL REY is a registered trademark and the Del Rey colophon is a trademark of Random House, Inc.

Publication rights arranged through Kodansha Ltd.

First published in Japan in 2001 by Kodansha Ltd., Tokyo

ISBN: 978-0-345-49138-1

Printed in the United States of America

www.delreymanga.com

3 4 5 6 7 8 9

Translator—Egan Loo
Adaptor—David Walsh
Lettering—Foltz Design
Cover Design—David Stevenson

CONTENTS

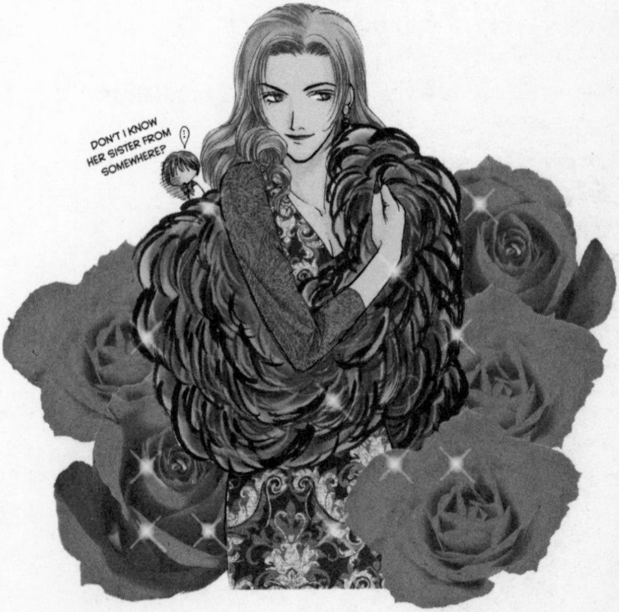
DON'T I KNOW HER SISTER FROM SOMEWHERE?

Honorifics Explained

Throughout the Del Rey Manga books, you will find Japanese honorifics left intact in the translations. For those not familiar with how the Japanese use honorifics, and, more important, how they differ from American honorifics, we present this brief overview.

Politeness has always been a critical facet of Japanese culture. Ever since the feudal era, when Japan was a highly stratified society, use of honorifics—which can be defined as polite speech that indicates relationship or status—has played an essential role in the Japanese language. When addressing someone in Japanese, an honorific usually takes the form of a suffix attached to one's name (example: "Asuna-san"), or as a title at the end of one's name, or in place of the name itself (example: "Negi-sensei" or simply "Sensei!").

Honorifics can be expressions of respect or endearment. In the context of manga and anime, honorifics give insight into the nature of the relationship between characters. Many translations into English leave out these important honorifics, and therefore distort the feel of the original Japanese. Because Japanese honorifics contain nuances that English honorifics lack, it is our policy at Del Rey not to translate them. Here, instead, is a guide to some of the honorifics you may encounter in Del Rey Manga.

-san: This is the most common honorific and is equivalent to Mr., Miss, Ms., Mrs. It is the all-purpose honorific and can be used in any situation where politeness is required.

-sama: This is one level higher than "-san" and is used to confer great respect.

-dono: This comes from the word "tono," which means "lord." It is even a higher level than "-sama" and confers utmost respect.

-kun: This suffix is used at the end of boys' names to express familiarity or endearment. It is also sometimes used by men amongst friends, or when addressing someone younger or of a lower station.

-chan: This is used to express endearment, mostly toward girls. It is also used for little boys, pets, and even among lovers. It gives a sense of childish cuteness.

Bozu: This is an informal way to refer to a boy, similar to the English terms "kid" or "squirt."

Sempai/ Senpai: This title suggests that the addressee is one's senior in a group or organization. It is most often used in a school setting, where underclassmen refer to their upperclassmen as "sempai." It can also be used in the workplace, such as when a newer employee addresses an employee who has seniority in the company.

Kohai: This is the opposite of "-sempai," and is used toward underclassmen in school or newcomers in the workplace. It connotes that the addressee is of a lower station.

Sensei: Literally meaning "one who has come before," this title is used for teachers, doctors, or masters of any profession or art.

-[blank]: This is usually forgotten in these lists, but it is perhaps the most significant difference between Japanese and English. The lack of honorific means that the speaker has permission to address the person in a very intimate way. Usually, only family, spouses, or very close friends have this kind of permission. Known as *yobisute*, it can be gratifying when someone who has earned the intimacy starts to call one by one's name without an honorific. But when that intimacy hasn't been earned, it can be very insulting.

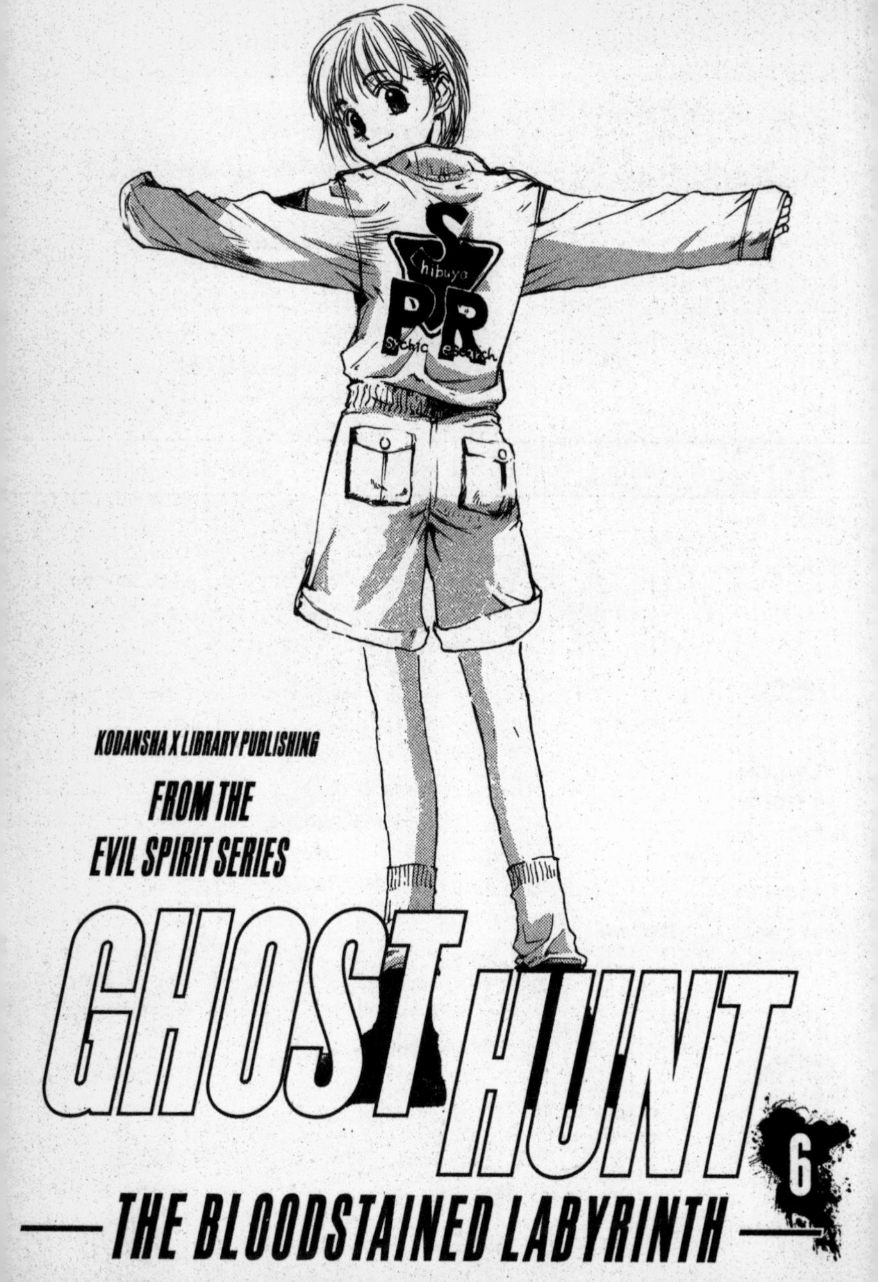
S
hibuya
P R
sychic esearch

KODANSHA X LIBRARY PUBLISHING

FROM THE
EVIL SPIRIT SERIES

GHOST HUNT 6

THE BLOODSTAINED LABYRINTH

GHOST HUNT

THIS IS WHAT SPR IS ALL ABOUT!

WHERE'S THE CASE NOW...?

SPR INVESTIGATED AND EXORCISED A POLTERGEIST PHENOMENON AT AN OLD MANSION, AND PREVIOUSLY SOLVED A SUPERNATURAL INCIDENT THAT CAUSED CHAOS AND PANIC AT A HIGH SCHOOL.

THE MEMBERS ARE...

WHEN SPR HAD INVESTIGATED MAI'S SCHOOL ON A PAST CASE, THESE MEMBERS JOINED FORCES TO EXORCISE IT.

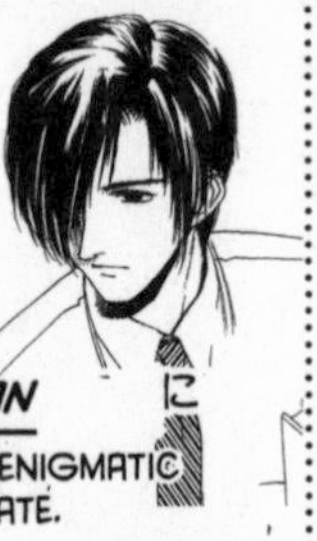

LIN-SAN

NARU'S ENIGMATIC ASSOCIATE.

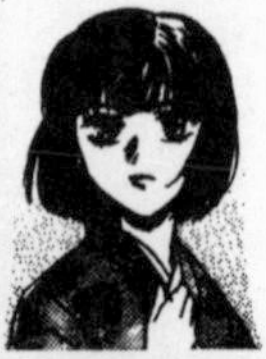

MASAKO HARA

A PSYCHIC MEDIUM. SHE IS WELL KNOWN IN THE PSYCHIC INDUSTRY.

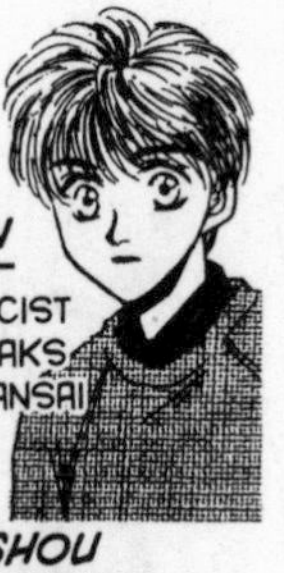

JOHN BROWN

AN EXORCIST WHO SPEAKS WITH A KANSAI DIALECT.

AYAKO MATSUZAKI

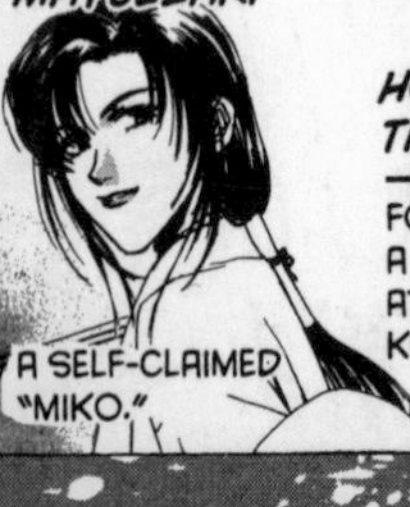

A SELF-CLAIMED "MIKO."

HOUSHOU TAKIGAWA

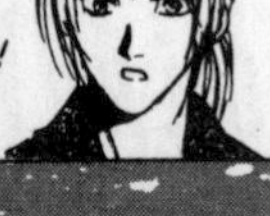

FORMERLY A MONK AT MT. KOUYA!

SHIBUYA PSYCHIC RESEARCH (SPR)

AVAILABLE FOR HIRE TO SCIENTIFICALLY RESEARCH AND SUBDUE UNEXPLAINABLE PHENOMENA

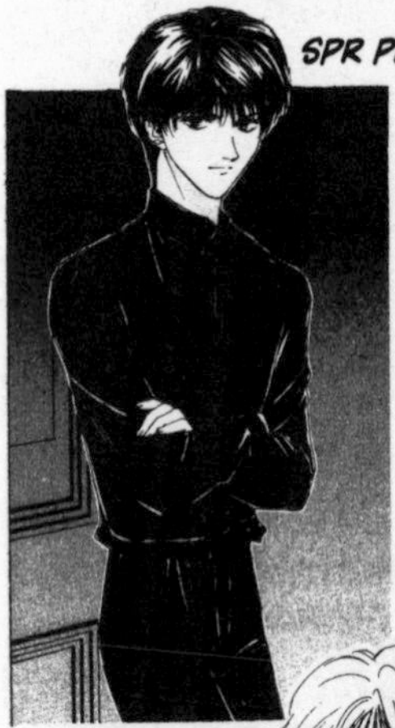

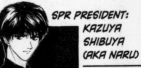

SPR PRESIDENT: KAZUYA SHIBUYA (AKA NARU)

17 YEARS OLD. HE'S COOL-HEADED, GOOD-LOOKING, AND SMART, BUT HE'S A SUPER NARCISSIST. SO HE HAS BEEN NICKNAMED NARU (SHORT FOR NARCISSIST).

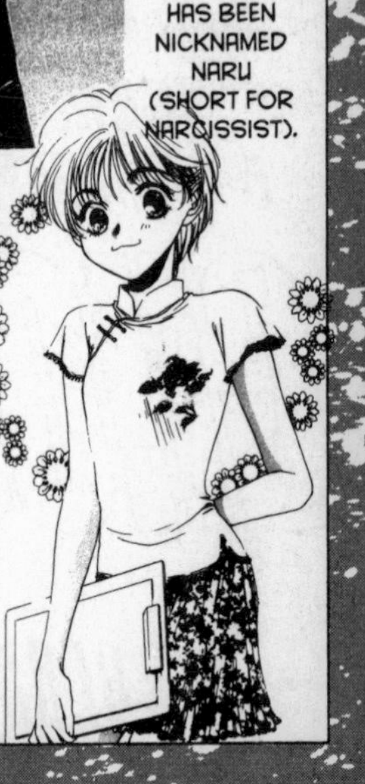

MAI TANIYAMA

A LIVELY 16-YEAR-OLD STUDENT WHO WORKS PART-TIME AT SPR. ENTHUSIASTIC, ALTHOUGH NARU ALWAYS GIVES HER A HARD TIME. (SHE'S ONLY SEEN NARU SMILE IN HER DREAMS!) BUT SHE MAY SECRETLY BE IN LOVE WITH HIM♡!

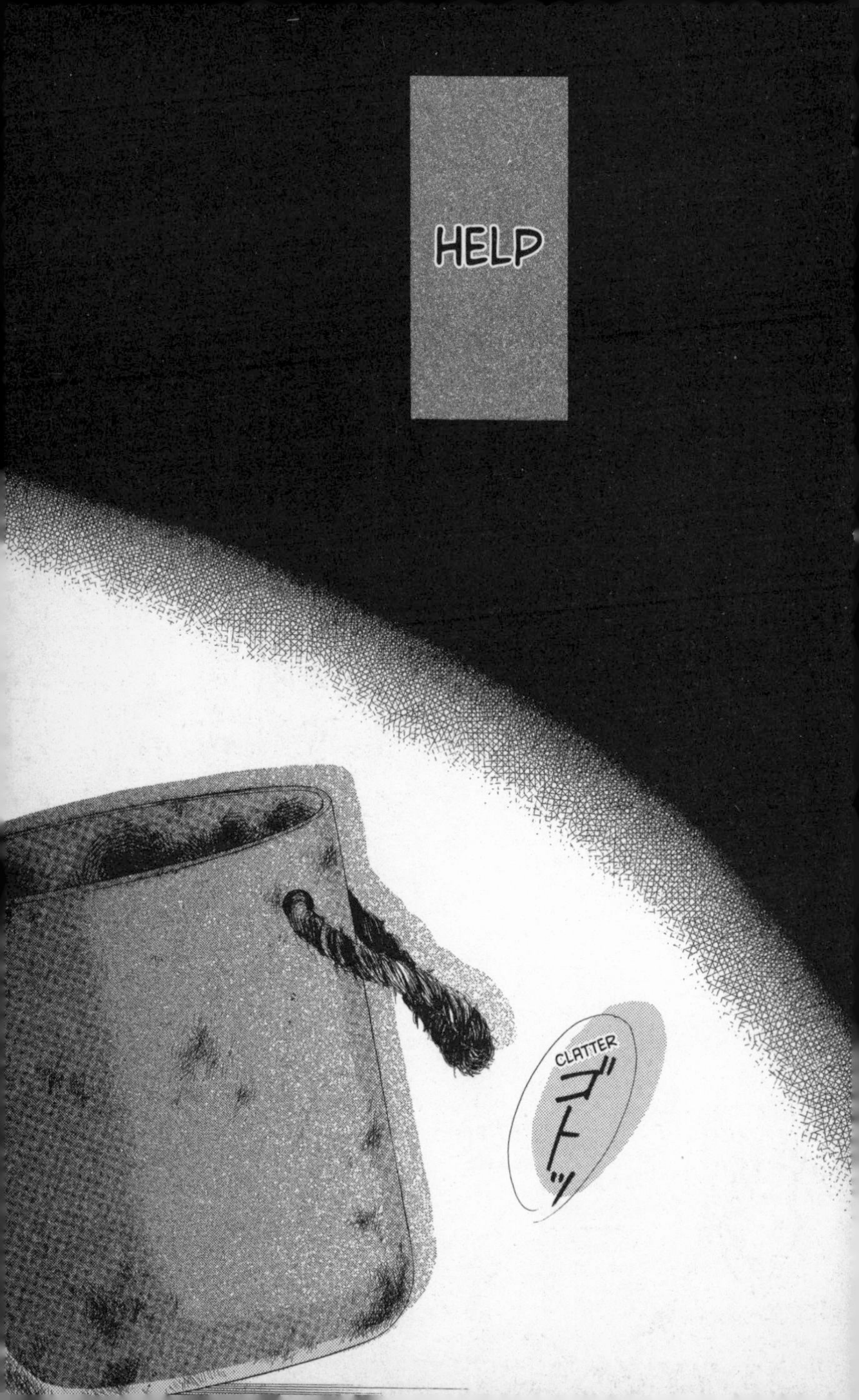
HELP
CLATTER
ゴトッ

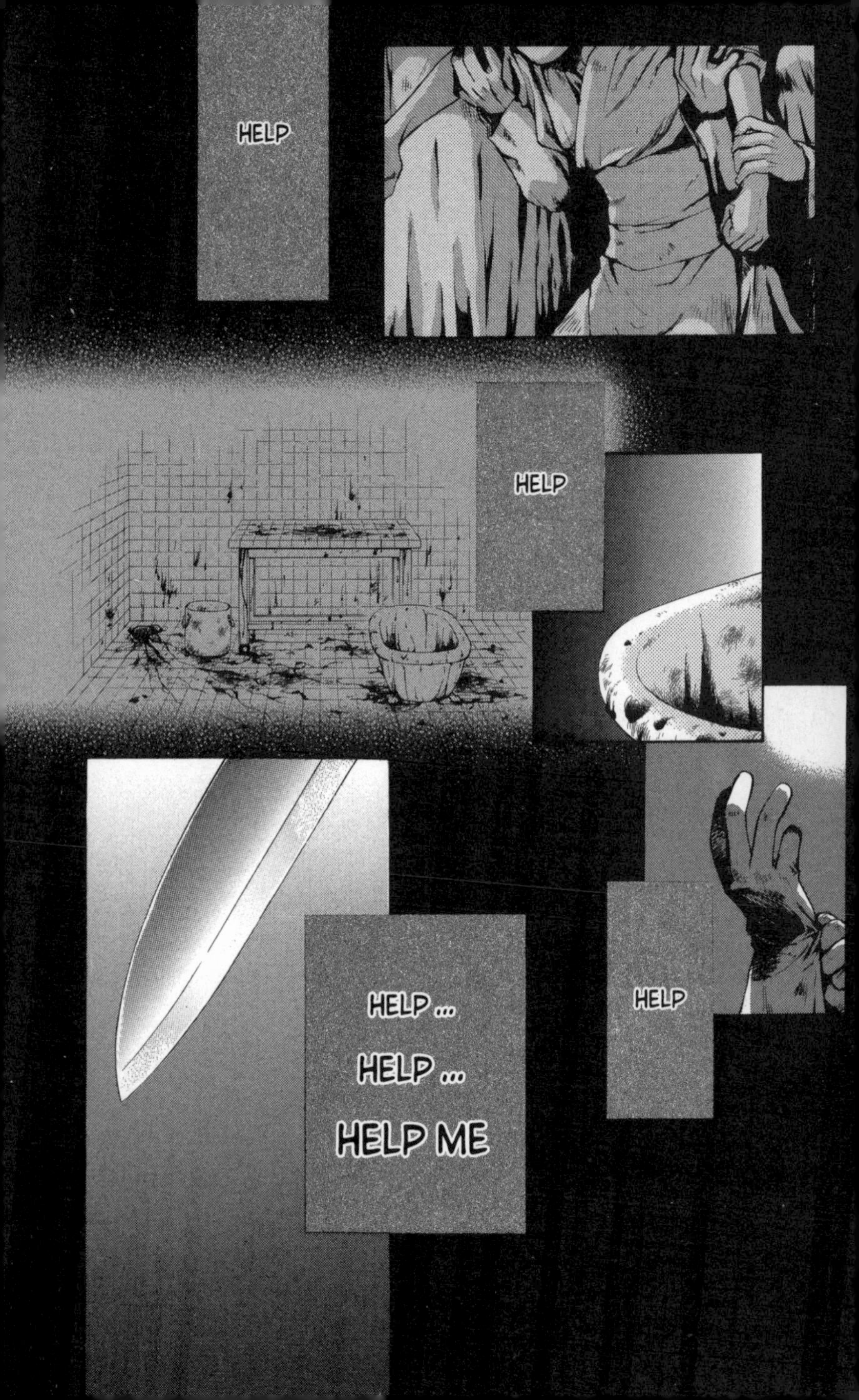
HELP
HELP
HELP
HELP ...
HELP ...
HELP ME

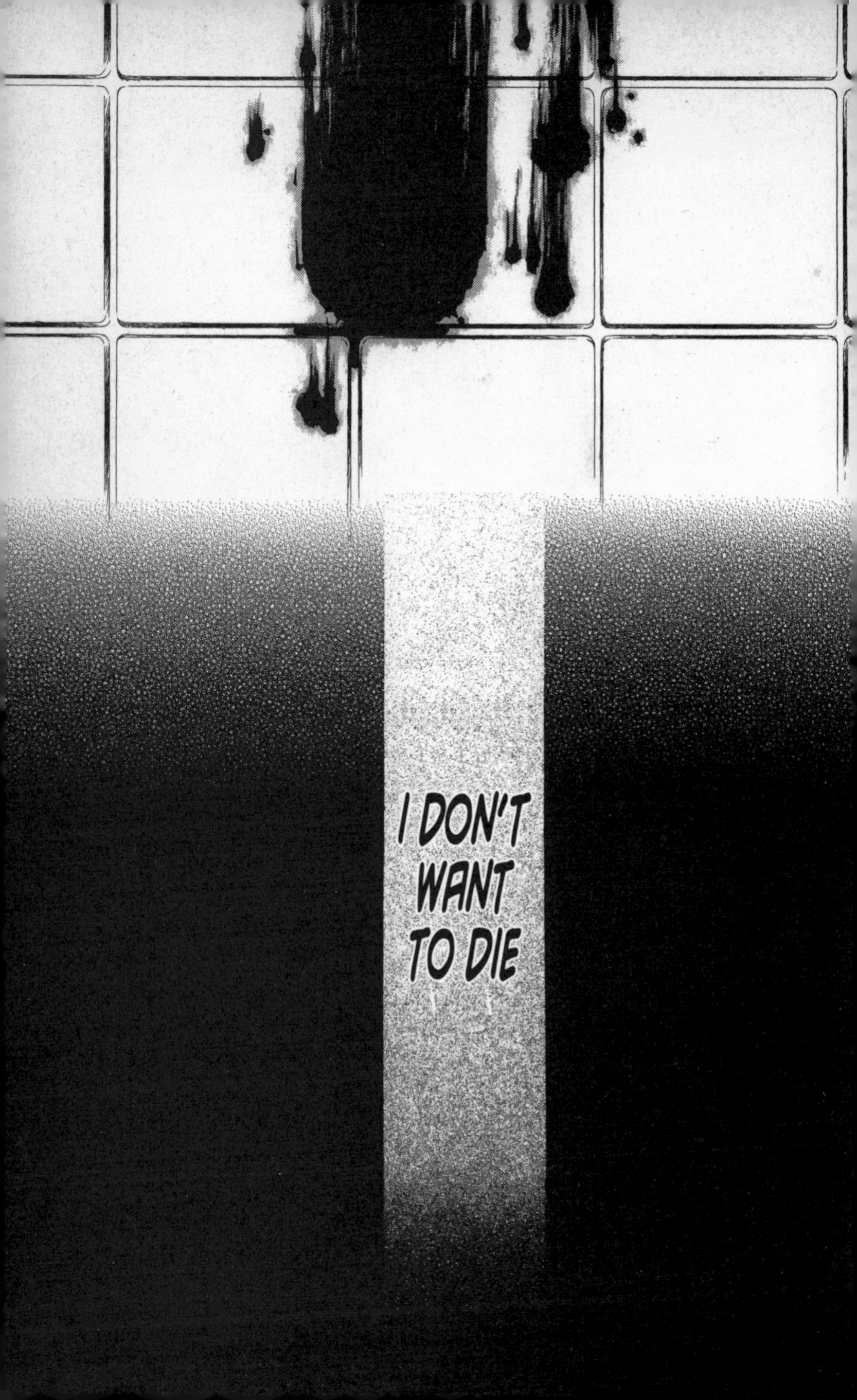
I DON'T WANT TO DIE

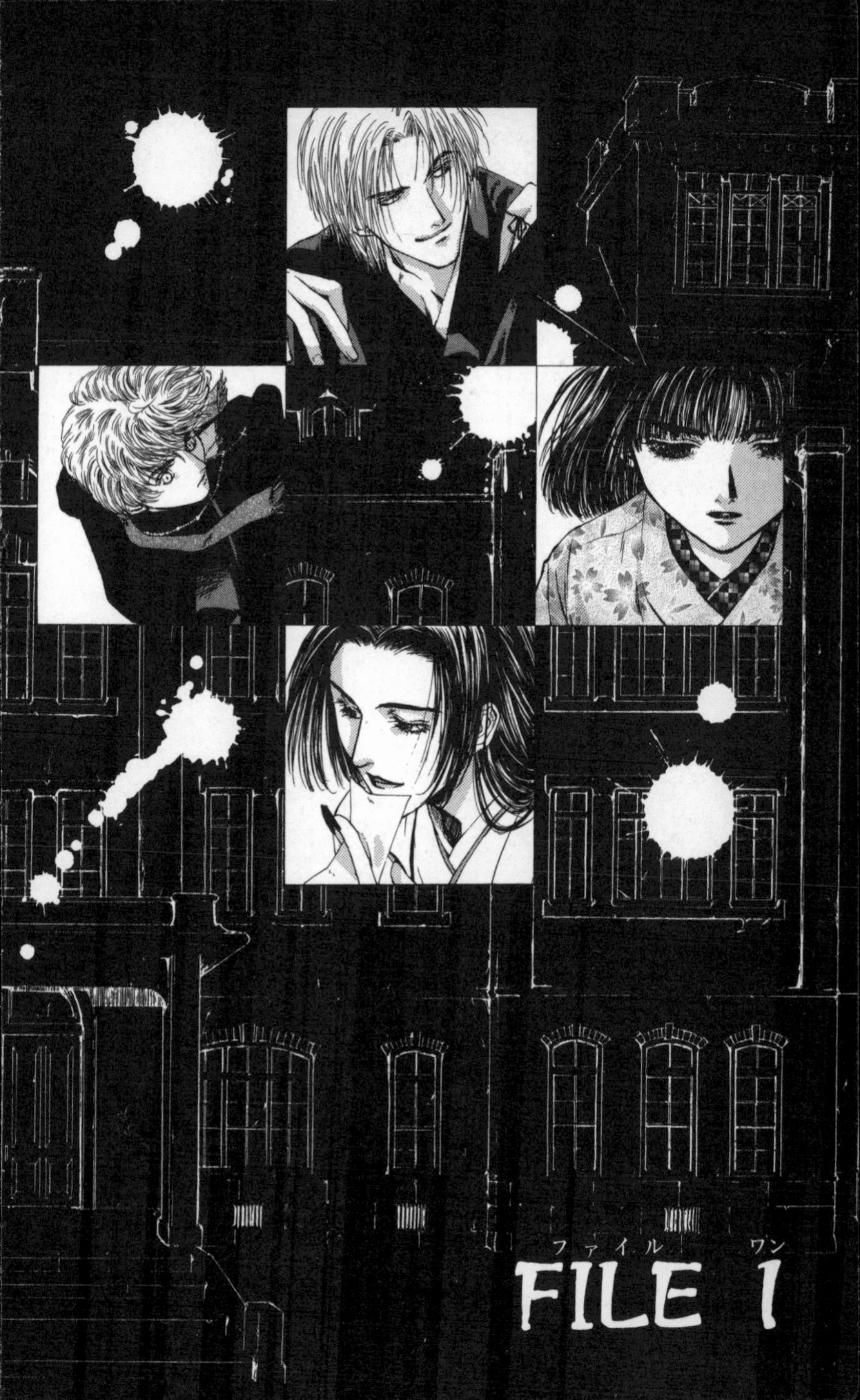
ファイル ワン
FILE 1

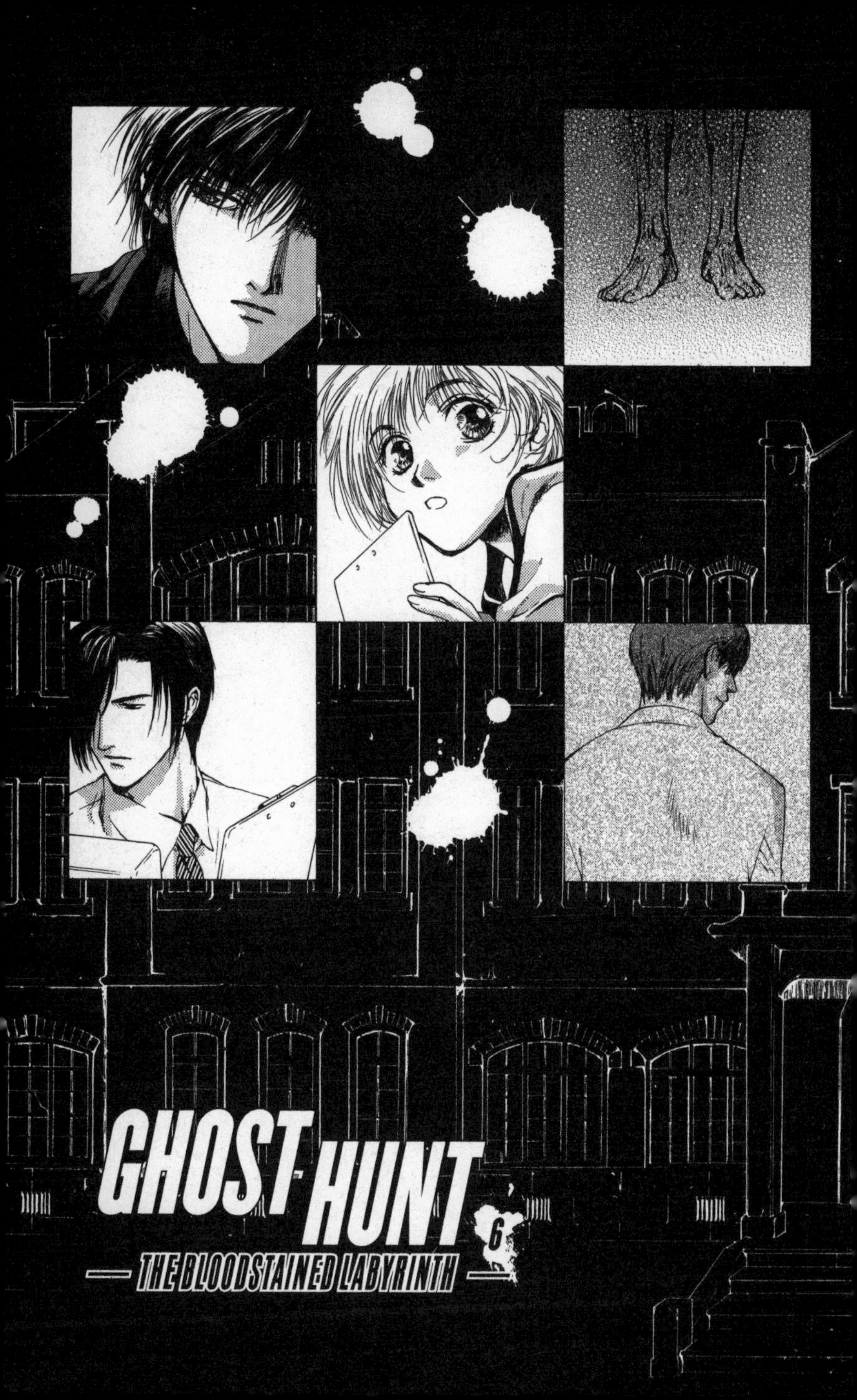
GHOST HUNT
6
— THE BLOODSTAINED LABYRINTH —

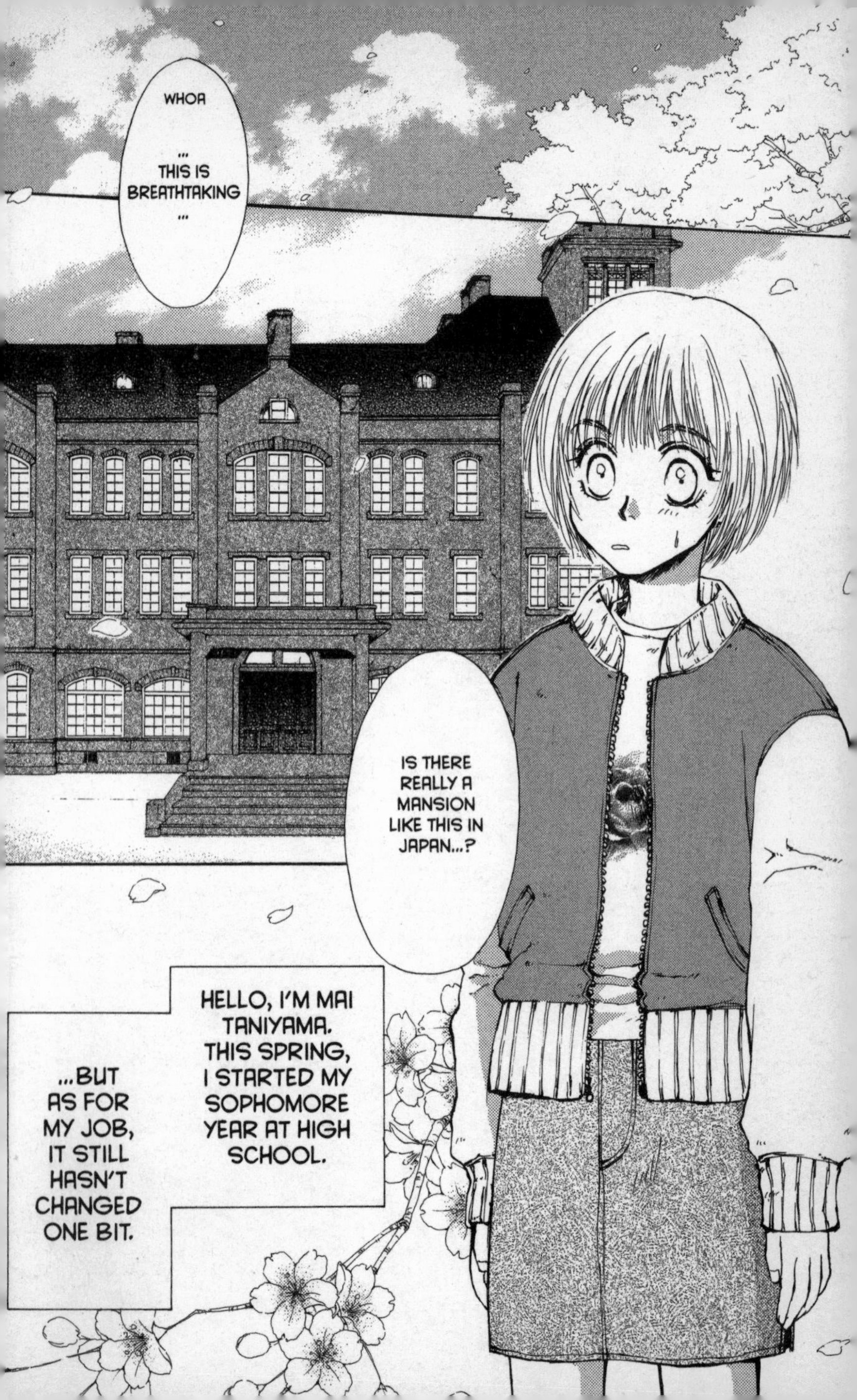

WHOA ... THIS IS BREATHTAKING ...
IS THERE REALLY A MANSION LIKE THIS IN JAPAN...?
HELLO, I'M MAI TANIYAMA. THIS SPRING, I STARTED MY SOPHOMORE YEAR AT HIGH SCHOOL.
...BUT AS FOR MY JOB, IT STILL HASN'T CHANGED ONE BIT.

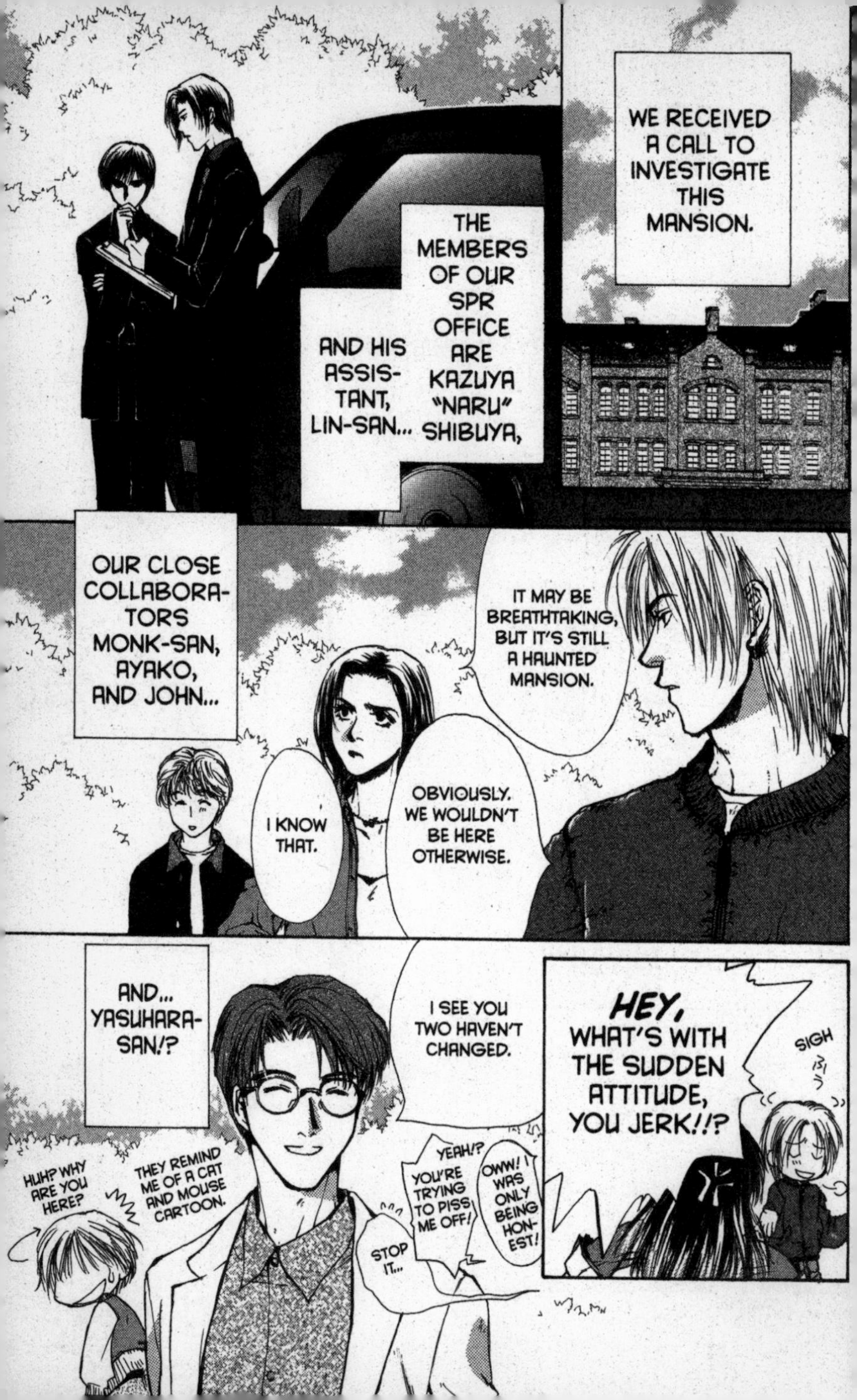
WE RECEIVED A CALL TO INVESTIGATE THIS MANSION.
THE MEMBERS OF OUR SPR OFFICE ARE KAZUYA "NARU" SHIBUYA,
AND HIS ASSIS-TANT, LIN-SAN...
OUR CLOSE COLLABORA-TORS MONK-SAN, AYAKO, AND JOHN...
IT MAY BE BREATHTAKING, BUT IT'S STILL A HAUNTED MANSION.
OBVIOUSLY. WE WOULDN'T BE HERE OTHERWISE.
I KNOW THAT.
HEY, WHAT'S WITH THE SUDDEN ATTITUDE, YOU JERK!!?
SIGH
AND... YASUHARA-SAN!?
I SEE YOU TWO HAVEN'T CHANGED.
YEAH!? YOU'RE TRYING TO PISS ME OFF!
OWW! I WAS ONLY BEING HON-EST!
STOP IT...
THEY REMIND ME OF A CAT AND MOUSE CARTOON.
HUH? WHY ARE YOU HERE?

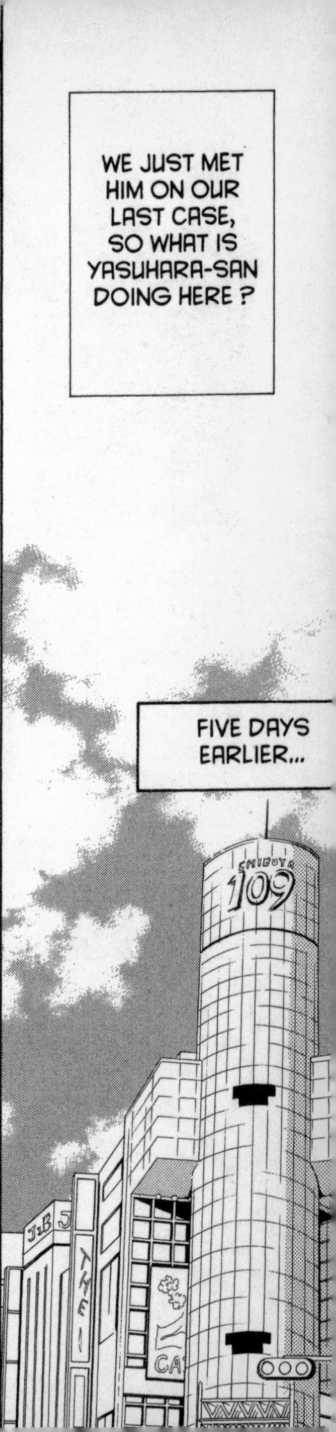
WE JUST MET HIM ON OUR LAST CASE, SO WHAT IS YASUHARA-SAN DOING HERE?
FIVE DAYS EARLIER...
109
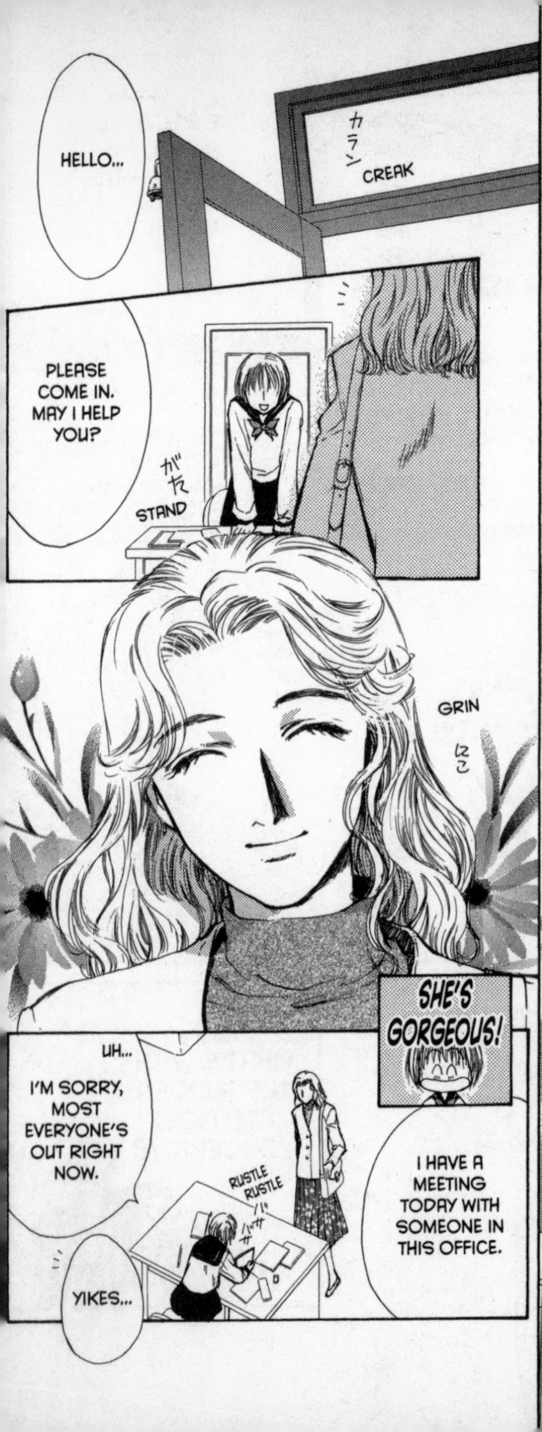
HELLO...
カラン
CREAK
PLEASE COME IN. MAY I HELP YOU?
ガタ
STAND
GRIN
ニコ
SHE'S GORGEOUS!
I HAVE A MEETING TODAY WITH SOMEONE IN THIS OFFICE.
UH...
I'M SORRY, MOST EVERYONE'S OUT RIGHT NOW.
RUSTLE RUSTLE
YIKES...

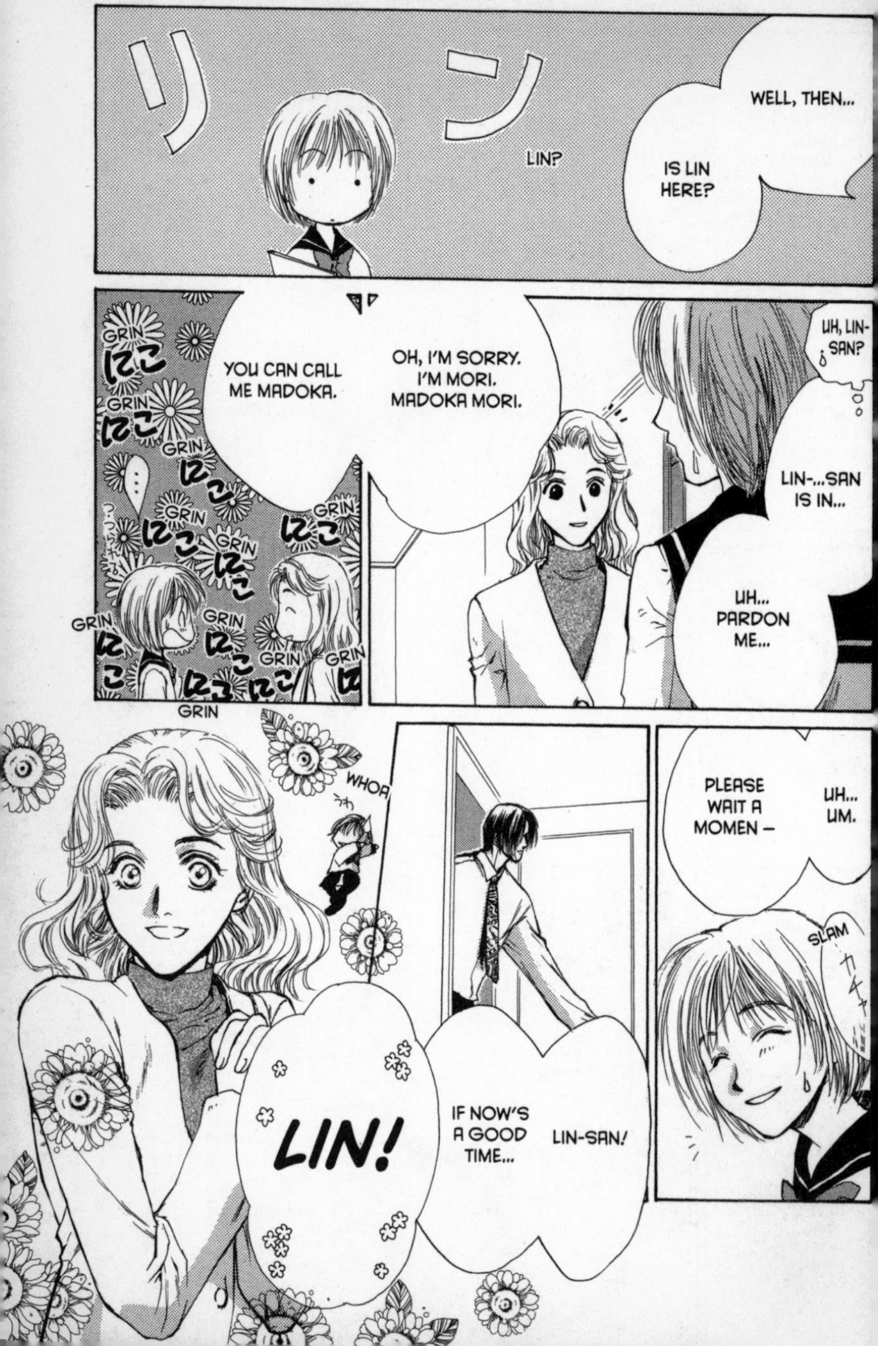
WELL, THEN...
IS LIN HERE?
LIN?
リン
UH, LIN-SAN?
LIN-...SAN IS IN...
UH... PARDON ME...
OH, I'M SORRY. I'M MORI. MADOKA MORI.
YOU CAN CALL ME MADOKA.
GRIN にこ
GRIN にこ
GRIN にこ
GRIN にこ
GRIN にこ
GRIN にこ
GRIN にこ
GRIN にこ
GRIN にこ
GRIN にこ
GRIN
UH... UM.
PLEASE WAIT A MOMEN –
SLAM
カチャ
LIN-SAN!
IF NOW'S A GOOD TIME...
LIN!
WHOA
うわ

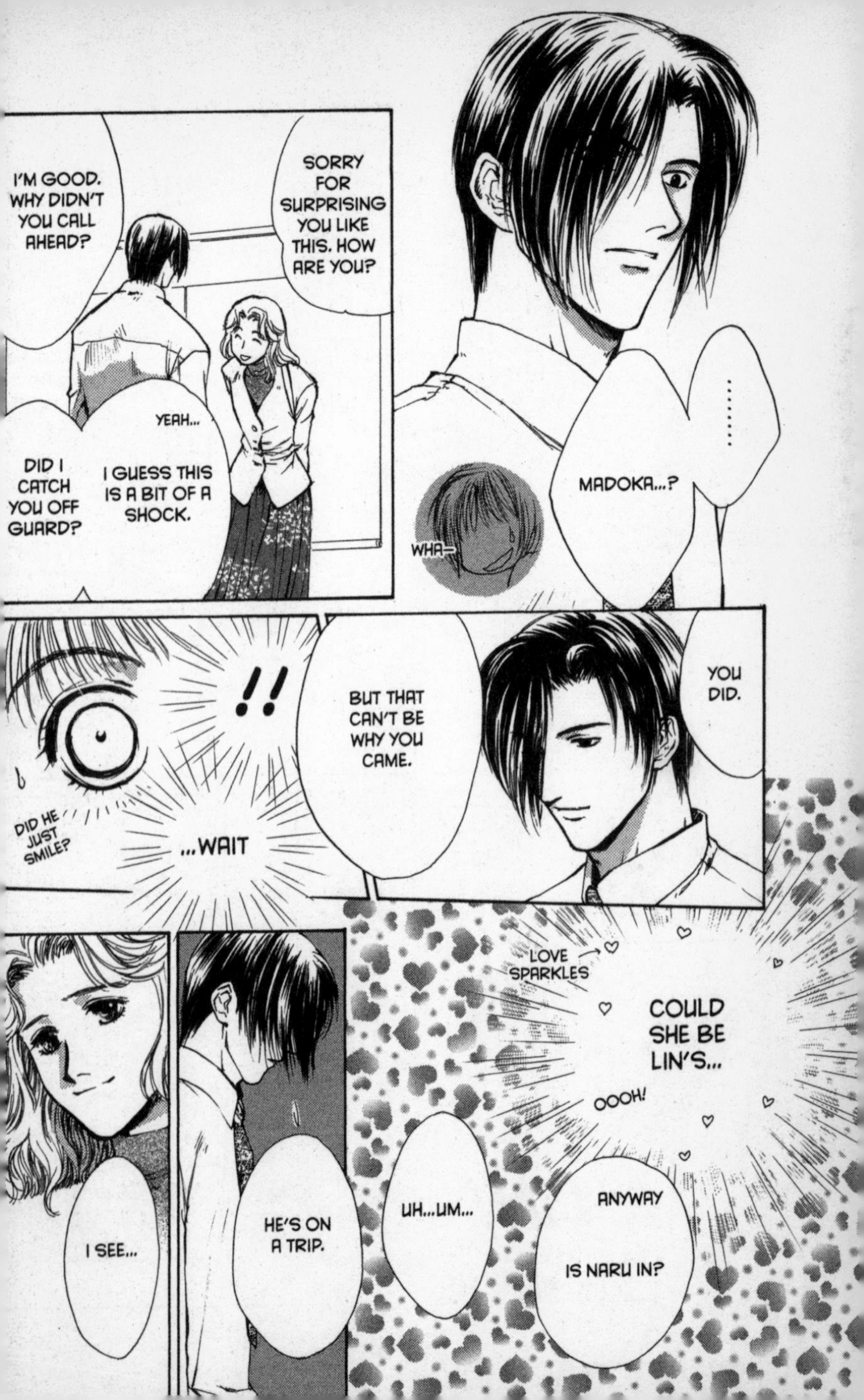
......
MADOKA...?
WHA–
SORRY FOR SURPRISING YOU LIKE THIS. HOW ARE YOU?
I'M GOOD. WHY DIDN'T YOU CALL AHEAD?
YEAH...
I GUESS THIS IS A BIT OF A SHOCK.
DID I CATCH YOU OFF GUARD?
YOU DID.
BUT THAT CAN'T BE WHY YOU CAME.
!!
...WAIT
DID HE JUST SMILE?
LOVE SPARKLES
COULD SHE BE LIN'S...
OOOH!
ANYWAY
IS NARU IN?
UH...UM...
HE'S ON A TRIP.
I SEE...

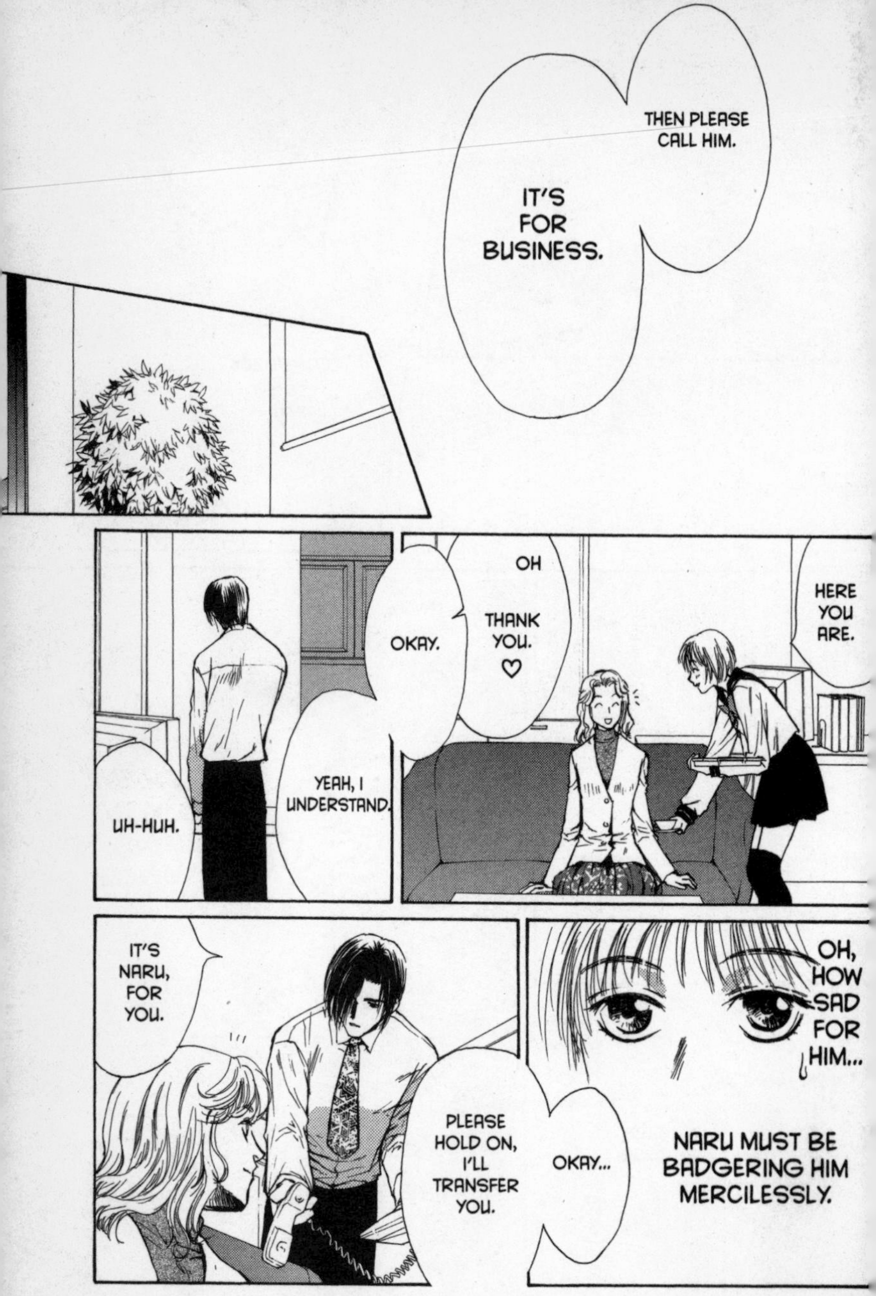
THEN PLEASE CALL HIM.
IT'S FOR BUSINESS.
HERE YOU ARE.
OH
THANK YOU. ♡
OKAY.
YEAH, I UNDERSTAND.
UH-HUH.
OH, HOW SAD FOR HIM...
NARU MUST BE BADGERING HIM MERCILESSLY.
PLEASE HOLD ON, I'LL TRANSFER YOU.
IT'S NARU, FOR YOU.
OKAY...

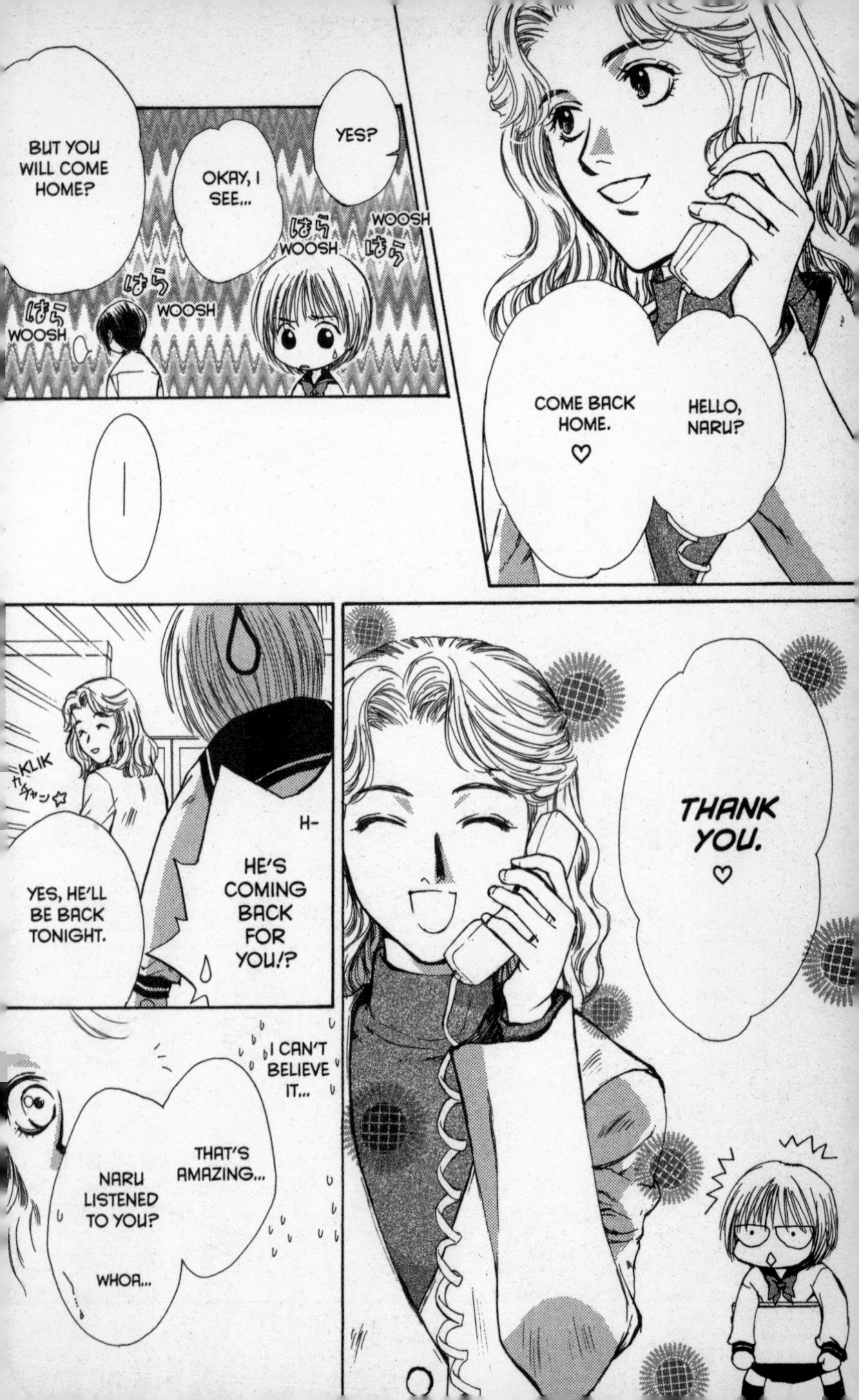
HELLO, NARU?
COME BACK HOME. ♡
YES?
OKAY, I SEE...
BUT YOU WILL COME HOME?
WOOSH はら
はら WOOSH
はら WOOSH
はら WOOSH
—
THANK YOU. ♡
H-
HE'S COMING BACK FOR YOU!?
KLIK ガチャン☆
YES, HE'LL BE BACK TONIGHT.
I CAN'T BELIEVE IT...
THAT'S AMAZING...
NARU LISTENED TO YOU?
WHOA...

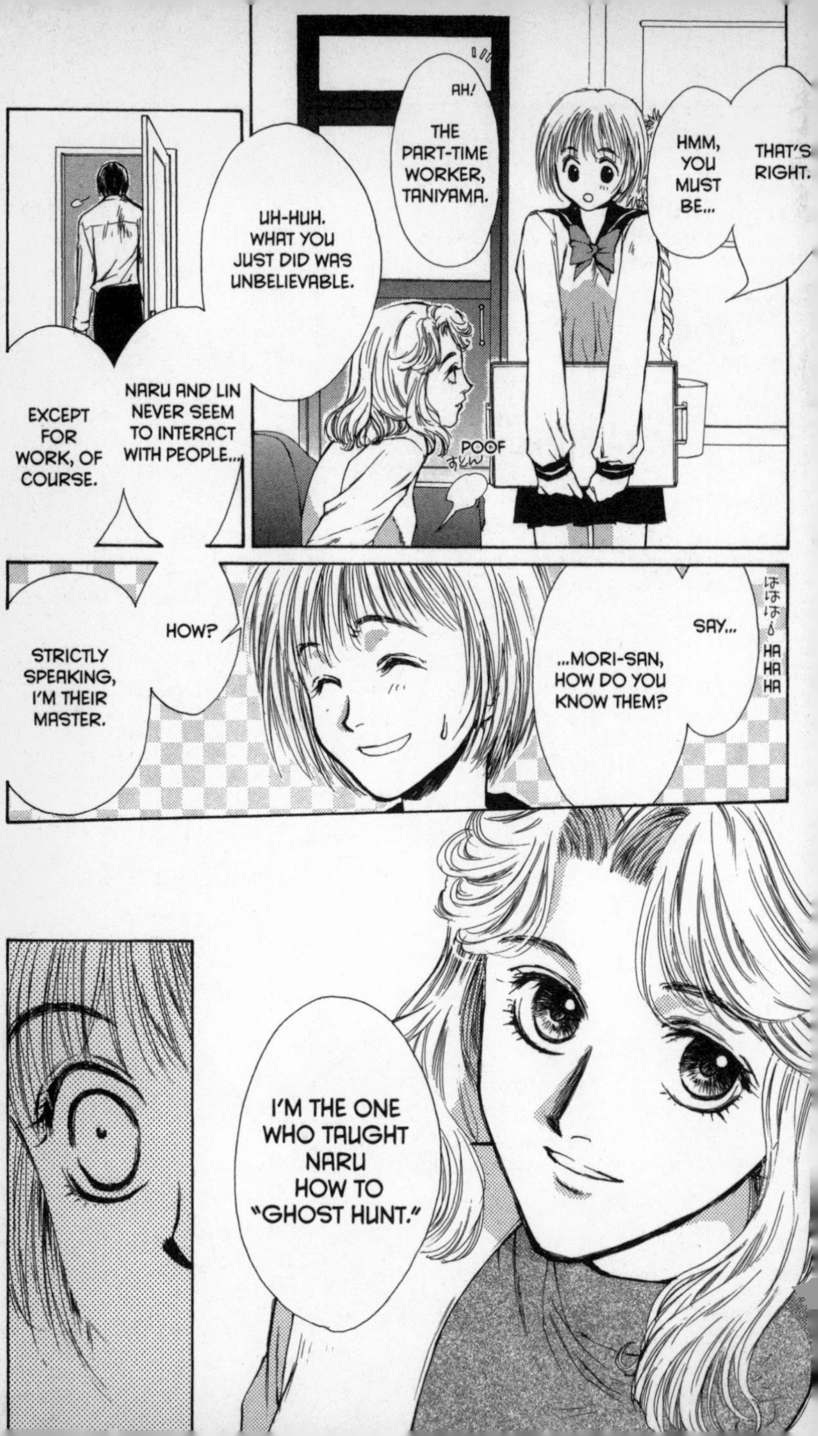
HMM, YOU MUST BE...
THAT'S RIGHT.
AH!
THE PART-TIME WORKER, TANIYAMA.
UH-HUH. WHAT YOU JUST DID WAS UNBELIEVABLE.
POOF
すとん
NARU AND LIN NEVER SEEM TO INTERACT WITH PEOPLE...
EXCEPT FOR WORK, OF COURSE.
ははは
HA HA HA
SAY...
...MORI-SAN, HOW DO YOU KNOW THEM?
HOW?
STRICTLY SPEAKING, I'M THEIR MASTER.
I'M THE ONE WHO TAUGHT NARU HOW TO "GHOST HUNT."

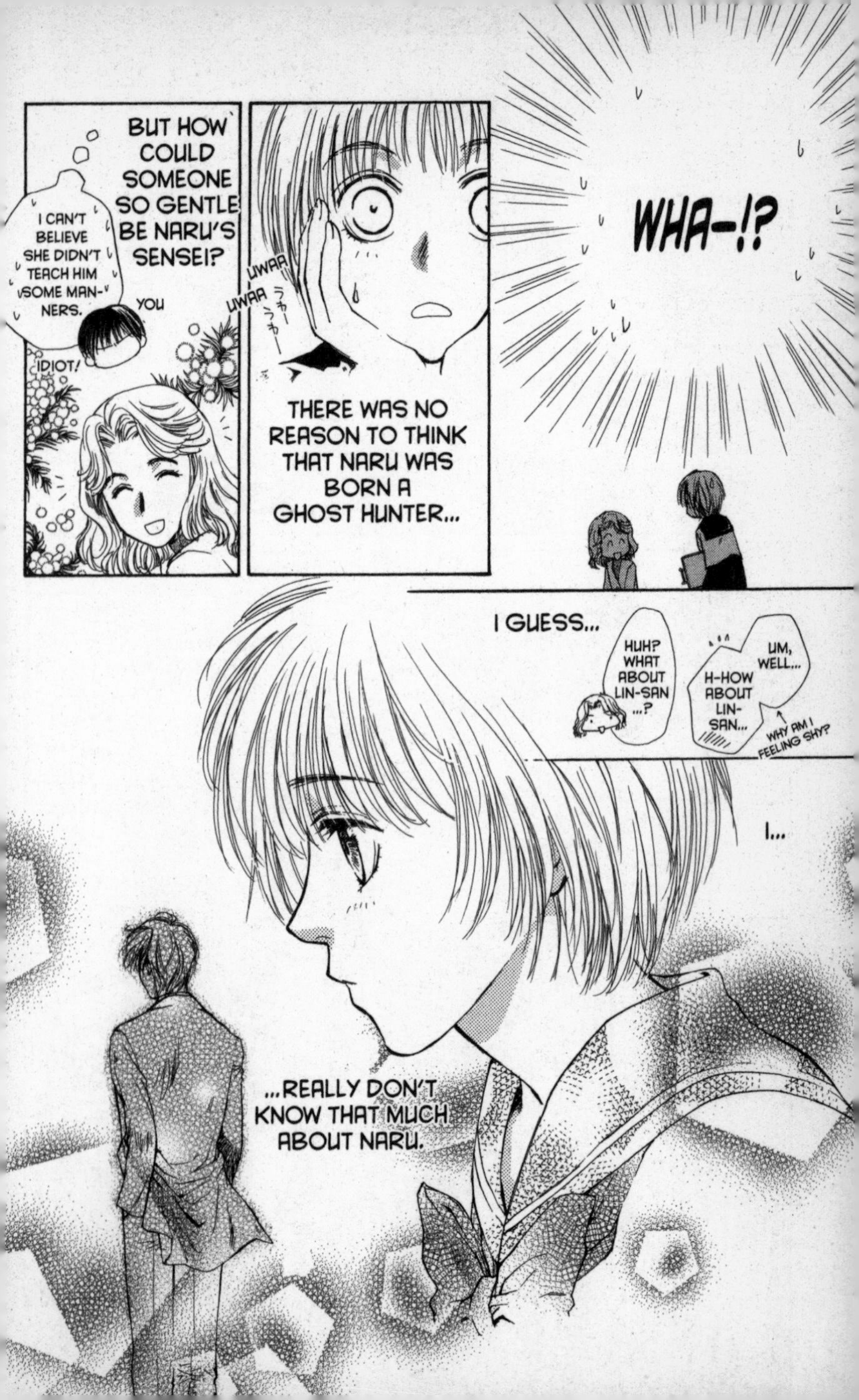

WHA-!?
UWAA
UWAA
THERE WAS NO REASON TO THINK THAT NARU WAS BORN A GHOST HUNTER...
BUT HOW COULD SOMEONE SO GENTLE BE NARU'S SENSEI?
I CAN'T BELIEVE SHE DIDN'T TEACH HIM SOME MAN-NERS.
YOU
IDIOT!
UM, WELL...
H-HOW ABOUT LIN-SAN...
WHY AM I FEELING SHY?
HUH? WHAT ABOUT LIN-SAN ...?
I GUESS...
I...
...REALLY DON'T KNOW THAT MUCH ABOUT NARU.

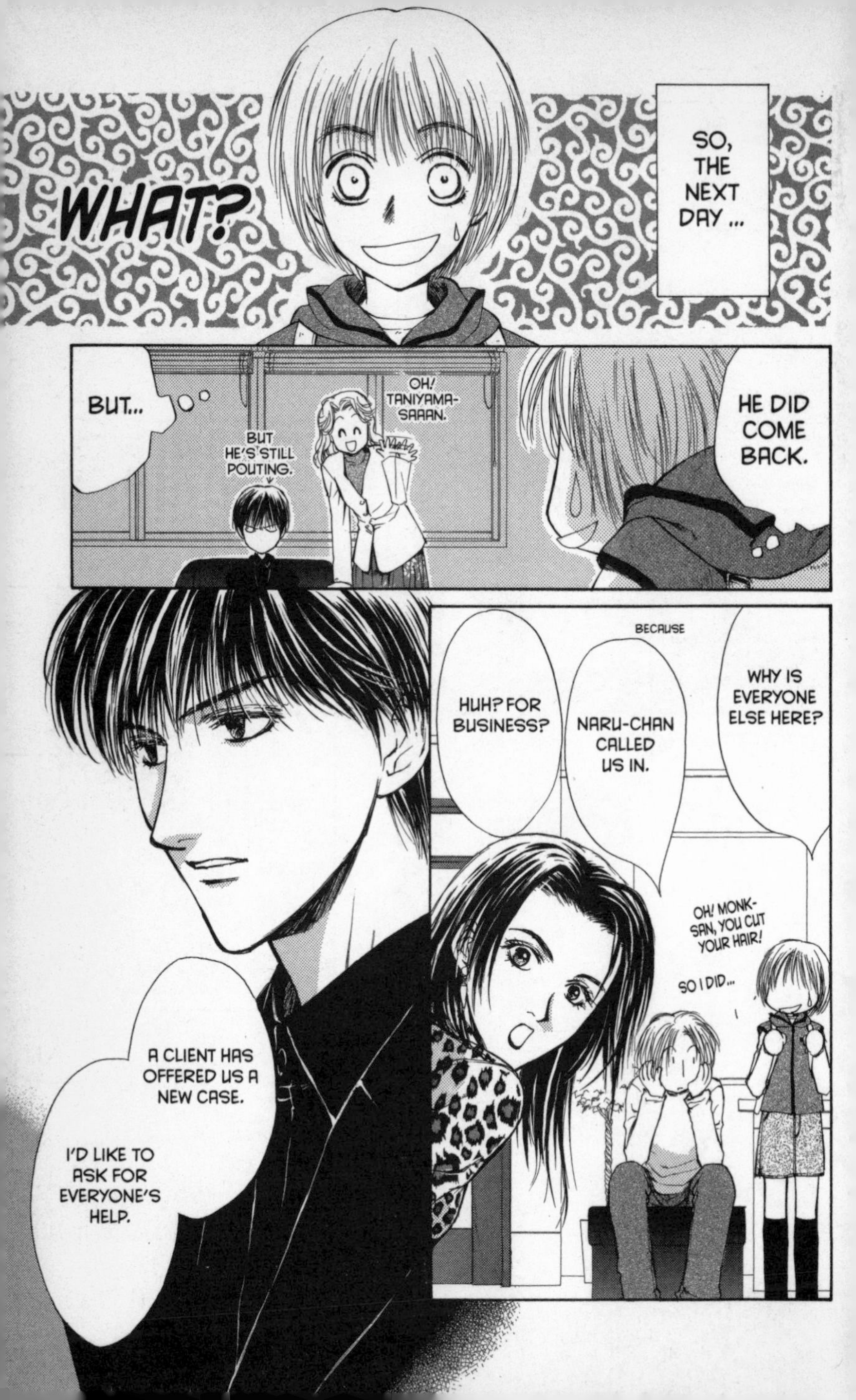
SO, THE NEXT DAY ...
WHAT?
HE DID COME BACK.
OH! TANIYAMA-SAAAN.
BUT HE'S STILL POUTING.
BUT...
WHY IS EVERYONE ELSE HERE?
BECAUSE
NARU-CHAN CALLED US IN.
HUH? FOR BUSINESS?
OH! MONK-SAN, YOU CUT YOUR HAIR!
SO I DID...
A CLIENT HAS OFFERED US A NEW CASE.
I'D LIKE TO ASK FOR EVERYONE'S HELP.

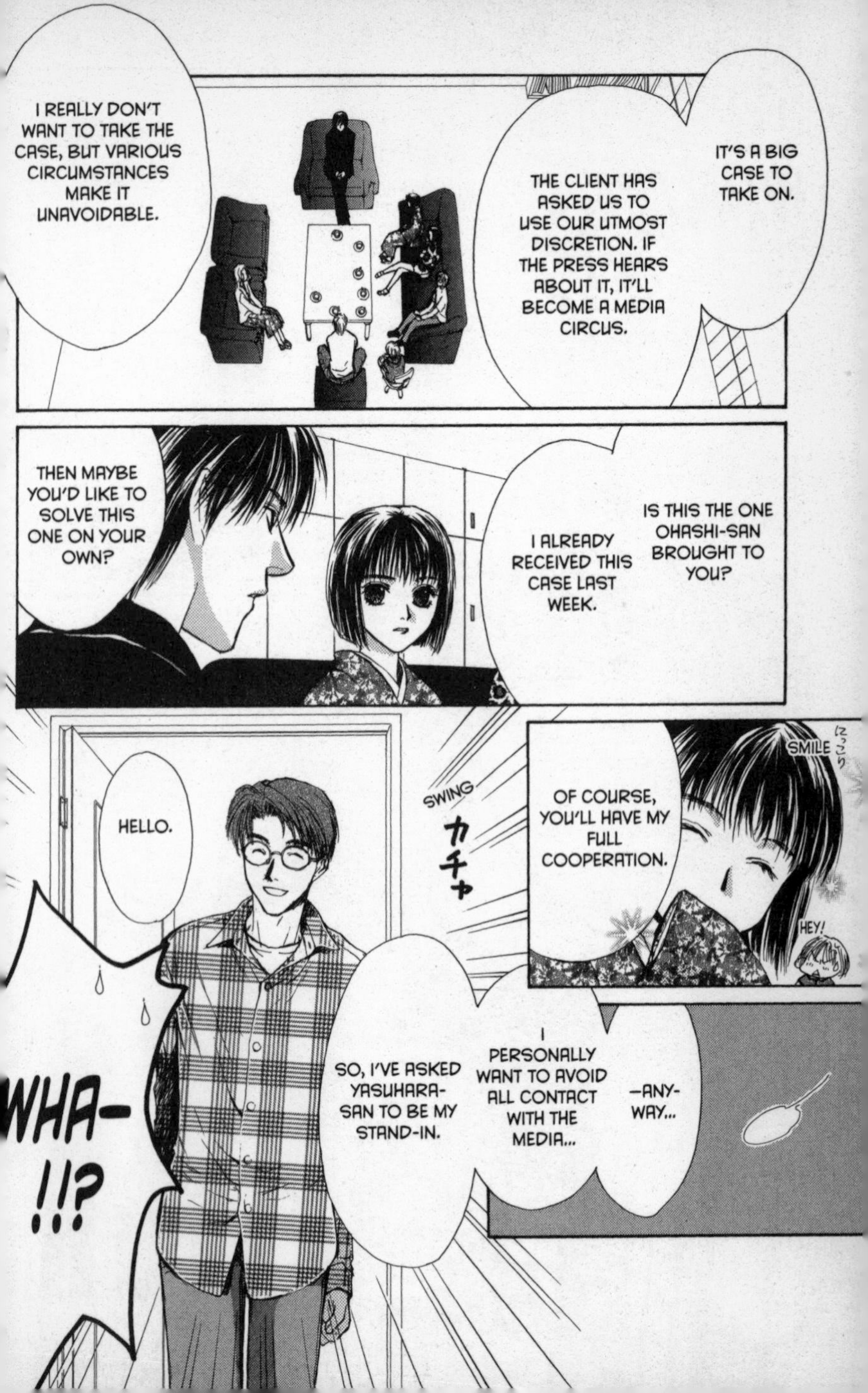
IT'S A BIG CASE TO TAKE ON.
THE CLIENT HAS ASKED US TO USE OUR UTMOST DISCRETION. IF THE PRESS HEARS ABOUT IT, IT'LL BECOME A MEDIA CIRCUS.
I REALLY DON'T WANT TO TAKE THE CASE, BUT VARIOUS CIRCUMSTANCES MAKE IT UNAVOIDABLE.
IS THIS THE ONE OHASHI-SAN BROUGHT TO YOU?
I ALREADY RECEIVED THIS CASE LAST WEEK.
THEN MAYBE YOU'D LIKE TO SOLVE THIS ONE ON YOUR OWN?
にっこり
SMILE
OF COURSE, YOU'LL HAVE MY FULL COOPERATION.
HEY!
—ANY-WAY...
I PERSONALLY WANT TO AVOID ALL CONTACT WITH THE MEDIA...
SO, I'VE ASKED YASUHARA-SAN TO BE MY STAND-IN.
SWING
カチャ
HELLO.
WHA-!!?

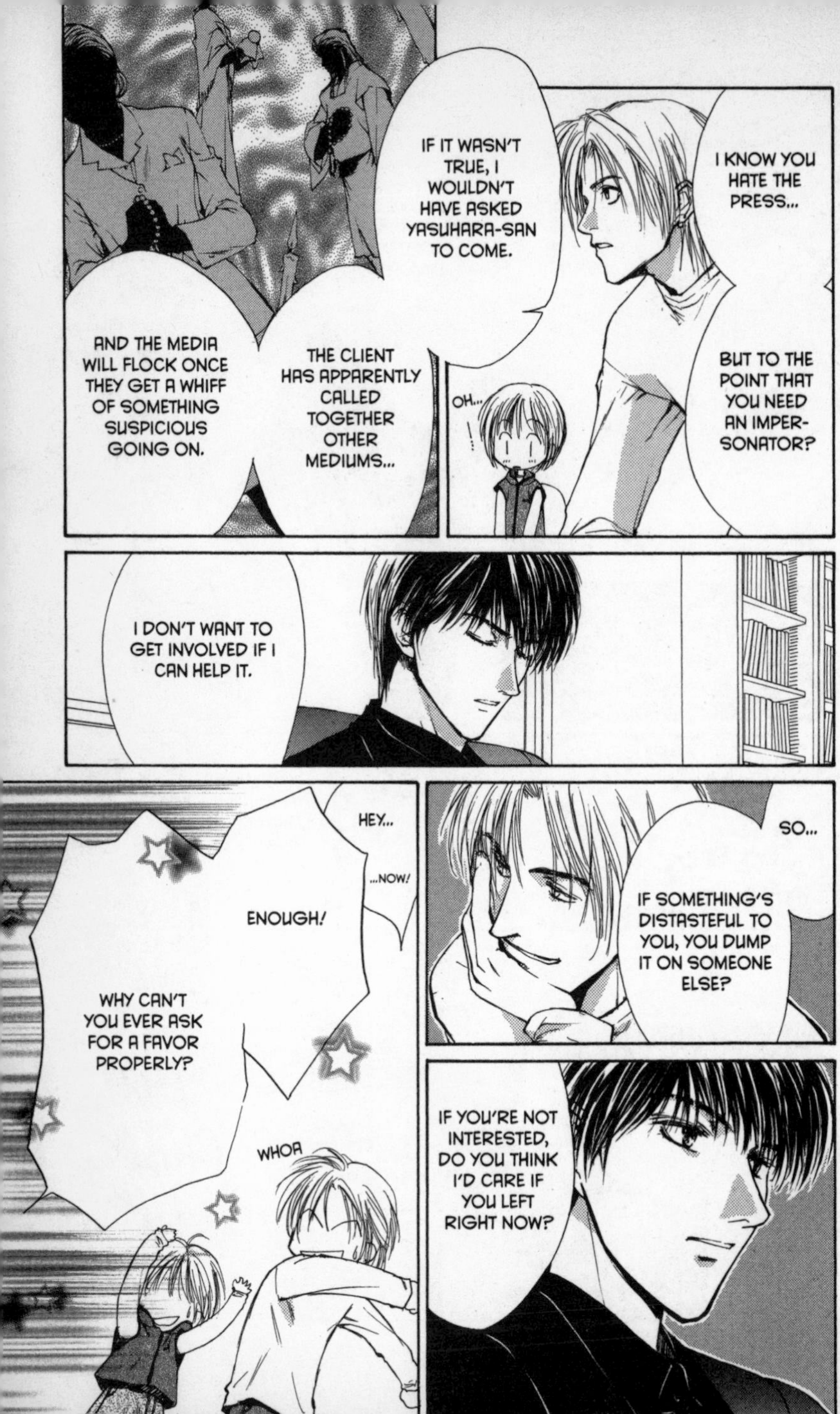

I KNOW YOU HATE THE PRESS...
BUT TO THE POINT THAT YOU NEED AN IMPER-SONATOR?
IF IT WASN'T TRUE, I WOULDN'T HAVE ASKED YASUHARA-SAN TO COME.
OH...
!
THE CLIENT HAS APPARENTLY CALLED TOGETHER OTHER MEDIUMS...
AND THE MEDIA WILL FLOCK ONCE THEY GET A WHIFF OF SOMETHING SUSPICIOUS GOING ON.
I DON'T WANT TO GET INVOLVED IF I CAN HELP IT.
SO...
IF SOMETHING'S DISTASTEFUL TO YOU, YOU DUMP IT ON SOMEONE ELSE?
IF YOU'RE NOT INTERESTED, DO YOU THINK I'D CARE IF YOU LEFT RIGHT NOW?
HEY...
...NOW!
ENOUGH!
WHY CAN'T YOU EVER ASK FOR A FAVOR PROPERLY?
WHOA

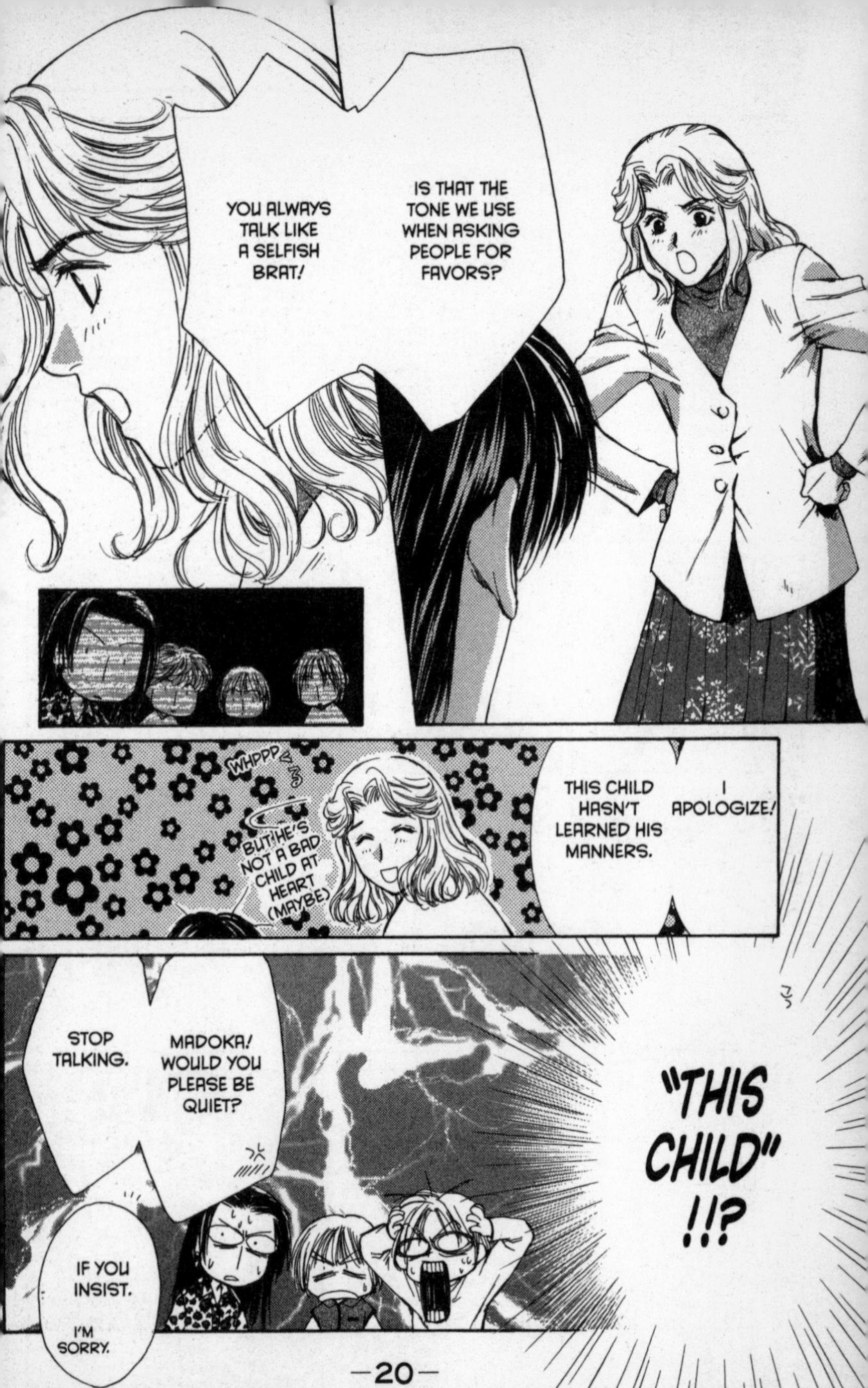
IS THAT THE TONE WE USE WHEN ASKING PEOPLE FOR FAVORS?
YOU ALWAYS TALK LIKE A SELFISH BRAT!
I APOLOGIZE!
THIS CHILD HASN'T LEARNED HIS MANNERS.
WHPPP
BUT HE'S NOT A BAD CHILD AT HEART (MAYBE)
"THIS CHILD" !!?
MADOKA! WOULD YOU PLEASE BE QUIET?
STOP TALKING.
IF YOU INSIST.
I'M SORRY.

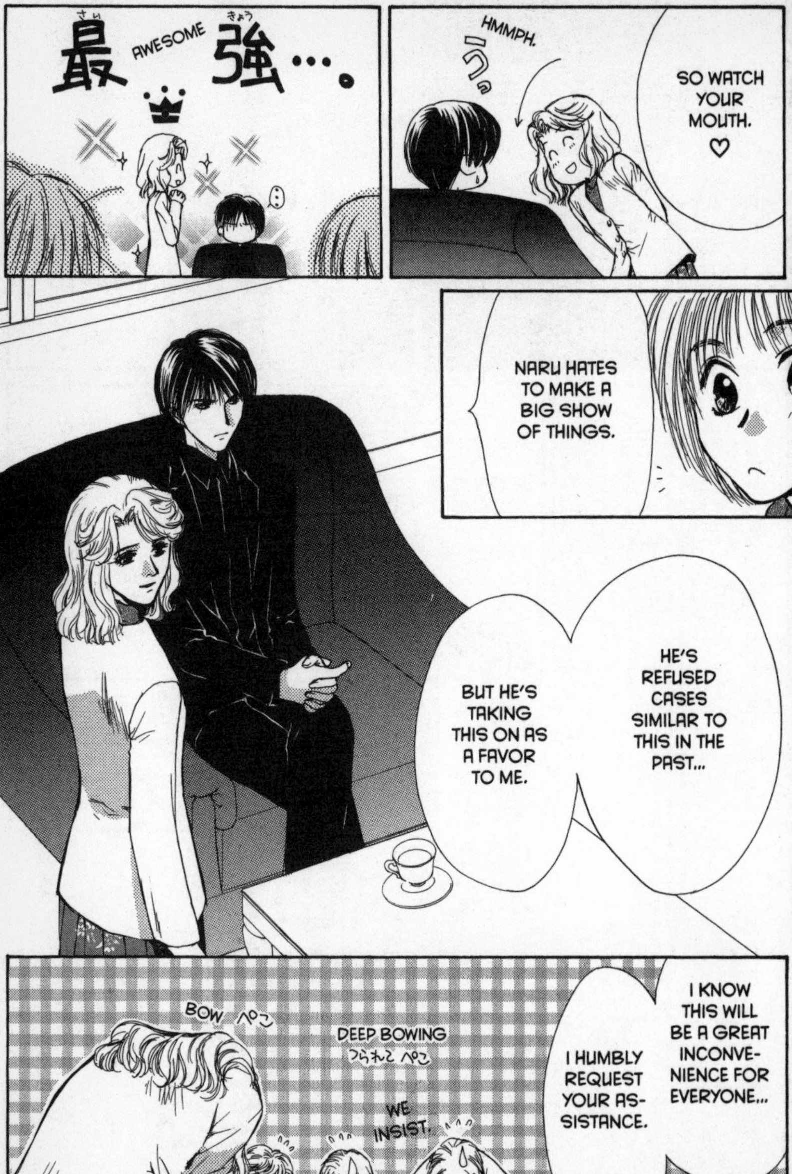
SO WATCH YOUR MOUTH. ♡
HMMPH.
う
AWESOME
最強…。
NARU HATES TO MAKE A BIG SHOW OF THINGS.
HE'S REFUSED CASES SIMILAR TO THIS IN THE PAST...
BUT HE'S TAKING THIS ON AS A FAVOR TO ME.
I KNOW THIS WILL BE A GREAT INCONVENIENCE FOR EVERYONE...
I HUMBLY REQUEST YOUR ASSISTANCE.
WE INSIST.
DEEP BOWING
つられてぺこ
BOW
ぺこ

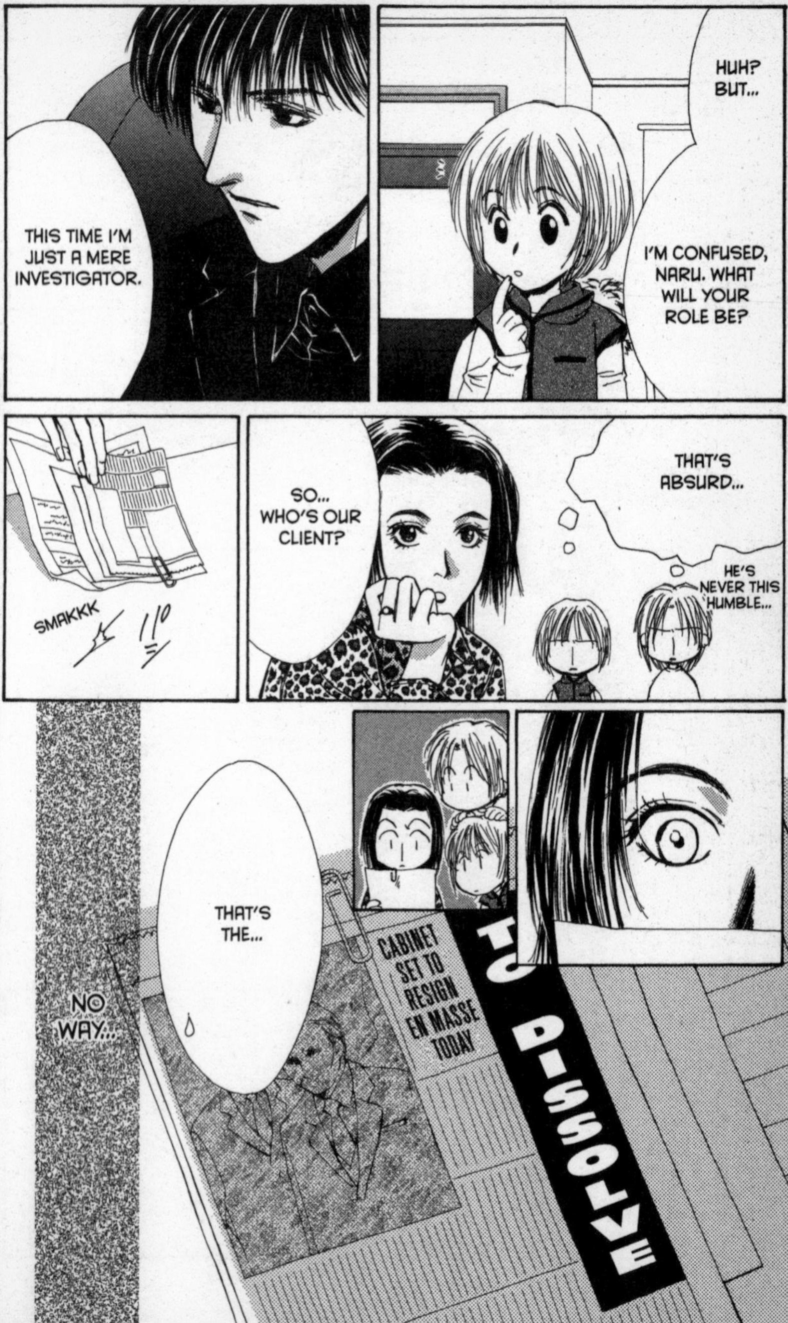
HUH? BUT...
I'M CONFUSED, NARU. WHAT WILL YOUR ROLE BE?
THIS TIME I'M JUST A MERE INVESTIGATOR.
THAT'S ABSURD...
HE'S NEVER THIS HUMBLE...
SO... WHO'S OUR CLIENT?
SMAKKK
THAT'S THE...
TO DISSOLVE
CABINET SET TO RESIGN EN MASSE TODAY
NO WAY...

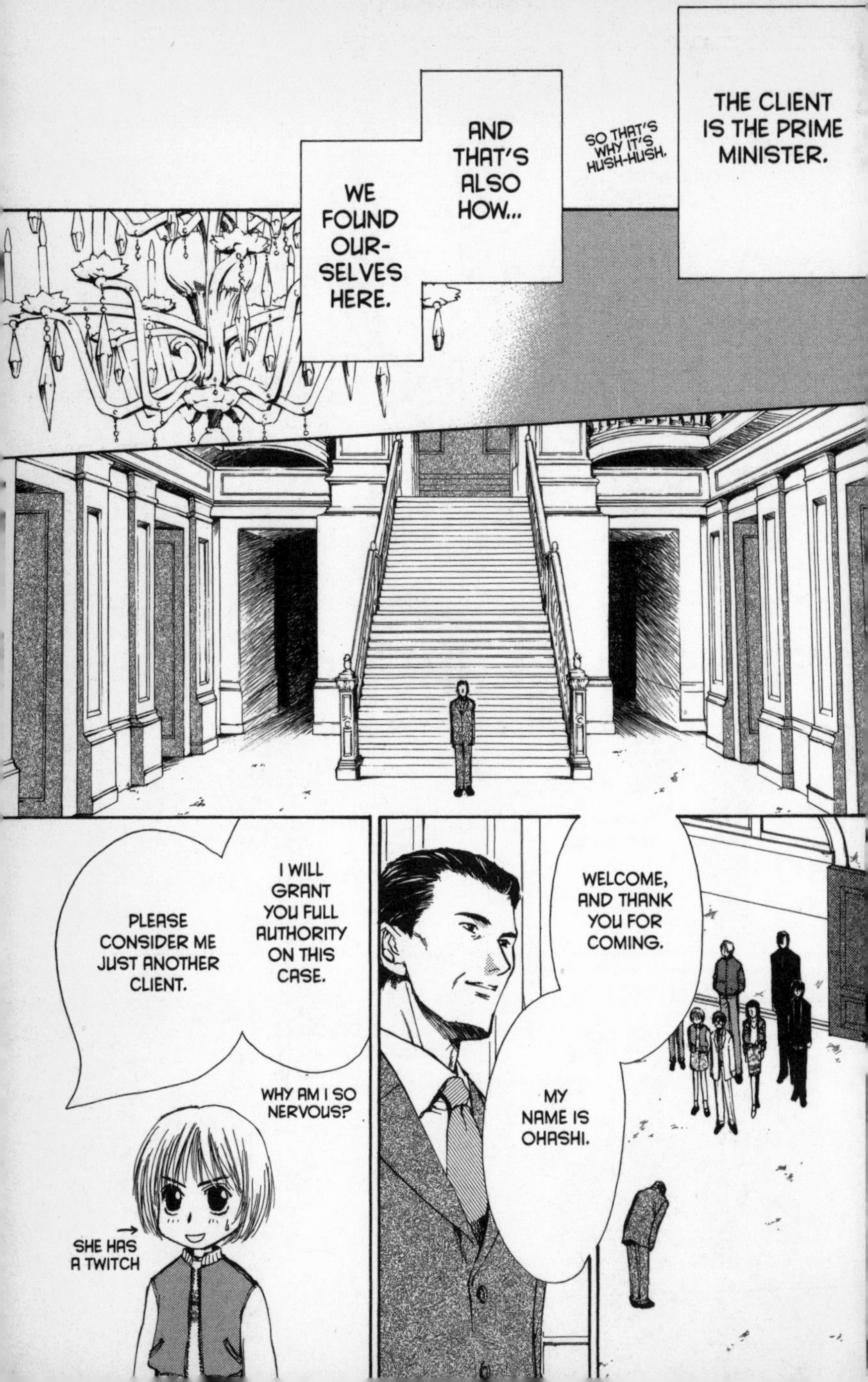
THE CLIENT IS THE PRIME MINISTER.
SO THAT'S WHY IT'S HUSH-HUSH.
AND THAT'S ALSO HOW...
WE FOUND OUR-SELVES HERE.
WELCOME, AND THANK YOU FOR COMING.
MY NAME IS OHASHI.
I WILL GRANT YOU FULL AUTHORITY ON THIS CASE.
PLEASE CONSIDER ME JUST ANOTHER CLIENT.
WHY AM I SO NERVOUS?
SHE HAS A TWITCH

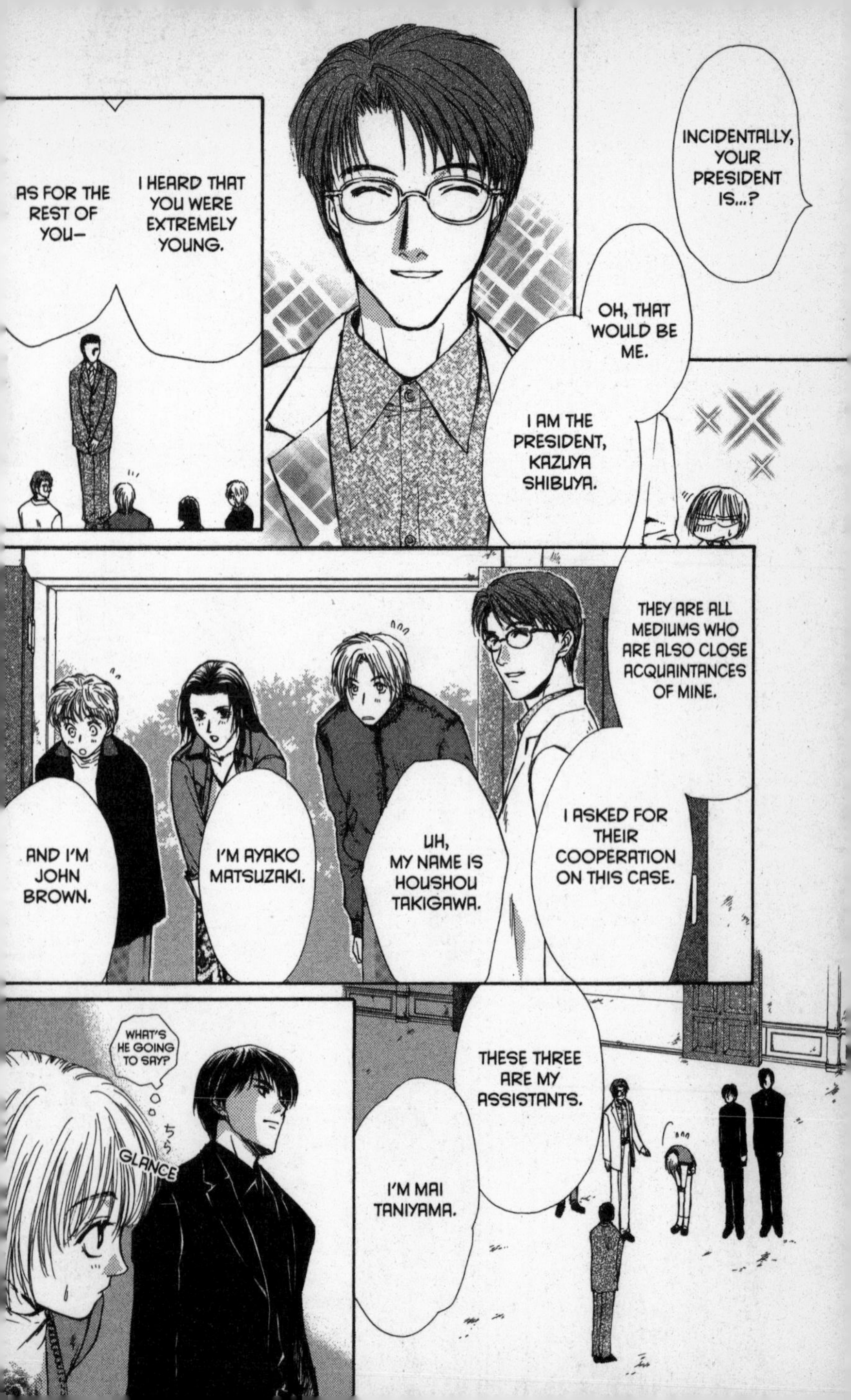
INCIDENTALLY, YOUR PRESIDENT IS...?
OH, THAT WOULD BE ME.
I AM THE PRESIDENT, KAZUYA SHIBUYA.
I HEARD THAT YOU WERE EXTREMELY YOUNG.
AS FOR THE REST OF YOU—
THEY ARE ALL MEDIUMS WHO ARE ALSO CLOSE ACQUAINTANCES OF MINE.
I ASKED FOR THEIR COOPERATION ON THIS CASE.
UH, MY NAME IS HOUSHOU TAKIGAWA.
I'M AYAKO MATSUZAKI.
AND I'M JOHN BROWN.
THESE THREE ARE MY ASSISTANTS.
I'M MAI TANIYAMA.
WHAT'S HE GOING TO SAY?
ちら
GLANCE

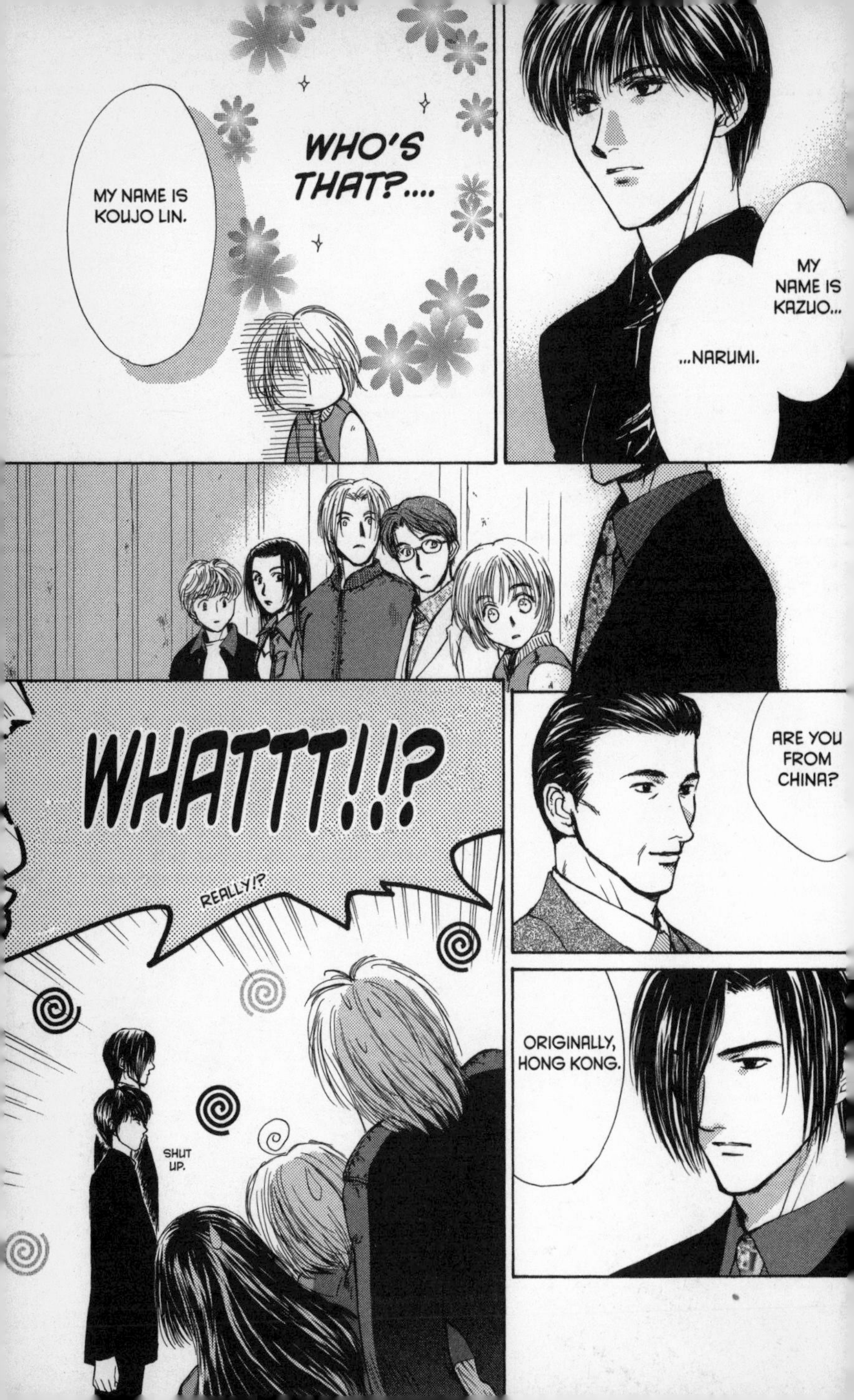
MY NAME IS KAZUO...
...NARUMI.
WHO'S THAT?....
MY NAME IS KOUJO LIN.
ARE YOU FROM CHINA?
ORIGINALLY, HONG KONG.
WHATTT!!?
REALLY!?
SHUT UP.

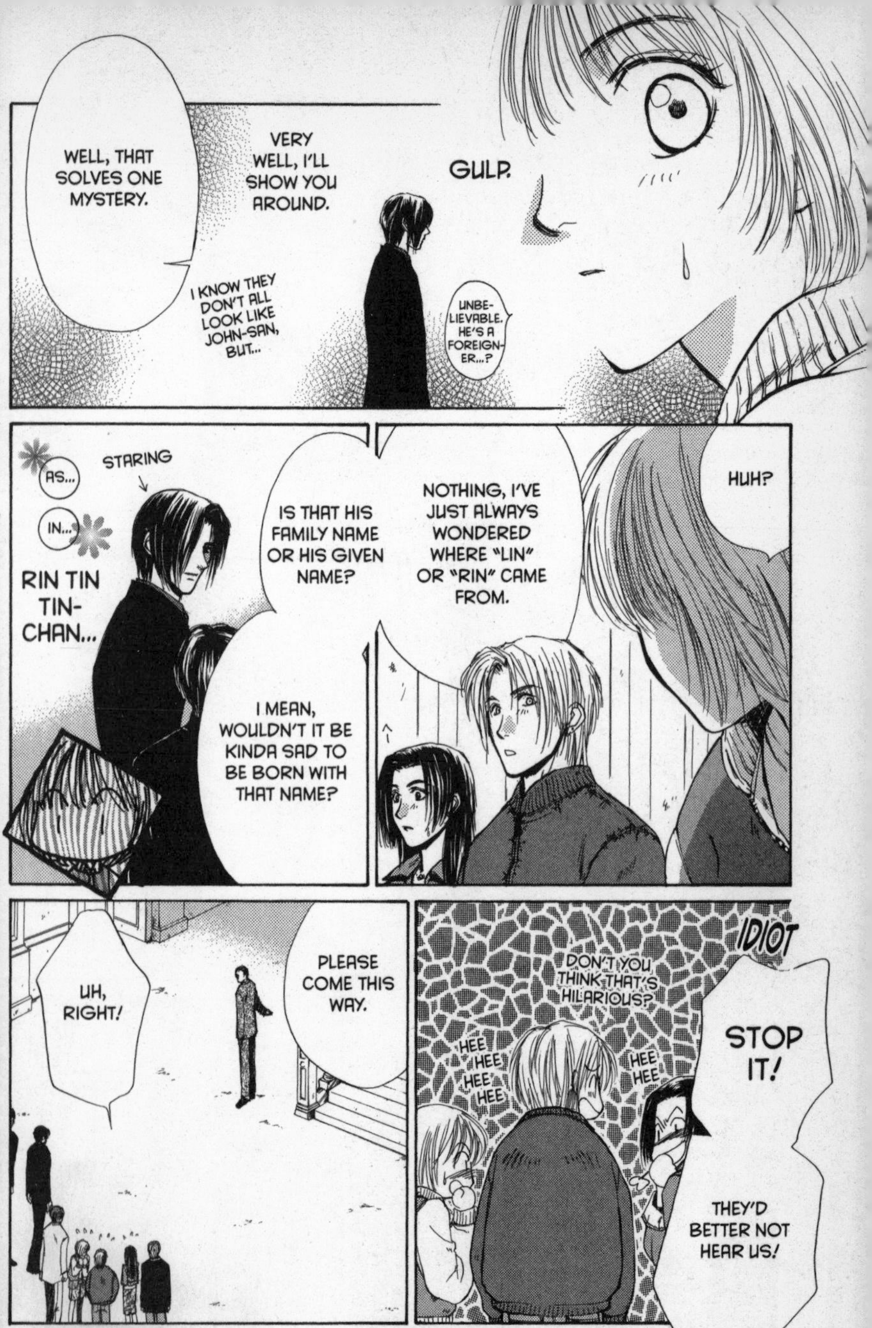
GULP.
VERY WELL, I'LL SHOW YOU AROUND.
WELL, THAT SOLVES ONE MYSTERY.
UNBE-LIEVABLE. HE'S A FOREIGN-ER...?
I KNOW THEY DON'T ALL LOOK LIKE JOHN-SAN, BUT...
HUH?
NOTHING, I'VE JUST ALWAYS WONDERED WHERE "LIN" OR "RIN" CAME FROM.
IS THAT HIS FAMILY NAME OR HIS GIVEN NAME?
I MEAN, WOULDN'T IT BE KINDA SAD TO BE BORN WITH THAT NAME?
STARING
AS...
IN...
RIN TIN TIN-CHAN...
IDIOT
DON'T YOU THINK THAT'S HILARIOUS?
STOP IT!
HEE HEE HEE HEE
HEE HEE
THEY'D BETTER NOT HEAR US!
PLEASE COME THIS WAY.
UH, RIGHT!

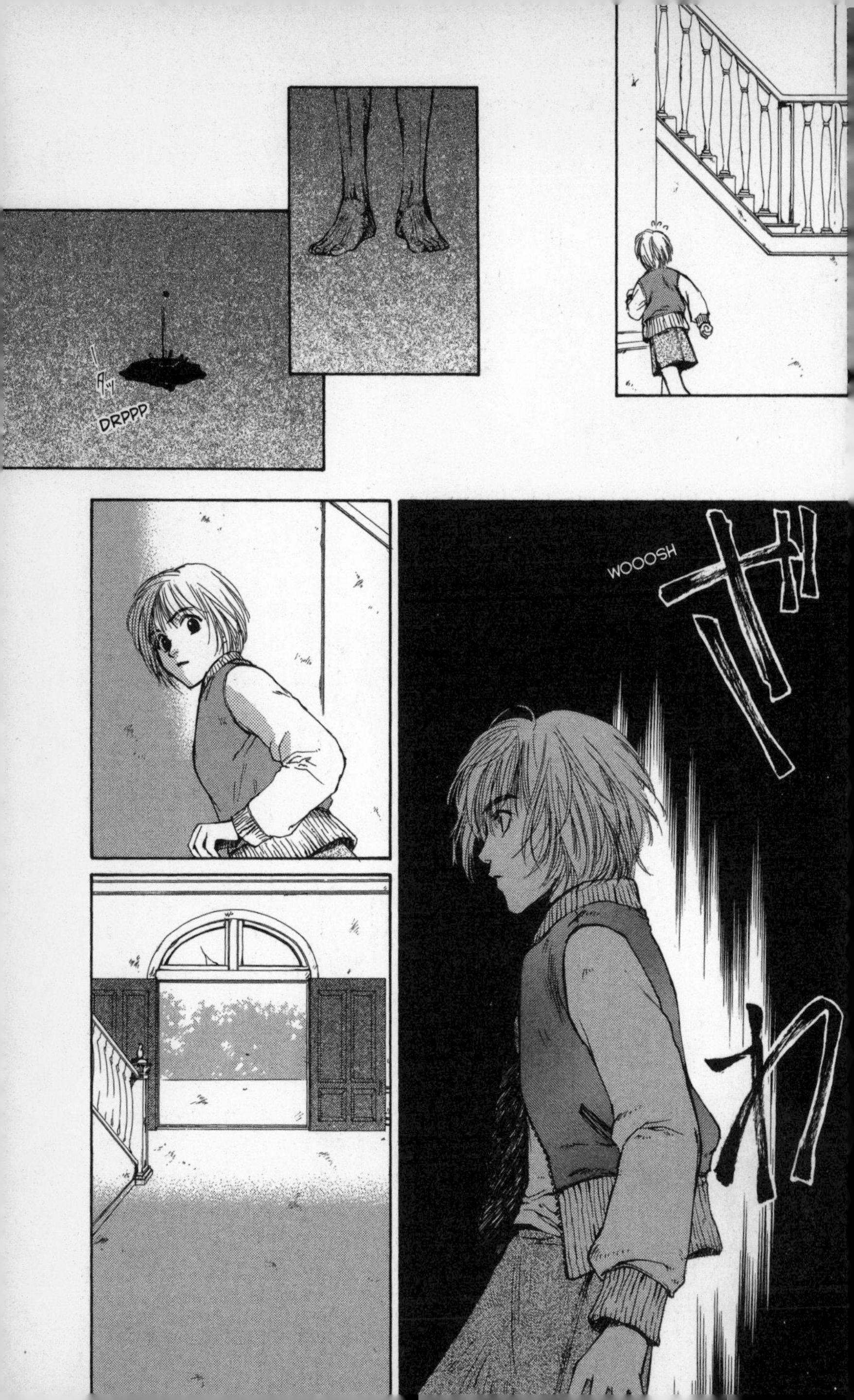
DRPPP
WOOOSH

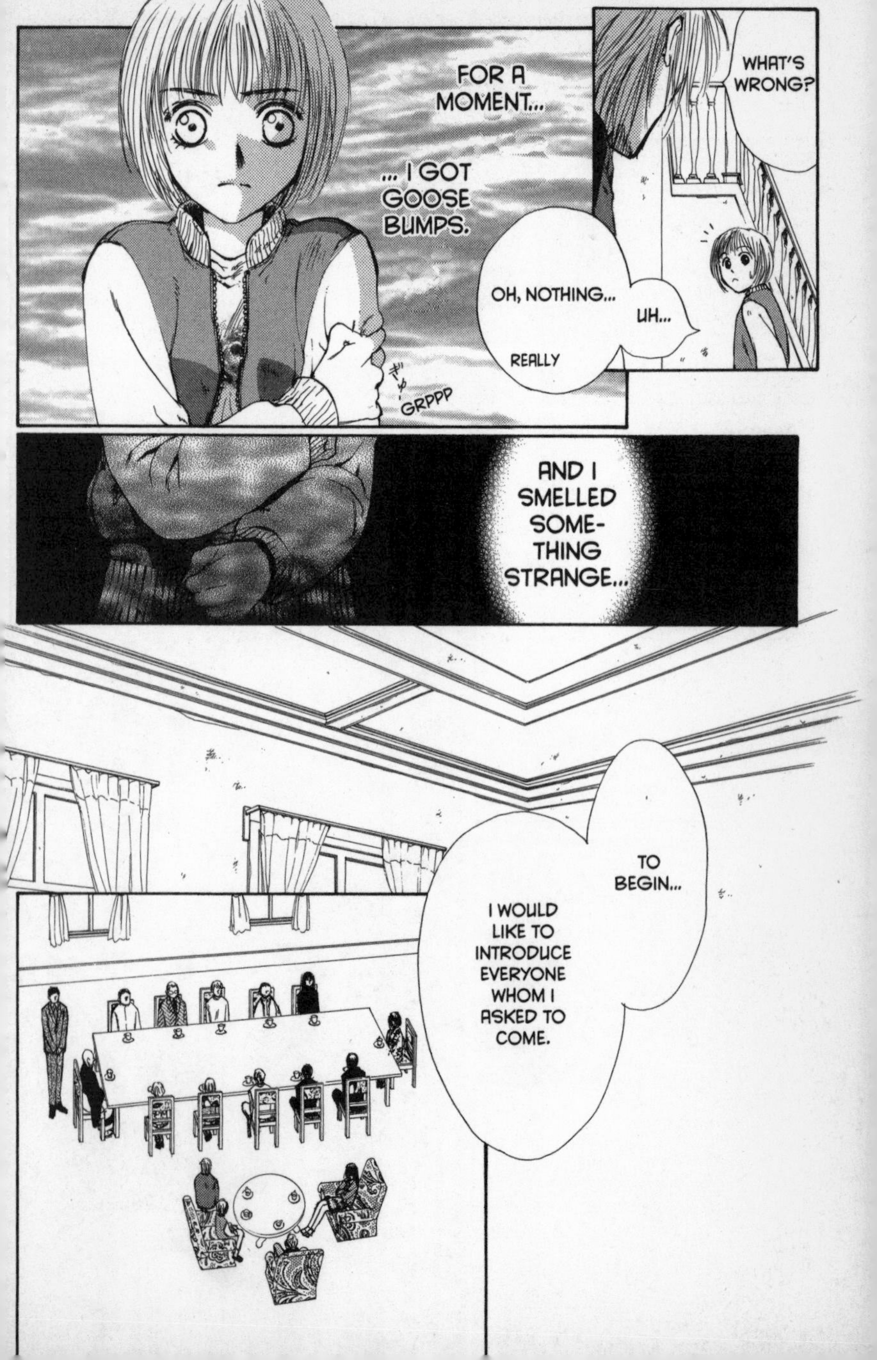
WHAT'S WRONG?
OH, NOTHING... UH... REALLY
FOR A MOMENT...
... I GOT GOOSE BUMPS.
GRPPP
AND I SMELLED SOME-THING STRANGE...
TO BEGIN...
I WOULD LIKE TO INTRODUCE EVERYONE WHOM I ASKED TO COME.

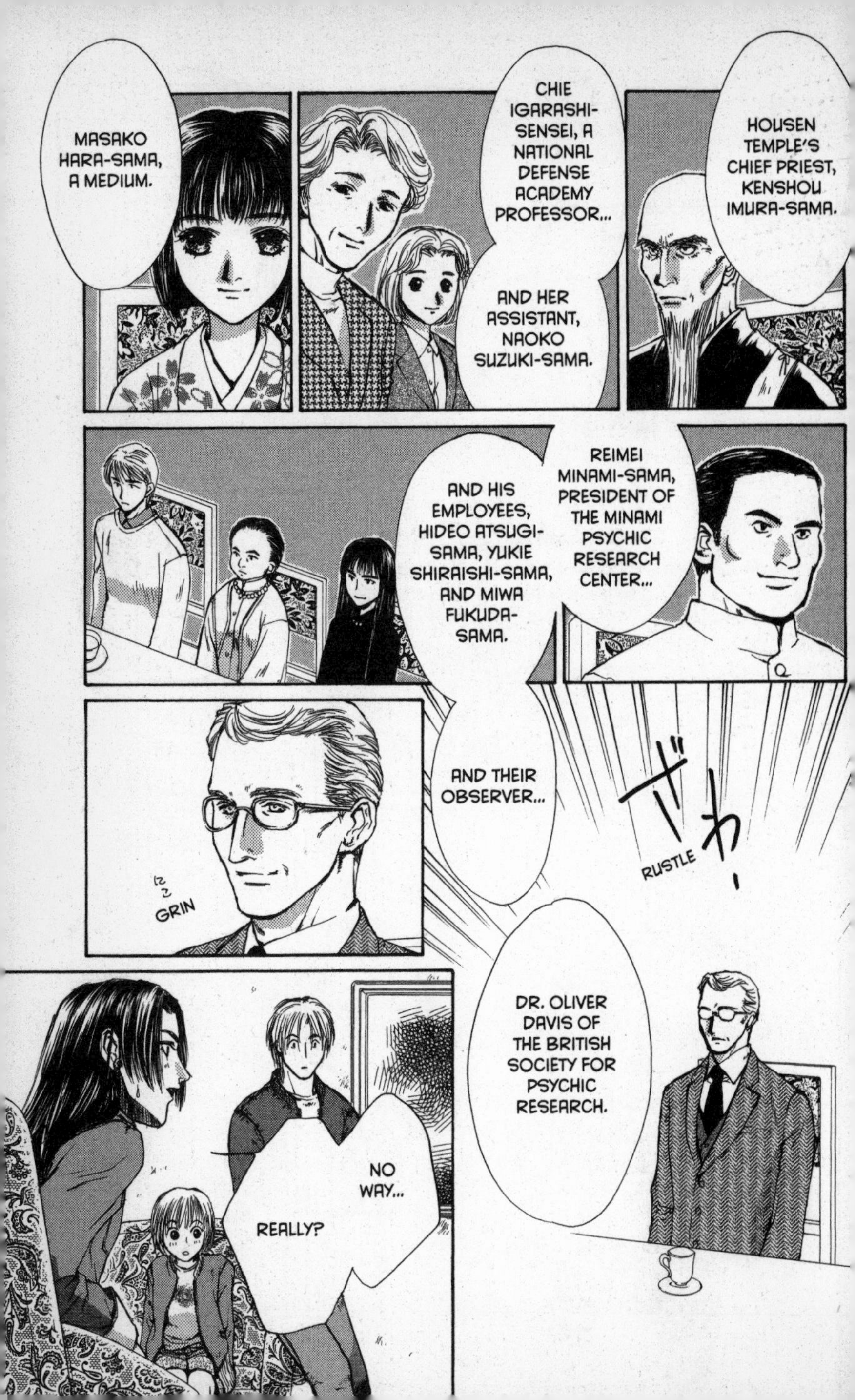
HOUSEN TEMPLE'S CHIEF PRIEST, KENSHOU IMURA-SAMA.
CHIE IGARASHI-SENSEI, A NATIONAL DEFENSE ACADEMY PROFESSOR...
AND HER ASSISTANT, NAOKO SUZUKI-SAMA.
MASAKO HARA-SAMA, A MEDIUM.
REIMEI MINAMI-SAMA, PRESIDENT OF THE MINAMI PSYCHIC RESEARCH CENTER...
AND HIS EMPLOYEES, HIDEO ATSUGI-SAMA, YUKIE SHIRAISHI-SAMA, AND MIWA FUKUDA-SAMA.
ざわ
RUSTLE
AND THEIR OBSERVER...
にこ
GRIN
DR. OLIVER DAVIS OF THE BRITISH SOCIETY FOR PSYCHIC RESEARCH.
NO WAY...
REALLY?

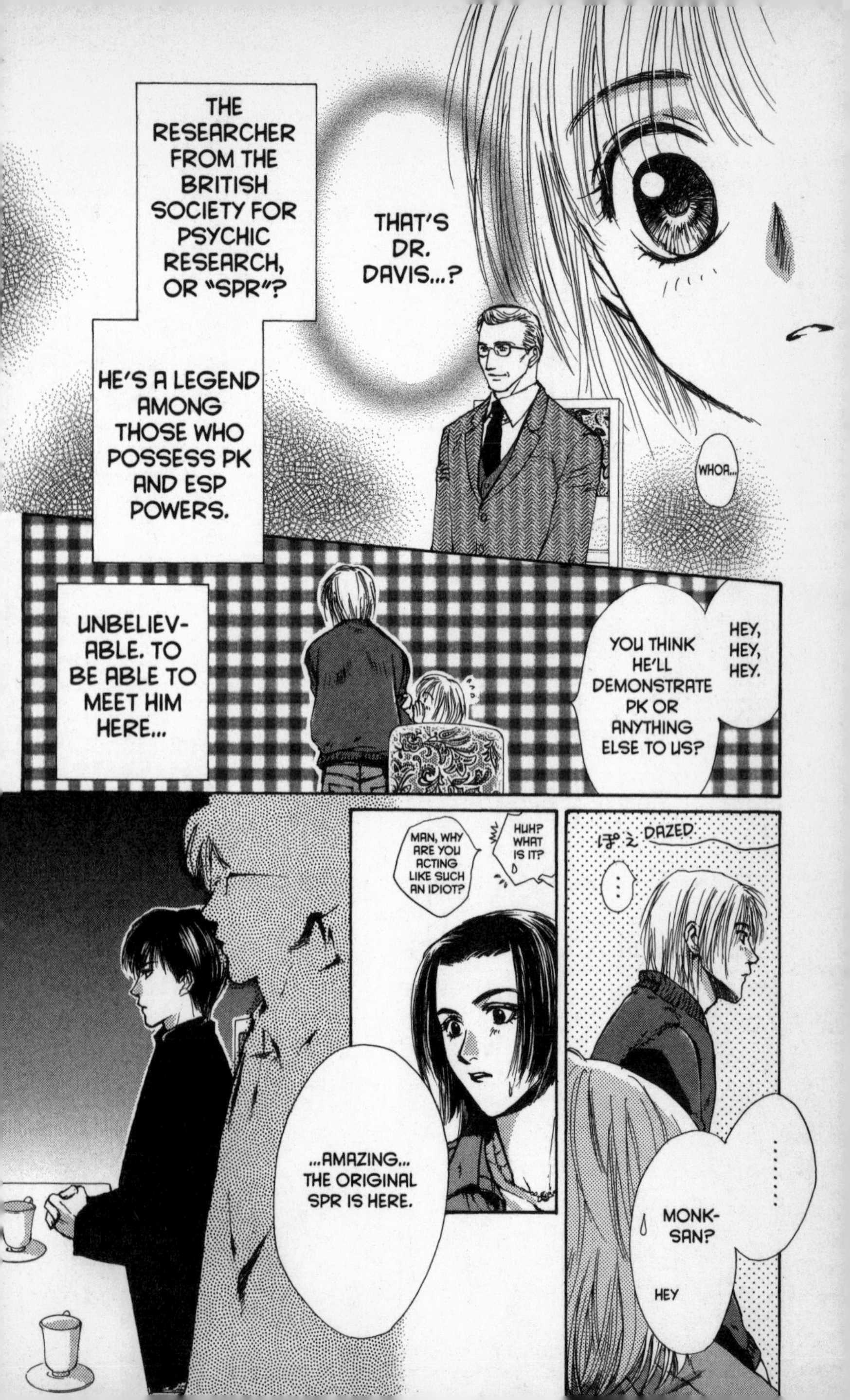
THAT'S DR. DAVIS...?
THE RESEARCHER FROM THE BRITISH SOCIETY FOR PSYCHIC RESEARCH, OR "SPR"?
HE'S A LEGEND AMONG THOSE WHO POSSESS PK AND ESP POWERS.
WHOA...
HEY, HEY, HEY.
YOU THINK HE'LL DEMONSTRATE PK OR ANYTHING ELSE TO US?
UNBELIEV-ABLE. TO BE ABLE TO MEET HIM HERE...
ぽえ DAZED
...
......
MONK-SAN?
HEY
HUH? WHAT IS IT?
MAN, WHY ARE YOU ACTING LIKE SUCH AN IDIOT?
...AMAZING... THE ORIGINAL SPR IS HERE.

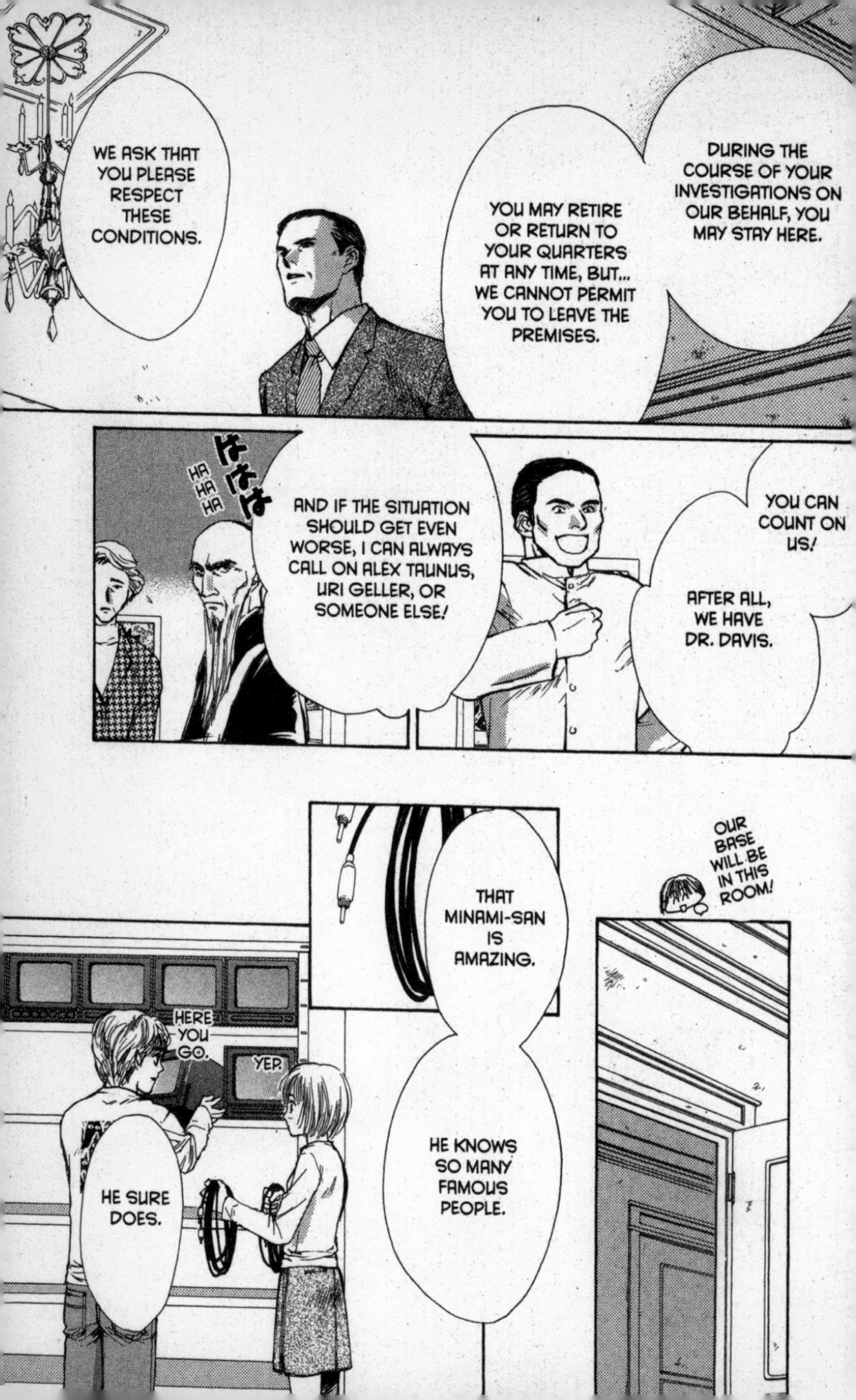
DURING THE COURSE OF YOUR INVESTIGATIONS ON OUR BEHALF, YOU MAY STAY HERE.
YOU MAY RETIRE OR RETURN TO YOUR QUARTERS AT ANY TIME, BUT... WE CANNOT PERMIT YOU TO LEAVE THE PREMISES.
WE ASK THAT YOU PLEASE RESPECT THESE CONDITIONS.
YOU CAN COUNT ON US!
AFTER ALL, WE HAVE DR. DAVIS.
HA HA HA
AND IF THE SITUATION SHOULD GET EVEN WORSE, I CAN ALWAYS CALL ON ALEX TAUNUS, URI GELLER, OR SOMEONE ELSE!
OUR BASE WILL BE IN THIS ROOM!
THAT MINAMI-SAN IS AMAZING.
HE KNOWS SO MANY FAMOUS PEOPLE.
HERE YOU GO.
YEP.
HE SURE DOES.

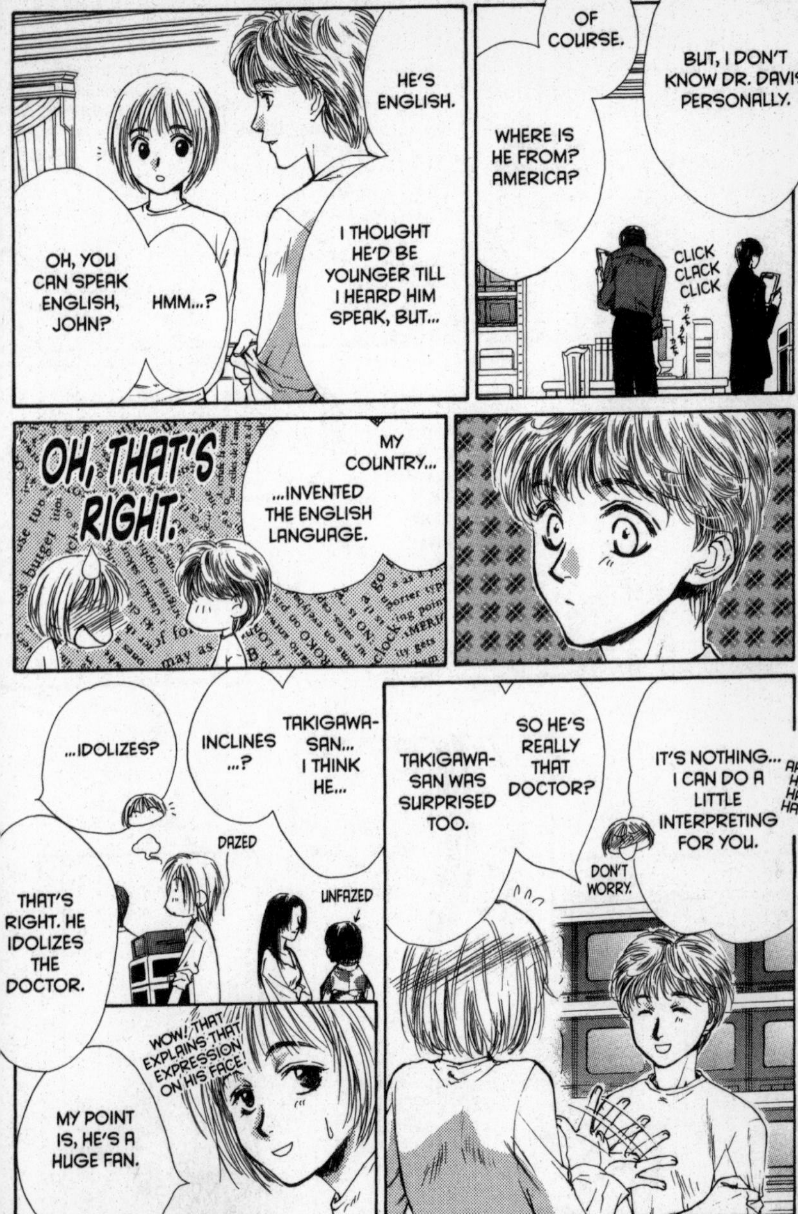
BUT, I DON'T KNOW DR. DAVIS PERSONALLY.
OF COURSE.
WHERE IS HE FROM? AMERICA?
CLICK CLACK CLICK
HE'S ENGLISH.
I THOUGHT HE'D BE YOUNGER TILL I HEARD HIM SPEAK, BUT...
HMM...?
OH, YOU CAN SPEAK ENGLISH, JOHN?
MY COUNTRY...
...INVENTED THE ENGLISH LANGUAGE.
OH, THAT'S RIGHT.
IT'S NOTHING... I CAN DO A LITTLE INTERPRETING FOR YOU.
AHA-HA HA HA.
SO HE'S REALLY THAT DOCTOR?
DON'T WORRY.
TAKIGAWA-SAN WAS SURPRISED TOO.
TAKIGAWA-SAN... I THINK HE...
INCLINES ...?
...IDOLIZES?
DAZED
UNFAZED
THAT'S RIGHT. HE IDOLIZES THE DOCTOR.
WOW! THAT EXPLAINS THAT EXPRESSION ON HIS FACE!
MY POINT IS, HE'S A HUGE FAN.

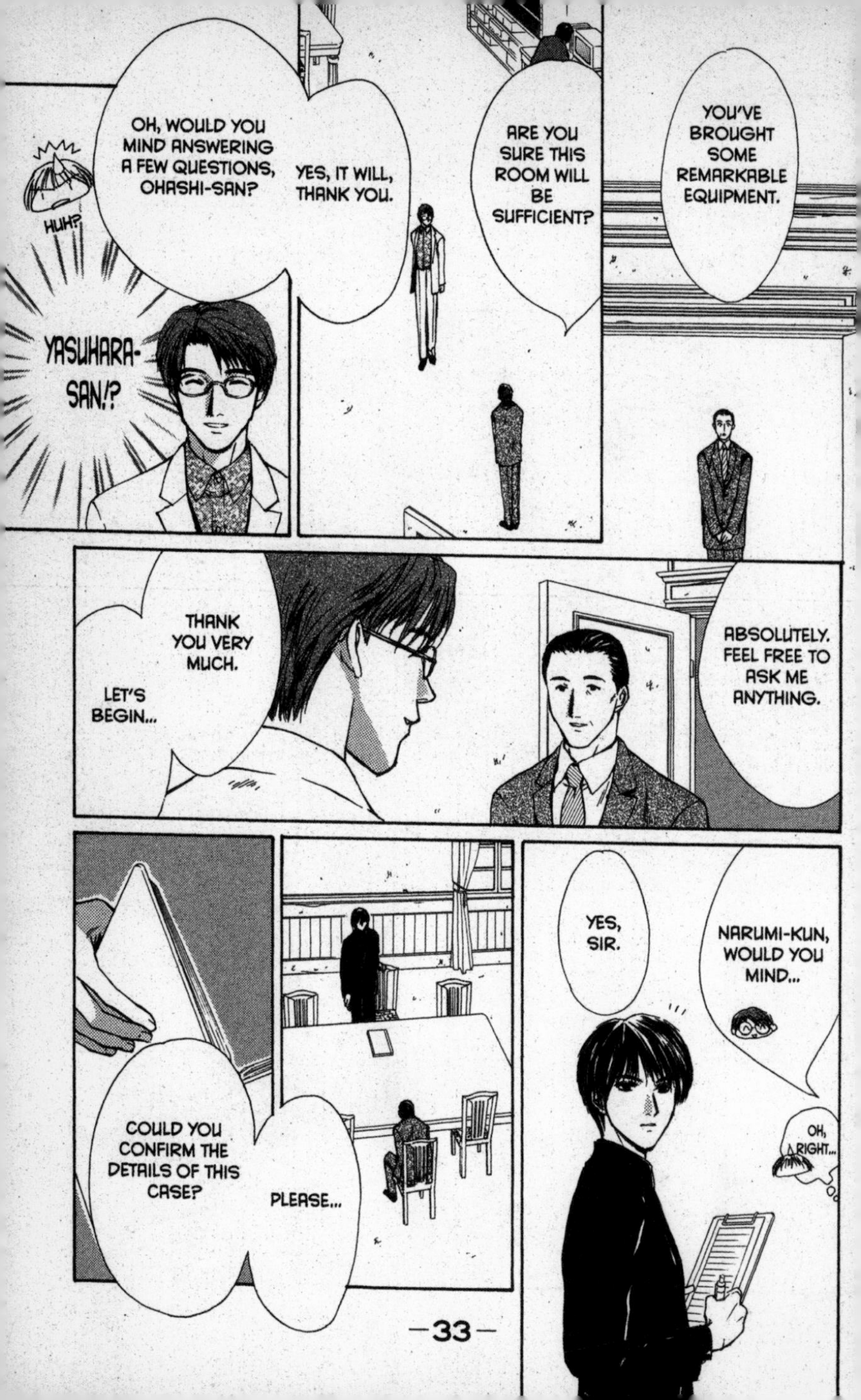

YOU'VE BROUGHT SOME REMARKABLE EQUIPMENT.
ARE YOU SURE THIS ROOM WILL BE SUFFICIENT?
YES, IT WILL, THANK YOU.
OH, WOULD YOU MIND ANSWERING A FEW QUESTIONS, OHASHI-SAN?
HUH?
YASUHARA-SAN!?
ABSOLUTELY. FEEL FREE TO ASK ME ANYTHING.
THANK YOU VERY MUCH.
LET'S BEGIN...
NARUMI-KUN, WOULD YOU MIND...
YES, SIR.
OH, RIGHT...
PLEASE...
COULD YOU CONFIRM THE DETAILS OF THIS CASE?

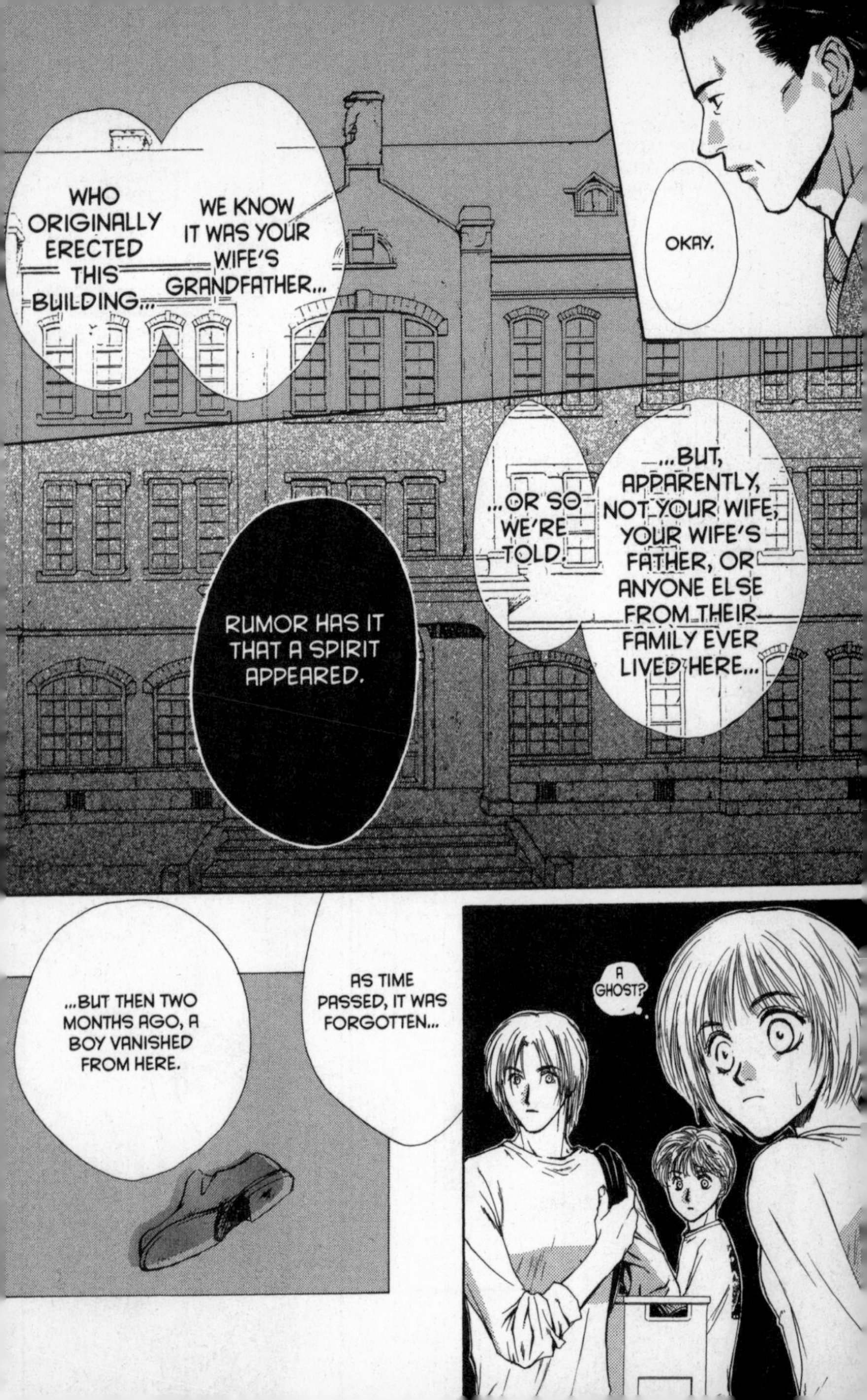
OKAY.
WE KNOW IT WAS YOUR WIFE'S GRANDFATHER...
WHO ORIGINALLY ERECTED THIS BUILDING...
...BUT, APPARENTLY, NOT YOUR WIFE, YOUR WIFE'S FATHER, OR ANYONE ELSE FROM THEIR FAMILY EVER LIVED HERE...
...OR SO WE'RE TOLD.
RUMOR HAS IT THAT A SPIRIT APPEARED.
A GHOST?
AS TIME PASSED, IT WAS FORGOTTEN...
...BUT THEN TWO MONTHS AGO, A BOY VANISHED FROM HERE.

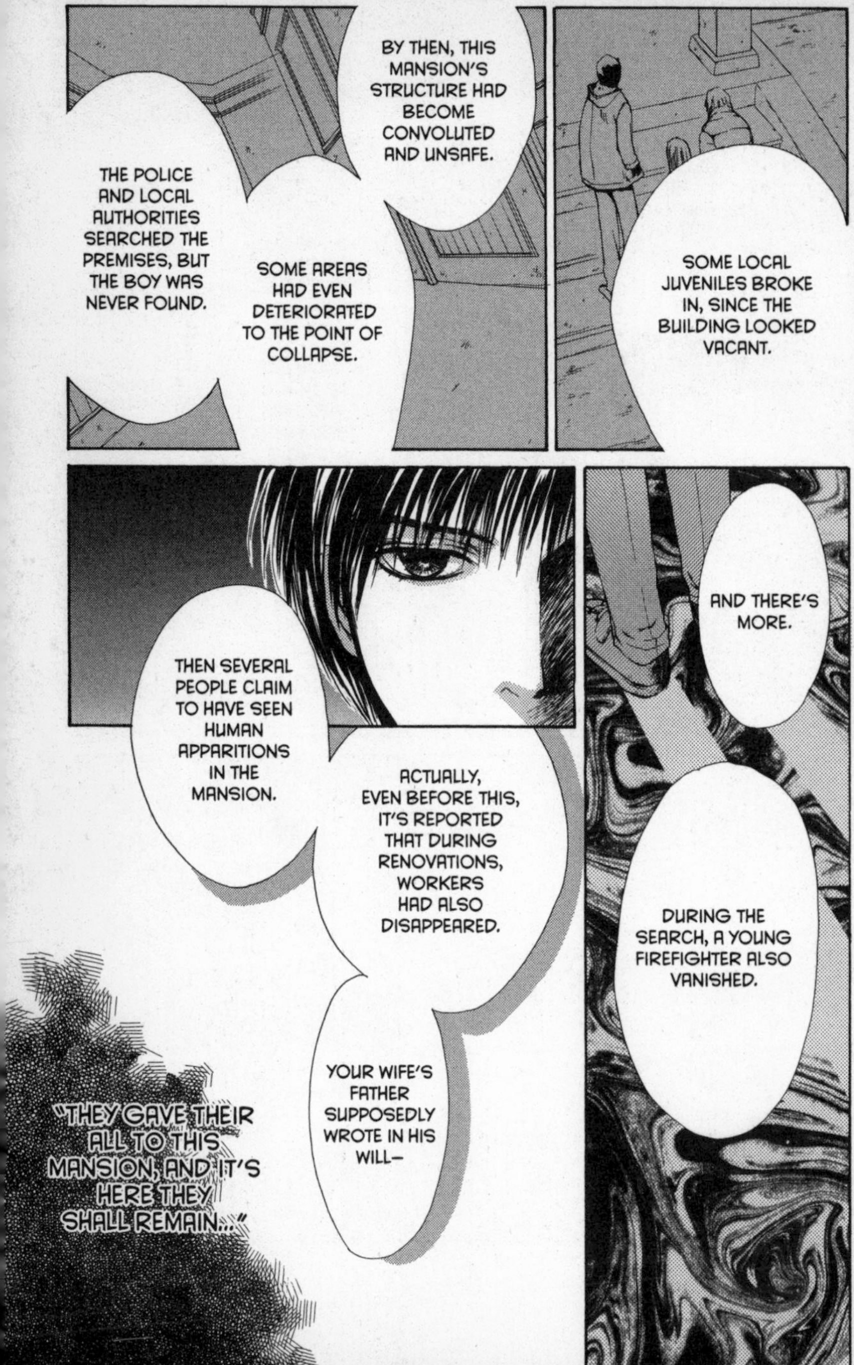
SOME LOCAL JUVENILES BROKE IN, SINCE THE BUILDING LOOKED VACANT.
BY THEN, THIS MANSION'S STRUCTURE HAD BECOME CONVOLUTED AND UNSAFE.
SOME AREAS HAD EVEN DETERIORATED TO THE POINT OF COLLAPSE.
THE POLICE AND LOCAL AUTHORITIES SEARCHED THE PREMISES, BUT THE BOY WAS NEVER FOUND.
AND THERE'S MORE.
DURING THE SEARCH, A YOUNG FIREFIGHTER ALSO VANISHED.
THEN SEVERAL PEOPLE CLAIM TO HAVE SEEN HUMAN APPARITIONS IN THE MANSION.
ACTUALLY, EVEN BEFORE THIS, IT'S REPORTED THAT DURING RENOVATIONS, WORKERS HAD ALSO DISAPPEARED.
YOUR WIFE'S FATHER SUPPOSEDLY WROTE IN HIS WILL—
"THEY GAVE THEIR ALL TO THIS MANSION, AND IT'S HERE THEY SHALL REMAIN..."

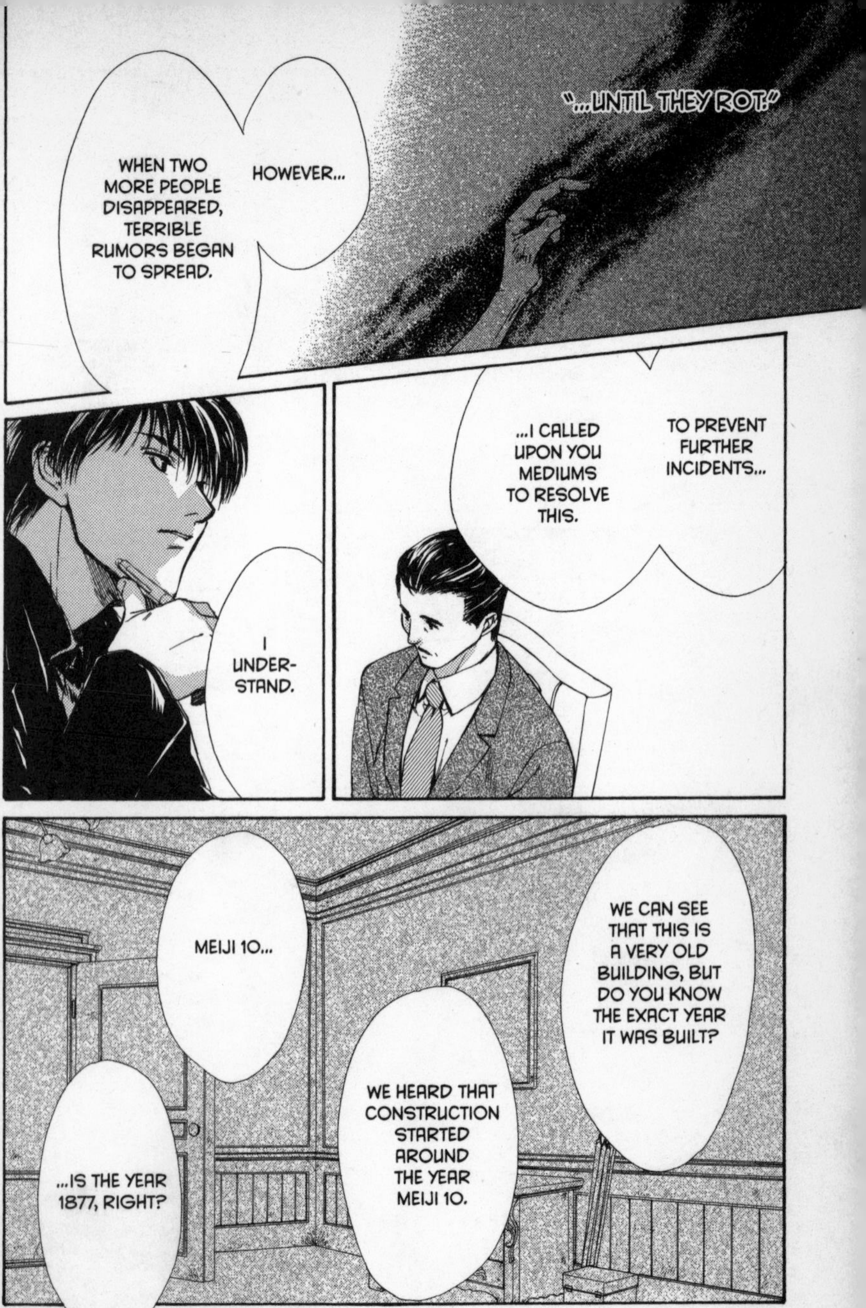
"...UNTIL THEY ROT."
HOWEVER...
WHEN TWO MORE PEOPLE DISAPPEARED, TERRIBLE RUMORS BEGAN TO SPREAD.
TO PREVENT FURTHER INCIDENTS...
...I CALLED UPON YOU MEDIUMS TO RESOLVE THIS.
I UNDER-STAND.
WE CAN SEE THAT THIS IS A VERY OLD BUILDING, BUT DO YOU KNOW THE EXACT YEAR IT WAS BUILT?
WE HEARD THAT CONSTRUCTION STARTED AROUND THE YEAR MEIJI 10.
MEIJI 10...
...IS THE YEAR 1877, RIGHT?

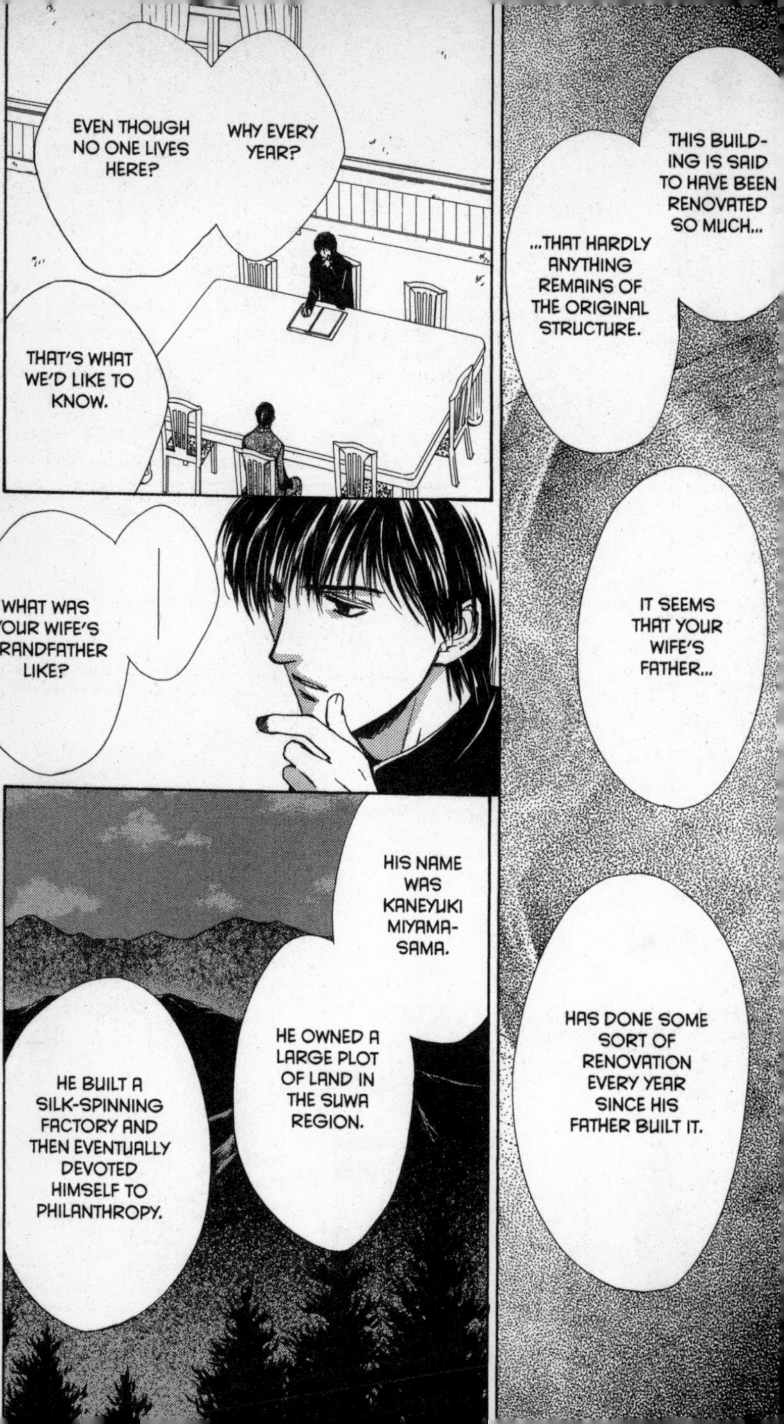
THIS BUILDING IS SAID TO HAVE BEEN RENOVATED SO MUCH...
...THAT HARDLY ANYTHING REMAINS OF THE ORIGINAL STRUCTURE.
IT SEEMS THAT YOUR WIFE'S FATHER...
HAS DONE SOME SORT OF RENOVATION EVERY YEAR SINCE HIS FATHER BUILT IT.
WHY EVERY YEAR?
EVEN THOUGH NO ONE LIVES HERE?
THAT'S WHAT WE'D LIKE TO KNOW.
WHAT WAS YOUR WIFE'S GRANDFATHER LIKE?
HIS NAME WAS KANEYUKI MIYAMA-SAMA.
HE OWNED A LARGE PLOT OF LAND IN THE SUWA REGION.
HE BUILT A SILK-SPINNING FACTORY AND THEN EVENTUALLY DEVOTED HIMSELF TO PHILANTHROPY.

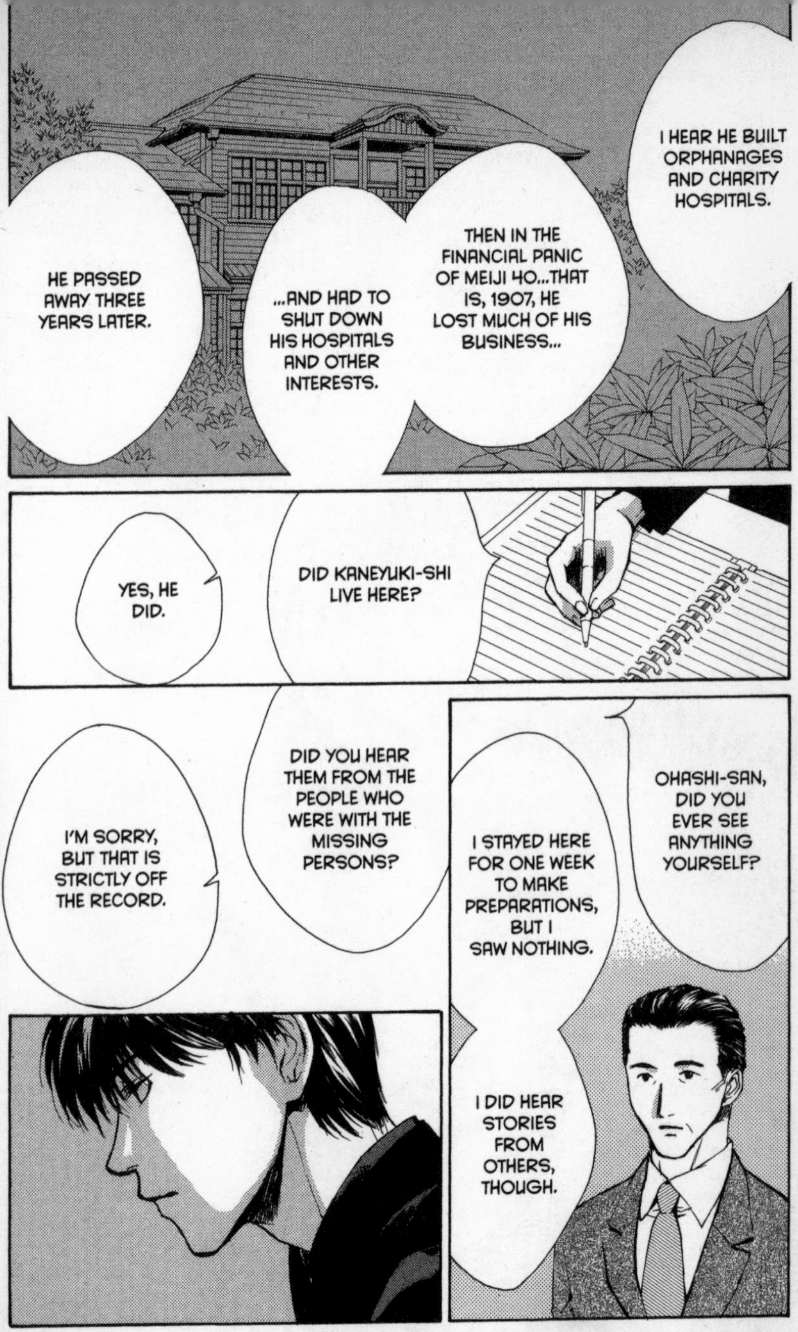
I HEAR HE BUILT ORPHANAGES AND CHARITY HOSPITALS.
THEN IN THE FINANCIAL PANIC OF MEIJI 40...THAT IS, 1907, HE LOST MUCH OF HIS BUSINESS...
...AND HAD TO SHUT DOWN HIS HOSPITALS AND OTHER INTERESTS.
HE PASSED AWAY THREE YEARS LATER.
DID KANEYUKI-SHI LIVE HERE?
YES, HE DID.
OHASHI-SAN, DID YOU EVER SEE ANYTHING YOURSELF?
I STAYED HERE FOR ONE WEEK TO MAKE PREPARATIONS, BUT I SAW NOTHING.
I DID HEAR STORIES FROM OTHERS, THOUGH.
DID YOU HEAR THEM FROM THE PEOPLE WHO WERE WITH THE MISSING PERSONS?
I'M SORRY, BUT THAT IS STRICTLY OFF THE RECORD.

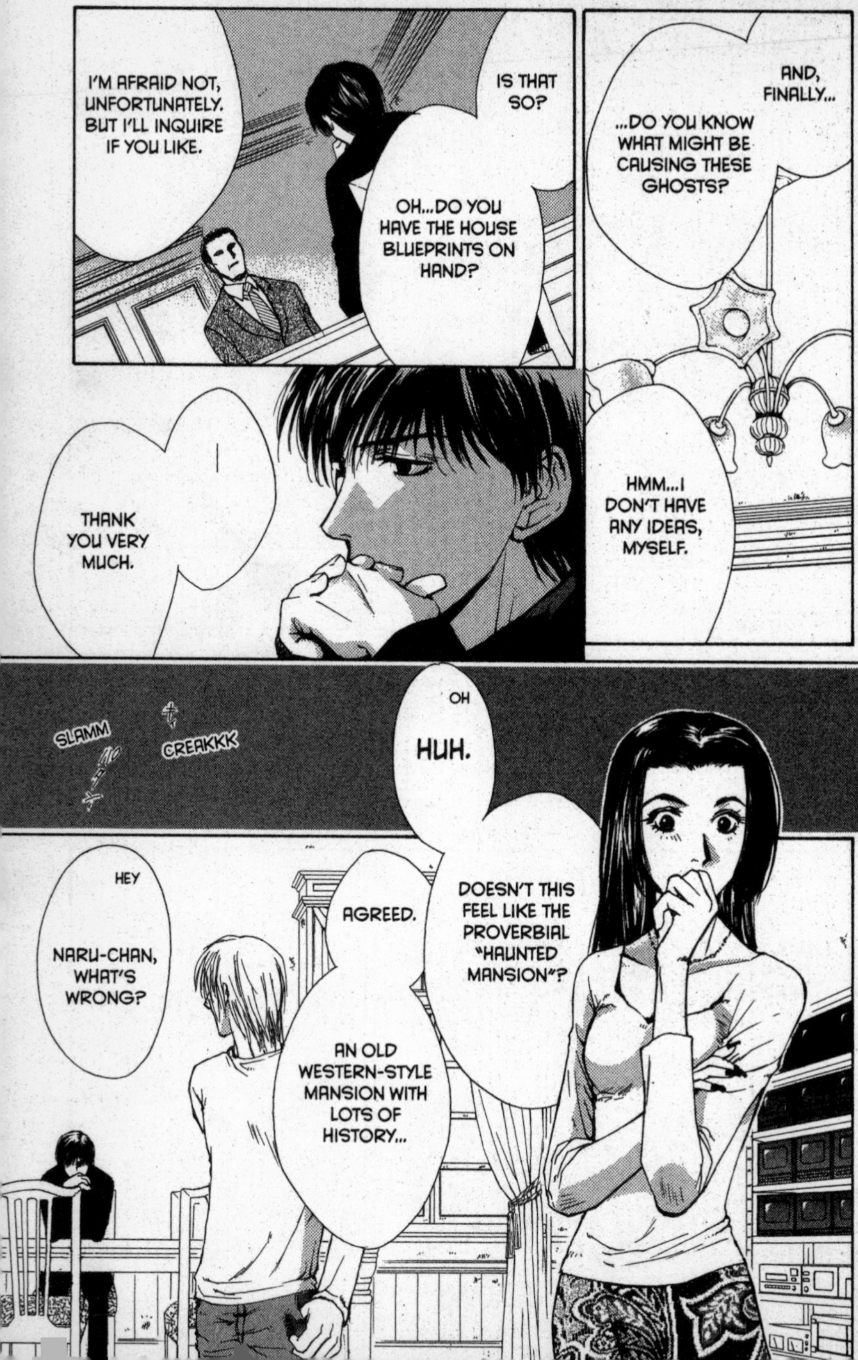
AND, FINALLY...
...DO YOU KNOW WHAT MIGHT BE CAUSING THESE GHOSTS?
HMM...I DON'T HAVE ANY IDEAS, MYSELF.
IS THAT SO?
OH...DO YOU HAVE THE HOUSE BLUEPRINTS ON HAND?
I'M AFRAID NOT, UNFORTUNATELY. BUT I'LL INQUIRE IF YOU LIKE.
THANK YOU VERY MUCH.
OH
HUH.
CREAKKK
SLAMM
DOESN'T THIS FEEL LIKE THE PROVERBIAL "HAUNTED MANSION"?
AGREED.
AN OLD WESTERN-STYLE MANSION WITH LOTS OF HISTORY...
HEY
NARU-CHAN, WHAT'S WRONG?

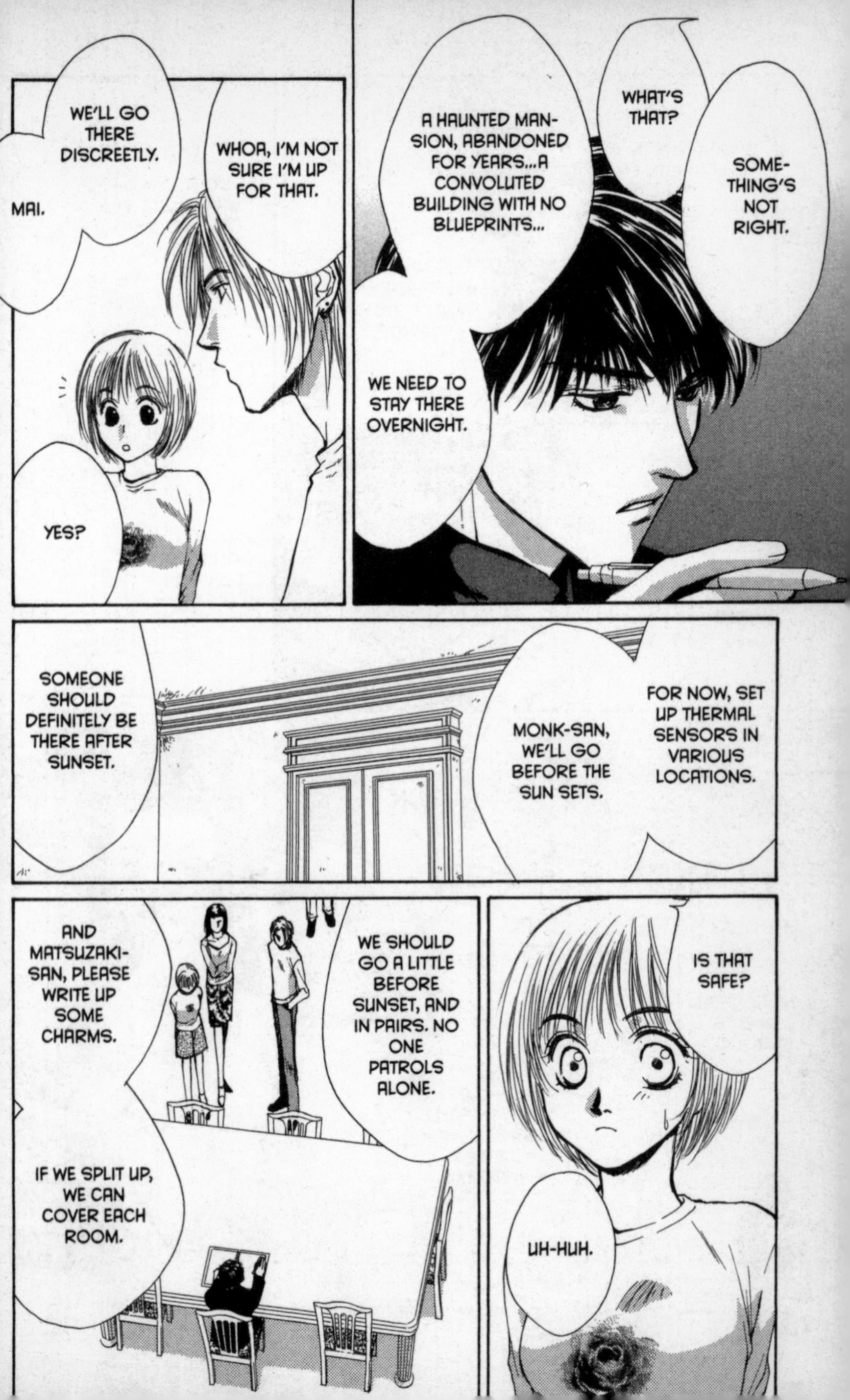

WHAT'S THAT?
SOMETHING'S NOT RIGHT.
A HAUNTED MANSION, ABANDONED FOR YEARS...A CONVOLUTED BUILDING WITH NO BLUEPRINTS...
WE NEED TO STAY THERE OVERNIGHT.
WHOA, I'M NOT SURE I'M UP FOR THAT.
WE'LL GO THERE DISCREETLY.
MAI.
YES?
FOR NOW, SET UP THERMAL SENSORS IN VARIOUS LOCATIONS.
MONK-SAN, WE'LL GO BEFORE THE SUN SETS.
SOMEONE SHOULD DEFINITELY BE THERE AFTER SUNSET.
IS THAT SAFE?
UH-HUH.
WE SHOULD GO A LITTLE BEFORE SUNSET, AND IN PAIRS. NO ONE PATROLS ALONE.
AND MATSUZAKI-SAN, PLEASE WRITE UP SOME CHARMS.
IF WE SPLIT UP, WE CAN COVER EACH ROOM.

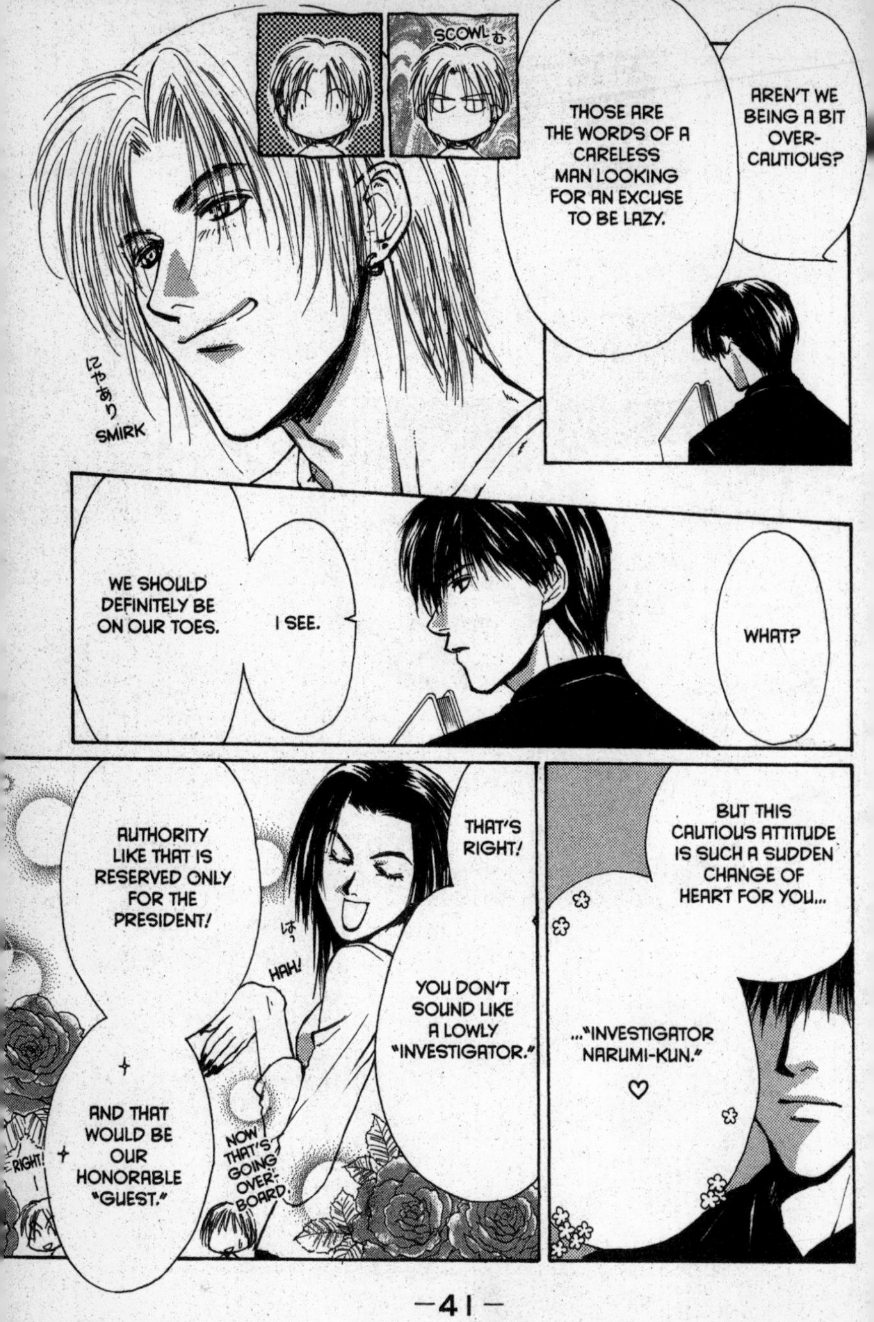
AREN'T WE BEING A BIT OVER-CAUTIOUS?
THOSE ARE THE WORDS OF A CARELESS MAN LOOKING FOR AN EXCUSE TO BE LAZY.
SCOWL む
にやあり
SMIRK
WHAT?
I SEE.
WE SHOULD DEFINITELY BE ON OUR TOES.
BUT THIS CAUTIOUS ATTITUDE IS SUCH A SUDDEN CHANGE OF HEART FOR YOU...
..."INVESTIGATOR NARUMI-KUN." ♡
THAT'S RIGHT!
YOU DON'T SOUND LIKE A LOWLY "INVESTIGATOR."
はっ
HAH!
AUTHORITY LIKE THAT IS RESERVED ONLY FOR THE PRESIDENT!
NOW THAT'S GOING OVERBOARD.
AND THAT WOULD BE OUR HONORABLE "GUEST."
RIGHT!

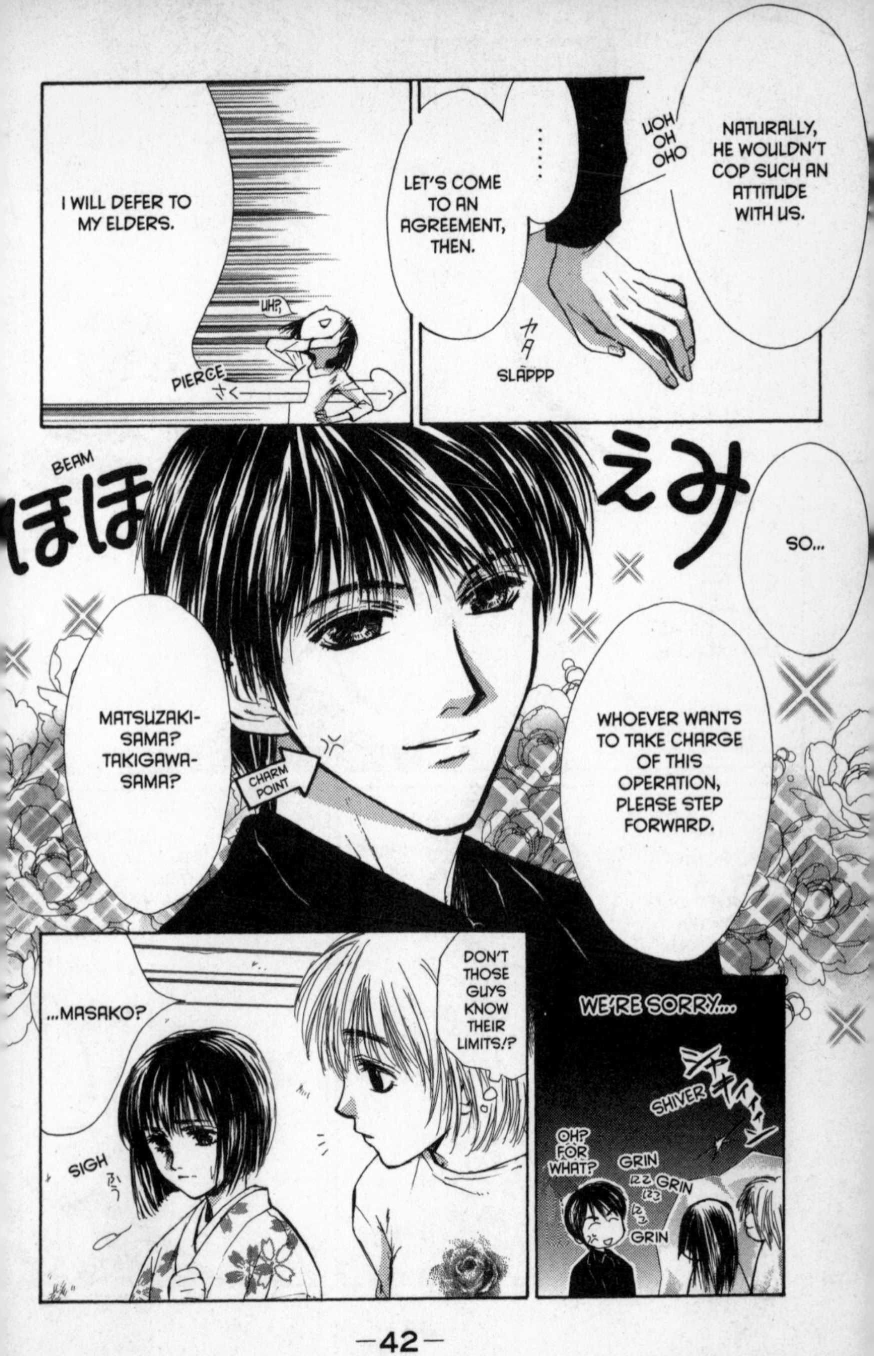
NATURALLY, HE WOULDN'T COP SUCH AN ATTITUDE WITH US.
UOH OH OHO
......
LET'S COME TO AN AGREEMENT, THEN.
カタ
SLAPPP
I WILL DEFER TO MY ELDERS.
UH?
PIERCE
さく
SO...
えみ
ほほ
BEAM
WHOEVER WANTS TO TAKE CHARGE OF THIS OPERATION, PLEASE STEP FORWARD.
MATSUZAKI-SAMA? TAKIGAWA-SAMA?
CHARM POINT
WE'RE SORRY....
SHIVER
GRIN
GRIN
GRIN
OH? FOR WHAT?
DON'T THOSE GUYS KNOW THEIR LIMITS!?
...MASAKO?
SIGH
ふう

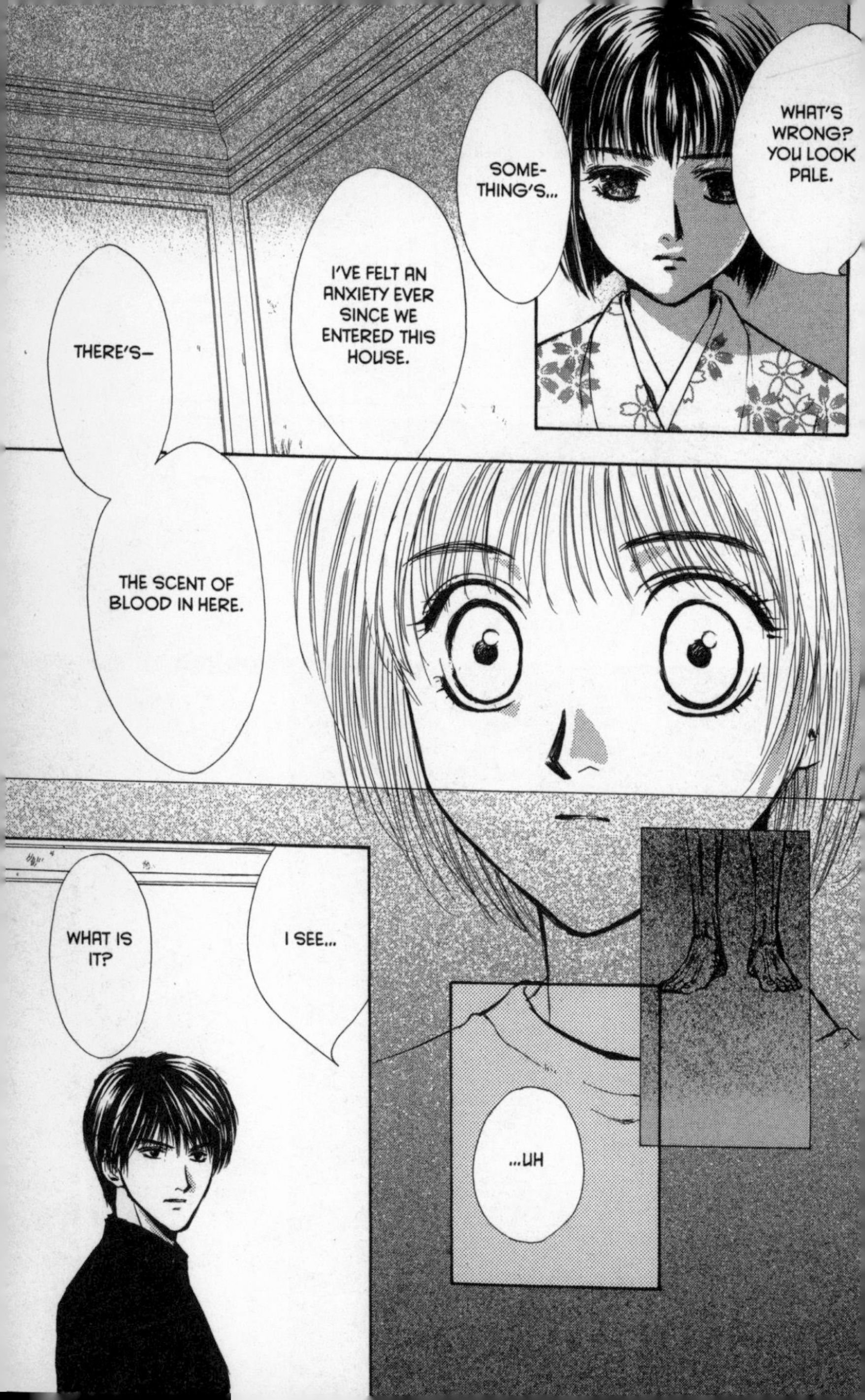
WHAT'S WRONG? YOU LOOK PALE.
SOME-THING'S...
I'VE FELT AN ANXIETY EVER SINCE WE ENTERED THIS HOUSE.
THERE'S—
THE SCENT OF BLOOD IN HERE.
...UH
I SEE...
WHAT IS IT?

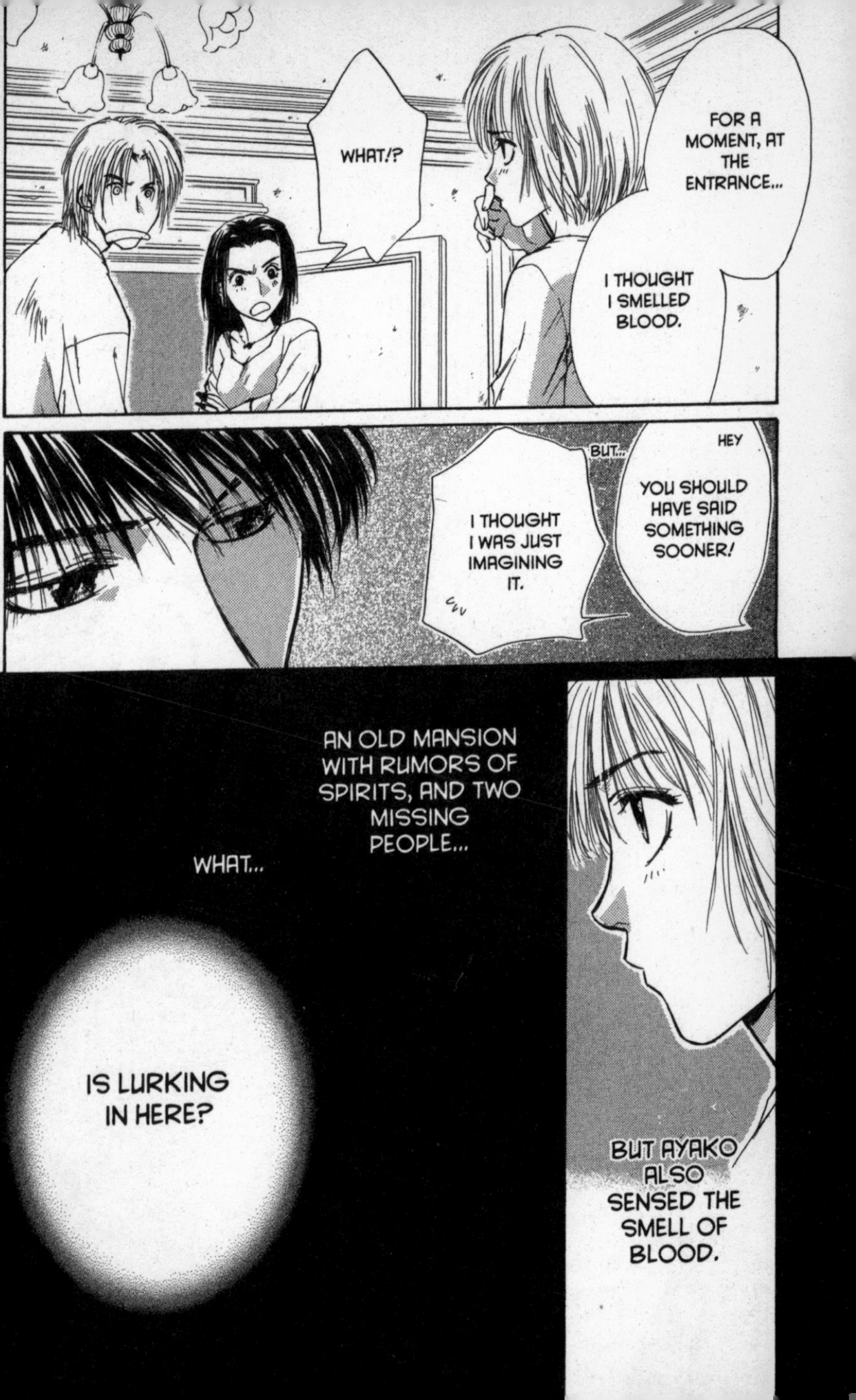
FOR A MOMENT, AT THE ENTRANCE...
I THOUGHT I SMELLED BLOOD.
WHAT!?
HEY
YOU SHOULD HAVE SAID SOMETHING SOONER!
BUT...
I THOUGHT I WAS JUST IMAGINING IT.
AN OLD MANSION WITH RUMORS OF SPIRITS, AND TWO MISSING PEOPLE...
WHAT...
IS LURKING IN HERE?
BUT AYAKO ALSO SENSED THE SMELL OF BLOOD.

GHOST HUNT
— THE BLOODSTAINED LABYRINTH —

FILE 2

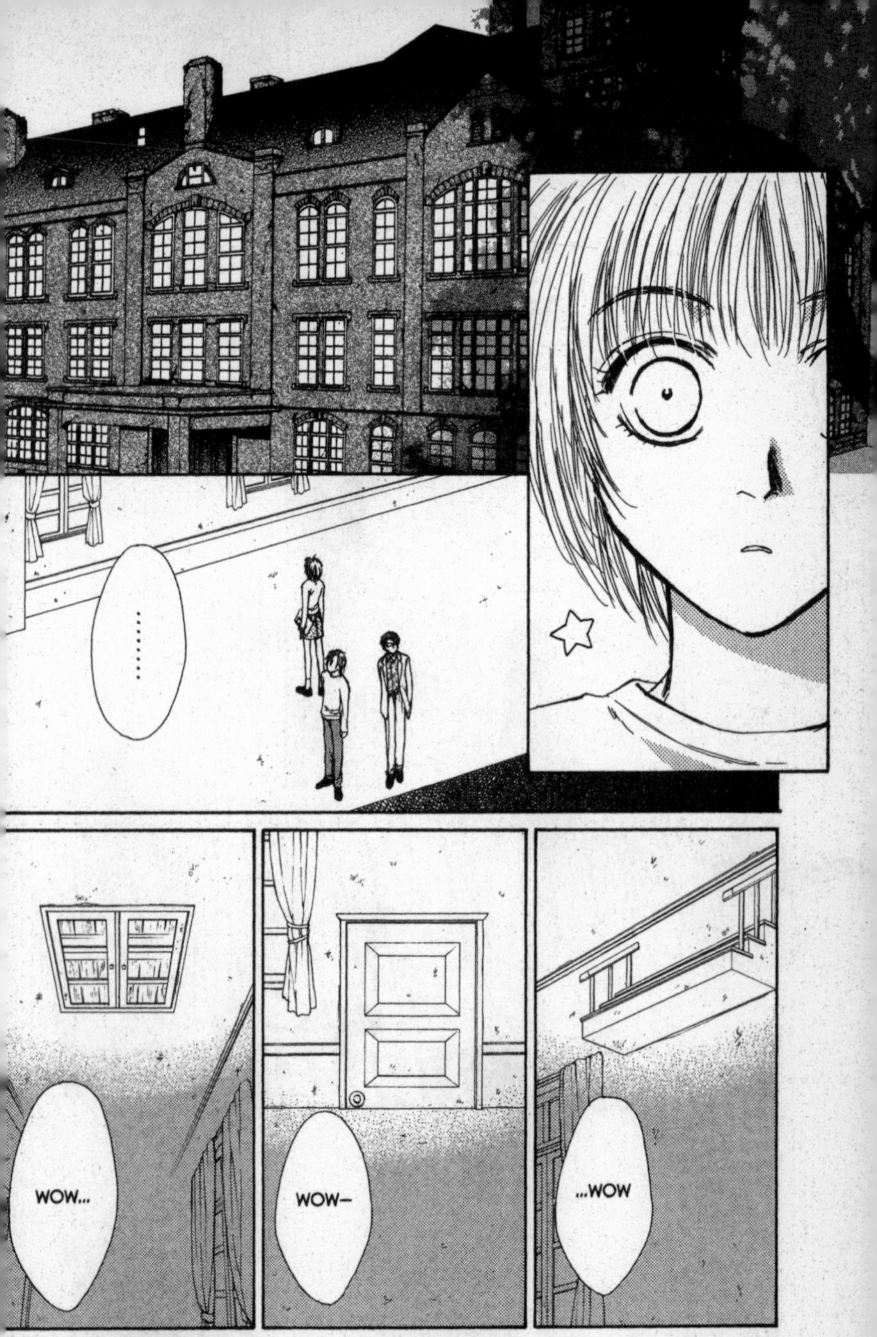
......
...WOW
WOW—
WOW...

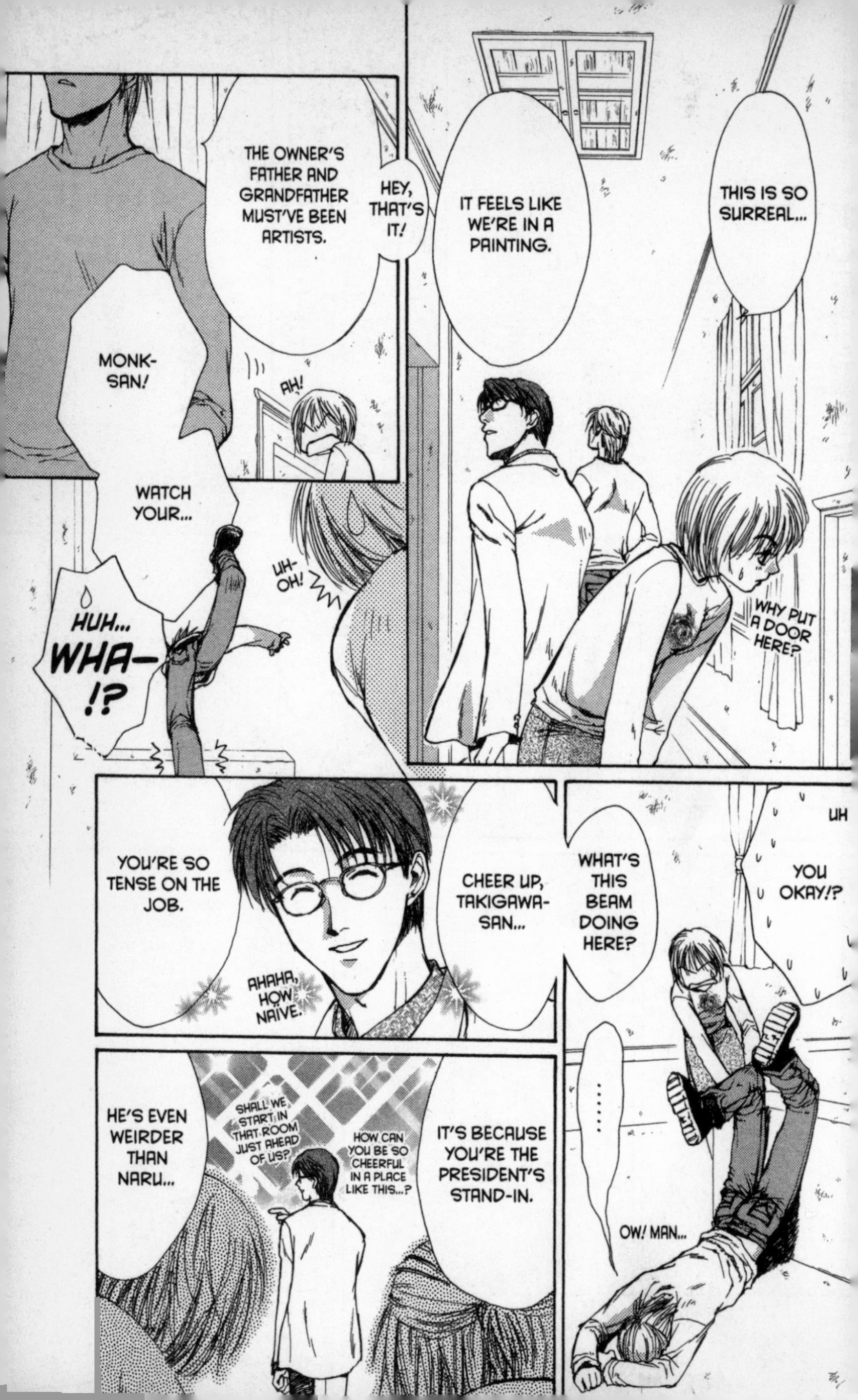

THIS IS SO SURREAL...
IT FEELS LIKE WE'RE IN A PAINTING.
WHY PUT A DOOR HERE?
HEY, THAT'S IT!
THE OWNER'S FATHER AND GRANDFATHER MUST'VE BEEN ARTISTS.
AH!
MONK-SAN!
UH-OH!
WATCH YOUR...
HUH... WHA-!?
UH
YOU OKAY!?
WHAT'S THIS BEAM DOING HERE?
......
OW! MAN...
CHEER UP, TAKIGAWA-SAN...
AHAHA, HOW NAÏVE.
YOU'RE SO TENSE ON THE JOB.
IT'S BECAUSE YOU'RE THE PRESIDENT'S STAND-IN.
HOW CAN YOU BE SO CHEERFUL IN A PLACE LIKE THIS...?
SHALL WE START IN THAT ROOM JUST AHEAD OF US?
HE'S EVEN WEIRDER THAN NARU...

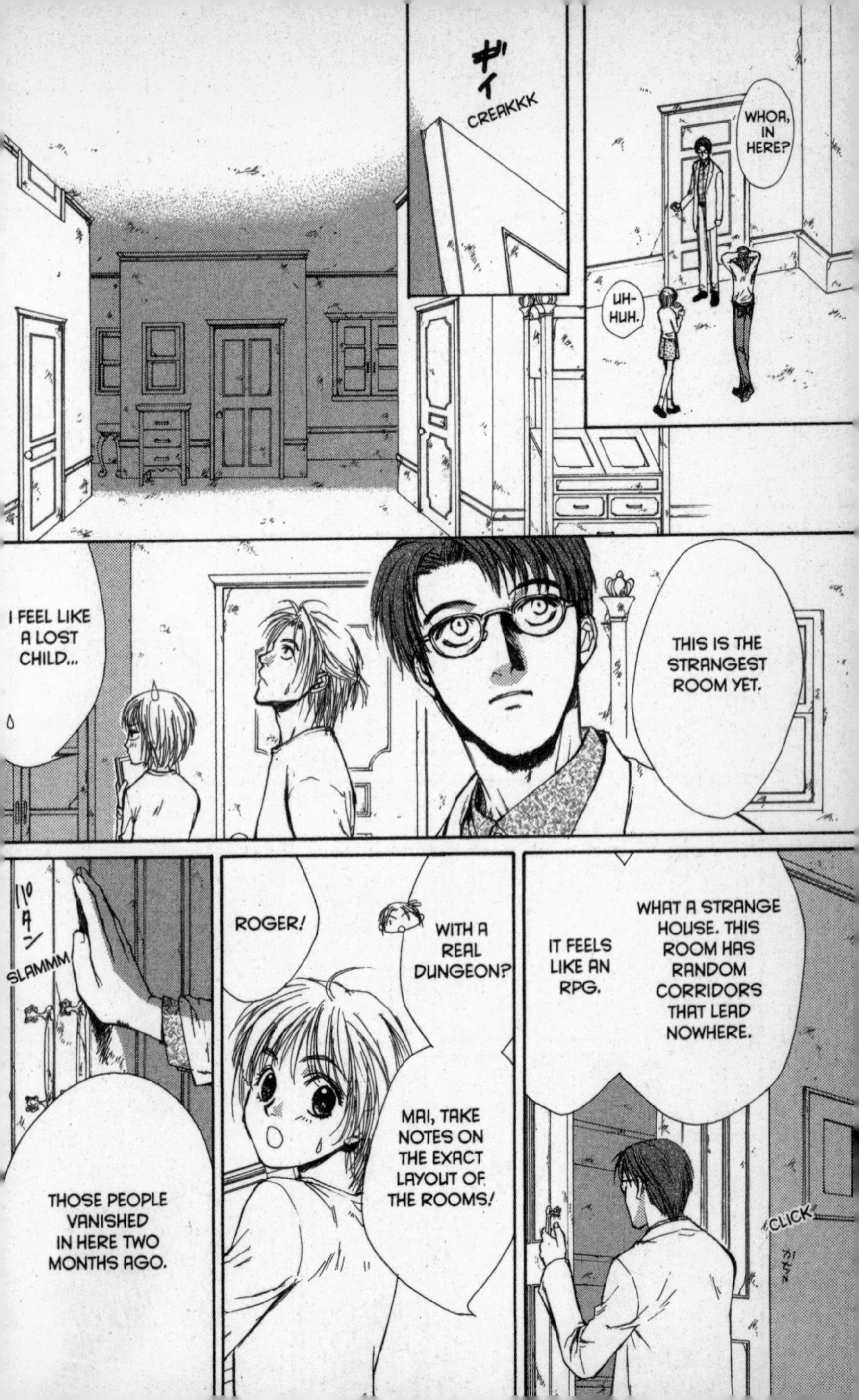

WHOA, IN HERE?
UH-HUH.
CREAKKK
THIS IS THE STRANGEST ROOM YET.
I FEEL LIKE A LOST CHILD...
WHAT A STRANGE HOUSE. THIS ROOM HAS RANDOM CORRIDORS THAT LEAD NOWHERE.
IT FEELS LIKE AN RPG.
CLICK
WITH A REAL DUNGEON?
ROGER!
MAI, TAKE NOTES ON THE EXACT LAYOUT OF THE ROOMS!
SLAMMM
THOSE PEOPLE VANISHED IN HERE TWO MONTHS AGO.

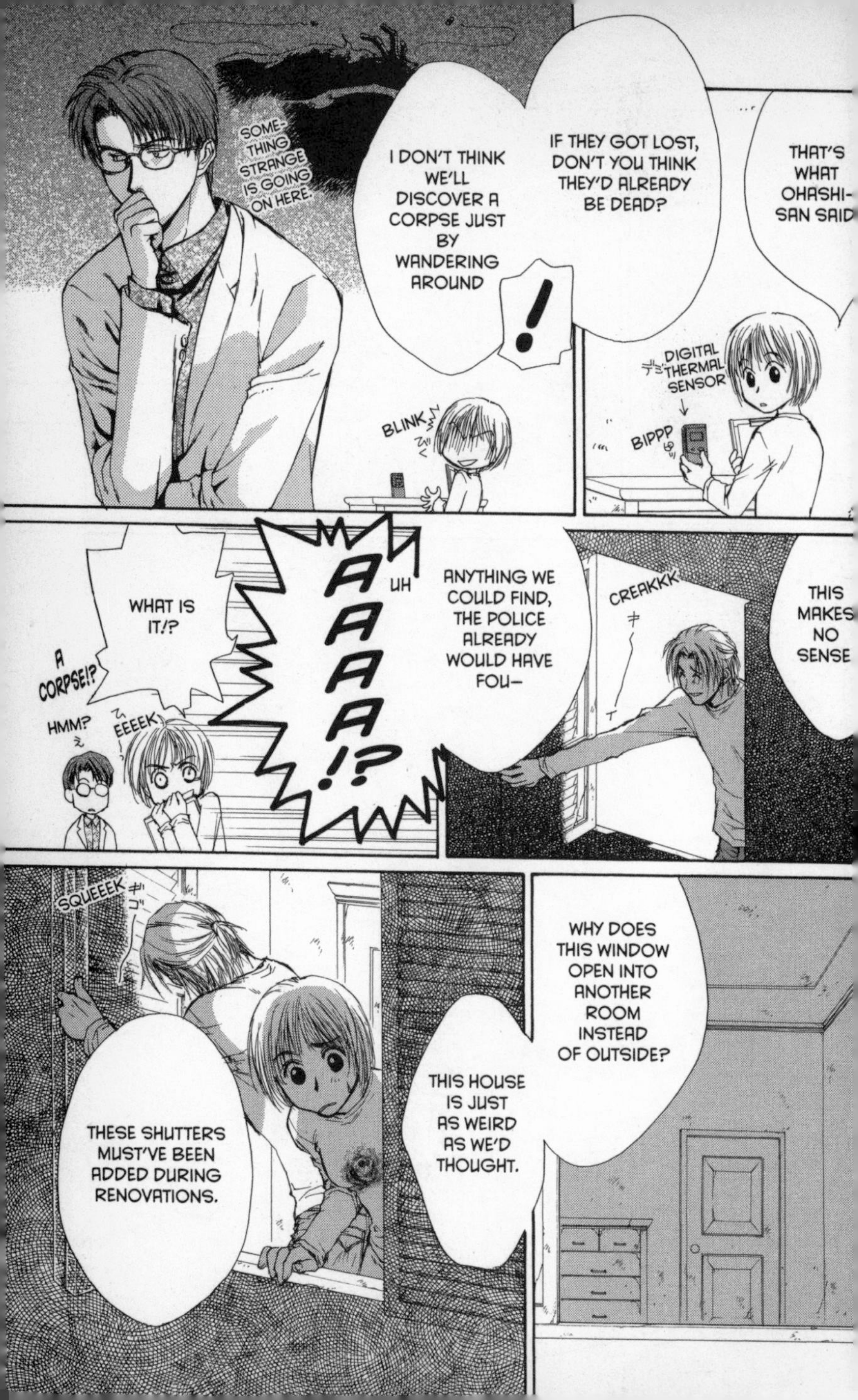
...
THAT'S WHAT OHASHI-SAN SAID
DIGITAL THERMAL SENSOR
BIPPP
IF THEY GOT LOST, DON'T YOU THINK THEY'D ALREADY BE DEAD?
I DON'T THINK WE'LL DISCOVER A CORPSE JUST BY WANDERING AROUND
!
BLINK
SOME-THING STRANGE IS GOING ON HERE.
THIS MAKES NO SENSE
CREAKKK
ANYTHING WE COULD FIND, THE POLICE ALREADY WOULD HAVE FOU—
UH
AAAAA!?
WHAT IS IT!?
A CORPSE!?
EEEEK
HMM?
WHY DOES THIS WINDOW OPEN INTO ANOTHER ROOM INSTEAD OF OUTSIDE?
THIS HOUSE IS JUST AS WEIRD AS WE'D THOUGHT.
SQUEEEK
THESE SHUTTERS MUST'VE BEEN ADDED DURING RENOVATIONS.

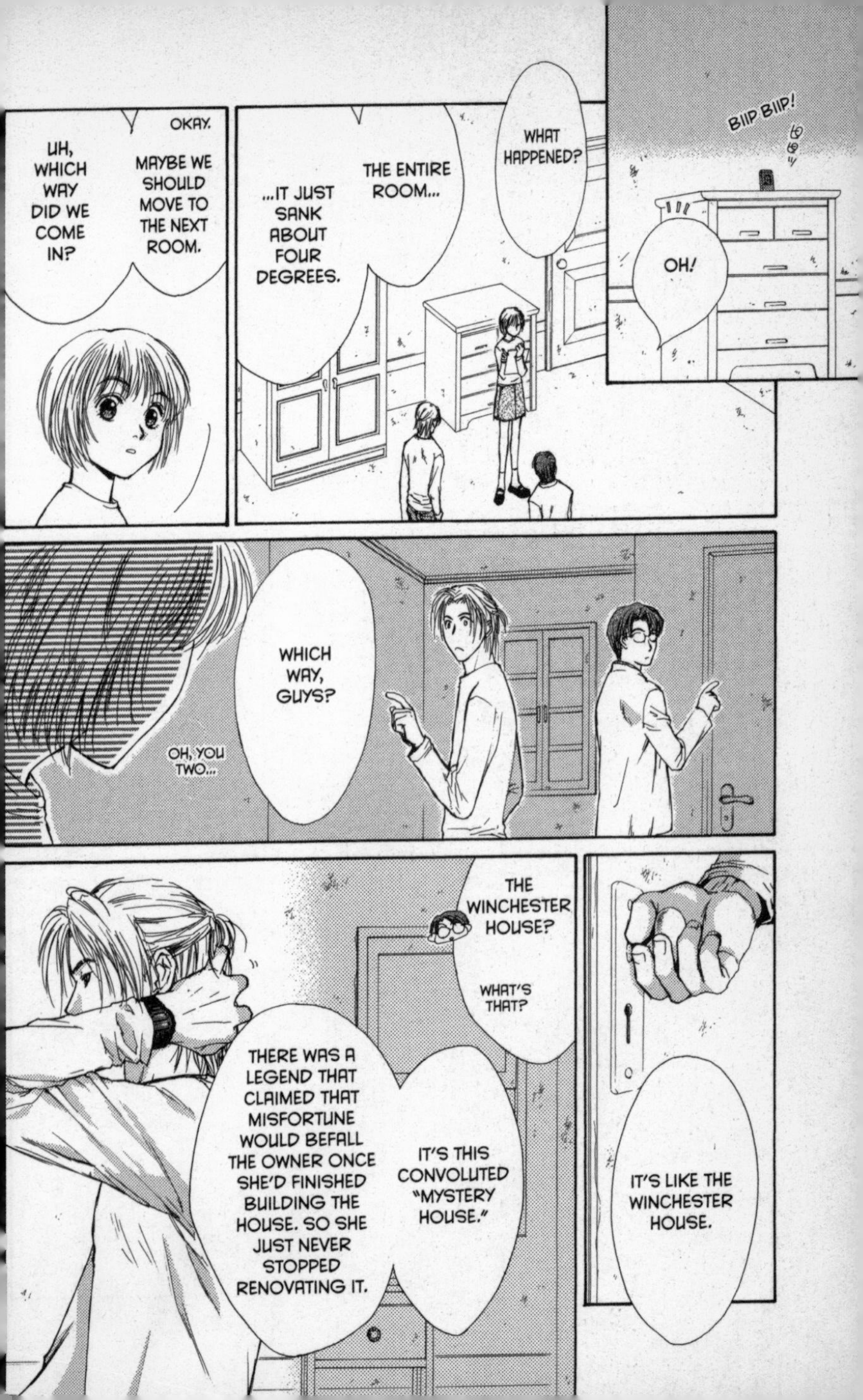
BIIP BIIP!
OH!
WHAT HAPPENED?
THE ENTIRE ROOM...
...IT JUST SANK ABOUT FOUR DEGREES.
OKAY. MAYBE WE SHOULD MOVE TO THE NEXT ROOM.
UH, WHICH WAY DID WE COME IN?
WHICH WAY, GUYS?
OH, YOU TWO...
IT'S LIKE THE WINCHESTER HOUSE.
THE WINCHESTER HOUSE?
WHAT'S THAT?
IT'S THIS CONVOLUTED "MYSTERY HOUSE."
THERE WAS A LEGEND THAT CLAIMED THAT MISFORTUNE WOULD BEFALL THE OWNER ONCE SHE'D FINISHED BUILDING THE HOUSE. SO SHE JUST NEVER STOPPED RENOVATING IT.

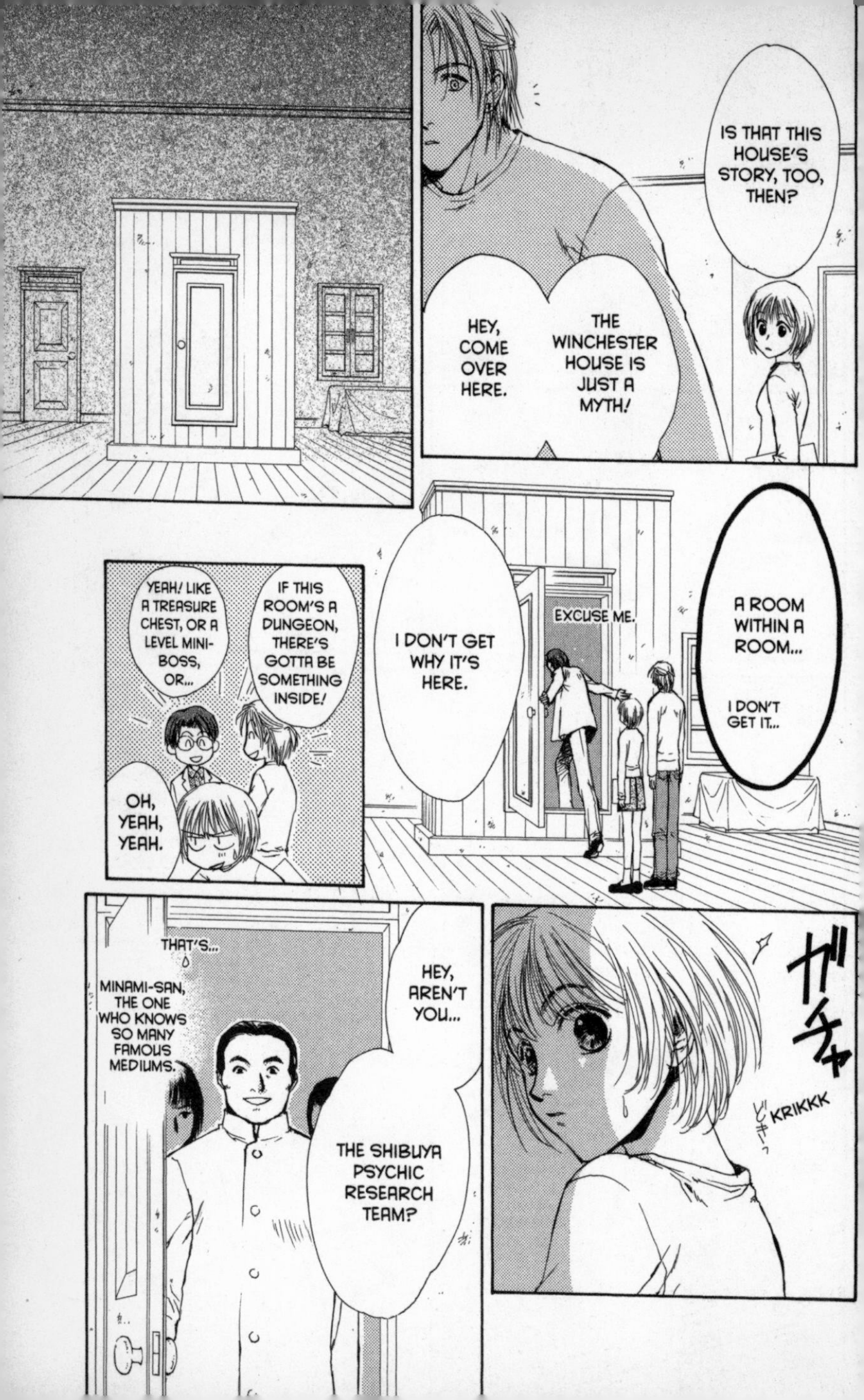
IS THAT THIS HOUSE'S STORY, TOO, THEN?
THE WINCHESTER HOUSE IS JUST A MYTH!
HEY, COME OVER HERE.
A ROOM WITHIN A ROOM...
I DON'T GET IT...
EXCUSE ME.
I DON'T GET WHY IT'S HERE.
IF THIS ROOM'S A DUNGEON, THERE'S GOTTA BE SOMETHING INSIDE!
YEAH! LIKE A TREASURE CHEST, OR A LEVEL MINI-BOSS, OR...
OH, YEAH, YEAH.
ガチャ
KRIKKK
どきっ
HEY, AREN'T YOU...
THE SHIBUYA PSYCHIC RESEARCH TEAM?
THAT'S...
MINAMI-SAN, THE ONE WHO KNOWS SO MANY FAMOUS MEDIUMS.

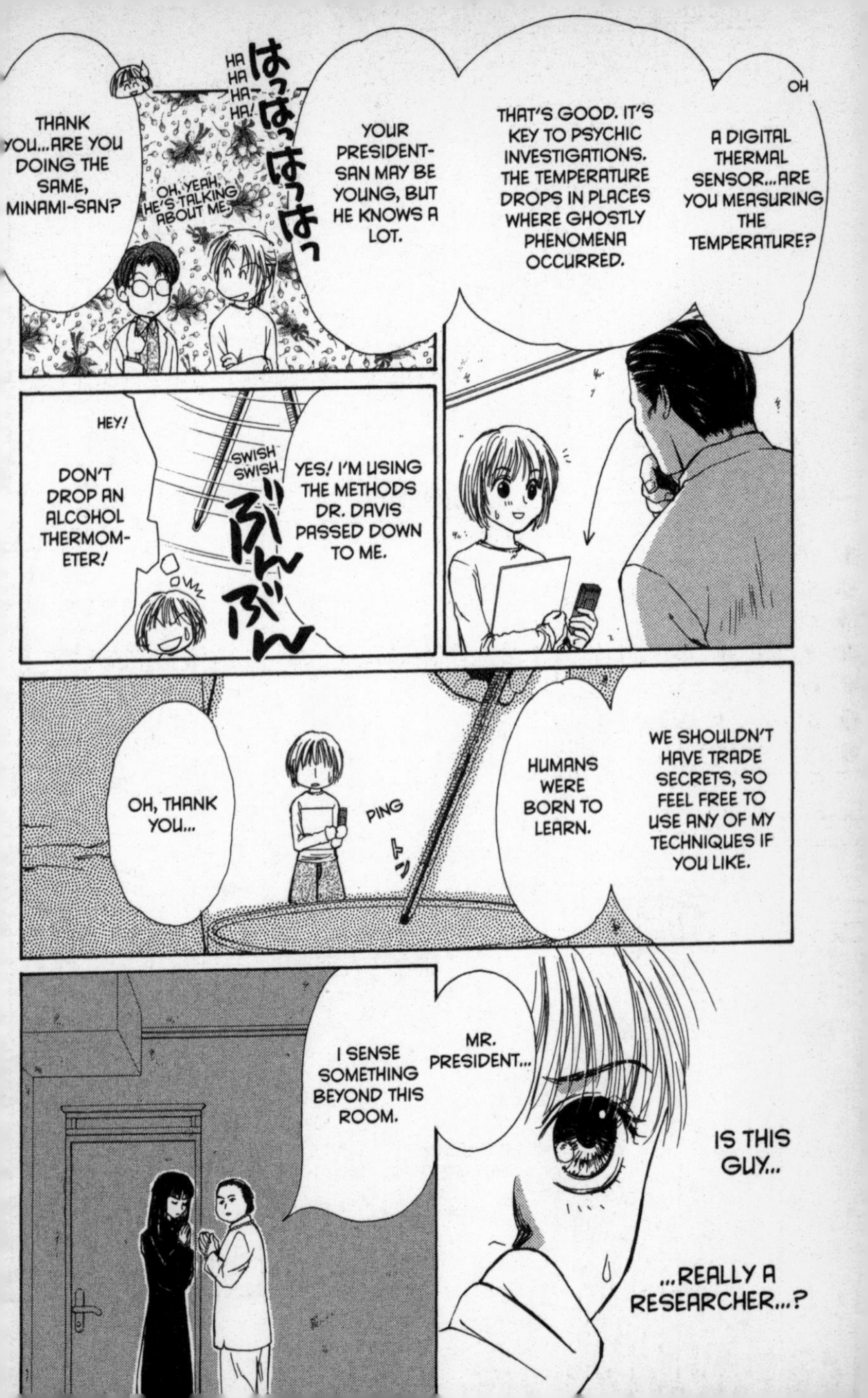
OH
A DIGITAL THERMAL SENSOR...ARE YOU MEASURING THE TEMPERATURE?
THAT'S GOOD. IT'S KEY TO PSYCHIC INVESTIGATIONS. THE TEMPERATURE DROPS IN PLACES WHERE GHOSTLY PHENOMENA OCCURRED.
YOUR PRESIDENT-SAN MAY BE YOUNG, BUT HE KNOWS A LOT.
HA HA HA HA!
OH, YEAH, HE'S TALKING ABOUT ME.
THANK YOU...ARE YOU DOING THE SAME, MINAMI-SAN?
YES! I'M USING THE METHODS DR. DAVIS PASSED DOWN TO ME.
SWISH SWISH
HEY!
DON'T DROP AN ALCOHOL THERMOM-ETER!
WE SHOULDN'T HAVE TRADE SECRETS, SO FEEL FREE TO USE ANY OF MY TECHNIQUES IF YOU LIKE.
HUMANS WERE BORN TO LEARN.
PING
OH, THANK YOU...
IS THIS GUY...
...REALLY A RESEARCHER...?
MR. PRESIDENT...
I SENSE SOMETHING BEYOND THIS ROOM.

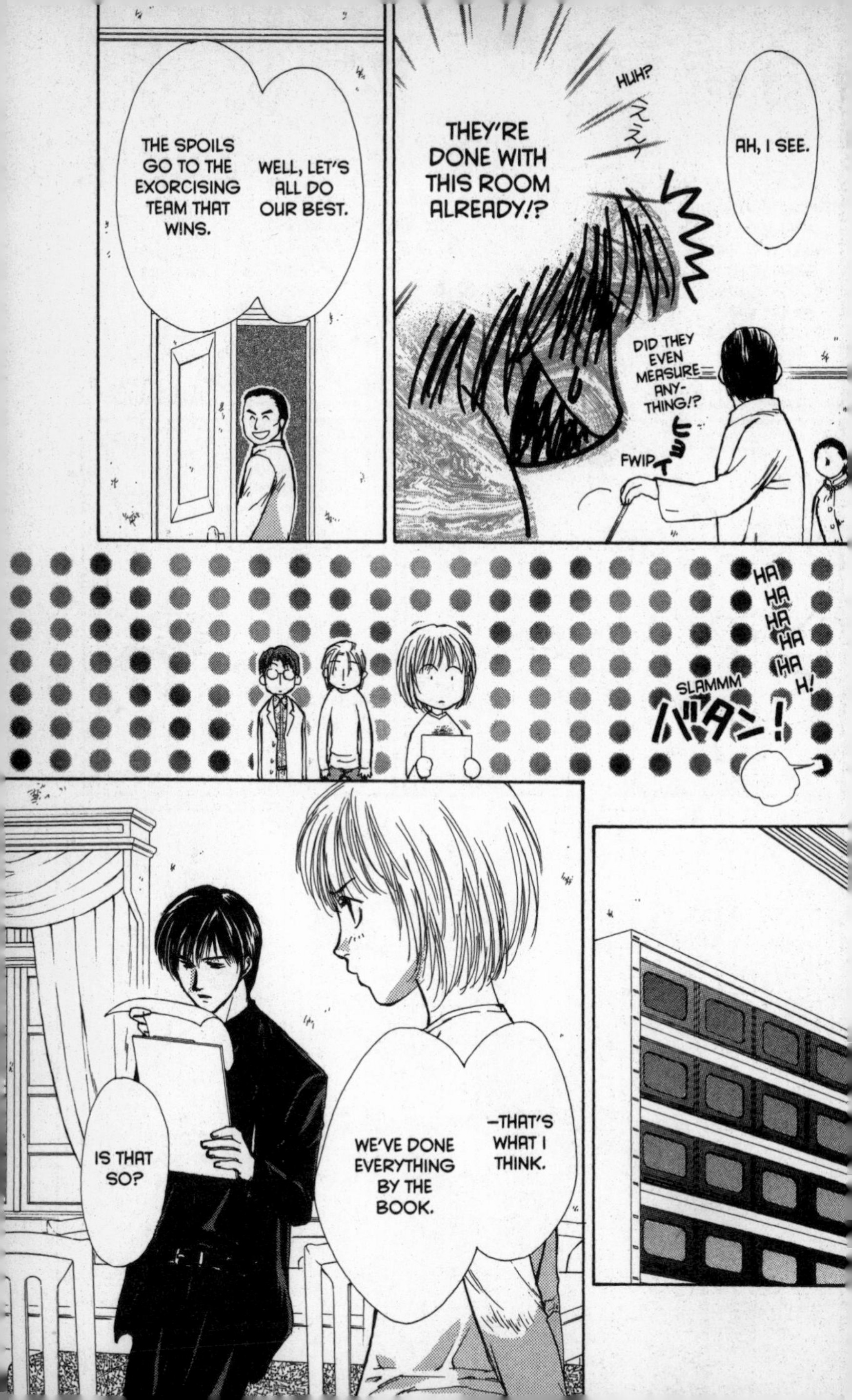

AH, I SEE.
HUH?
THEY'RE DONE WITH THIS ROOM ALREADY!?
DID THEY EVEN MEASURE ANY-THING!?
FWIP
ヒョイ
THE SPOILS GO TO THE EXORCISING TEAM THAT WINS. WELL, LET'S ALL DO OUR BEST.
HA HA HA HA HA H!
SLAMMM
バタン!
WE'VE DONE EVERYTHING BY THE BOOK. —THAT'S WHAT I THINK.
IS THAT SO?

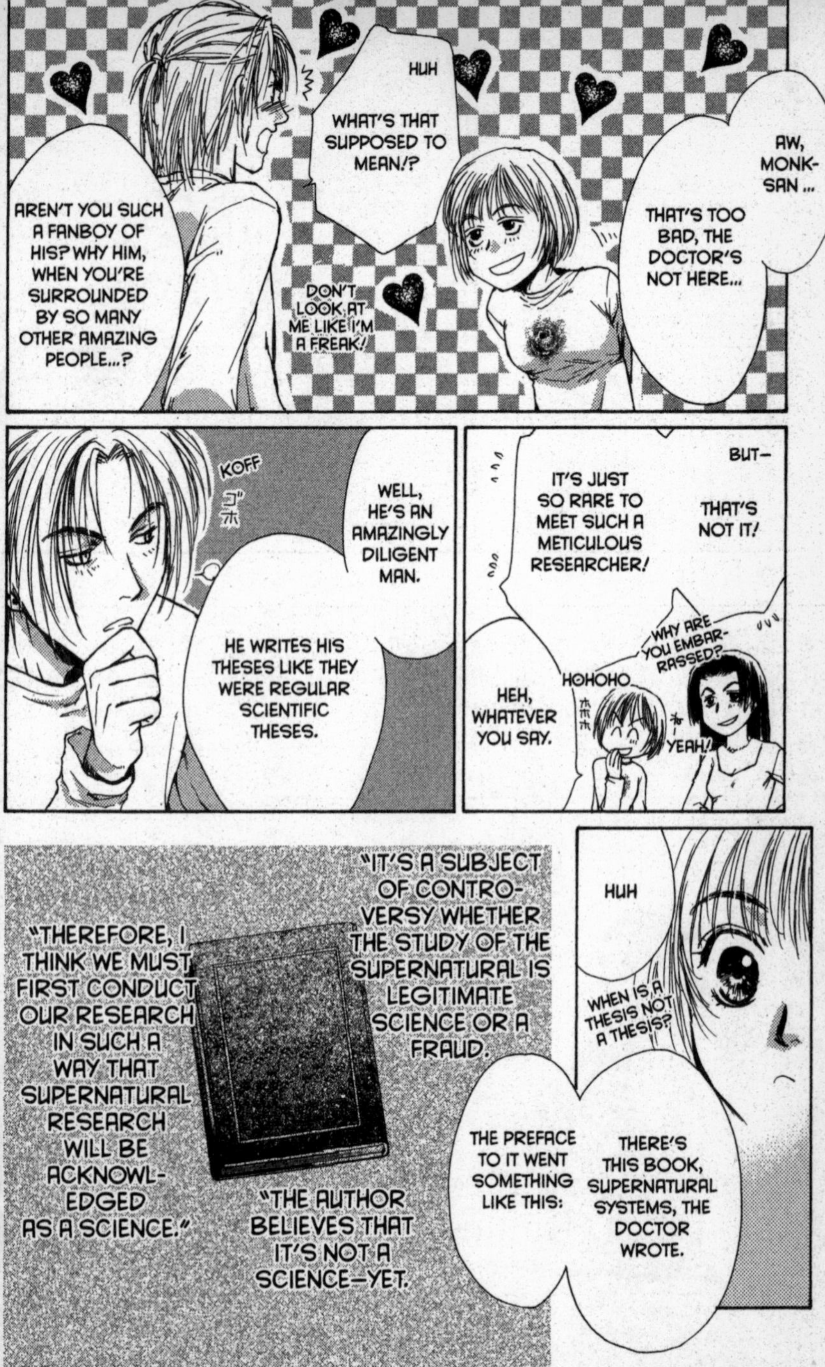
AW, MONK-SAN ...
THAT'S TOO BAD, THE DOCTOR'S NOT HERE...
HUH
WHAT'S THAT SUPPOSED TO MEAN!?
AREN'T YOU SUCH A FANBOY OF HIS? WHY HIM, WHEN YOU'RE SURROUNDED BY SO MANY OTHER AMAZING PEOPLE...?
DON'T LOOK AT ME LIKE I'M A FREAK!
BUT—
THAT'S NOT IT!
IT'S JUST SO RARE TO MEET SUCH A METICULOUS RESEARCHER!
WHY ARE YOU EMBARRASSED?
YEAH!
HOHOHO
HEH, WHATEVER YOU SAY.
KOFF
WELL, HE'S AN AMAZINGLY DILIGENT MAN.
HE WRITES HIS THESES LIKE THEY WERE REGULAR SCIENTIFIC THESES.
HUH
WHEN IS A THESIS NOT A THESIS?
THERE'S THIS BOOK, SUPERNATURAL SYSTEMS, THE DOCTOR WROTE.
THE PREFACE TO IT WENT SOMETHING LIKE THIS:
"IT'S A SUBJECT OF CONTROVERSY WHETHER THE STUDY OF THE SUPERNATURAL IS LEGITIMATE SCIENCE OR A FRAUD.
"THE AUTHOR BELIEVES THAT IT'S NOT A SCIENCE—YET.
"THEREFORE, I THINK WE MUST FIRST CONDUCT OUR RESEARCH IN SUCH A WAY THAT SUPERNATURAL RESEARCH WILL BE ACKNOWLEDGED AS A SCIENCE."

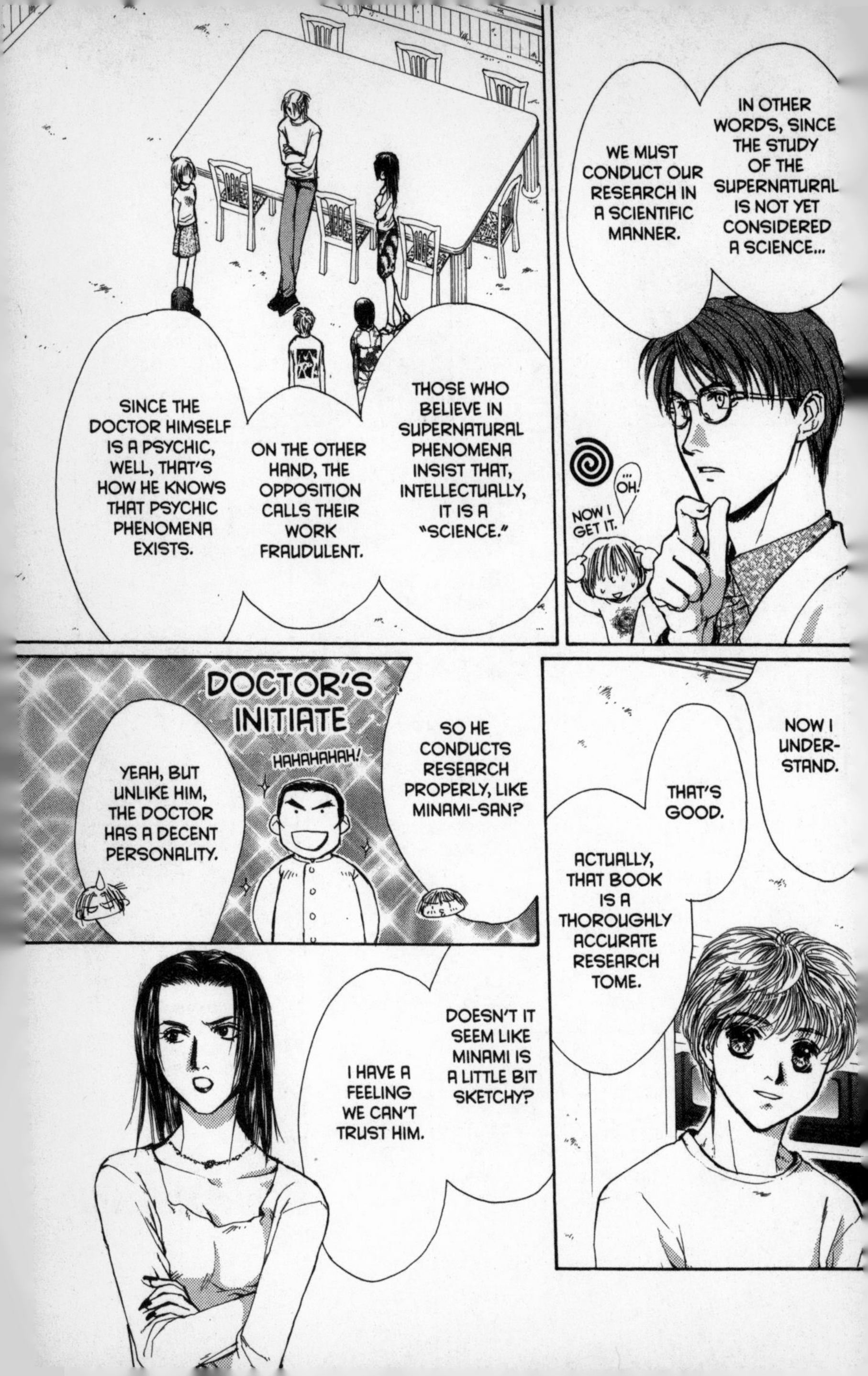
IN OTHER WORDS, SINCE THE STUDY OF THE SUPERNATURAL IS NOT YET CONSIDERED A SCIENCE...
WE MUST CONDUCT OUR RESEARCH IN A SCIENTIFIC MANNER.
...OH!
NOW I GET IT.
THOSE WHO BELIEVE IN SUPERNATURAL PHENOMENA INSIST THAT, INTELLECTUALLY, IT IS A "SCIENCE."
ON THE OTHER HAND, THE OPPOSITION CALLS THEIR WORK FRAUDULENT.
SINCE THE DOCTOR HIMSELF IS A PSYCHIC, WELL, THAT'S HOW HE KNOWS THAT PSYCHIC PHENOMENA EXISTS.
NOW I UNDER-STAND.
THAT'S GOOD.
ACTUALLY, THAT BOOK IS A THOROUGHLY ACCURATE RESEARCH TOME.
DOCTOR'S INITIATE
SO HE CONDUCTS RESEARCH PROPERLY, LIKE MINAMI-SAN?
HAHAHAHAH!
YEAH, BUT UNLIKE HIM, THE DOCTOR HAS A DECENT PERSONALITY.
DOESN'T IT SEEM LIKE MINAMI IS A LITTLE BIT SKETCHY?
I HAVE A FEELING WE CAN'T TRUST HIM.

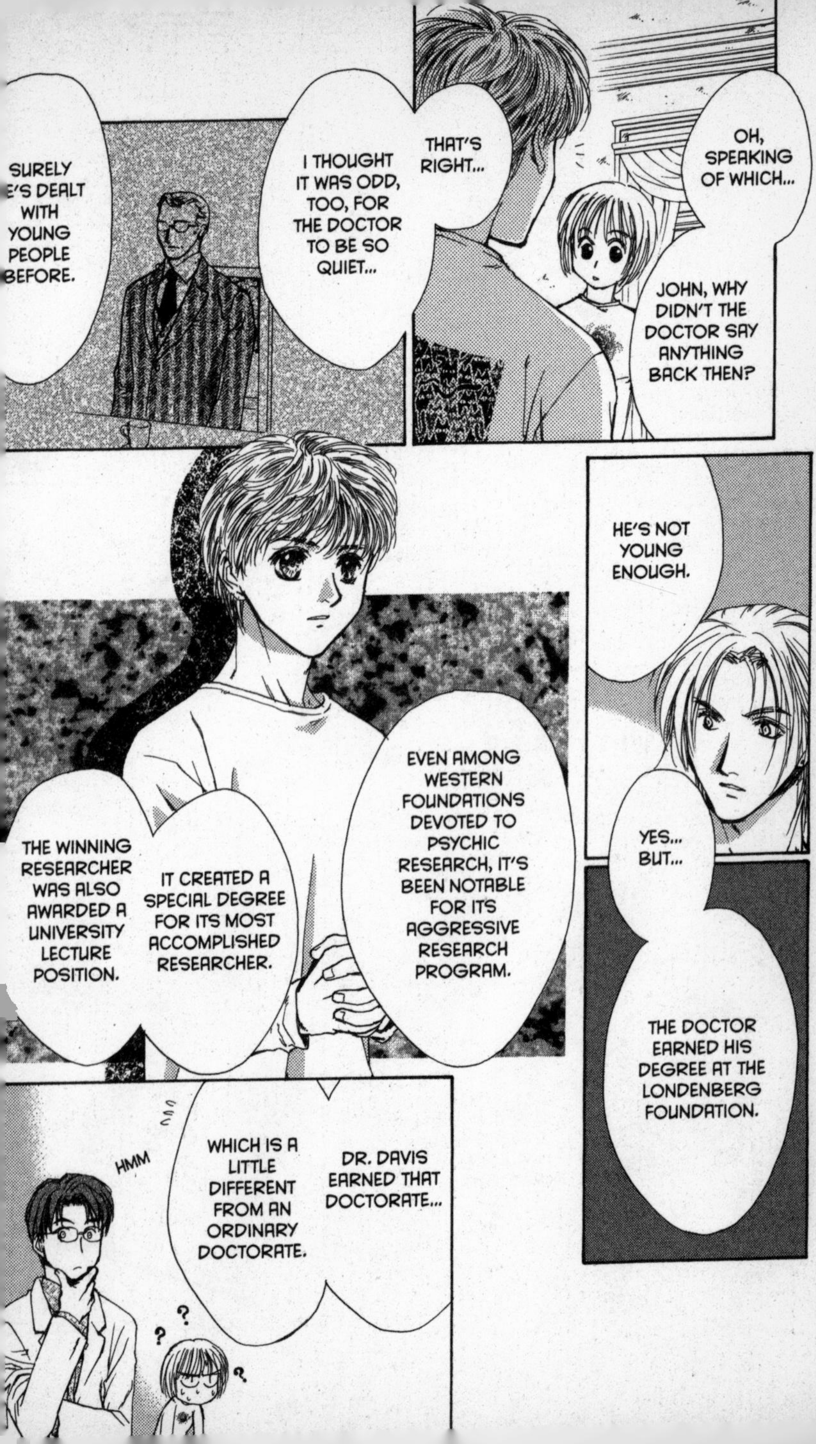
OH, SPEAKING OF WHICH...
JOHN, WHY DIDN'T THE DOCTOR SAY ANYTHING BACK THEN?
THAT'S RIGHT...
I THOUGHT IT WAS ODD, TOO, FOR THE DOCTOR TO BE SO QUIET...
SURELY E'S DEALT WITH YOUNG PEOPLE BEFORE.
HE'S NOT YOUNG ENOUGH.
YES... BUT...
THE DOCTOR EARNED HIS DEGREE AT THE LONDENBERG FOUNDATION.
EVEN AMONG WESTERN FOUNDATIONS DEVOTED TO PSYCHIC RESEARCH, IT'S BEEN NOTABLE FOR ITS AGGRESSIVE RESEARCH PROGRAM.
IT CREATED A SPECIAL DEGREE FOR ITS MOST ACCOMPLISHED RESEARCHER.
THE WINNING RESEARCHER WAS ALSO AWARDED A UNIVERSITY LECTURE POSITION.
DR. DAVIS EARNED THAT DOCTORATE...
WHICH IS A LITTLE DIFFERENT FROM AN ORDINARY DOCTORATE.
HMM

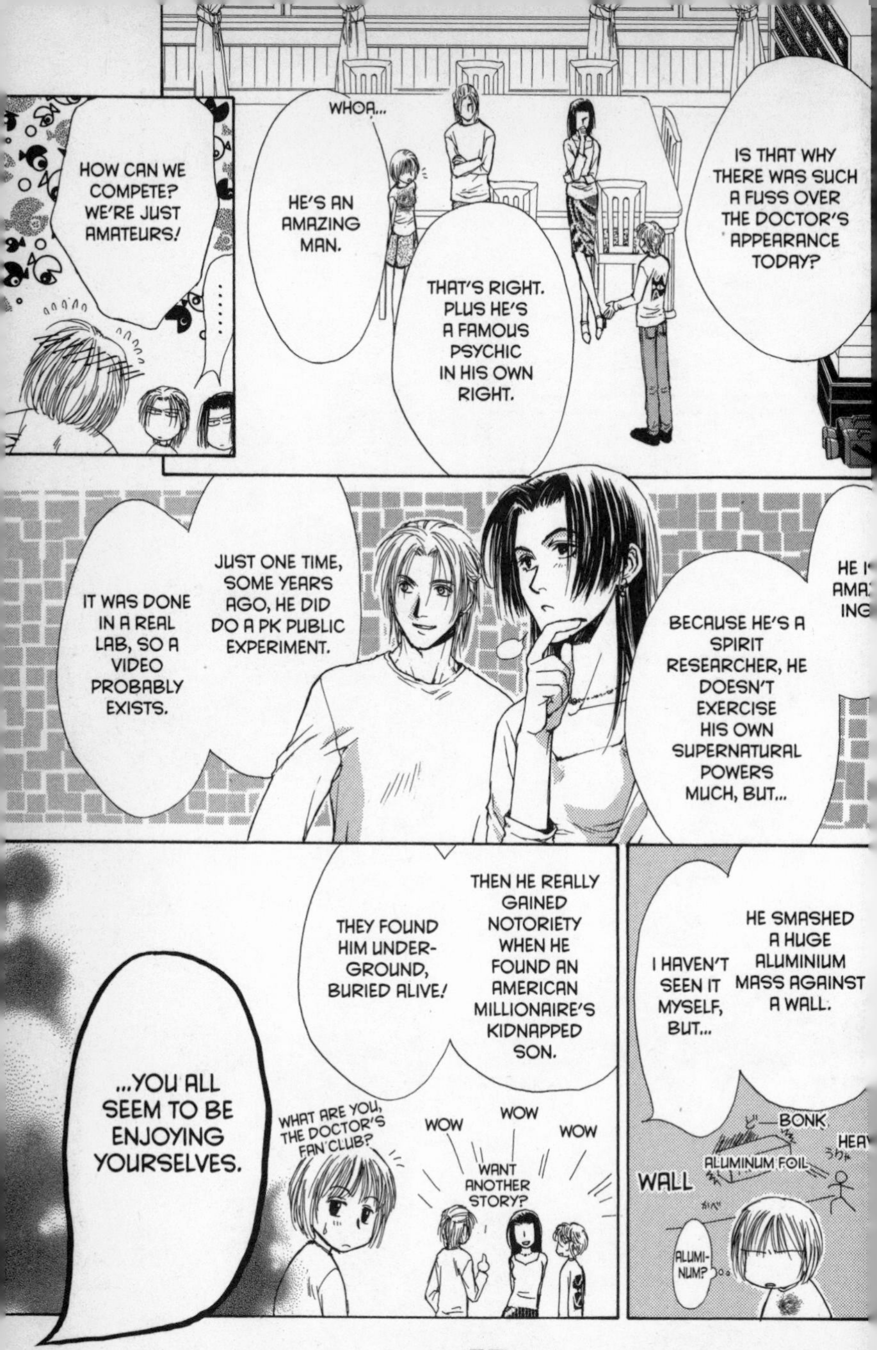
IS THAT WHY THERE WAS SUCH A FUSS OVER THE DOCTOR'S APPEARANCE TODAY?
WHOA...
HE'S AN AMAZING MAN.
THAT'S RIGHT. PLUS HE'S A FAMOUS PSYCHIC IN HIS OWN RIGHT.
HOW CAN WE COMPETE? WE'RE JUST AMATEURS!
......
HE I AMA ING
BECAUSE HE'S A SPIRIT RESEARCHER, HE DOESN'T EXERCISE HIS OWN SUPERNATURAL POWERS MUCH, BUT...
JUST ONE TIME, SOME YEARS AGO, HE DID DO A PK PUBLIC EXPERIMENT.
IT WAS DONE IN A REAL LAB, SO A VIDEO PROBABLY EXISTS.
HE SMASHED A HUGE ALUMINIUM MASS AGAINST A WALL.
I HAVEN'T SEEN IT MYSELF, BUT...
BONK
HEA
ALUMINUM FOIL
WALL
ALUMI-NUM?
THEN HE REALLY GAINED NOTORIETY WHEN HE FOUND AN AMERICAN MILLIONAIRE'S KIDNAPPED SON.
THEY FOUND HIM UNDER-GROUND, BURIED ALIVE!
WOW
WOW
WOW
WANT ANOTHER STORY?
WHAT ARE YOU, THE DOCTOR'S FAN CLUB?
...YOU ALL SEEM TO BE ENJOYING YOURSELVES.

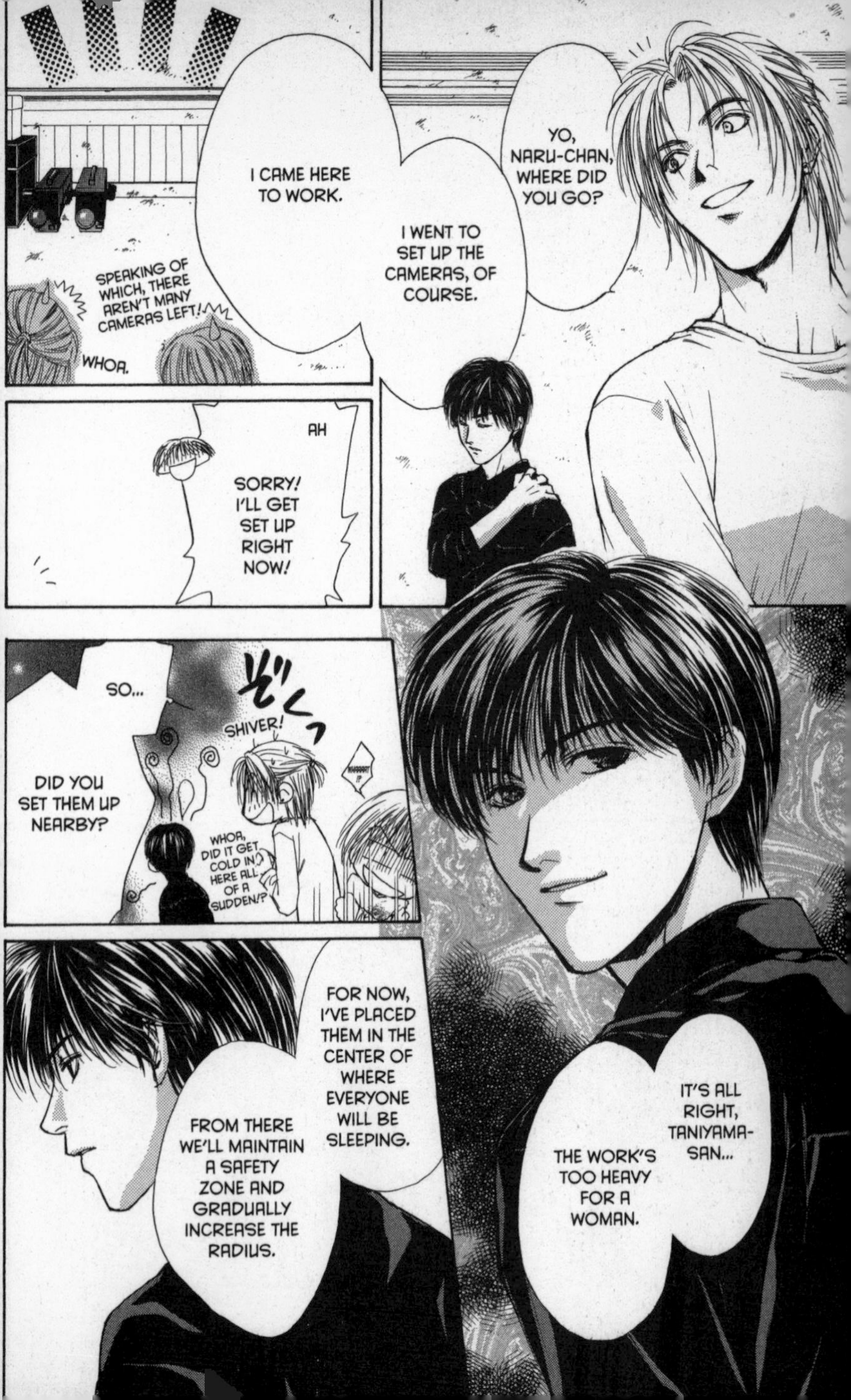

YO, NARU-CHAN, WHERE DID YOU GO?
I WENT TO SET UP THE CAMERAS, OF COURSE.
I CAME HERE TO WORK.
SPEAKING OF WHICH, THERE AREN'T MANY CAMERAS LEFT!
WHOA.
AH
SORRY! I'LL GET SET UP RIGHT NOW!
IT'S ALL RIGHT, TANIYAMA-SAN...
THE WORK'S TOO HEAVY FOR A WOMAN.
SO...
DID YOU SET THEM UP NEARBY?
ぞくっ
SHIVER!
WHAAAAT !?
WHOA, DID IT GET COLD IN HERE ALL OF A SUDDEN!?
FOR NOW, I'VE PLACED THEM IN THE CENTER OF WHERE EVERYONE WILL BE SLEEPING.
FROM THERE WE'LL MAINTAIN A SAFETY ZONE AND GRADUALLY INCREASE THE RADIUS.

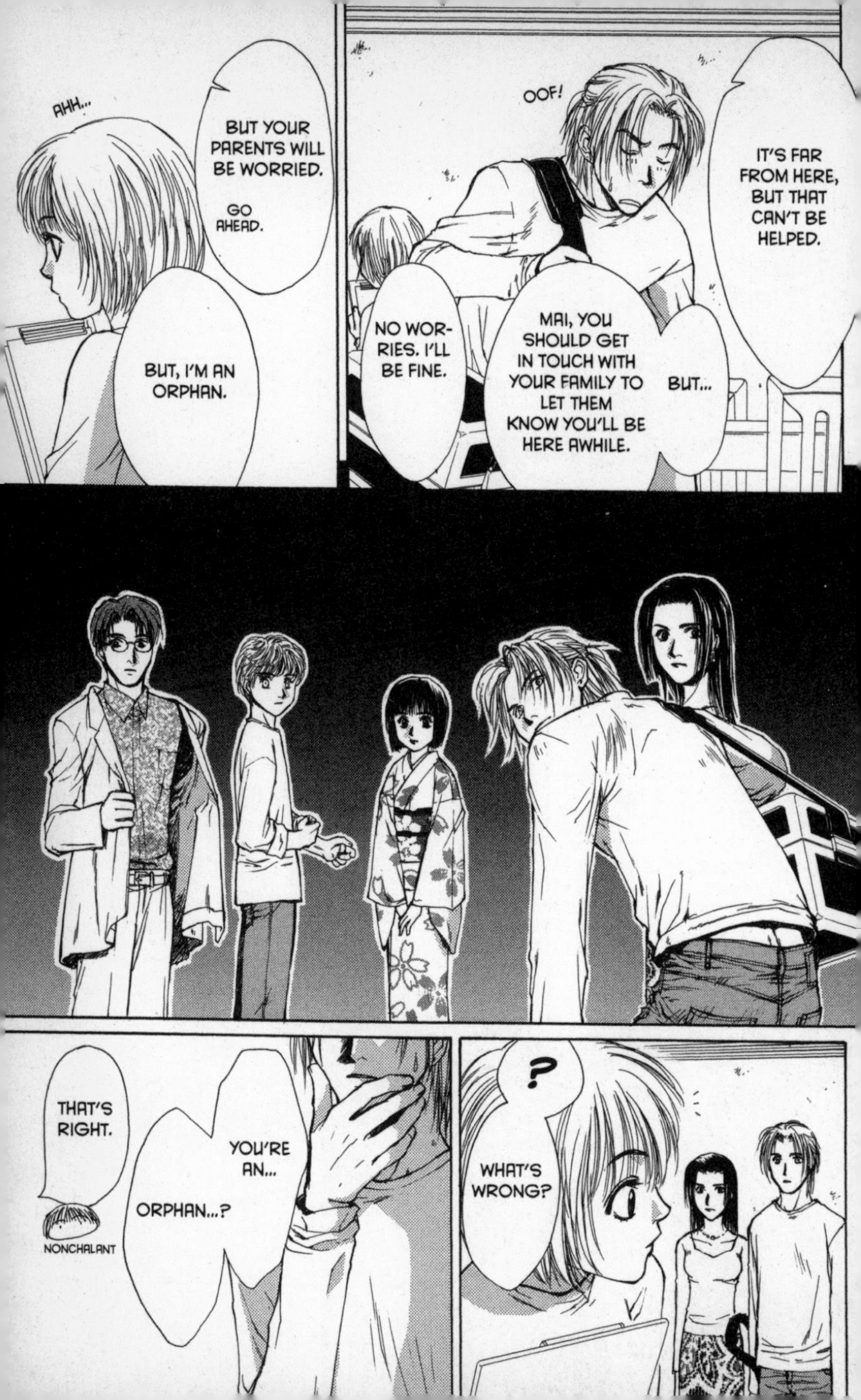
IT'S FAR FROM HERE, BUT THAT CAN'T BE HELPED.
OOF!
BUT...
MAI, YOU SHOULD GET IN TOUCH WITH YOUR FAMILY TO LET THEM KNOW YOU'LL BE HERE AWHILE.
NO WORRIES. I'LL BE FINE.
BUT YOUR PARENTS WILL BE WORRIED.
GO AHEAD.
AHH...
BUT, I'M AN ORPHAN.
?
WHAT'S WRONG?
YOU'RE AN...
ORPHAN...?
THAT'S RIGHT.
NONCHALANT

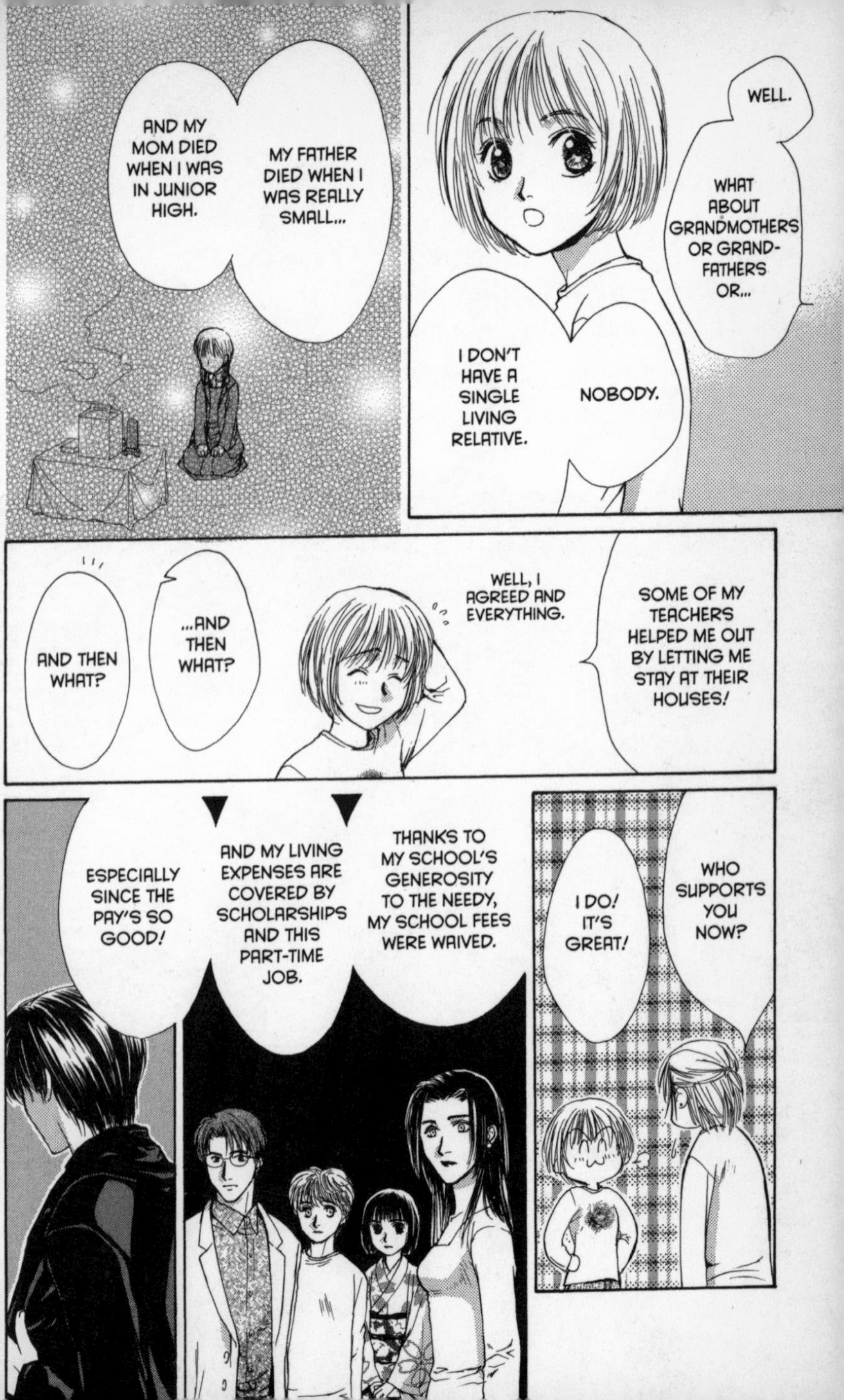
WELL.
WHAT ABOUT GRANDMOTHERS OR GRAND-FATHERS OR...
NOBODY.
I DON'T HAVE A SINGLE LIVING RELATIVE.
MY FATHER DIED WHEN I WAS REALLY SMALL...
AND MY MOM DIED WHEN I WAS IN JUNIOR HIGH.
SOME OF MY TEACHERS HELPED ME OUT BY LETTING ME STAY AT THEIR HOUSES!
WELL, I AGREED AND EVERYTHING.
...AND THEN WHAT?
AND THEN WHAT?
WHO SUPPORTS YOU NOW?
I DO! IT'S GREAT!
THANKS TO MY SCHOOL'S GENEROSITY TO THE NEEDY, MY SCHOOL FEES WERE WAIVED.
AND MY LIVING EXPENSES ARE COVERED BY SCHOLARSHIPS AND THIS PART-TIME JOB.
ESPECIALLY SINCE THE PAY'S SO GOOD!

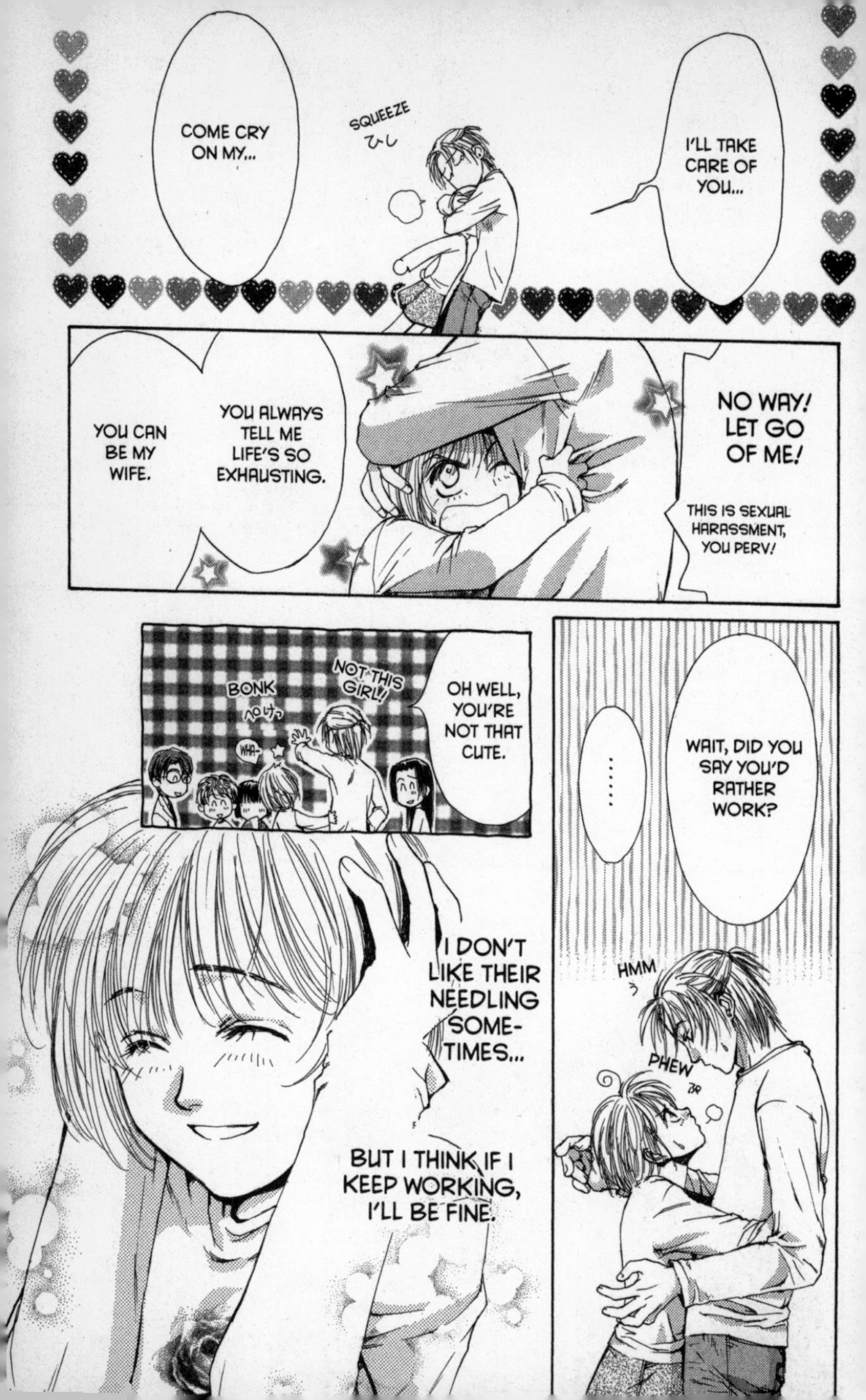
I'LL TAKE CARE OF YOU...
SQUEEZE
ひし
COME CRY ON MY...
NO WAY! LET GO OF ME!
THIS IS SEXUAL HARASSMENT, YOU PERV!
YOU ALWAYS TELL ME LIFE'S SO EXHAUSTING.
YOU CAN BE MY WIFE.
WAIT, DID YOU SAY YOU'D RATHER WORK?
......
HMM
PHEW
OH WELL, YOU'RE NOT THAT CUTE.
NOT THIS GIRL!
BONK
WHA-
I DON'T LIKE THEIR NEEDLING SOMETIMES...
BUT I THINK IF I KEEP WORKING, I'LL BE FINE.

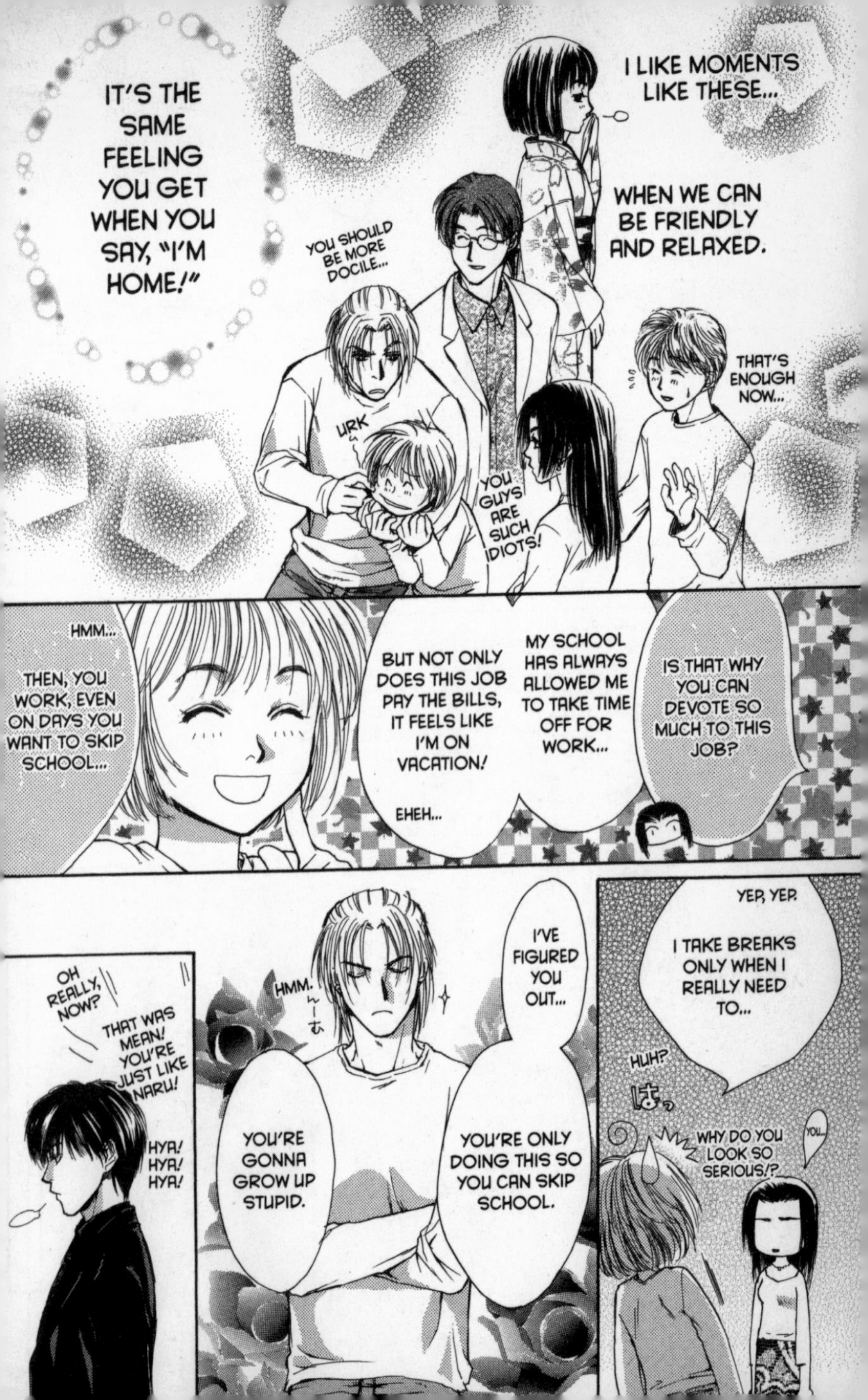
I LIKE MOMENTS LIKE THESE...
WHEN WE CAN BE FRIENDLY AND RELAXED.
IT'S THE SAME FEELING YOU GET WHEN YOU SAY, "I'M HOME!"
THAT'S ENOUGH NOW...
YOU SHOULD BE MORE DOCILE...
URK
YOU GUYS ARE SUCH IDIOTS!
IS THAT WHY YOU CAN DEVOTE SO MUCH TO THIS JOB?
MY SCHOOL HAS ALWAYS ALLOWED ME TO TAKE TIME OFF FOR WORK...
BUT NOT ONLY DOES THIS JOB PAY THE BILLS, IT FEELS LIKE I'M ON VACATION!
EHEH...
HMM...
THEN, YOU WORK, EVEN ON DAYS YOU WANT TO SKIP SCHOOL...
YEP, YEP.
I TAKE BREAKS ONLY WHEN I REALLY NEED TO...
HUH?
WHY DO YOU LOOK SO SERIOUS!?
YOU...
I'VE FIGURED YOU OUT...
HMM.
YOU'RE ONLY DOING THIS SO YOU CAN SKIP SCHOOL.
YOU'RE GONNA GROW UP STUPID.
OH REALLY, NOW?
THAT WAS MEAN! YOU'RE JUST LIKE NARU!
HYA! HYA! HYA!

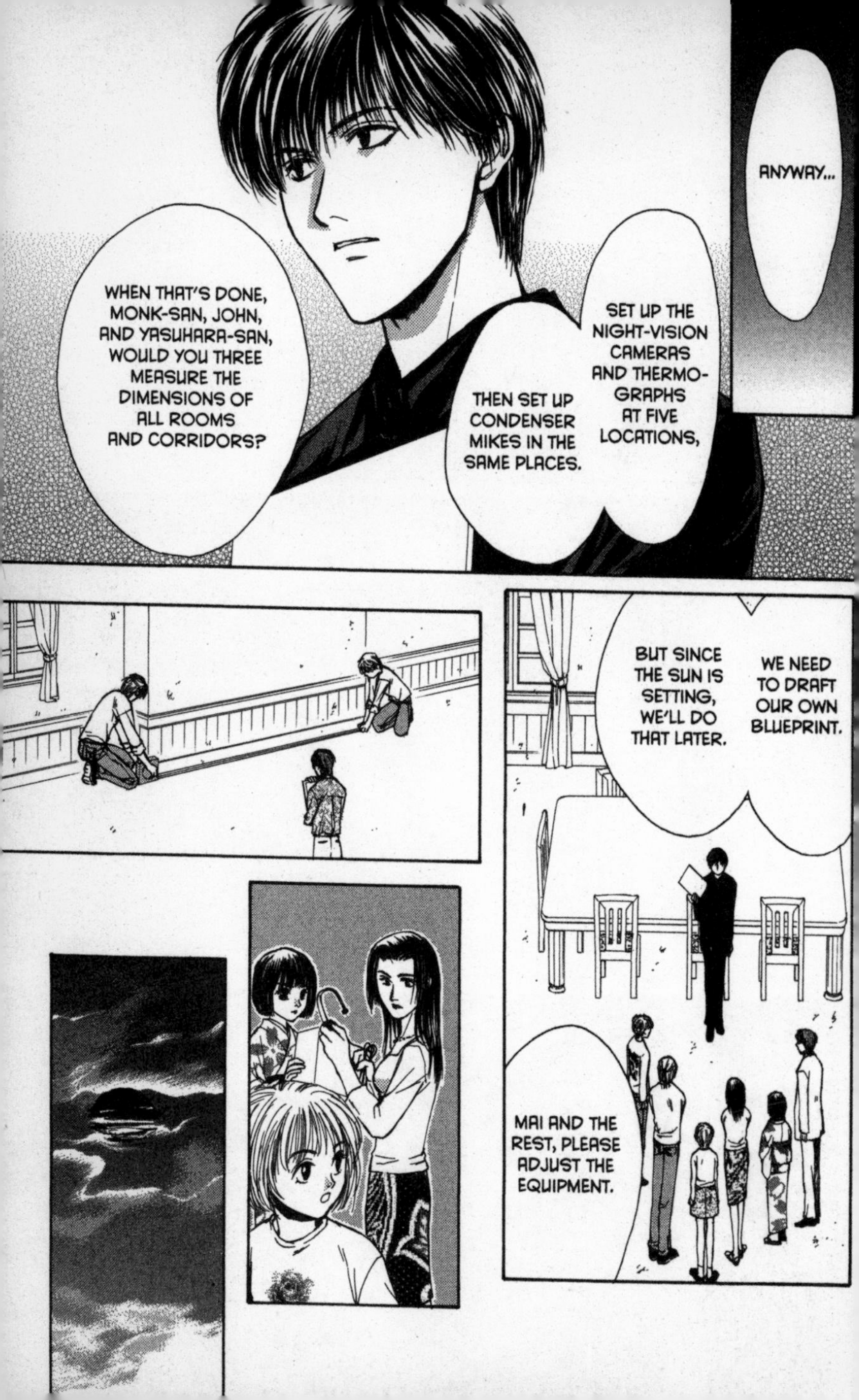
ANYWAY...
SET UP THE NIGHT-VISION CAMERAS AND THERMOGRAPHS AT FIVE LOCATIONS,
THEN SET UP CONDENSER MIKES IN THE SAME PLACES.
WHEN THAT'S DONE, MONK-SAN, JOHN, AND YASUHARA-SAN, WOULD YOU THREE MEASURE THE DIMENSIONS OF ALL ROOMS AND CORRIDORS?
WE NEED TO DRAFT OUR OWN BLUEPRINT.
BUT SINCE THE SUN IS SETTING, WE'LL DO THAT LATER.
MAI AND THE REST, PLEASE ADJUST THE EQUIPMENT.

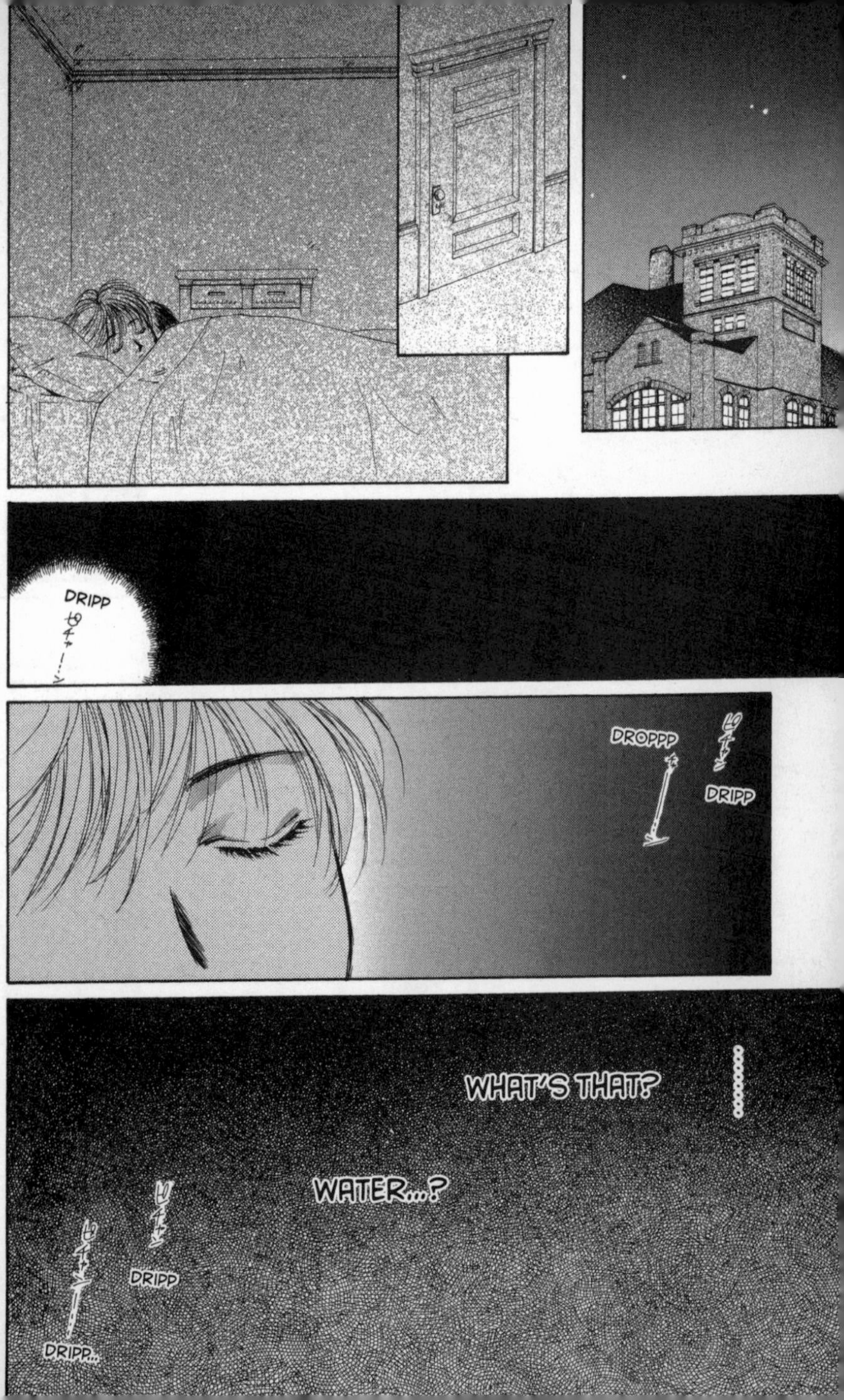
DRIPP
DROPPP
DRIPP
......
WHAT'S THAT?
WATER...?
DRIPP
DRIPP...

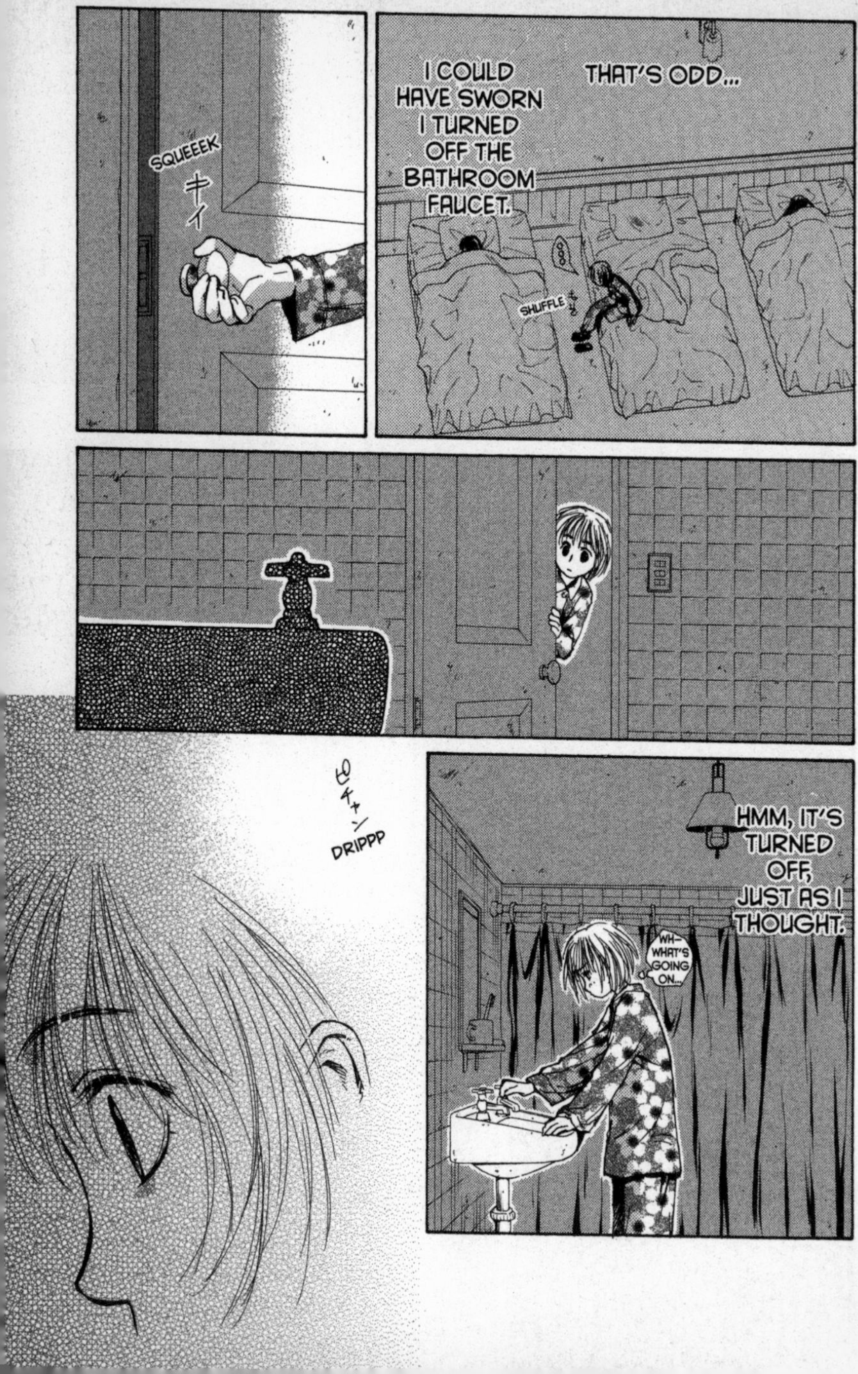
THAT'S ODD...
I COULD HAVE SWORN I TURNED OFF THE BATHROOM FAUCET.
SHUFFLE
SQUEEEK
キイ
HMM, IT'S TURNED OFF, JUST AS I THOUGHT.
WH- WHAT'S GOING ON...
ピチャン
DRIPPP

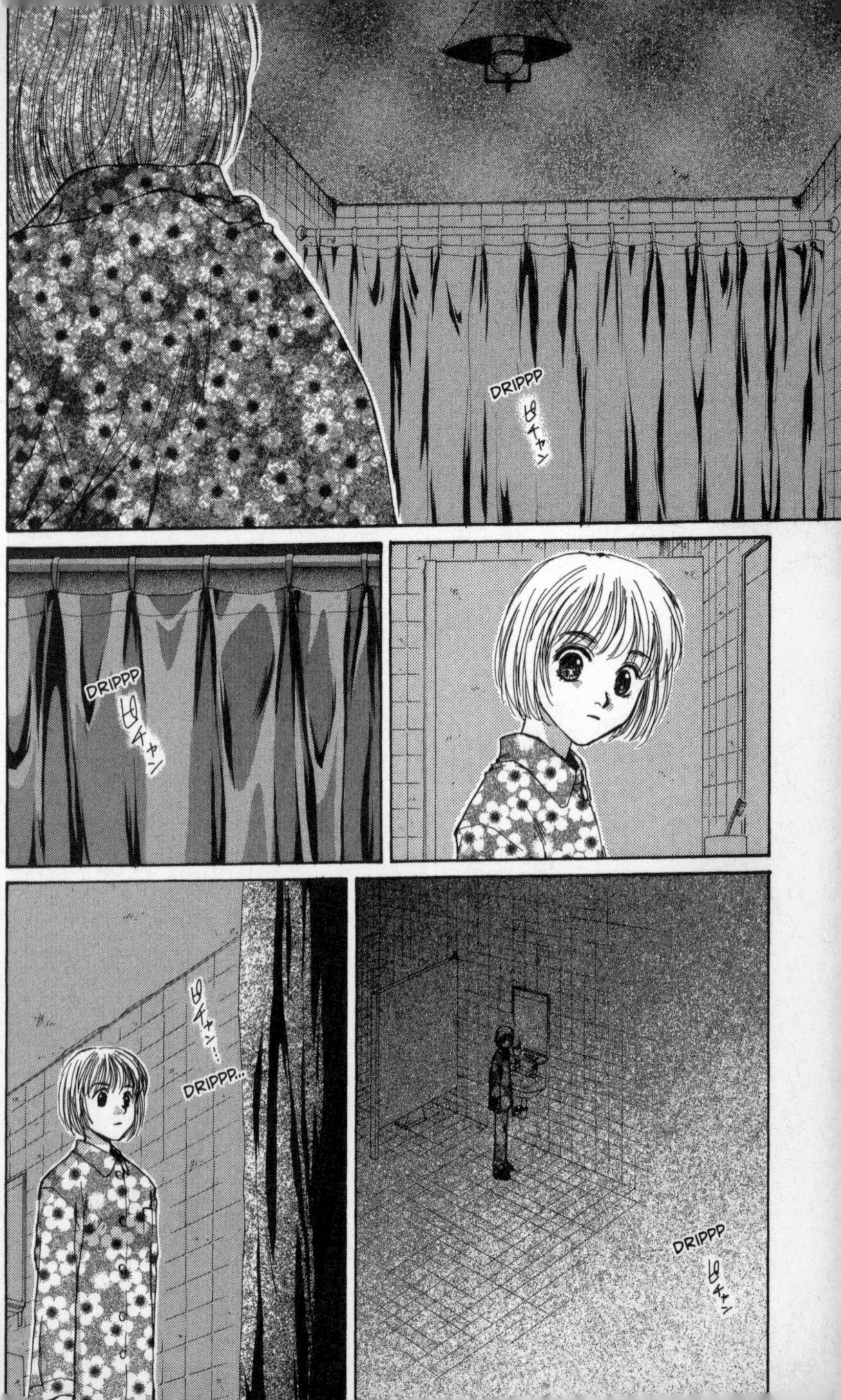
DRIPPP
ピチャン
DRIPPP
ピチャン
DRIPPP
ピチャン
ピチャン…
DRIPPP...

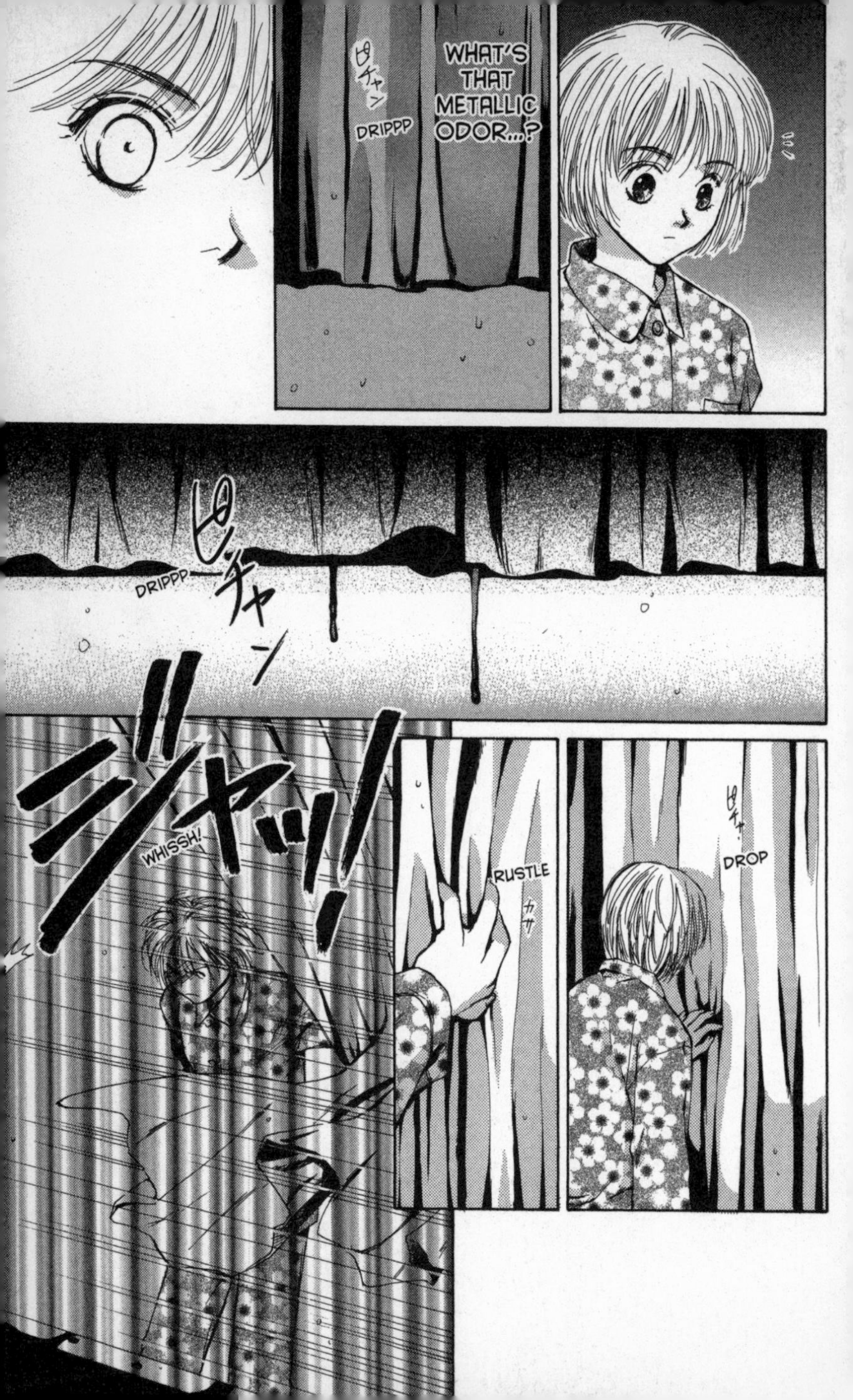
WHAT'S THAT METALLIC ODOR...?
ピチャン
DRIPPP
ピチャン
DRIPPP
ピチャ
DROP
カサ
RUSTLE
ジャッ!!
WHISSH!

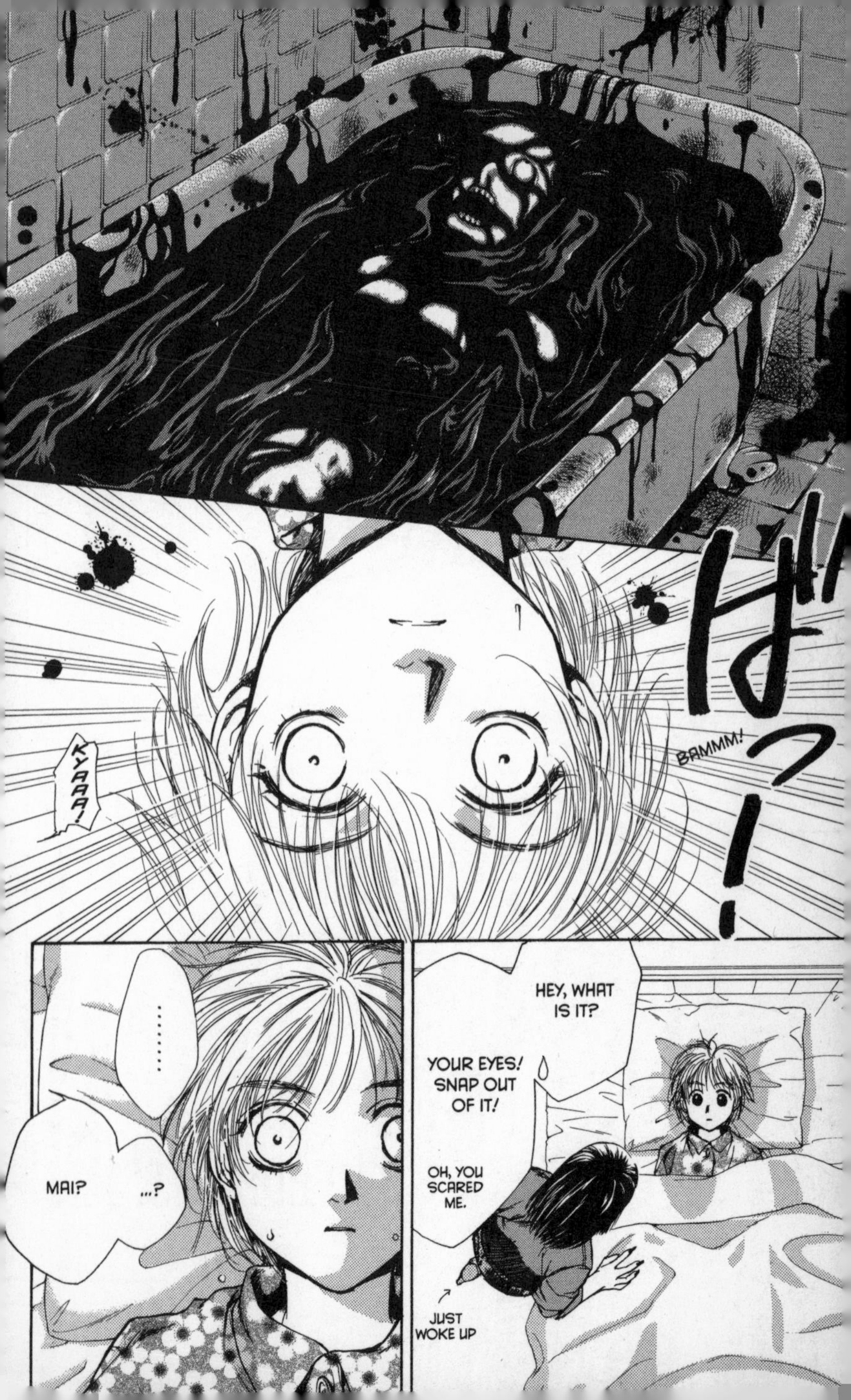
ばっ!
BAMMM!
KYAAA!
HEY, WHAT IS IT?
YOUR EYES! SNAP OUT OF IT!
OH, YOU SCARED ME.
JUST WOKE UP
......
...?
MAI?

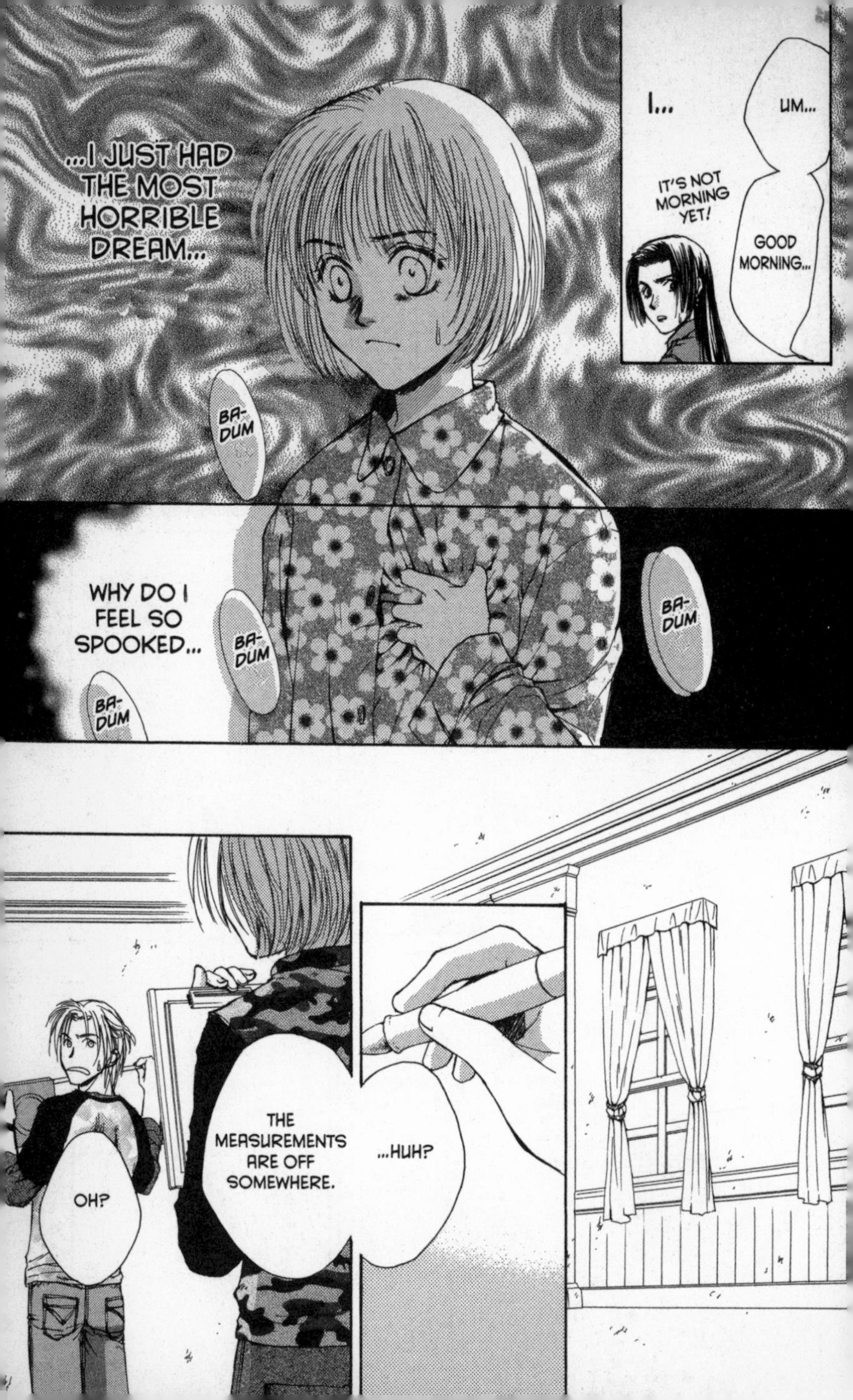
UM...
I...
GOOD MORNING...
IT'S NOT MORNING YET!
...I JUST HAD THE MOST HORRIBLE DREAM...
BA-DUM
BA-DUM
BA-DUM
WHY DO I FEEL SO SPOOKED...
BA-DUM
...HUH?
THE MEASUREMENTS ARE OFF SOMEWHERE.
OH?

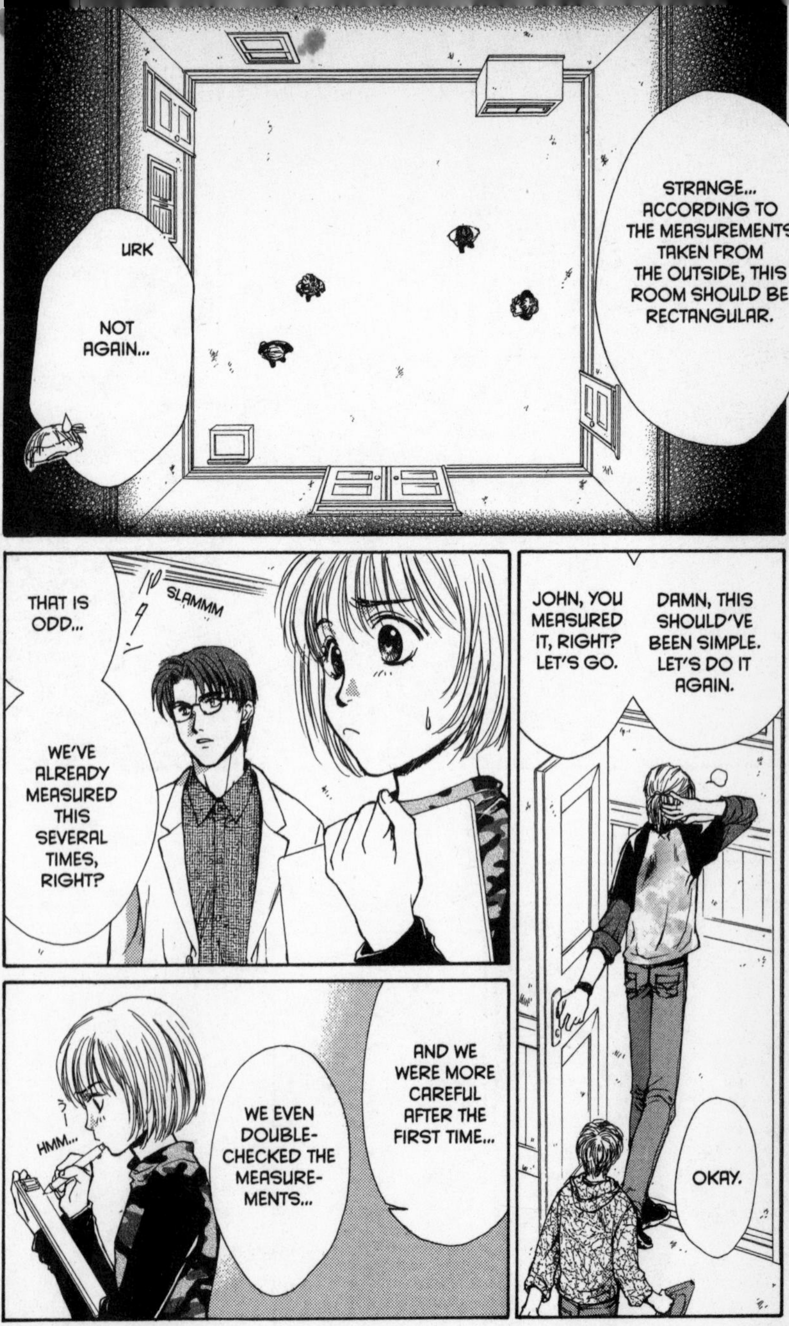
STRANGE... ACCORDING TO THE MEASUREMENTS TAKEN FROM THE OUTSIDE, THIS ROOM SHOULD BE RECTANGULAR.
URK
NOT AGAIN...
DAMN, THIS SHOULD'VE BEEN SIMPLE. LET'S DO IT AGAIN.
JOHN, YOU MEASURED IT, RIGHT? LET'S GO.
OKAY.
SLAMMM
THAT IS ODD...
WE'VE ALREADY MEASURED THIS SEVERAL TIMES, RIGHT?
AND WE WERE MORE CAREFUL AFTER THE FIRST TIME...
WE EVEN DOUBLE-CHECKED THE MEASUREMENTS...
HMM...

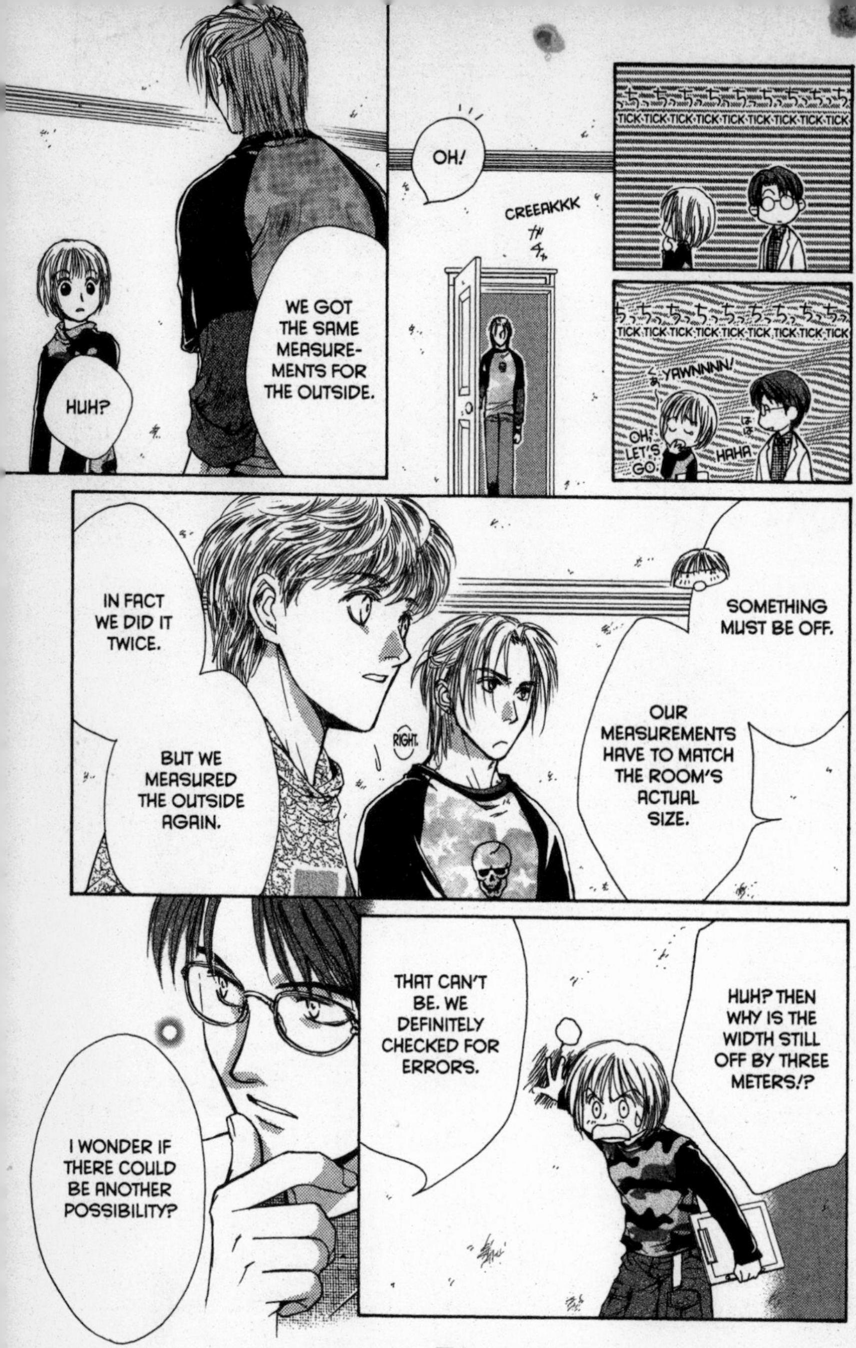
TICK-TICK-TICK-TICK-TICK-TICK-TICK-TICK-TICK
TICK-TICK-TICK-TICK-TICK-TICK-TICK-TICK
YAWNNNN!
OH! LET'S GO
HAHA
OH!
CREEAKKK
WE GOT THE SAME MEASUREMENTS FOR THE OUTSIDE.
HUH?
SOMETHING MUST BE OFF.
OUR MEASUREMENTS HAVE TO MATCH THE ROOM'S ACTUAL SIZE.
RIGHT.
IN FACT WE DID IT TWICE.
BUT WE MEASURED THE OUTSIDE AGAIN.
HUH? THEN WHY IS THE WIDTH STILL OFF BY THREE METERS!?
THAT CAN'T BE. WE DEFINITELY CHECKED FOR ERRORS.
I WONDER IF THERE COULD BE ANOTHER POSSIBILITY?

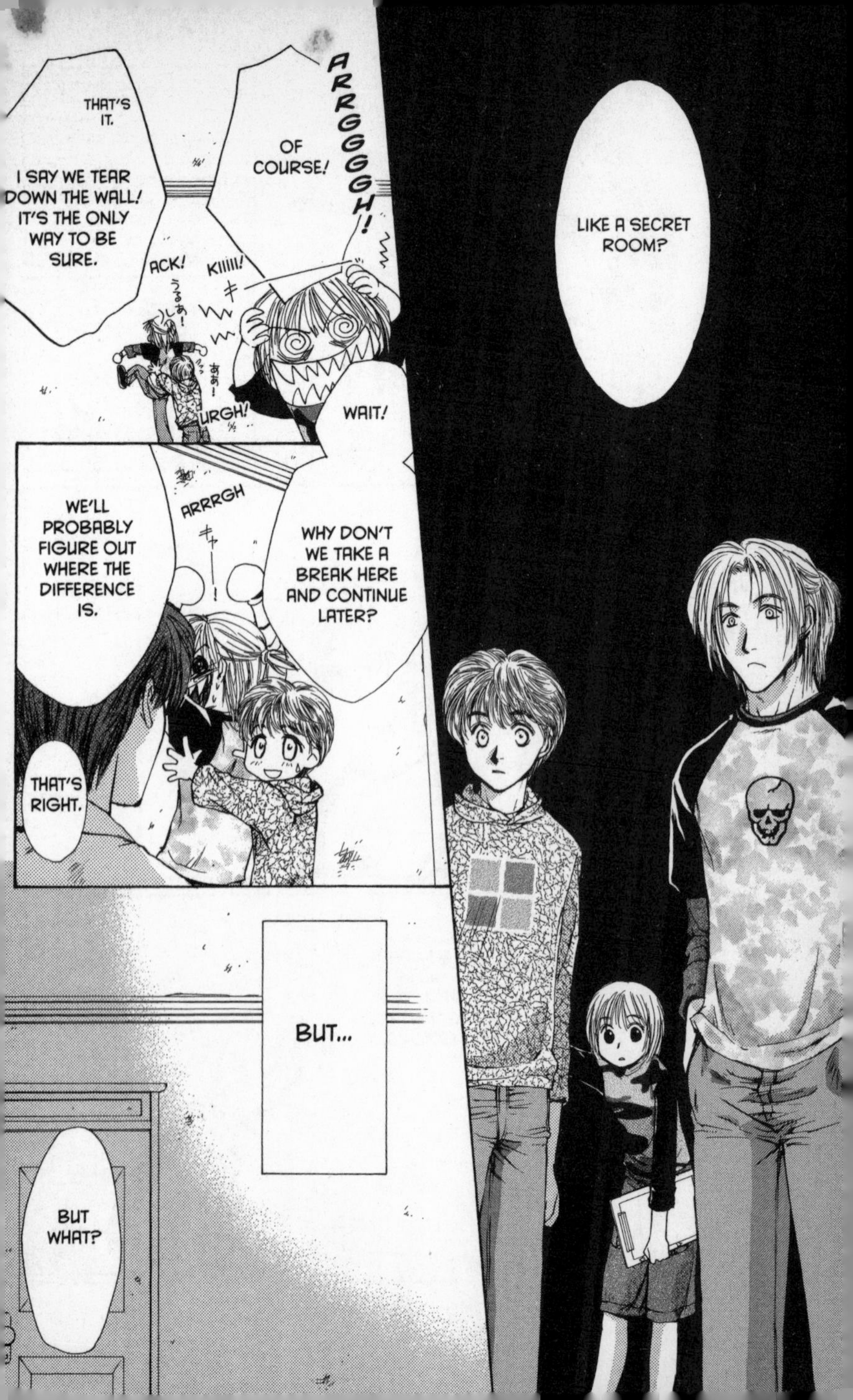
LIKE A SECRET ROOM?
ARRGGGGH!
OF COURSE!
THAT'S IT.
I SAY WE TEAR DOWN THE WALL! IT'S THE ONLY WAY TO BE SURE.
KIIIII!
ACK!
URGH!
WAIT!
WHY DON'T WE TAKE A BREAK HERE AND CONTINUE LATER?
ARRRGH
WE'LL PROBABLY FIGURE OUT WHERE THE DIFFERENCE IS.
THAT'S RIGHT.
BUT...
BUT WHAT?

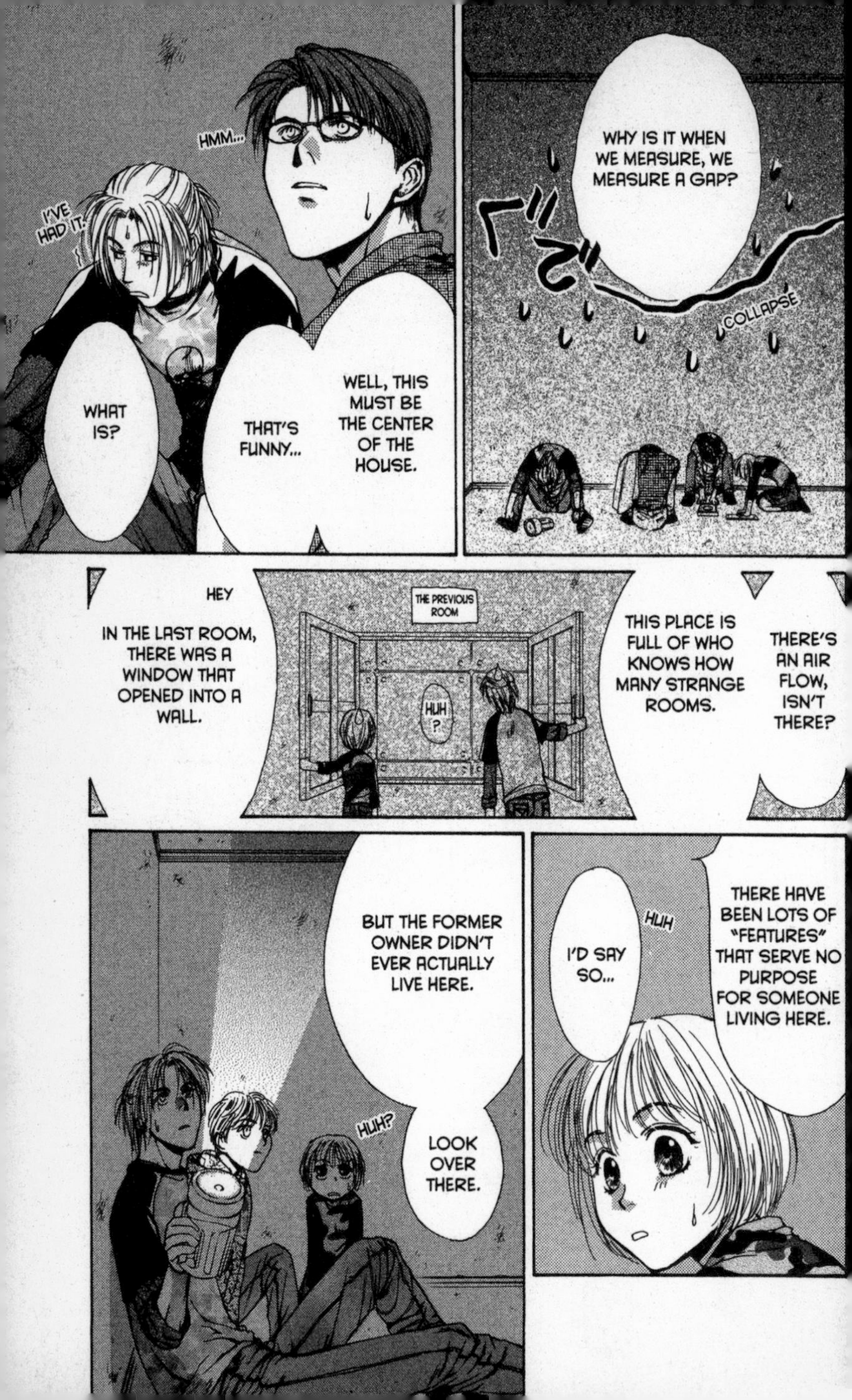
WHY IS IT WHEN WE MEASURE, WE MEASURE A GAP?
COLLAPSE
HMM...
I'VE HAD IT.
WELL, THIS MUST BE THE CENTER OF THE HOUSE.
THAT'S FUNNY...
WHAT IS?
THERE'S AN AIR FLOW, ISN'T THERE?
THIS PLACE IS FULL OF WHO KNOWS HOW MANY STRANGE ROOMS.
THE PREVIOUS ROOM
HUH?
HEY
IN THE LAST ROOM, THERE WAS A WINDOW THAT OPENED INTO A WALL.
THERE HAVE BEEN LOTS OF "FEATURES" THAT SERVE NO PURPOSE FOR SOMEONE LIVING HERE.
HUH
I'D SAY SO...
BUT THE FORMER OWNER DIDN'T EVER ACTUALLY LIVE HERE.
HUH?
LOOK OVER THERE.

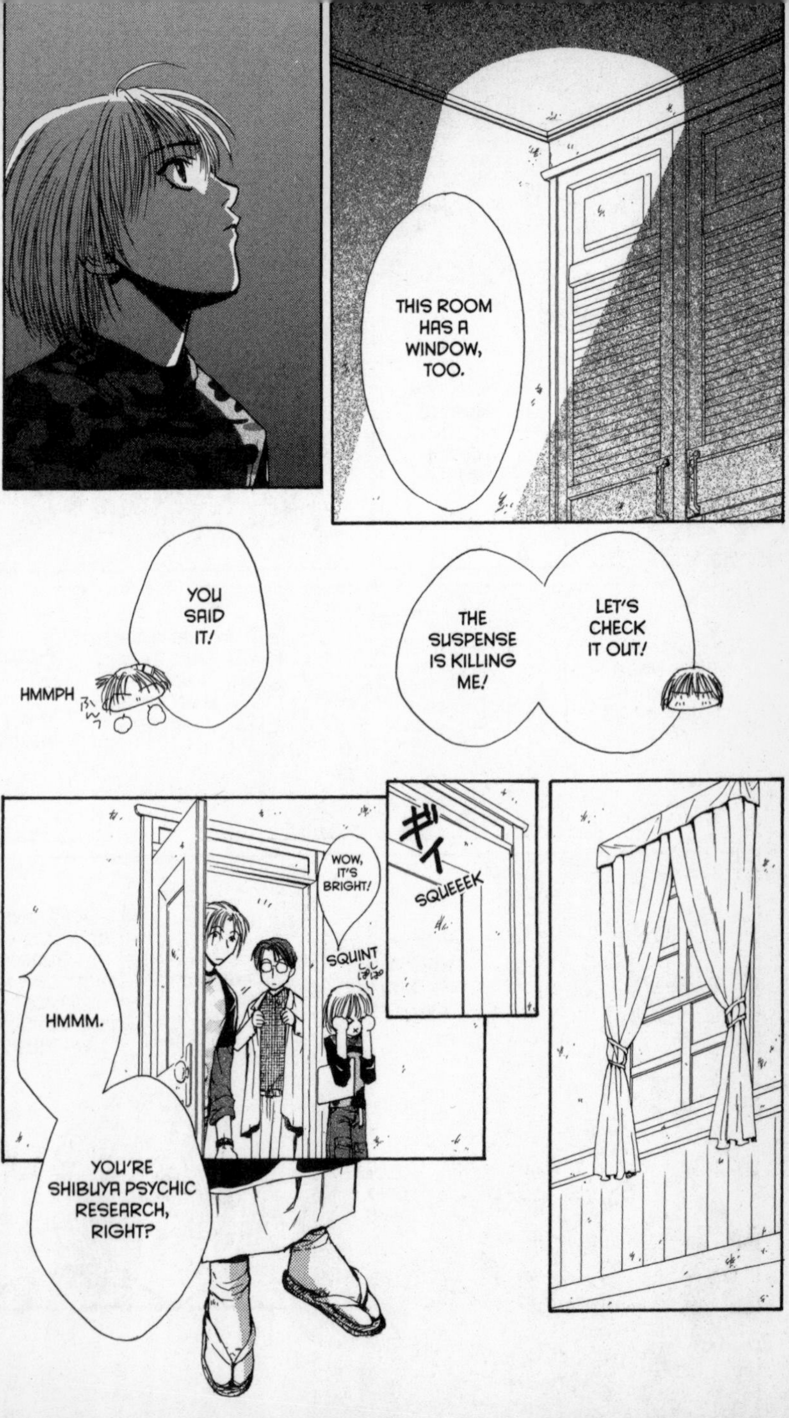
THIS ROOM HAS A WINDOW, TOO.
LET'S CHECK IT OUT!
THE SUSPENSE IS KILLING ME!
YOU SAID IT!
HMMPH
ギイ
SQUEEEK
WOW, IT'S BRIGHT!
SQUINT
HMMM.
YOU'RE SHIBUYA PSYCHIC RESEARCH, RIGHT?

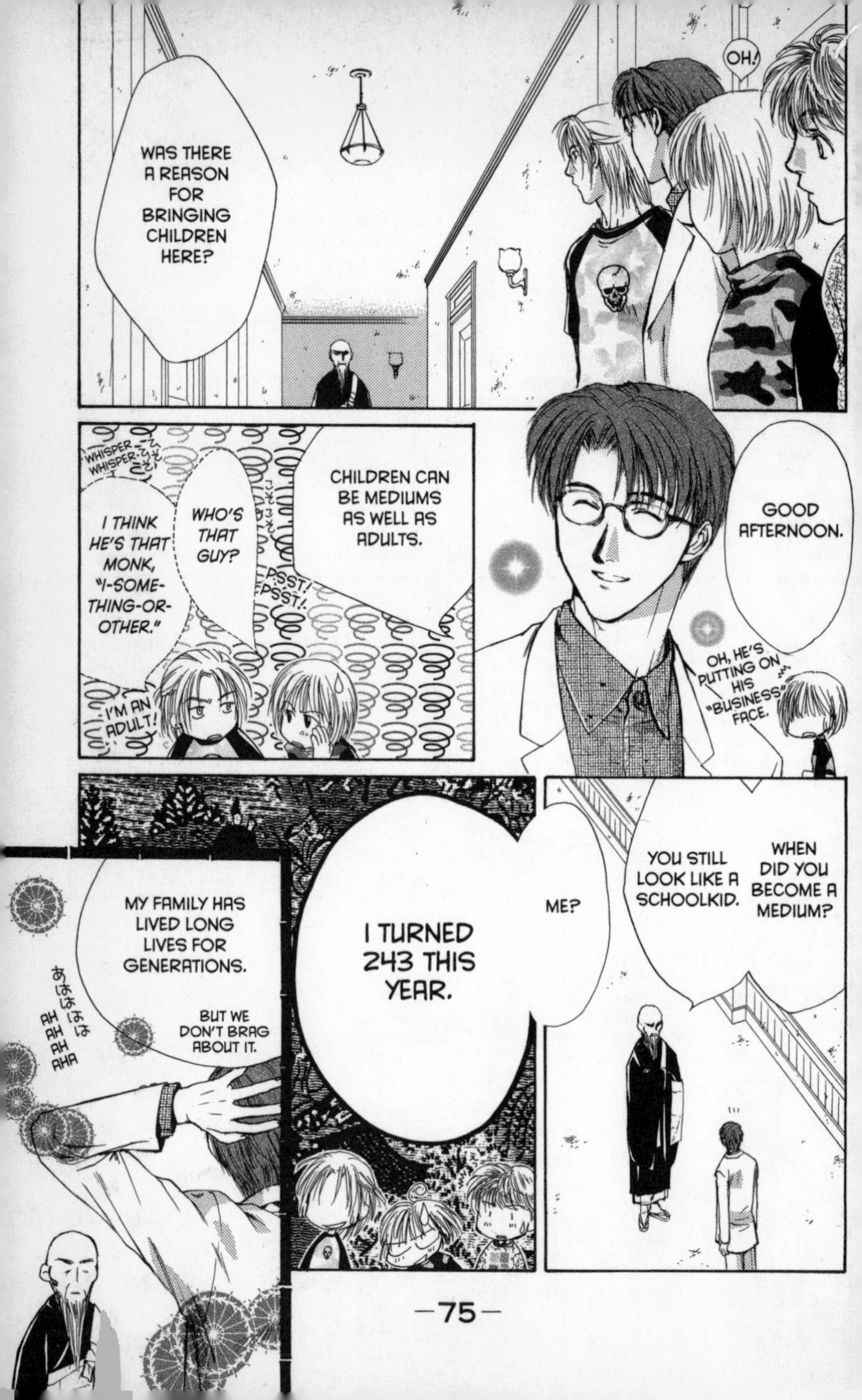
OH!
WAS THERE A REASON FOR BRINGING CHILDREN HERE?
GOOD AFTERNOON.
OH, HE'S PUTTING ON HIS "BUSINESS" FACE.
CHILDREN CAN BE MEDIUMS AS WELL AS ADULTS.
こそこそ
PSST! PSST!
WHISPER WHISPER ひそひそ
WHO'S THAT GUY?
I THINK HE'S THAT MONK, "I-SOME-THING-OR-OTHER."
I'M AN ADULT!
WHEN DID YOU BECOME A MEDIUM?
YOU STILL LOOK LIKE A SCHOOLKID.
ME?
I TURNED 243 THIS YEAR.
MY FAMILY HAS LIVED LONG LIVES FOR GENERATIONS.
BUT WE DON'T BRAG ABOUT IT.
あはははは AH AH AH AHA

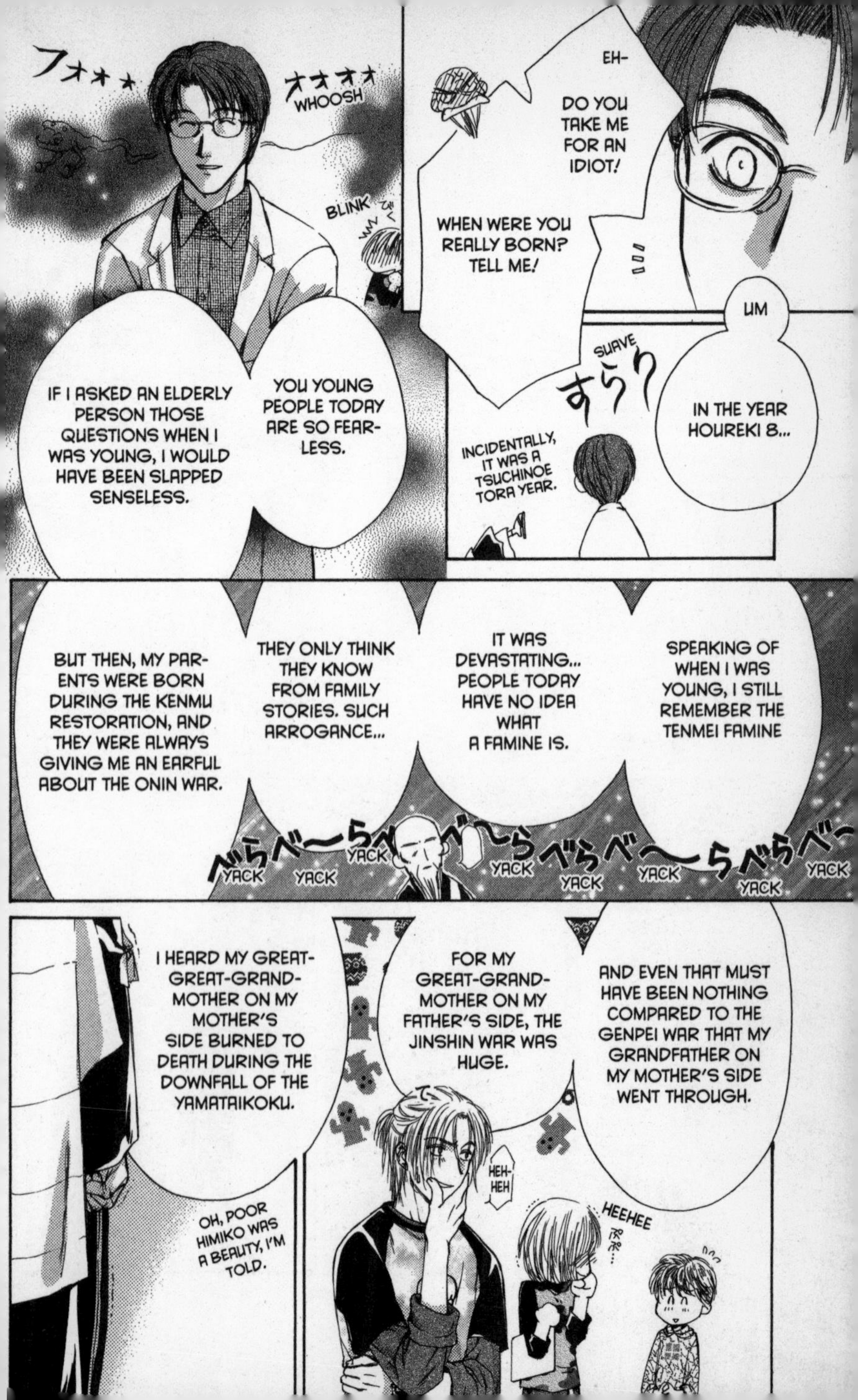
EH-
DO YOU TAKE ME FOR AN IDIOT!
WHEN WERE YOU REALLY BORN? TELL ME!
UM
IN THE YEAR HOUREKI 8...
SUAVE すらり
INCIDENTALLY, IT WAS A TSUCHINOE TORA YEAR.
オオオオ WHOOSH
フォォォ★
BLINK びく
YOU YOUNG PEOPLE TODAY ARE SO FEAR-LESS.
IF I ASKED AN ELDERLY PERSON THOSE QUESTIONS WHEN I WAS YOUNG, I WOULD HAVE BEEN SLAPPED SENSELESS.
SPEAKING OF WHEN I WAS YOUNG, I STILL REMEMBER THE TENMEI FAMINE
IT WAS DEVASTATING... PEOPLE TODAY HAVE NO IDEA WHAT A FAMINE IS.
THEY ONLY THINK THEY KNOW FROM FAMILY STORIES. SUCH ARROGANCE...
BUT THEN, MY PAR-ENTS WERE BORN DURING THE KENMU RESTORATION, AND THEY WERE ALWAYS GIVING ME AN EARFUL ABOUT THE ONIN WAR.
べらべ〜らべ YACK YACK YACK べ〜ら YACK べらべ〜 YACK YACK 〜らべらべ〜 YACK YACK
AND EVEN THAT MUST HAVE BEEN NOTHING COMPARED TO THE GENPEI WAR THAT MY GRANDFATHER ON MY MOTHER'S SIDE WENT THROUGH.
FOR MY GREAT-GRAND-MOTHER ON MY FATHER'S SIDE, THE JINSHIN WAR WAS HUGE.
I HEARD MY GREAT-GREAT-GRAND-MOTHER ON MY MOTHER'S SIDE BURNED TO DEATH DURING THE DOWNFALL OF THE YAMATAIKOKU.
HEH-HEH
HEEHEE
OH, POOR HIMIKO WAS A BEAUTY, I'M TOLD.

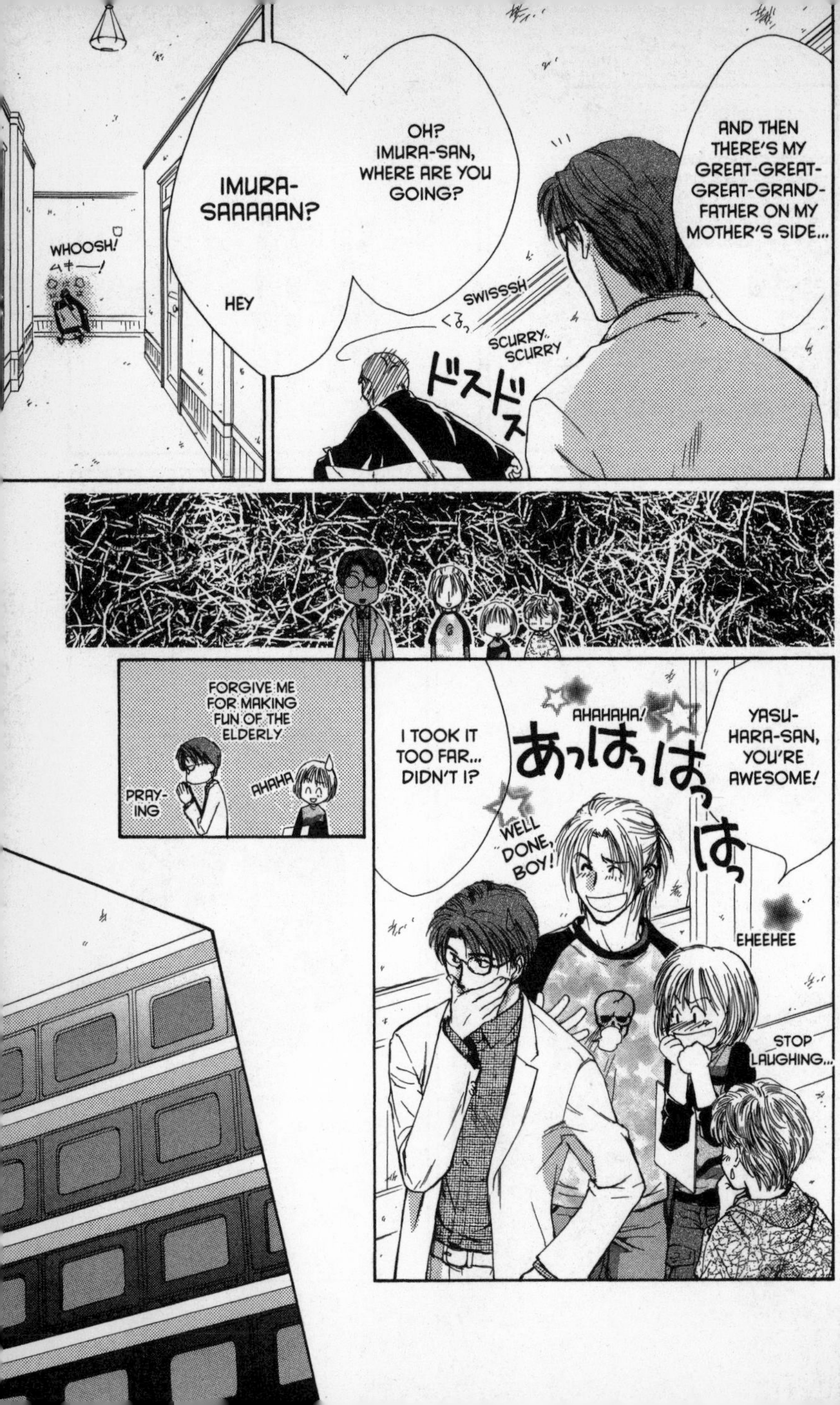
AND THEN THERE'S MY GREAT-GREAT-GREAT-GRAND-FATHER ON MY MOTHER'S SIDE...
SWISSSH
くるっ
SCURRY SCURRY
ドスドス
OH? IMURA-SAN, WHERE ARE YOU GOING?
IMURA-SAAAAAN?
HEY
WHOOSH!
ムキー—!
YASU-HARA-SAN, YOU'RE AWESOME!
あっはっはっ
AHAHAHA!
I TOOK IT TOO FAR... DIDN'T I?
WELL DONE, BOY!
EHEEHEE
STOP LAUGHING...
FORGIVE ME FOR MAKING FUN OF THE ELDERLY
AHAHA
PRAY-ING

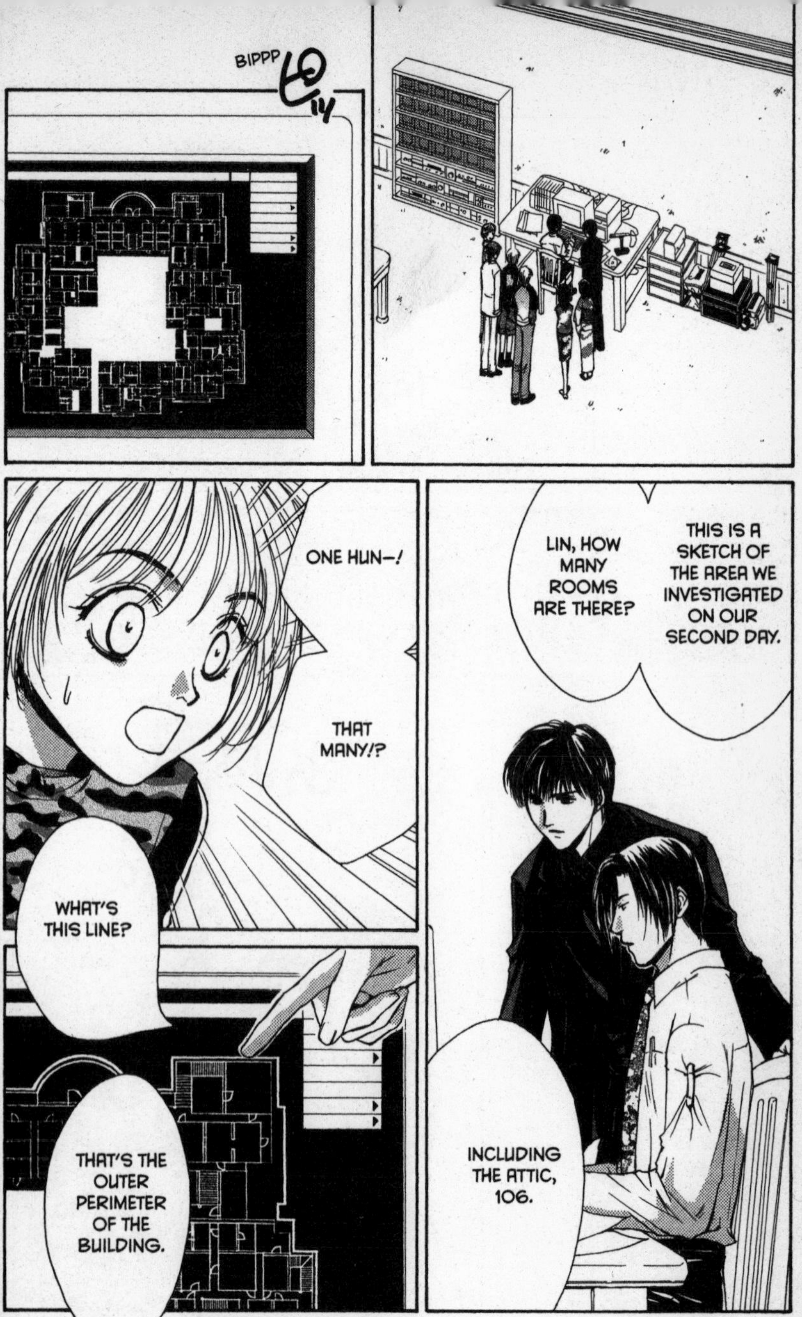
BIPPP
THIS IS A SKETCH OF THE AREA WE INVESTIGATED ON OUR SECOND DAY.
LIN, HOW MANY ROOMS ARE THERE?
INCLUDING THE ATTIC, 106.
ONE HUN—!
THAT MANY!?
WHAT'S THIS LINE?
THAT'S THE OUTER PERIMETER OF THE BUILDING.

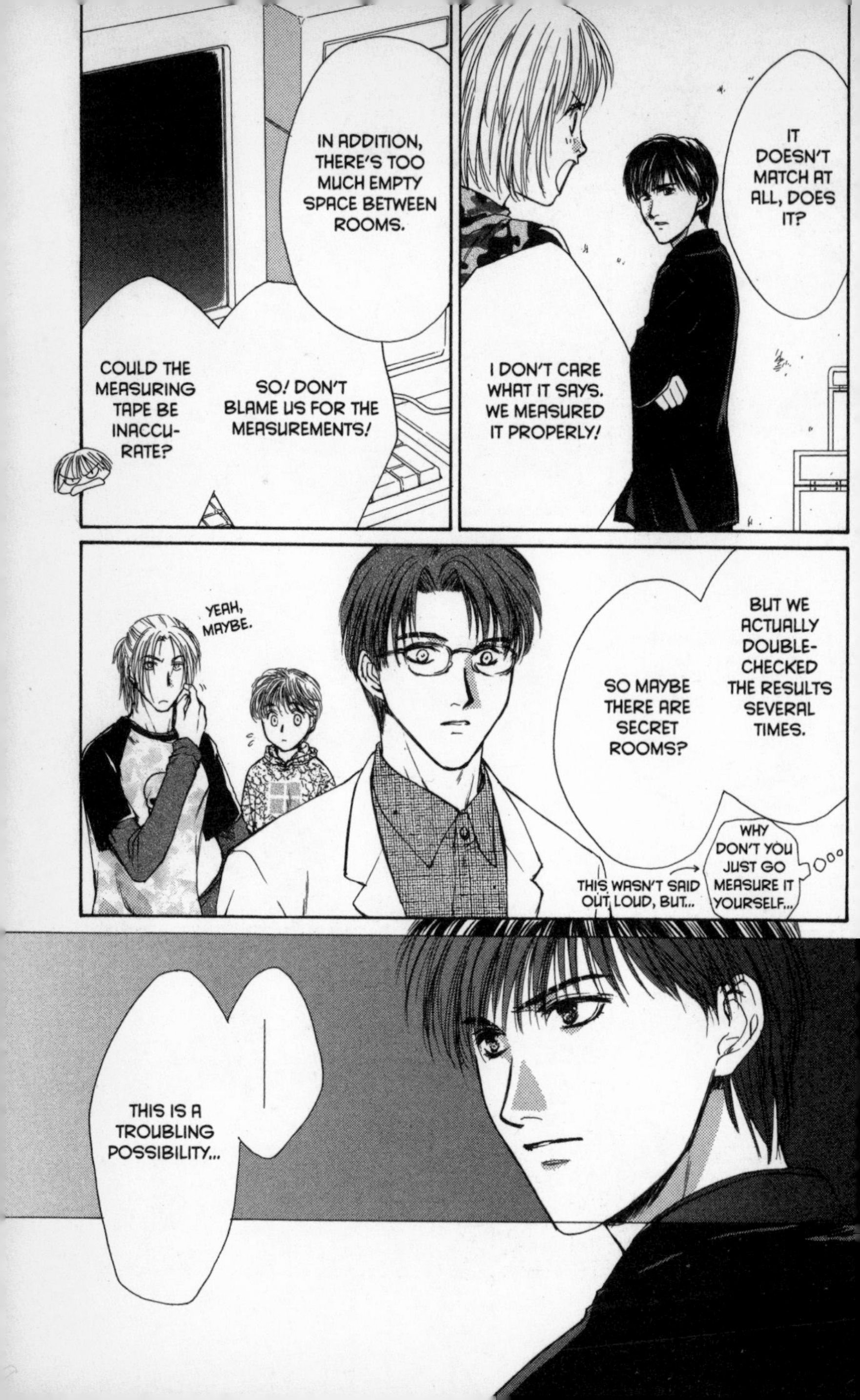
IT DOESN'T MATCH AT ALL, DOES IT?
I DON'T CARE WHAT IT SAYS. WE MEASURED IT PROPERLY!
IN ADDITION, THERE'S TOO MUCH EMPTY SPACE BETWEEN ROOMS.
SO! DON'T BLAME US FOR THE MEASUREMENTS!
COULD THE MEASURING TAPE BE INACCURATE?
BUT WE ACTUALLY DOUBLE-CHECKED THE RESULTS SEVERAL TIMES.
SO MAYBE THERE ARE SECRET ROOMS?
WHY DON'T YOU JUST GO MEASURE IT YOURSELF...
THIS WASN'T SAID OUT LOUD, BUT...
YEAH, MAYBE.
THIS IS A TROUBLING POSSIBILITY...

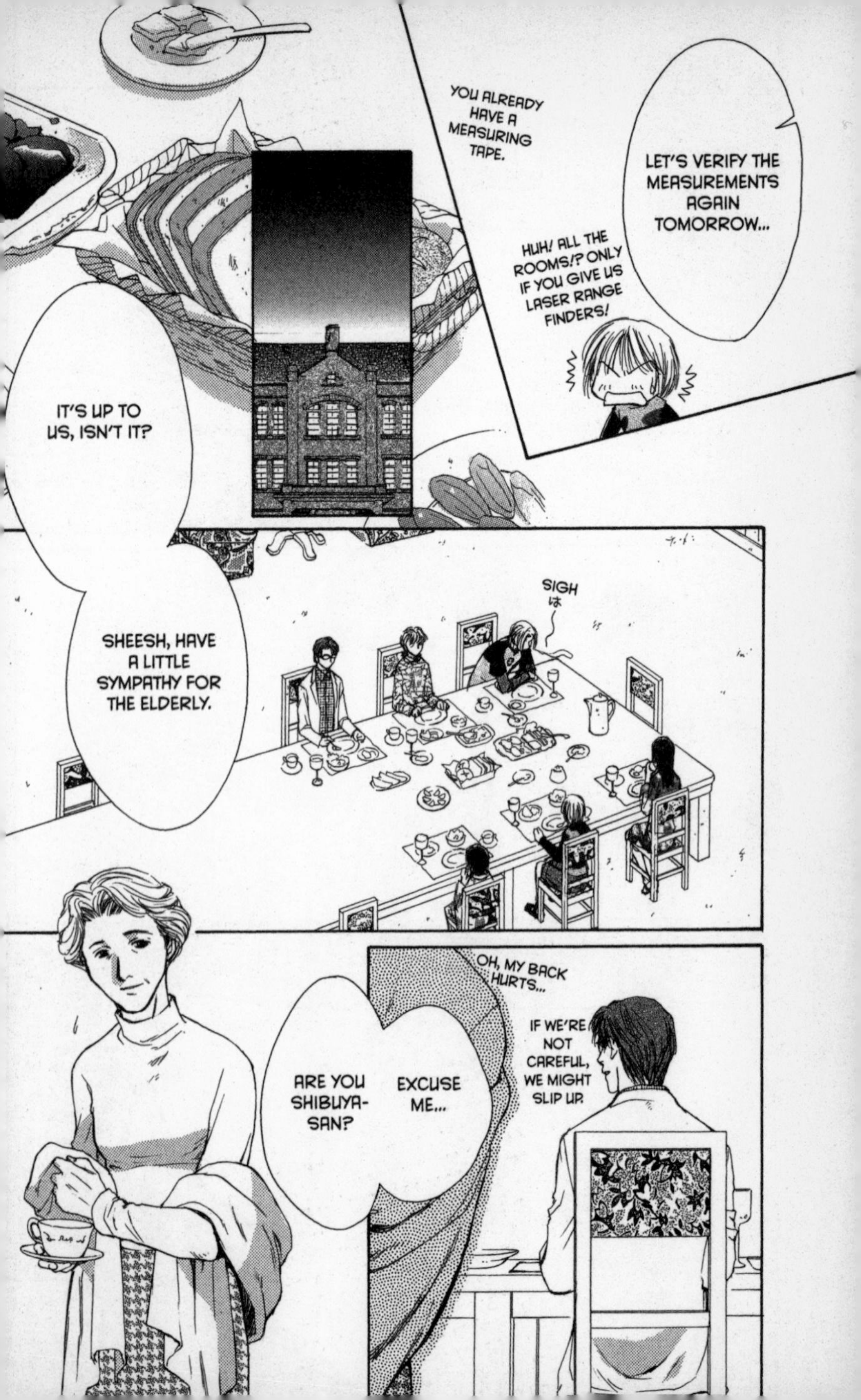
LET'S VERIFY THE MEASUREMENTS AGAIN TOMORROW...
YOU ALREADY HAVE A MEASURING TAPE.
HUH! ALL THE ROOMS!? ONLY IF YOU GIVE US LASER RANGE FINDERS!
IT'S UP TO US, ISN'T IT?
SHEESH, HAVE A LITTLE SYMPATHY FOR THE ELDERLY.
SIGH
は
OH, MY BACK HURTS...
IF WE'RE NOT CAREFUL, WE MIGHT SLIP UP.
EXCUSE ME...
ARE YOU SHIBUYA-SAN?

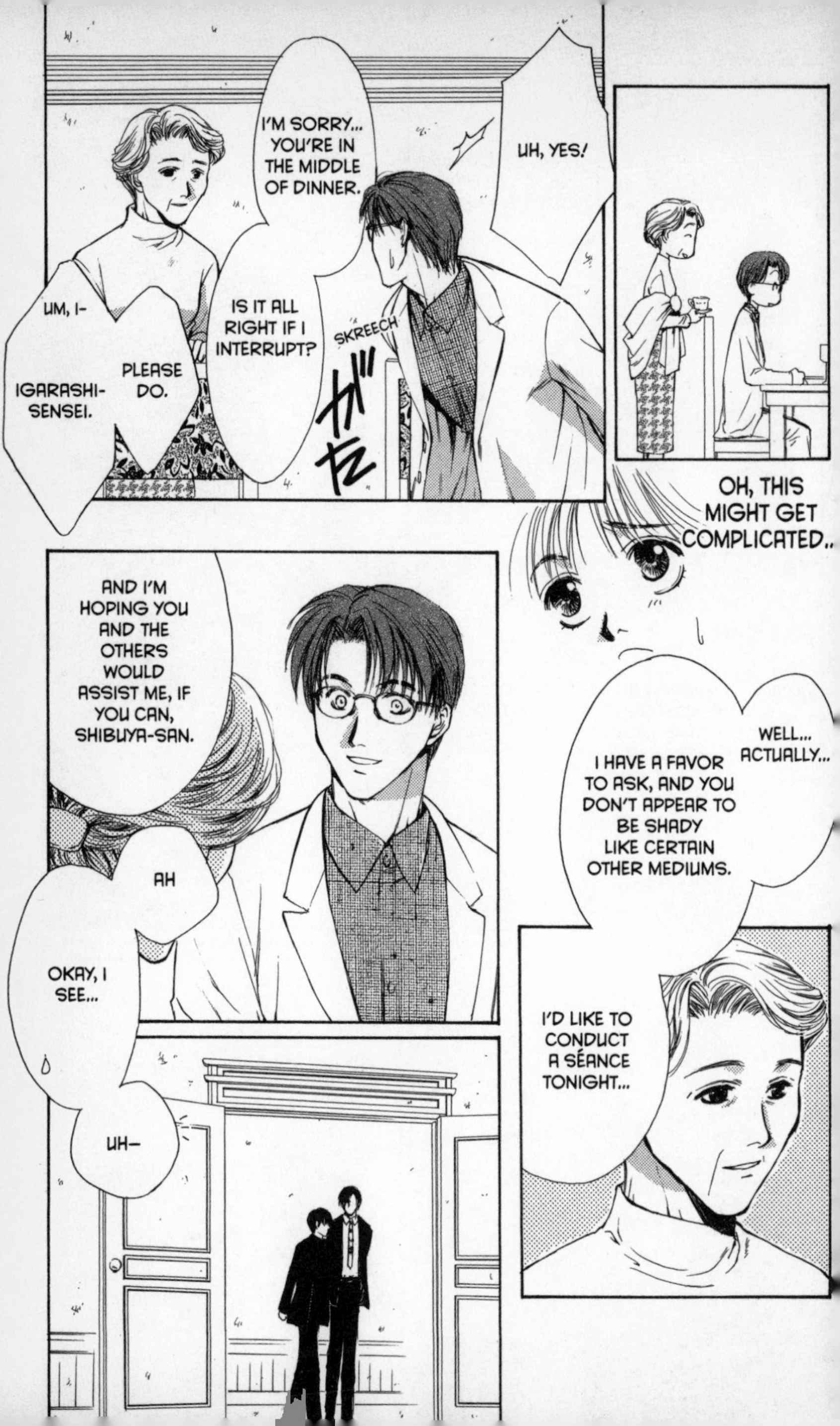
UH, YES!
I'M SORRY... YOU'RE IN THE MIDDLE OF DINNER.
IS IT ALL RIGHT IF I INTERRUPT?
SKREECH
PLEASE DO.
UM, I-
IGARASHI-SENSEI.
OH, THIS MIGHT GET COMPLICATED..
WELL... ACTUALLY...
I HAVE A FAVOR TO ASK, AND YOU DON'T APPEAR TO BE SHADY LIKE CERTAIN OTHER MEDIUMS.
I'D LIKE TO CONDUCT A SÉANCE TONIGHT...
AND I'M HOPING YOU AND THE OTHERS WOULD ASSIST ME, IF YOU CAN, SHIBUYA-SAN.
AH
OKAY, I SEE...
UH-

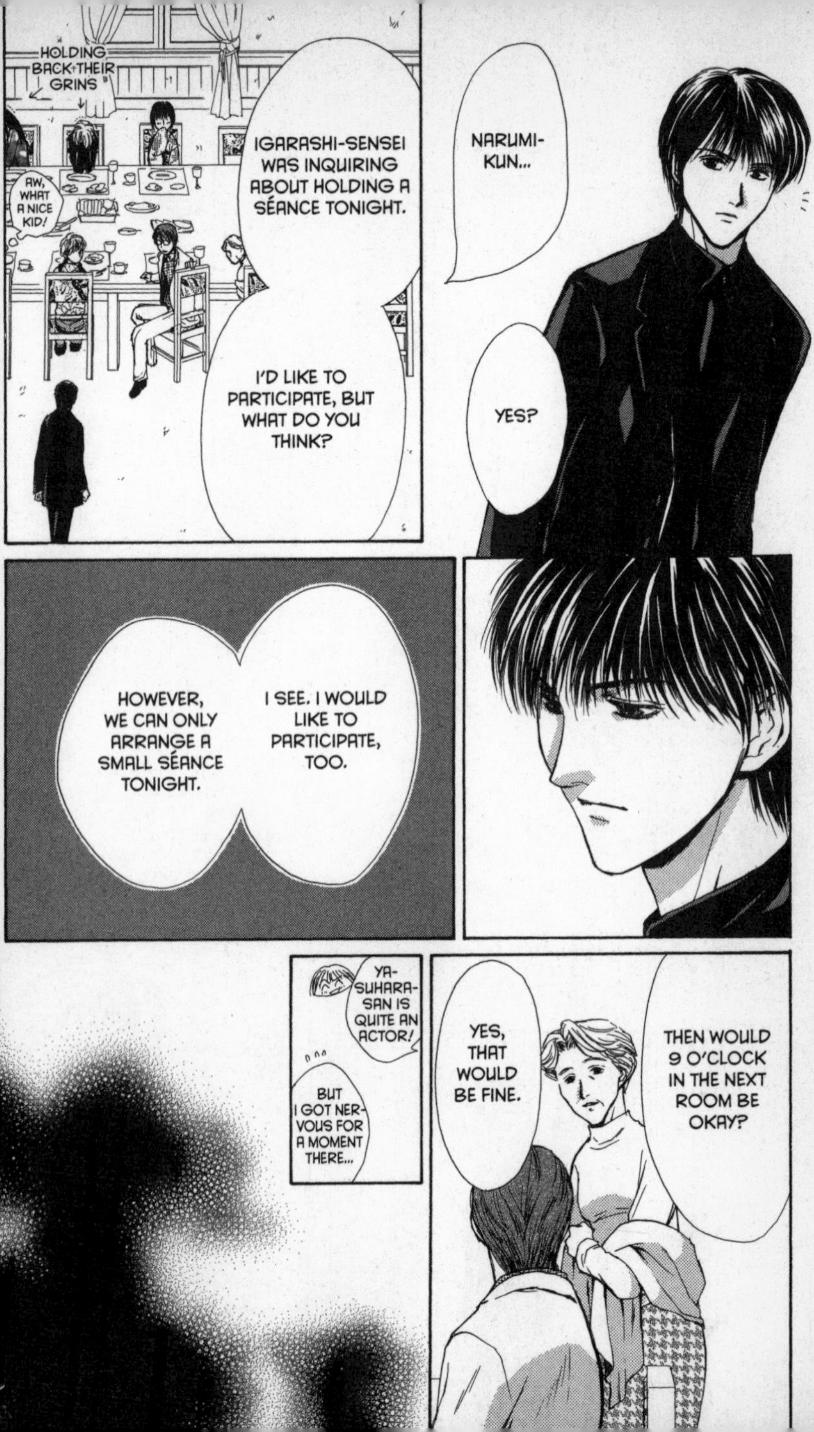
NARUMI-KUN...
YES?
IGARASHI-SENSEI WAS INQUIRING ABOUT HOLDING A SÉANCE TONIGHT.
I'D LIKE TO PARTICIPATE, BUT WHAT DO YOU THINK?
HOLDING BACK THEIR GRINS
AW, WHAT A NICE KID!
I SEE. I WOULD LIKE TO PARTICIPATE, TOO.
HOWEVER, WE CAN ONLY ARRANGE A SMALL SÉANCE TONIGHT.
THEN WOULD 9 O'CLOCK IN THE NEXT ROOM BE OKAY?
YES, THAT WOULD BE FINE.
YASUHARA-SAN IS QUITE AN ACTOR!
BUT I GOT NERVOUS FOR A MOMENT THERE...

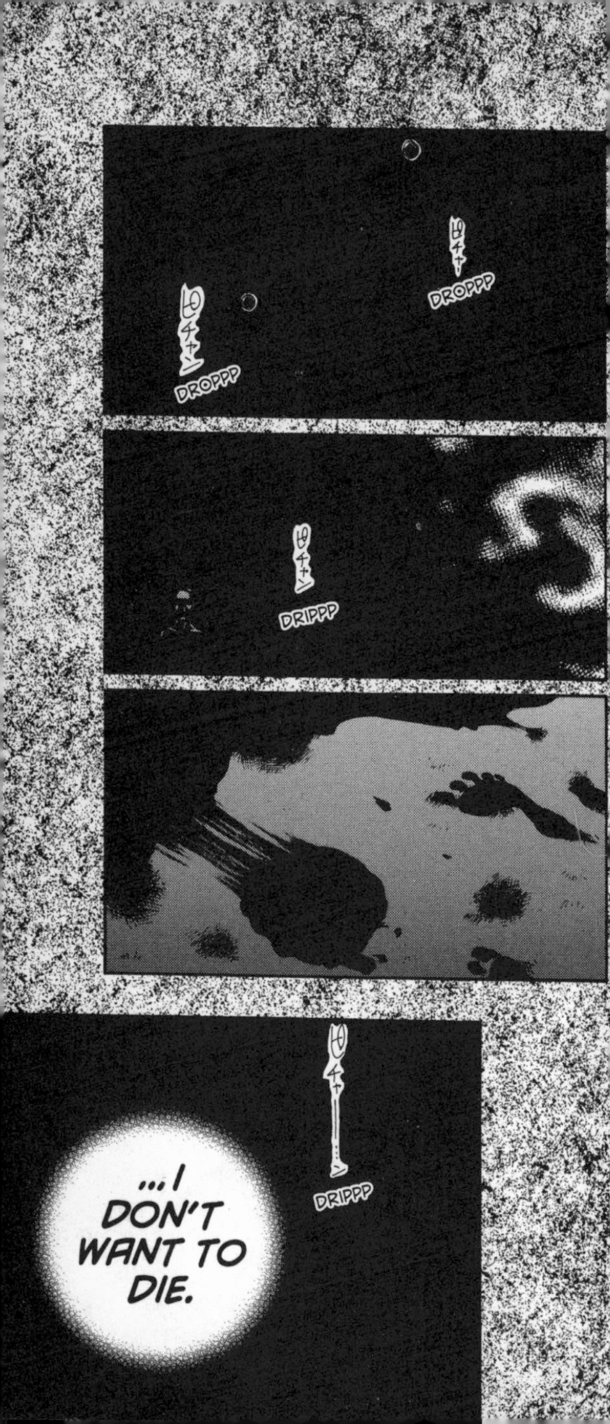
DROPPP
DROPPP
DRIPPP
DRIPPP
...I DON'T WANT TO DIE.

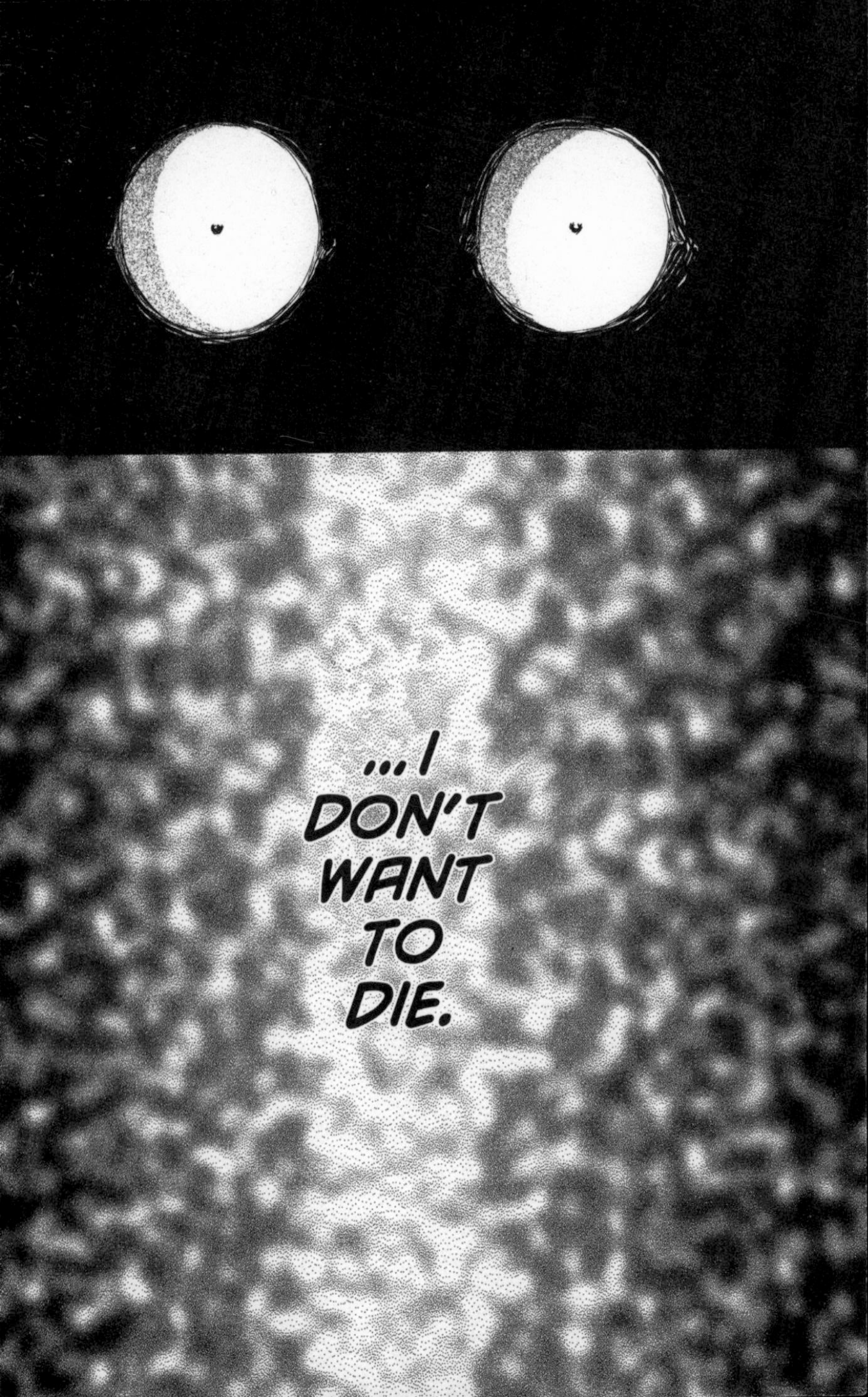
...I DON'T WANT TO DIE.

GHOST HUNT

— THE BLOODSTAINED LABYRINTH —

FILE 3

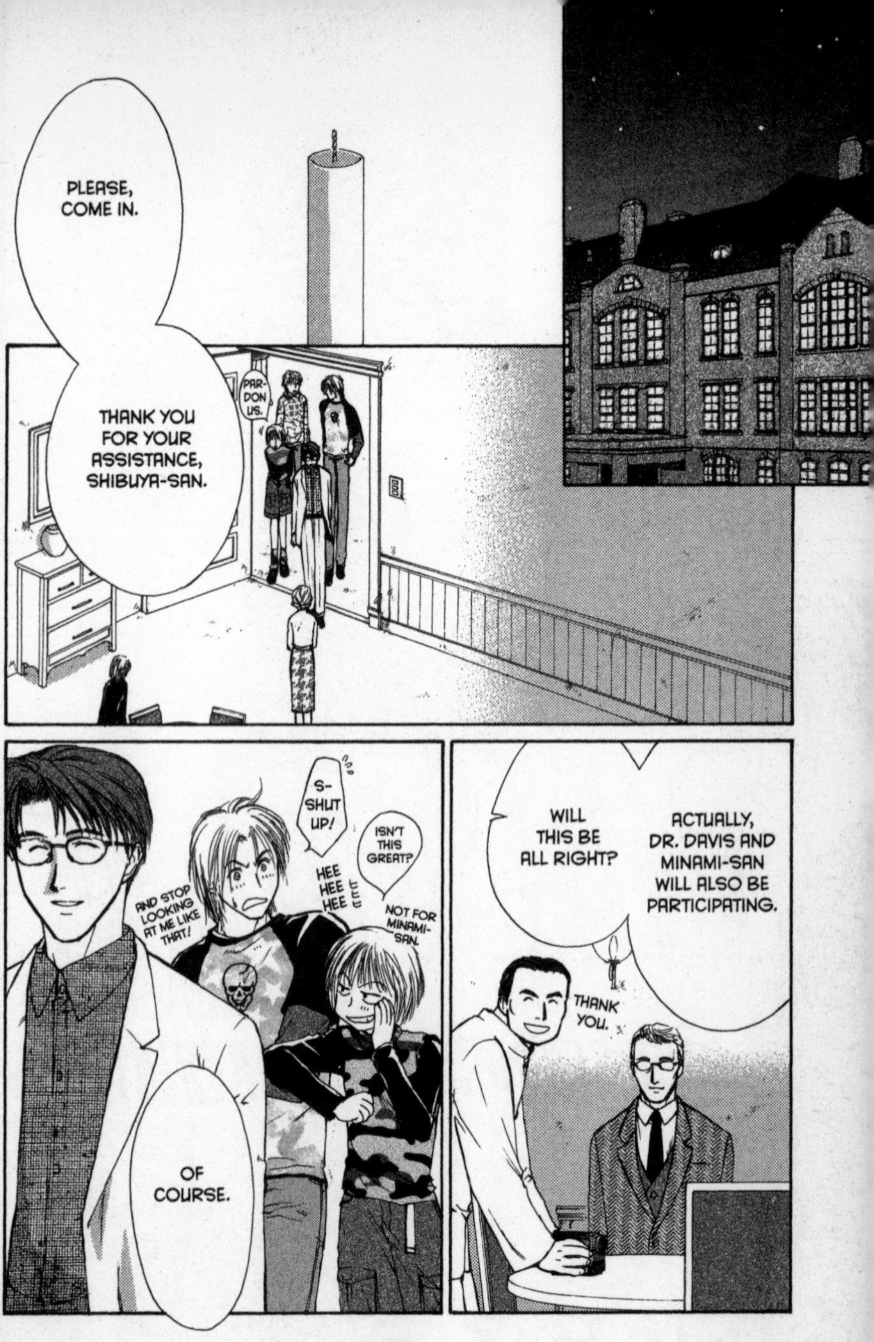
PLEASE, COME IN.
THANK YOU FOR YOUR ASSISTANCE, SHIBUYA-SAN.
PARDON US.
ACTUALLY, DR. DAVIS AND MINAMI-SAN WILL ALSO BE PARTICIPATING.
WILL THIS BE ALL RIGHT?
THANK YOU.
ISN'T THIS GREAT?
S-SHUT UP!
HEE HEE HEE
NOT FOR MINAMI-SAN.
AND STOP LOOKING AT ME LIKE THAT!
OF COURSE.

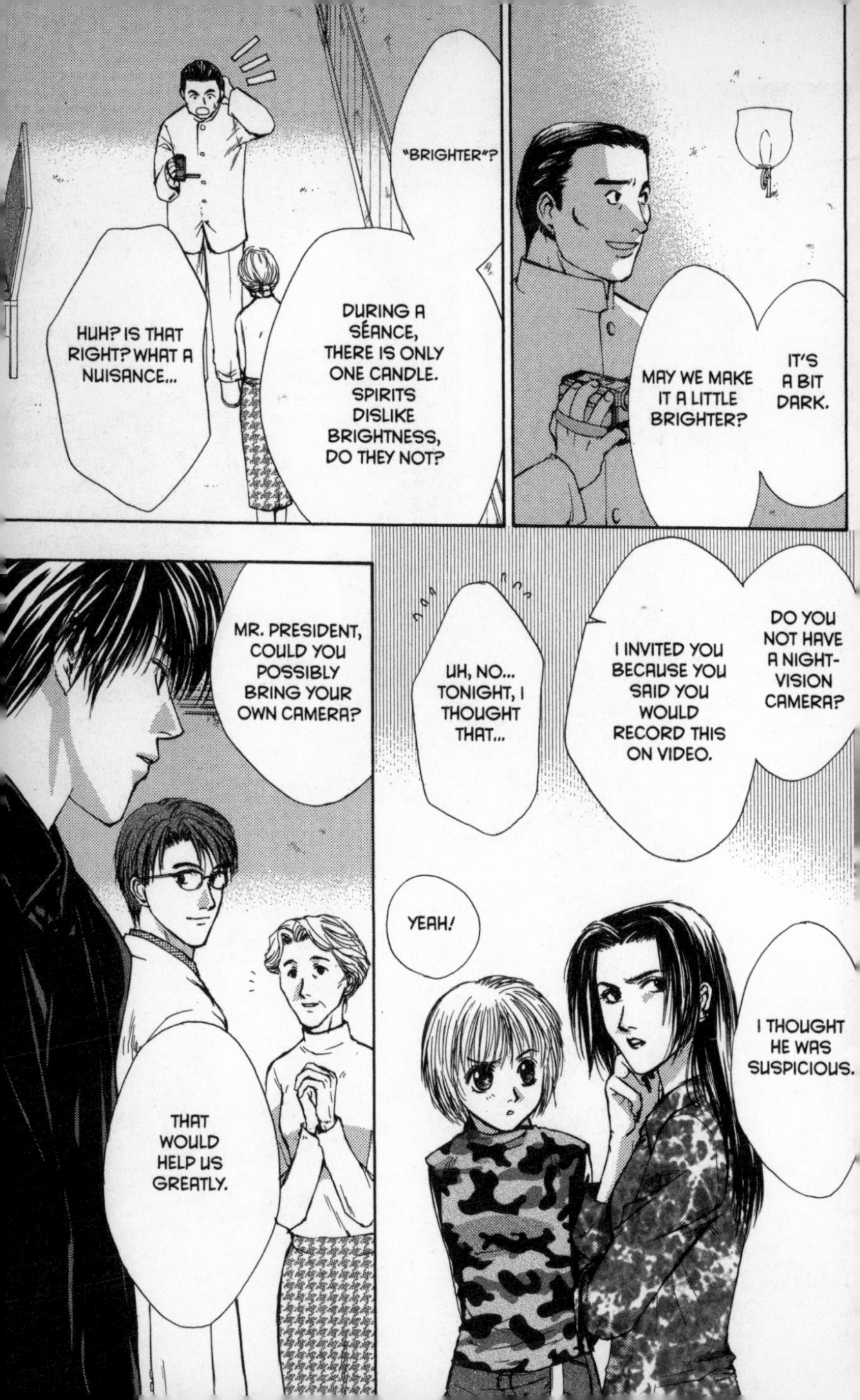
IT'S A BIT DARK.
MAY WE MAKE IT A LITTLE BRIGHTER?
"BRIGHTER"?
DURING A SÉANCE, THERE IS ONLY ONE CANDLE. SPIRITS DISLIKE BRIGHTNESS, DO THEY NOT?
HUH? IS THAT RIGHT? WHAT A NUISANCE...
DO YOU NOT HAVE A NIGHT-VISION CAMERA?
I INVITED YOU BECAUSE YOU SAID YOU WOULD RECORD THIS ON VIDEO.
UH, NO... TONIGHT, I THOUGHT THAT...
I THOUGHT HE WAS SUSPICIOUS.
YEAH!
MR. PRESIDENT, COULD YOU POSSIBLY BRING YOUR OWN CAMERA?
THAT WOULD HELP US GREATLY.

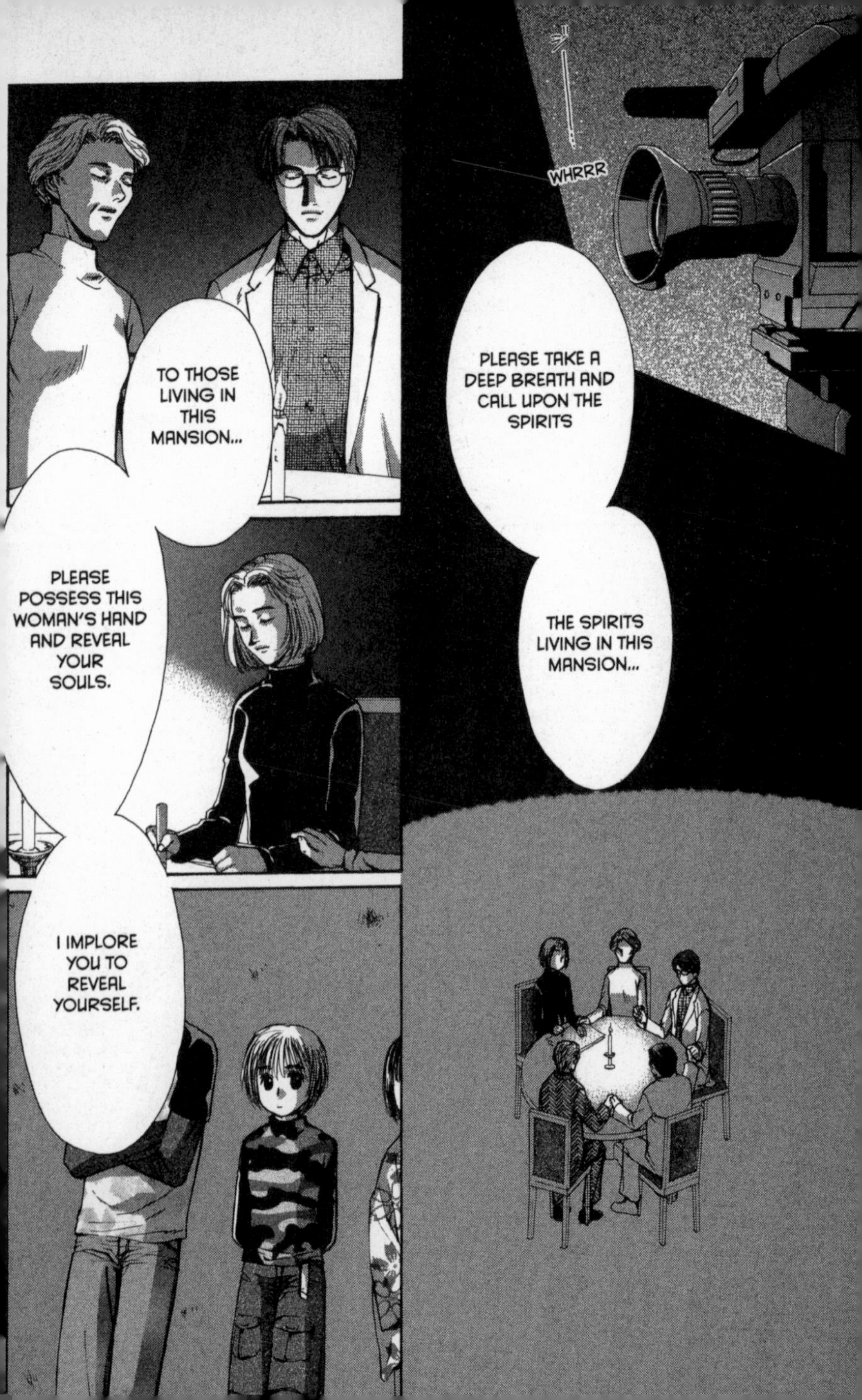
WHRRR
PLEASE TAKE A DEEP BREATH AND CALL UPON THE SPIRITS
THE SPIRITS LIVING IN THIS MANSION...
TO THOSE LIVING IN THIS MANSION...
PLEASE POSSESS THIS WOMAN'S HAND AND REVEAL YOUR SOULS.
I IMPLORE YOU TO REVEAL YOURSELF.

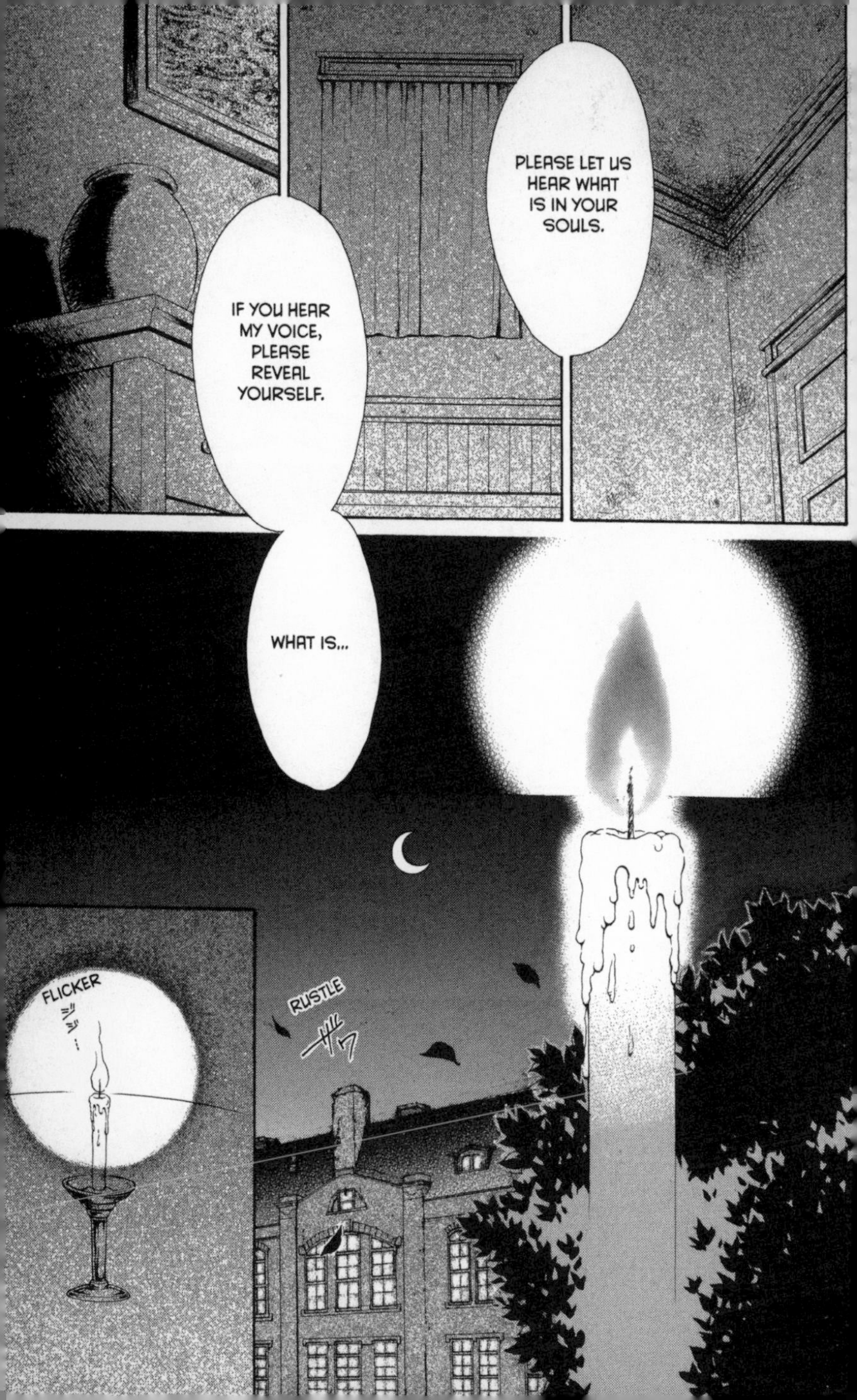
PLEASE LET US HEAR WHAT IS IN YOUR SOULS.
IF YOU HEAR MY VOICE, PLEASE REVEAL YOURSELF.
WHAT IS...
RUSTLE
ザワ
FLICKER
ジジ…

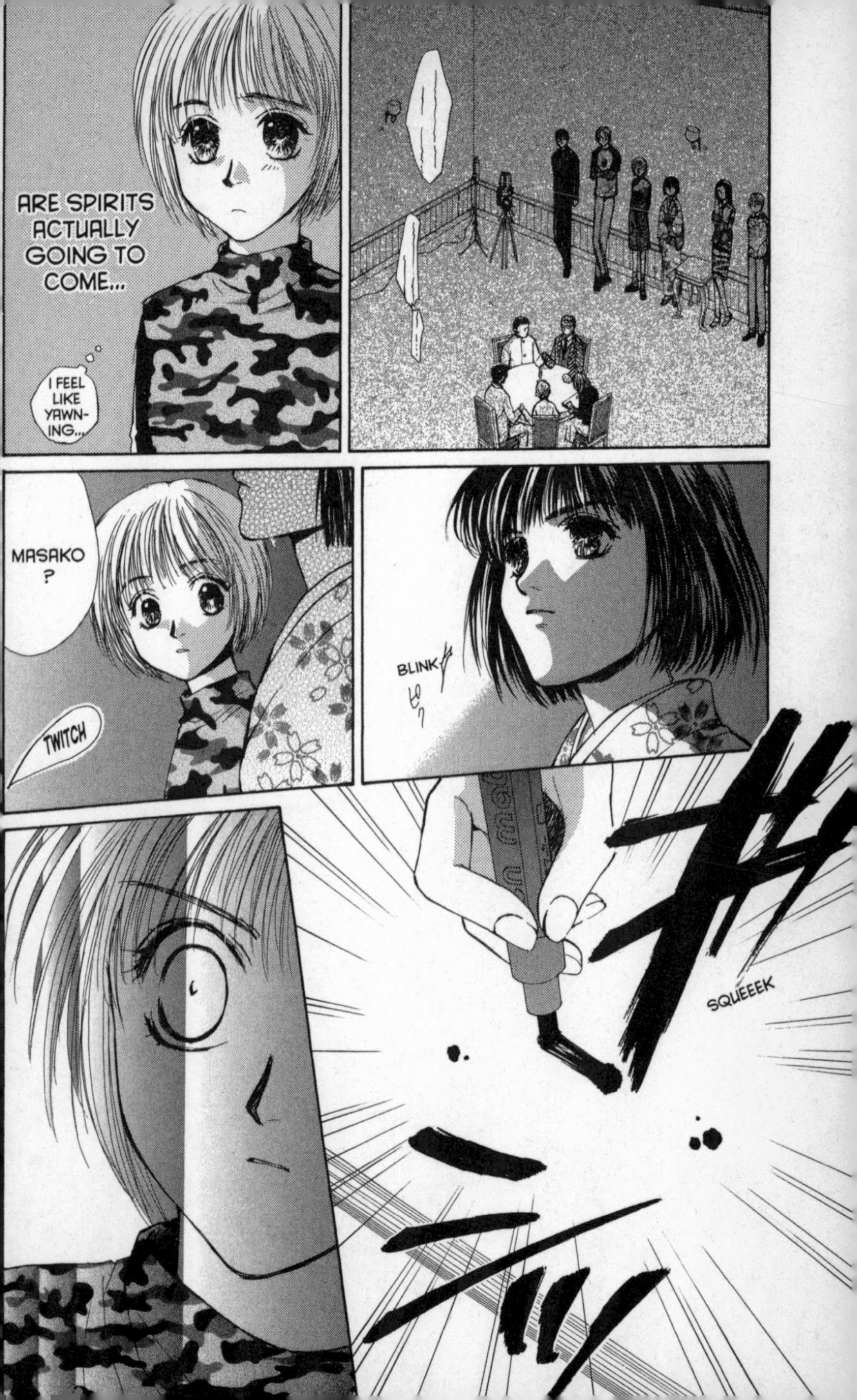
ARE SPIRITS ACTUALLY GOING TO COME...
I FEEL LIKE YAWN-ING...
BLINK
ピク
MASAKO ?
TWITCH
SQUEEEK

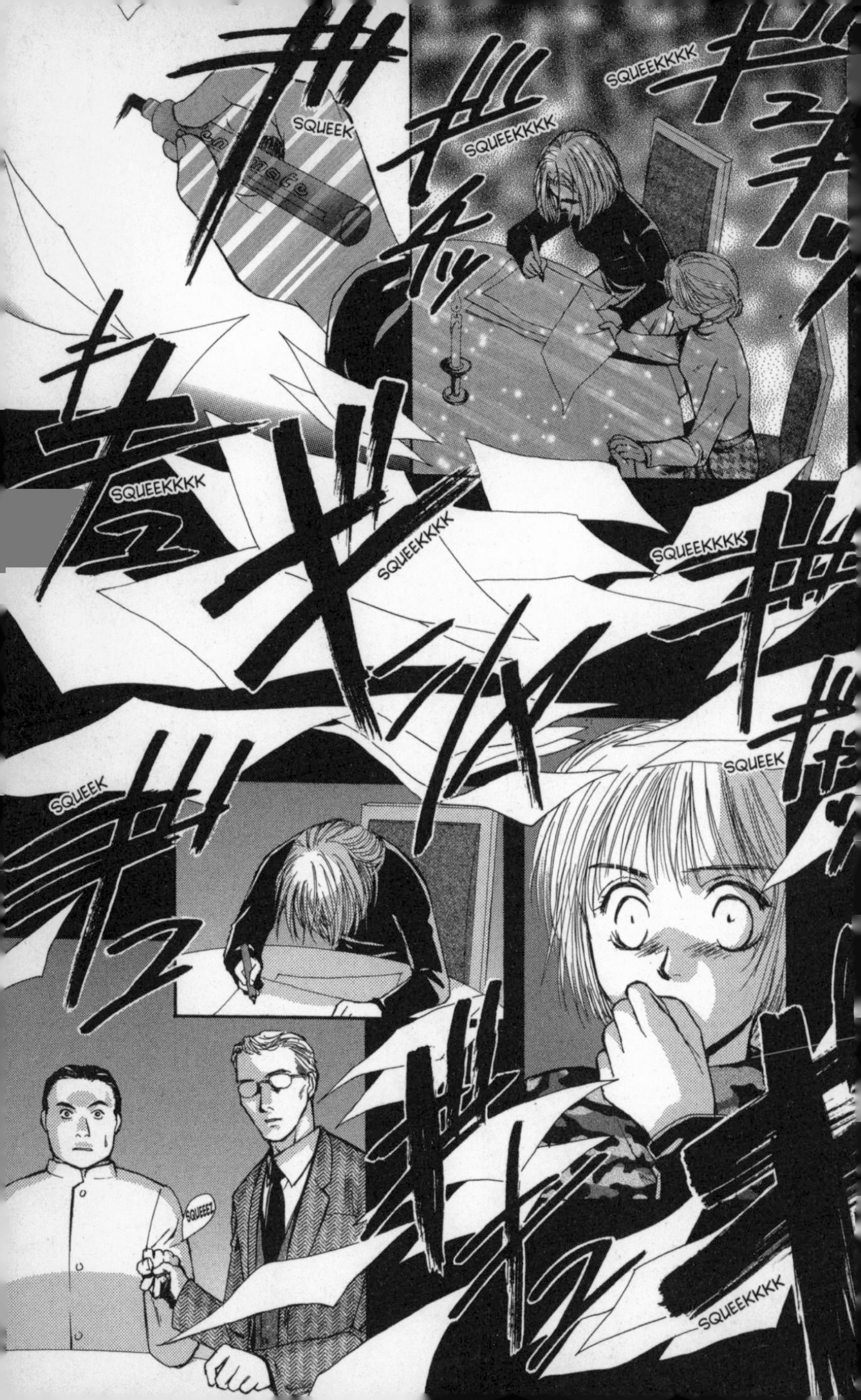
SQUEEKKKK
SQUEEKKKK
SQUEEK
SQUEEKKKK
SQUEEKKKK
SQUEEKKKK
SQUEEK
SQUEEK
SQUEEEZ
SQUEEKKKK

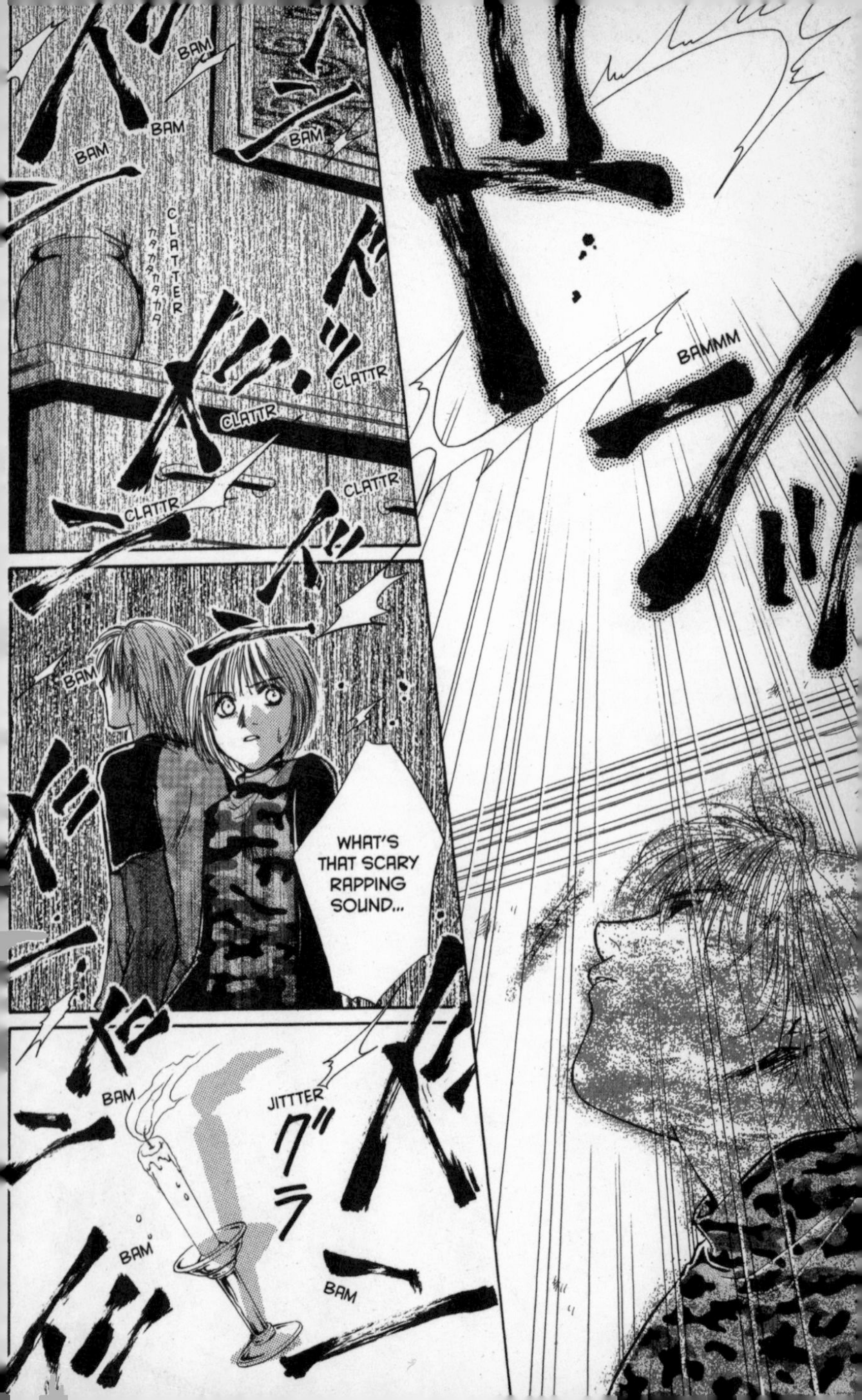
BAMMM
BAM
BAM
BAM
BAM
CLATTER
CLATTR
CLATTR
CLATTR
CLATTR
BAM
WHAT'S THAT SCARY RAPPING SOUND...
JITTER
グラ
BAM
BAM
BAM

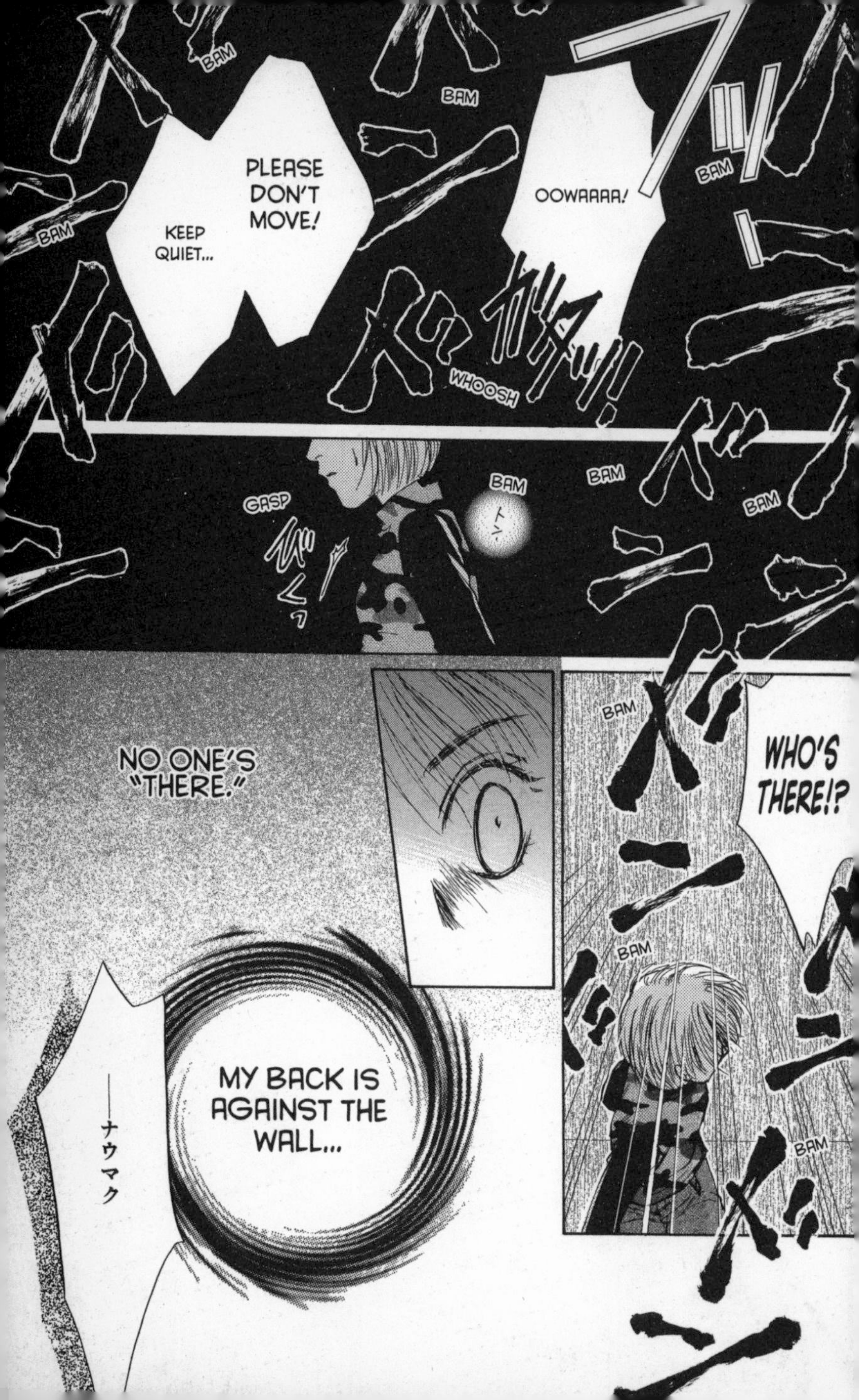
BAM
BAM
BAM
OOWAAAAA!
BAM
BAM
PLEASE DON'T MOVE!
KEEP QUIET...
WHOOSH
BAM
BAM
BAM
GASP
BAM
WHO'S THERE!?
BAM
BAM
NO ONE'S "THERE."
MY BACK IS AGAINST THE WALL...
――ナウマク

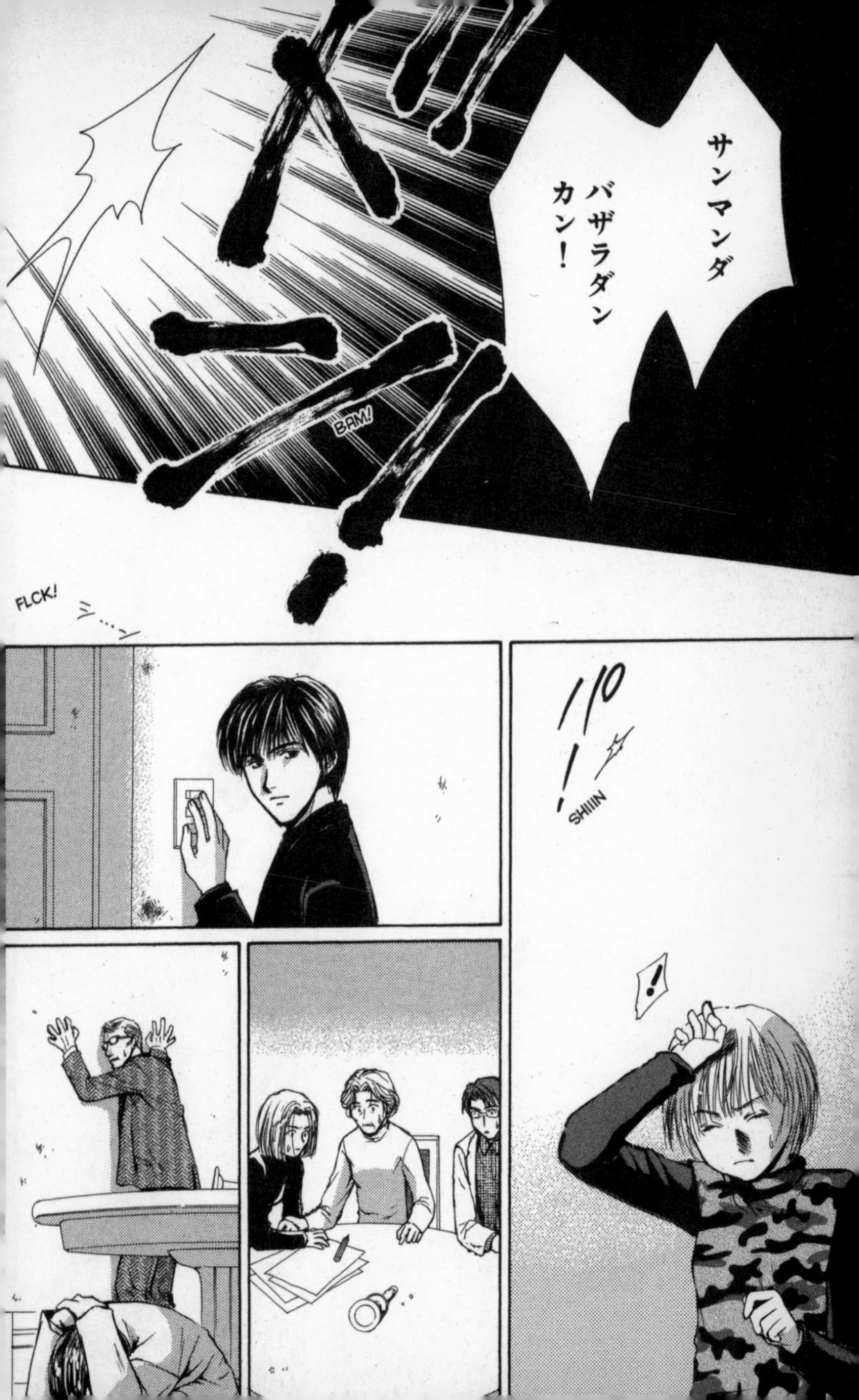
サンマンダ
バザラダン
カン!
BAM!
FLCK!
シ…ン
パ!
SHIIN
!

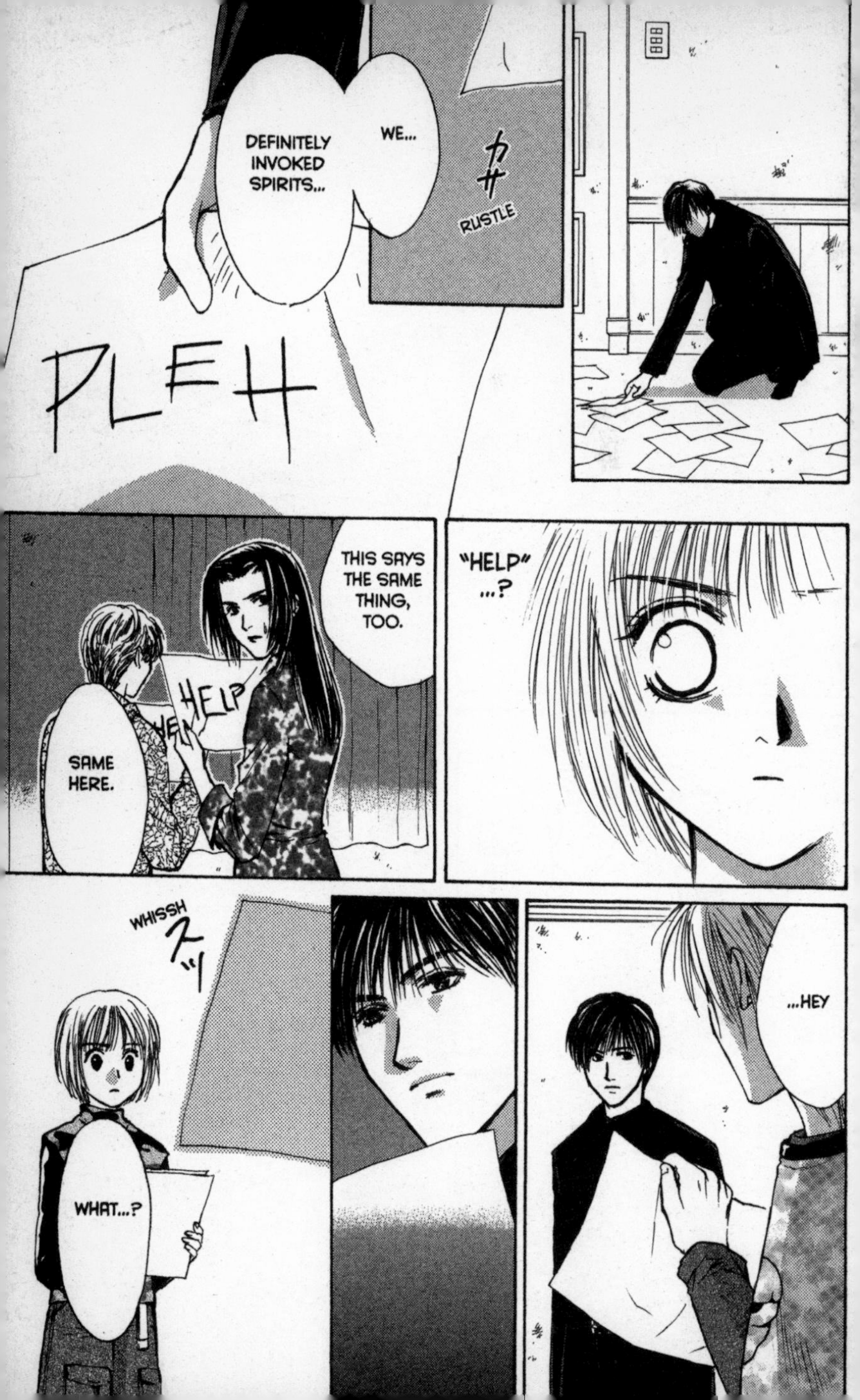
WE...
DEFINITELY INVOKED SPIRITS...
カサ
RUSTLE
PLEH
"HELP" ...?
THIS SAYS THE SAME THING, TOO.
HELP
SAME HERE.
...HEY
WHISSH
スッ
WHAT...?

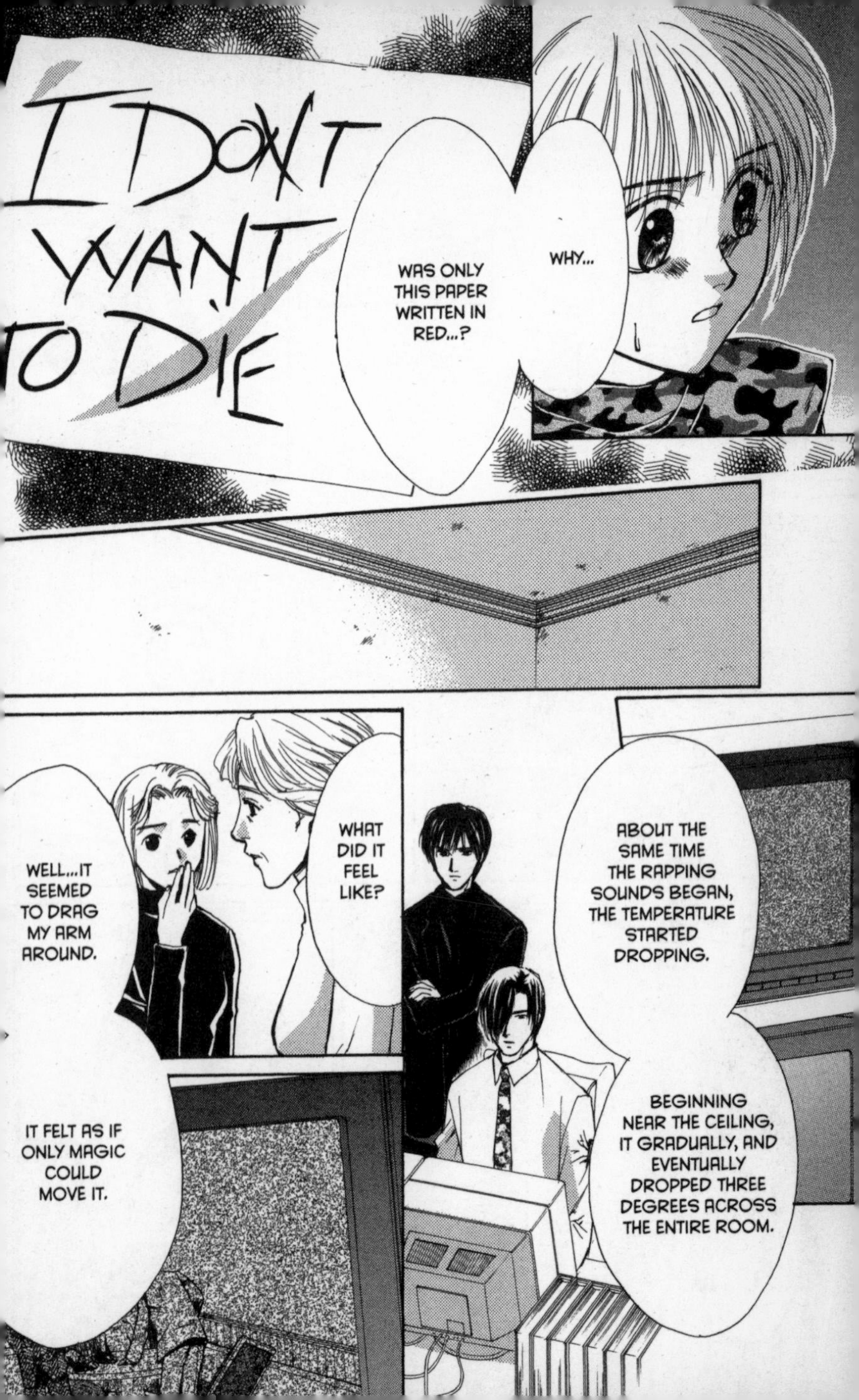
WHY...
WAS ONLY THIS PAPER WRITTEN IN RED...?
I DON'T WANT TO DIE
ABOUT THE SAME TIME THE RAPPING SOUNDS BEGAN, THE TEMPERATURE STARTED DROPPING.
BEGINNING NEAR THE CEILING, IT GRADUALLY, AND EVENTUALLY DROPPED THREE DEGREES ACROSS THE ENTIRE ROOM.
WHAT DID IT FEEL LIKE?
WELL...IT SEEMED TO DRAG MY ARM AROUND.
IT FELT AS IF ONLY MAGIC COULD MOVE IT.

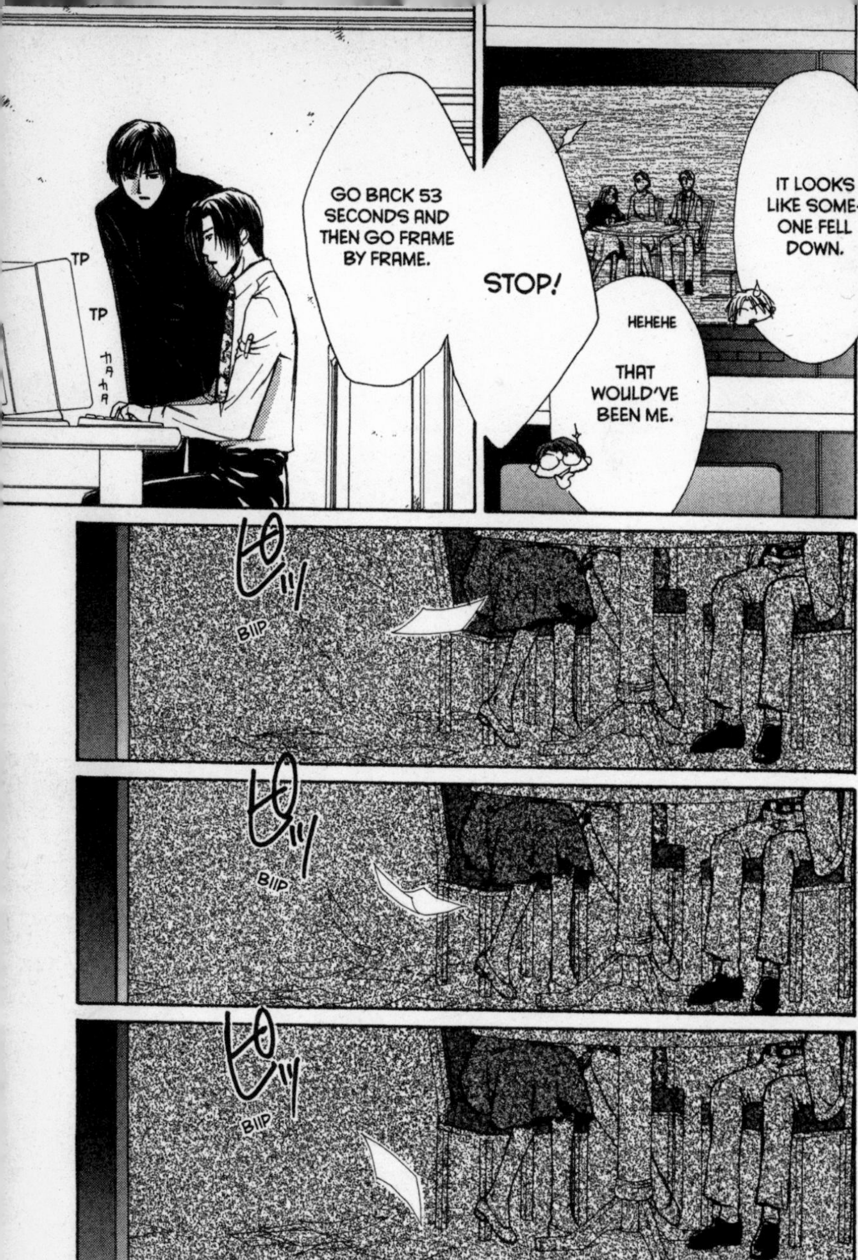

IT LOOKS LIKE SOME-ONE FELL DOWN.
HEHEHE
THAT WOULD'VE BEEN ME.
GO BACK 53 SECONDS AND THEN GO FRAME BY FRAME.
STOP!
TP
TP
カタカタ
ピピッ
BIIP
ピピッ
BIIP
ピピッ
BIIP

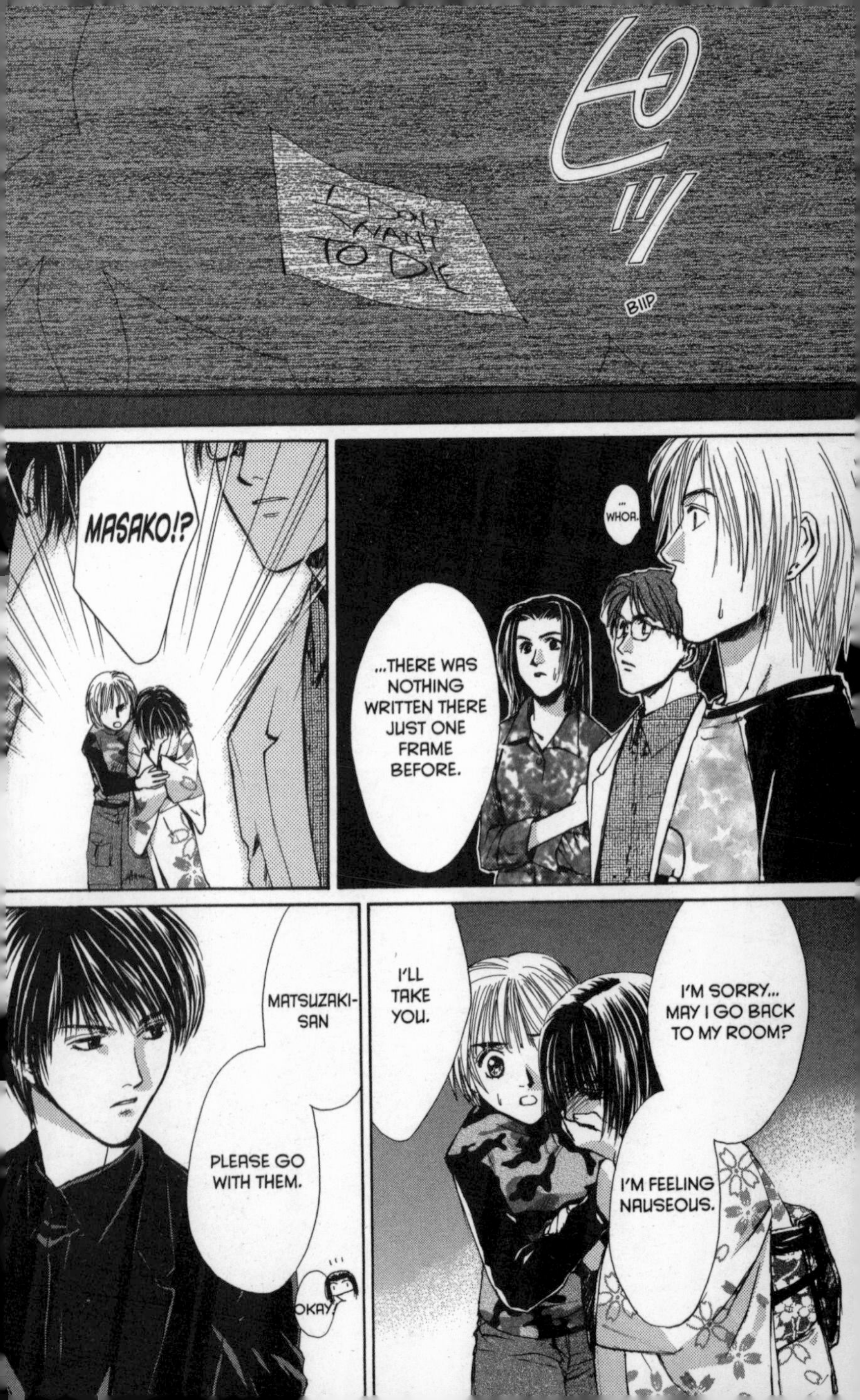
ピッ
BIIP
I DON'T WANT TO DIE
... WHOA.
...THERE WAS NOTHING WRITTEN THERE JUST ONE FRAME BEFORE.
MASAKO!?
I'M SORRY... MAY I GO BACK TO MY ROOM?
I'LL TAKE YOU.
I'M FEELING NAUSEOUS.
MATSUZAKI-SAN
PLEASE GO WITH THEM.
OKAY!

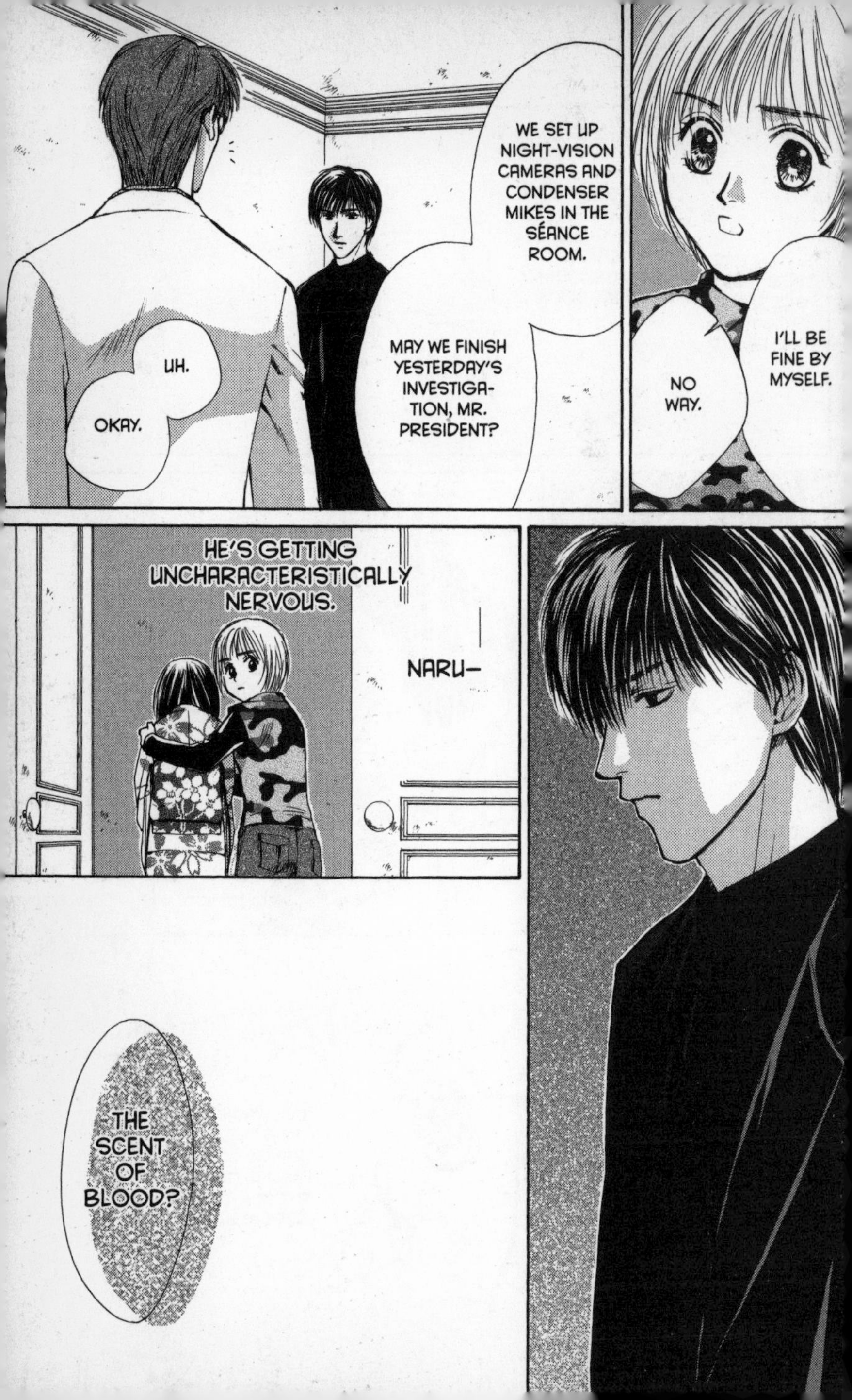
I'LL BE FINE BY MYSELF.
NO WAY.
WE SET UP NIGHT-VISION CAMERAS AND CONDENSER MIKES IN THE SÉANCE ROOM.
MAY WE FINISH YESTERDAY'S INVESTIGA-TION, MR. PRESIDENT?
UH.
OKAY.
HE'S GETTING UNCHARACTERISTICALLY NERVOUS.
NARU—
THE SCENT OF BLOOD?

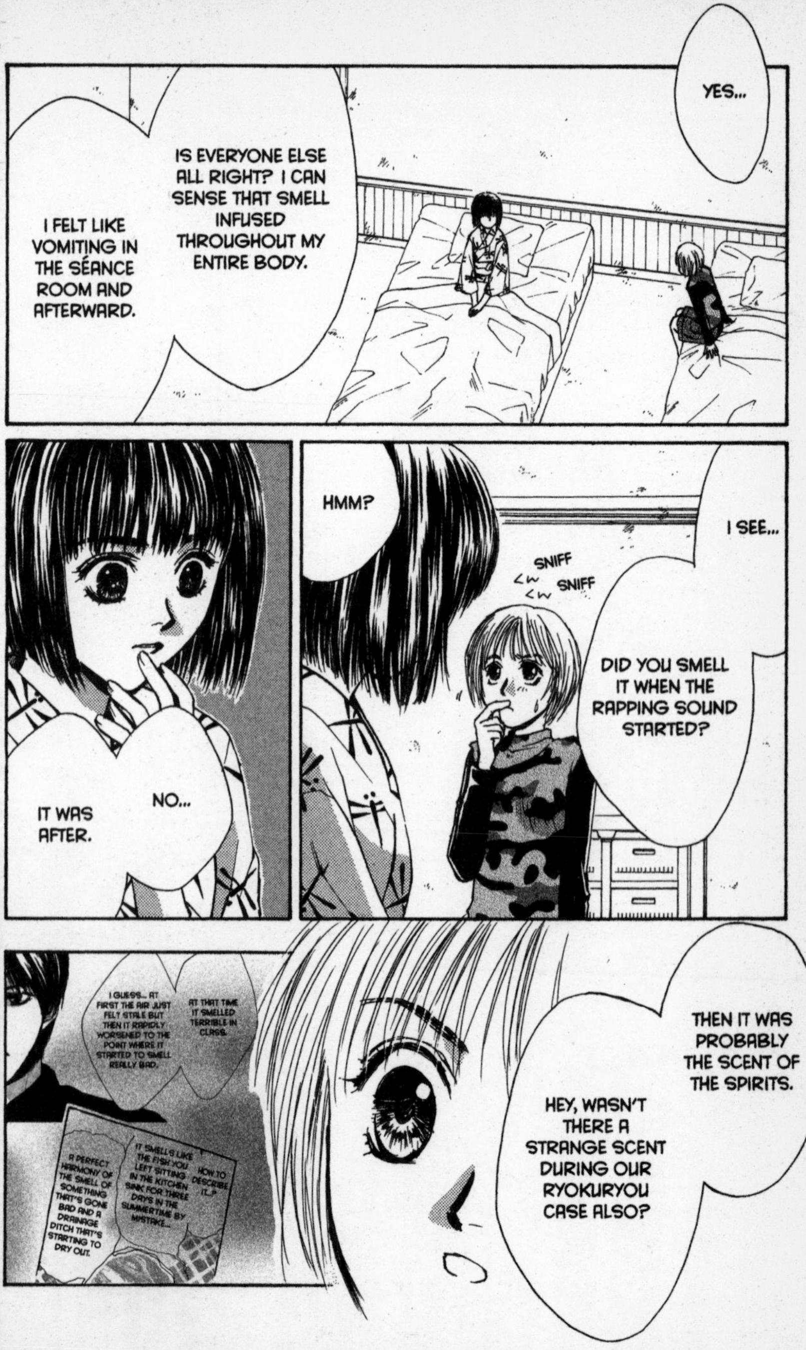
YES...
IS EVERYONE ELSE ALL RIGHT? I CAN SENSE THAT SMELL INFUSED THROUGHOUT MY ENTIRE BODY.
I FELT LIKE VOMITING IN THE SÉANCE ROOM AND AFTERWARD.
I SEE...
HMM?
SNIFF SNIFF
DID YOU SMELL IT WHEN THE RAPPING SOUND STARTED?
NO...
IT WAS AFTER.
THEN IT WAS PROBABLY THE SCENT OF THE SPIRITS.
HEY, WASN'T THERE A STRANGE SCENT DURING OUR RYOKURYOU CASE ALSO?
AT THAT TIME IT SMELLED TERRIBLE IN CLASS.
I GUESS... AT FIRST THE AIR JUST FELT STALE BUT THEN IT RAPIDLY WORSENED TO THE POINT WHERE IT STARTED TO SMELL REALLY BAD.
HOW TO DESCRIBE IT...?
IT SMELLS LIKE THE FISH YOU LEFT SITTING IN THE KITCHEN SINK FOR THREE DAYS IN THE SUMMERTIME BY MISTAKE...
A PERFECT HARMONY OF THE SMELL OF SOMETHING THAT'S GONE BAD AND A DRAINAGE DITCH THAT'S STARTING TO DRY OUT.

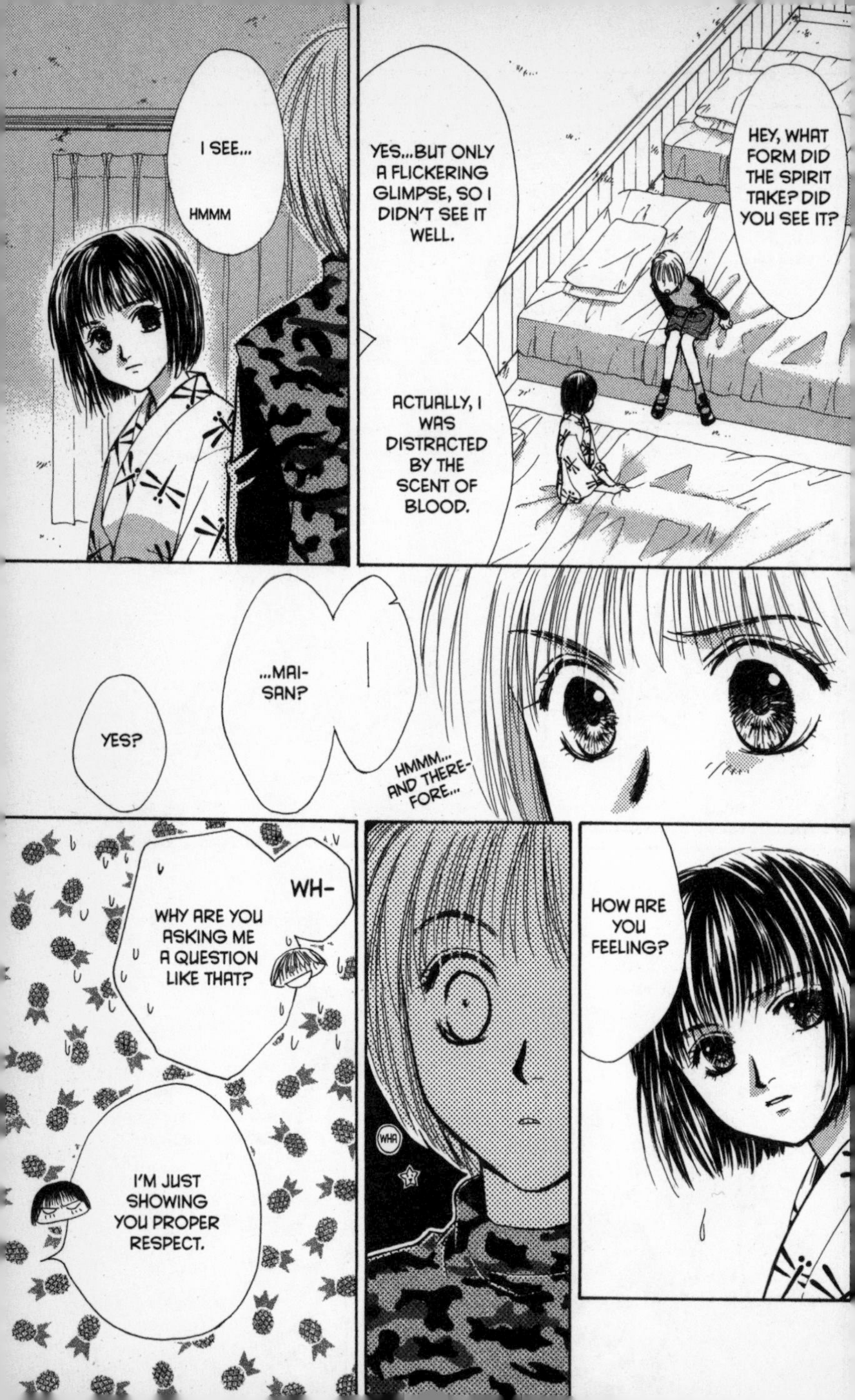
HEY, WHAT FORM DID THE SPIRIT TAKE? DID YOU SEE IT?
YES...BUT ONLY A FLICKERING GLIMPSE, SO I DIDN'T SEE IT WELL.
ACTUALLY, I WAS DISTRACTED BY THE SCENT OF BLOOD.
I SEE...
HMMM
HMMM... AND THERE-FORE...
...MAI-SAN?
YES?
HOW ARE YOU FEELING?
WHA
WH-
WHY ARE YOU ASKING ME A QUESTION LIKE THAT?
I'M JUST SHOWING YOU PROPER RESPECT.

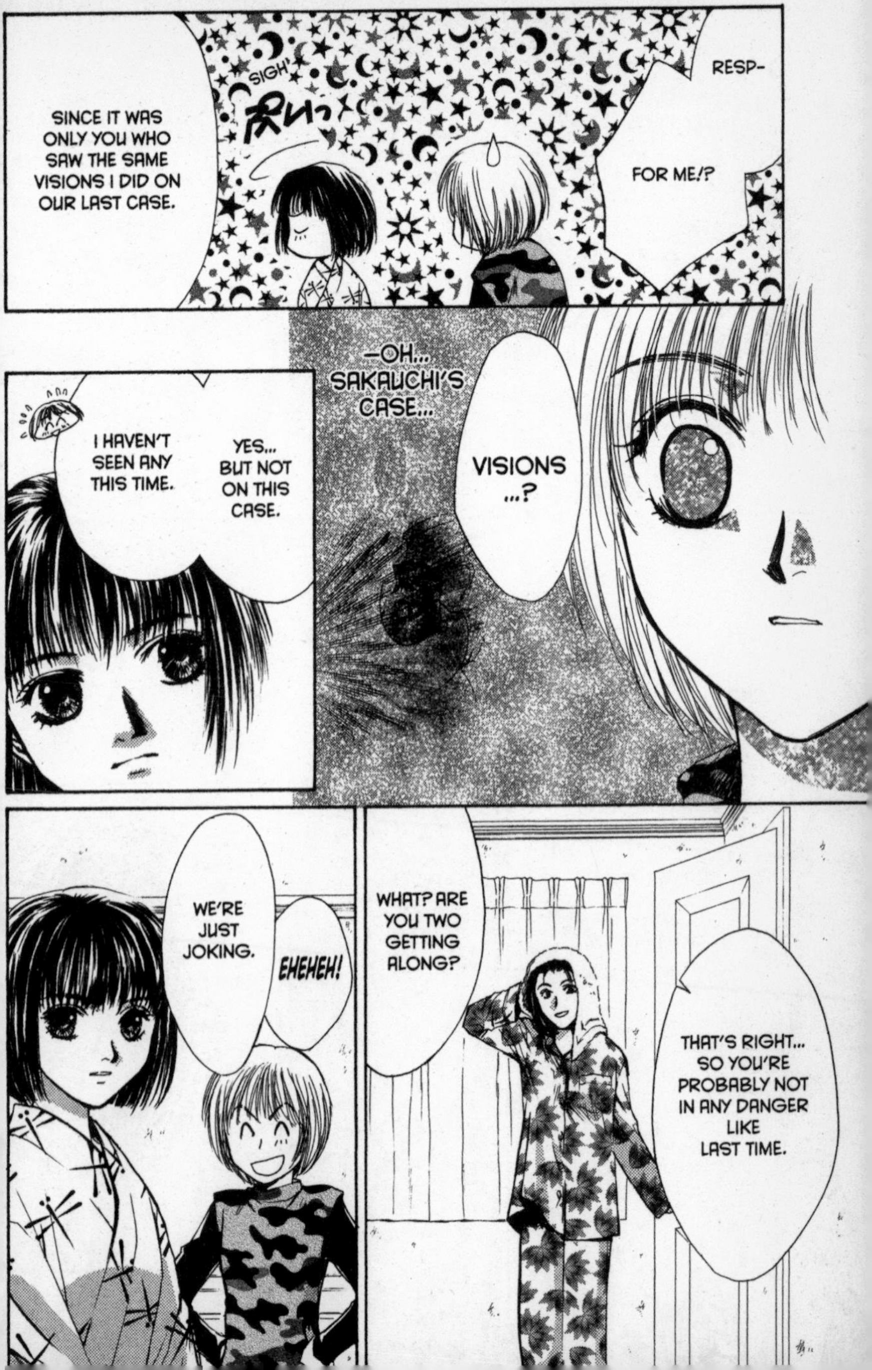
RESP-
FOR ME!?
SIGH
SINCE IT WAS ONLY YOU WHO SAW THE SAME VISIONS I DID ON OUR LAST CASE.
VISIONS ...?
—OH... SAKAUCHI'S CASE...
YES... BUT NOT ON THIS CASE.
I HAVEN'T SEEN ANY THIS TIME.
THAT'S RIGHT... SO YOU'RE PROBABLY NOT IN ANY DANGER LIKE LAST TIME.
WHAT? ARE YOU TWO GETTING ALONG?
EHEHEH!
WE'RE JUST JOKING.

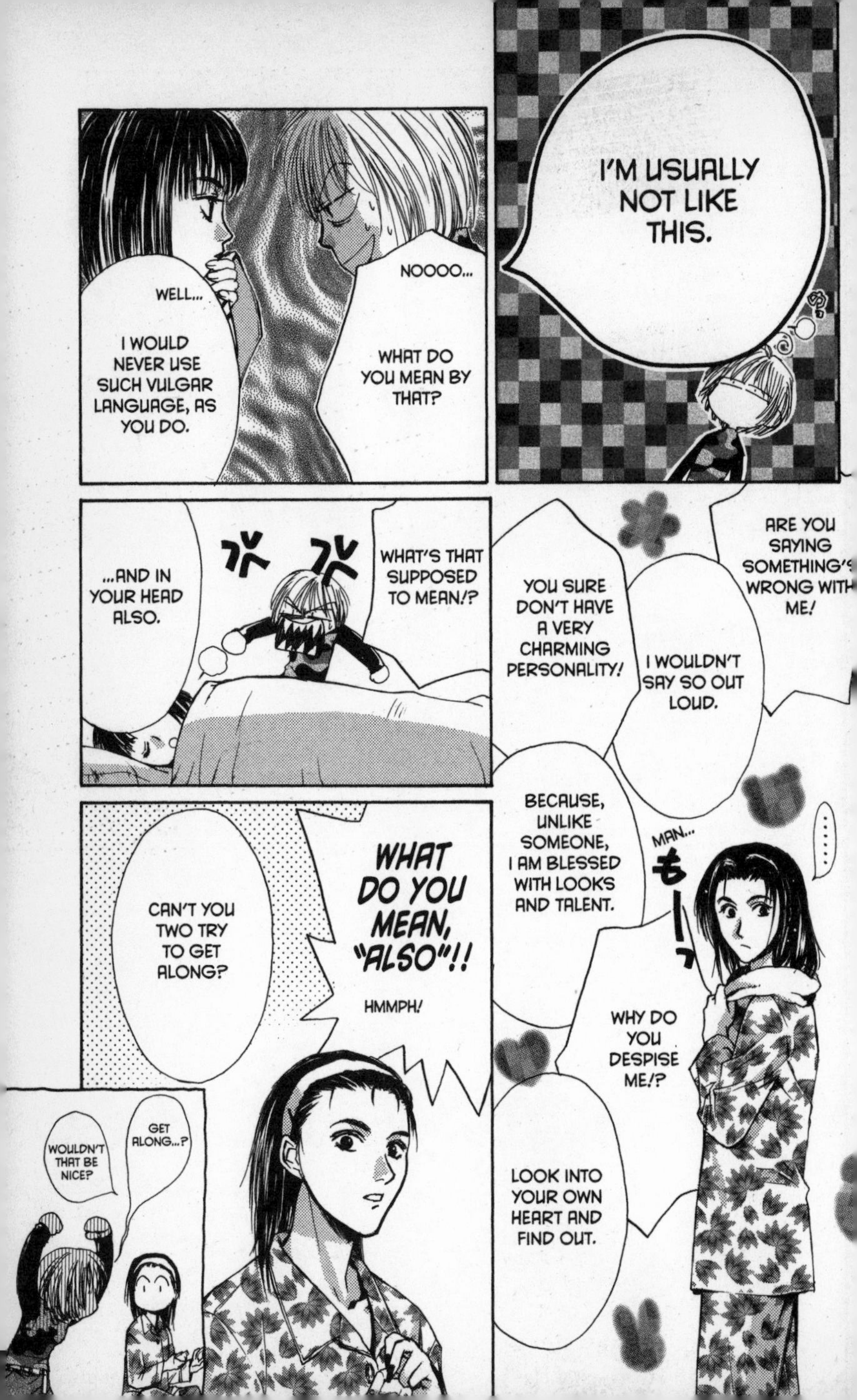
I'M USUALLY NOT LIKE THIS.
NOOOO...
WHAT DO YOU MEAN BY THAT?
WELL...
I WOULD NEVER USE SUCH VULGAR LANGUAGE, AS YOU DO.
ARE YOU SAYING SOMETHING'S WRONG WITH ME!
YOU SURE DON'T HAVE A VERY CHARMING PERSONALITY!
I WOULDN'T SAY SO OUT LOUD.
BECAUSE, UNLIKE SOMEONE, I AM BLESSED WITH LOOKS AND TALENT.
MAN...
......
WHY DO YOU DESPISE ME!?
LOOK INTO YOUR OWN HEART AND FIND OUT.
...AND IN YOUR HEAD ALSO.
WHAT'S THAT SUPPOSED TO MEAN!?
WHAT DO YOU MEAN, "ALSO"!!
HMMPH!
CAN'T YOU TWO TRY TO GET ALONG?
GET ALONG...?
WOULDN'T THAT BE NICE?

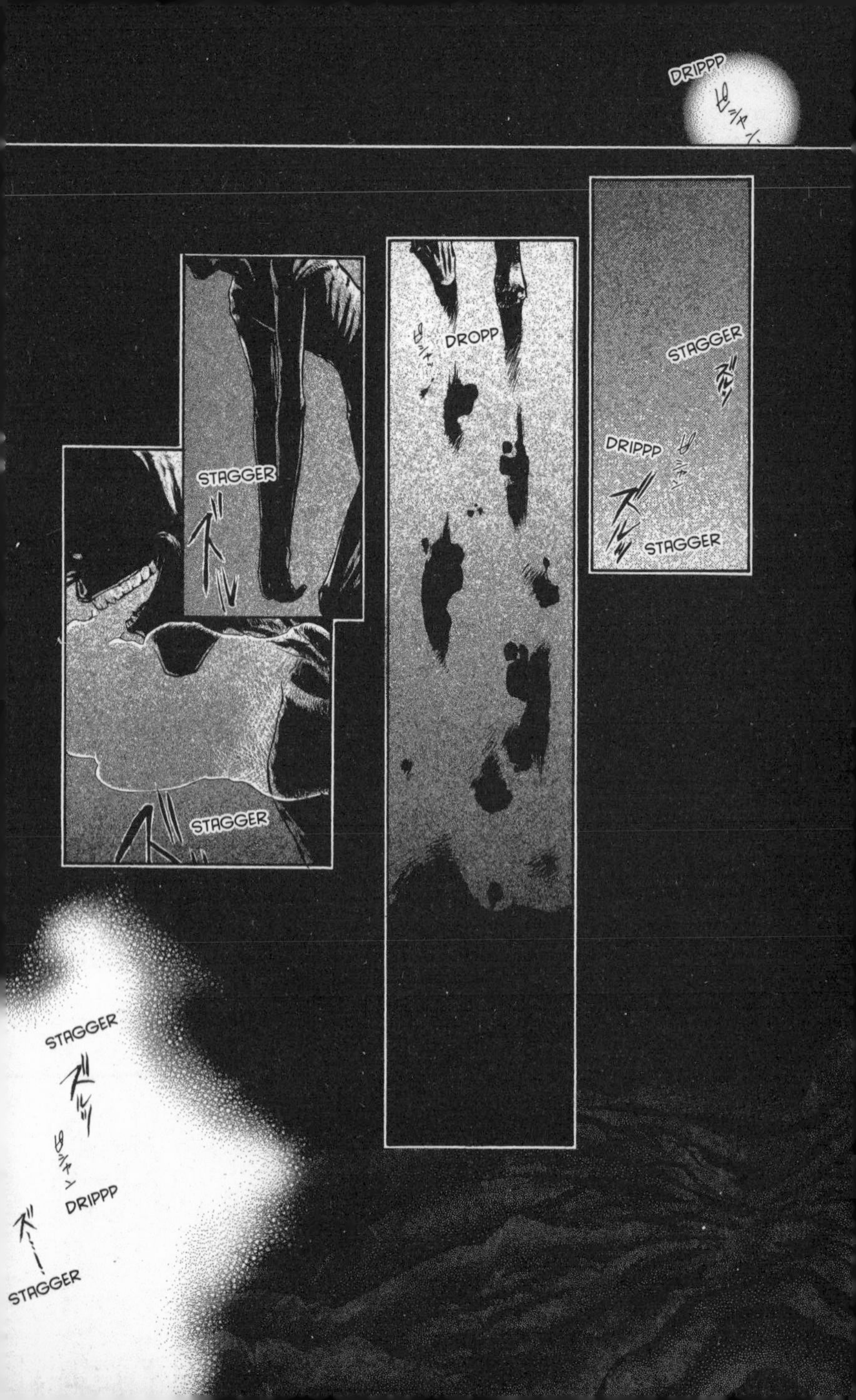
DRIPPP
STAGGER
DRIPPP
STAGGER
DROPP
STAGGER
STAGGER
STAGGER
DRIPPP
STAGGER

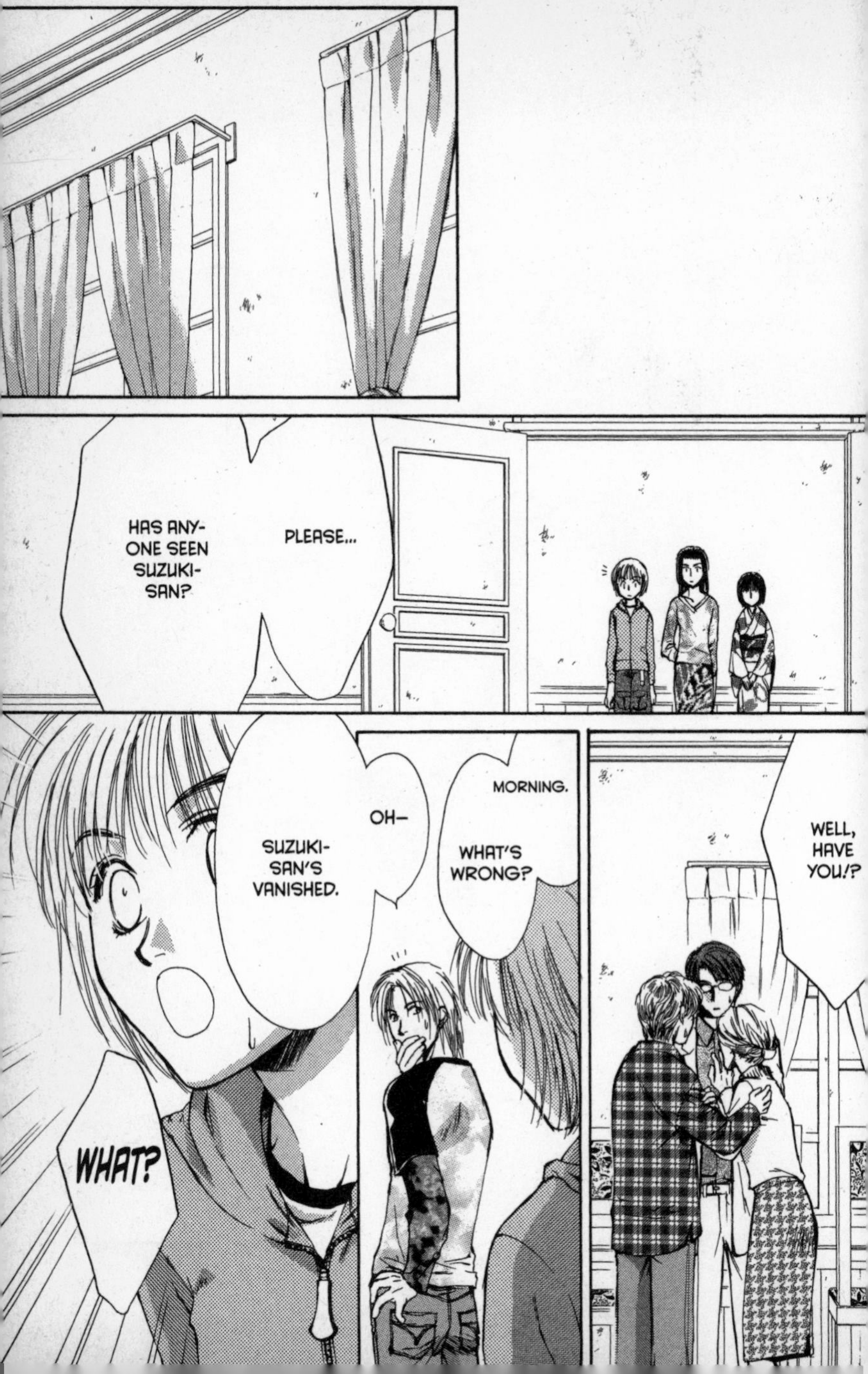
PLEASE...
HAS ANYONE SEEN SUZUKI-SAN?
WELL, HAVE YOU!?
MORNING.
WHAT'S WRONG?
OH—
SUZUKI-SAN'S VANISHED.
WHAT?

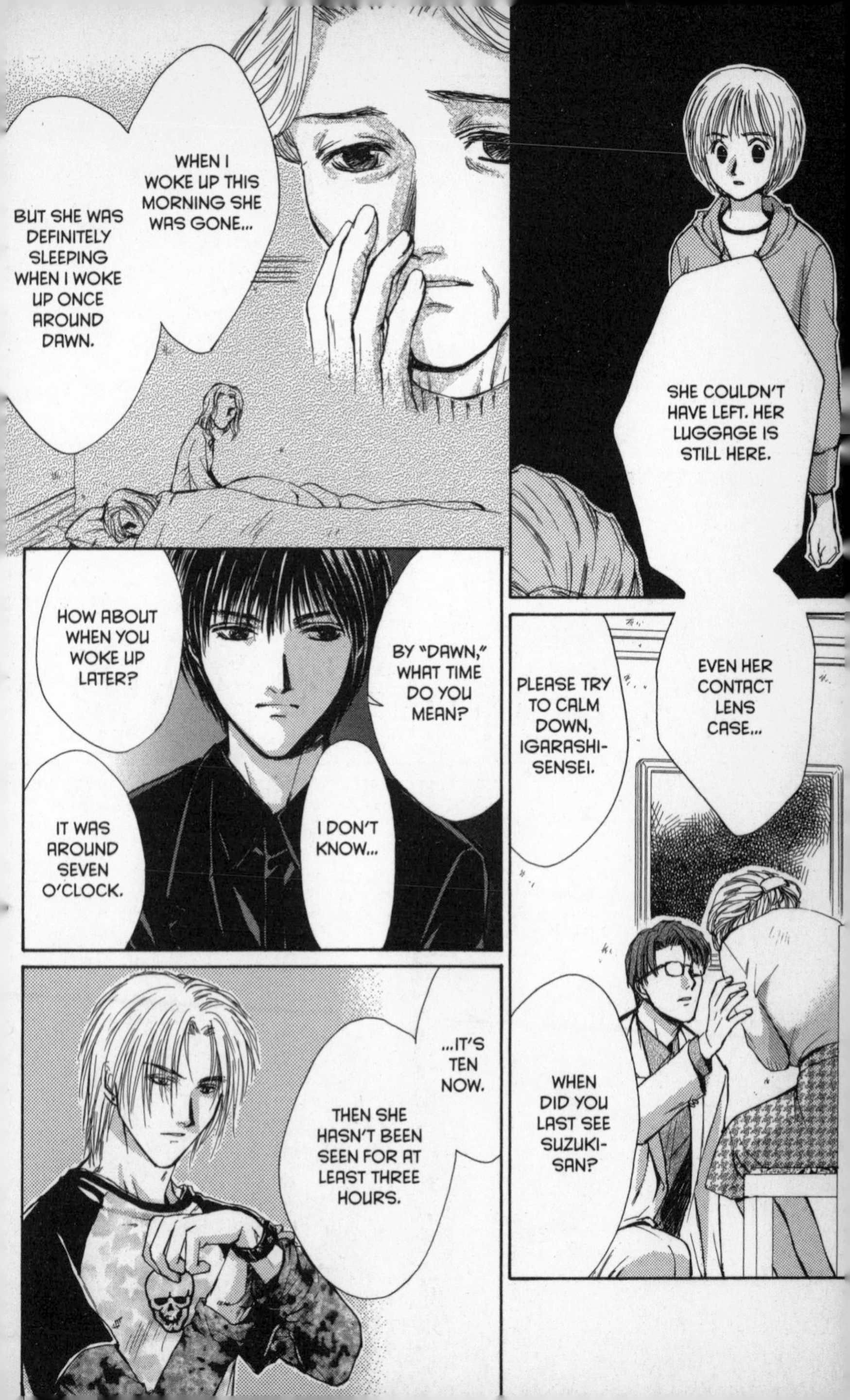
SHE COULDN'T HAVE LEFT. HER LUGGAGE IS STILL HERE.
EVEN HER CONTACT LENS CASE...
PLEASE TRY TO CALM DOWN, IGARASHI-SENSEI.
WHEN DID YOU LAST SEE SUZUKI-SAN?
WHEN I WOKE UP THIS MORNING SHE WAS GONE...
BUT SHE WAS DEFINITELY SLEEPING WHEN I WOKE UP ONCE AROUND DAWN.
BY "DAWN," WHAT TIME DO YOU MEAN?
I DON'T KNOW...
HOW ABOUT WHEN YOU WOKE UP LATER?
IT WAS AROUND SEVEN O'CLOCK.
...IT'S TEN NOW.
THEN SHE HASN'T BEEN SEEN FOR AT LEAST THREE HOURS.

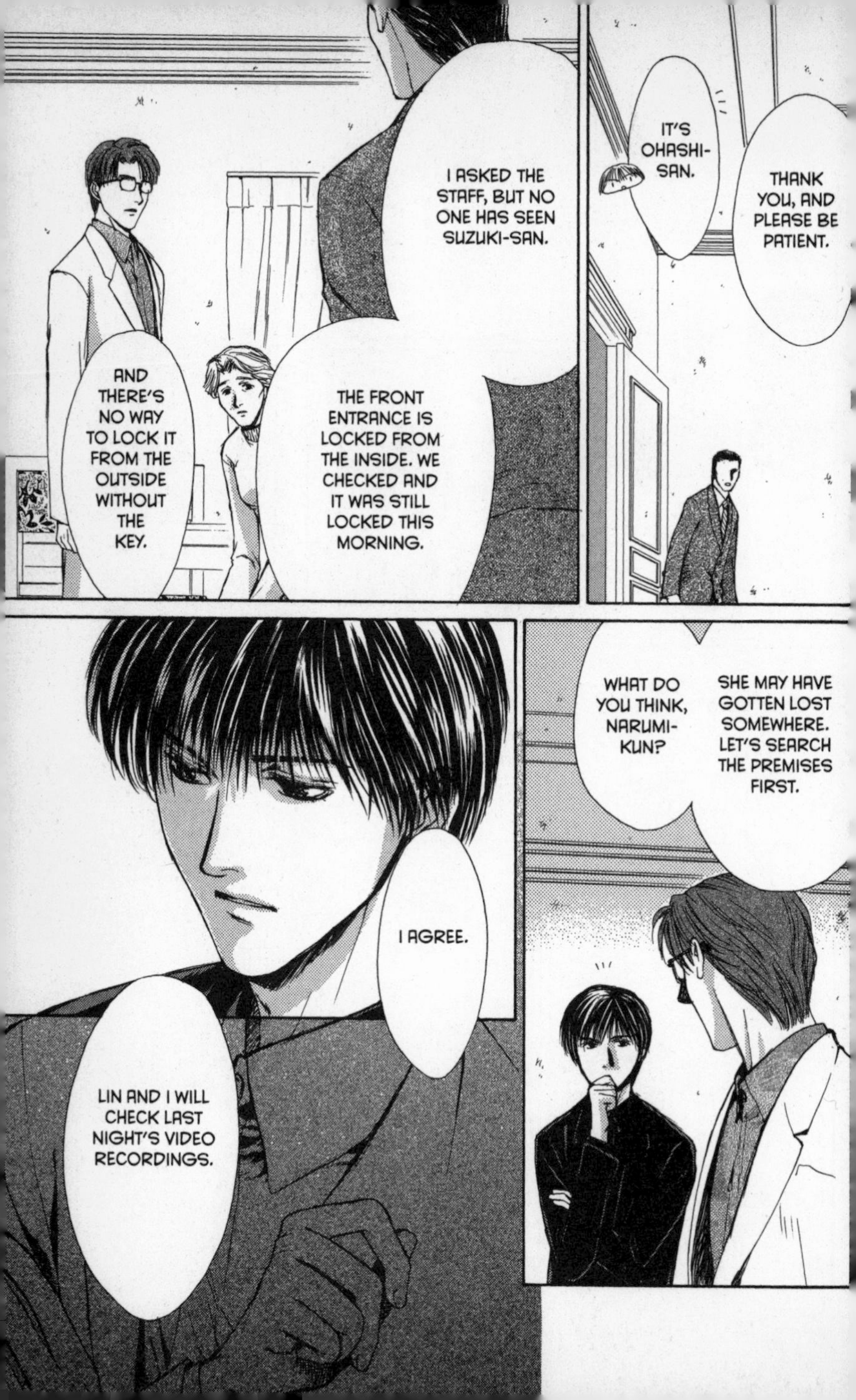

IT'S OHASHI-SAN.
THANK YOU, AND PLEASE BE PATIENT.
I ASKED THE STAFF, BUT NO ONE HAS SEEN SUZUKI-SAN.
THE FRONT ENTRANCE IS LOCKED FROM THE INSIDE. WE CHECKED AND IT WAS STILL LOCKED THIS MORNING.
AND THERE'S NO WAY TO LOCK IT FROM THE OUTSIDE WITHOUT THE KEY.
SHE MAY HAVE GOTTEN LOST SOMEWHERE. LET'S SEARCH THE PREMISES FIRST.
WHAT DO YOU THINK, NARUMI-KUN?
I AGREE.
LIN AND I WILL CHECK LAST NIGHT'S VIDEO RECORDINGS.

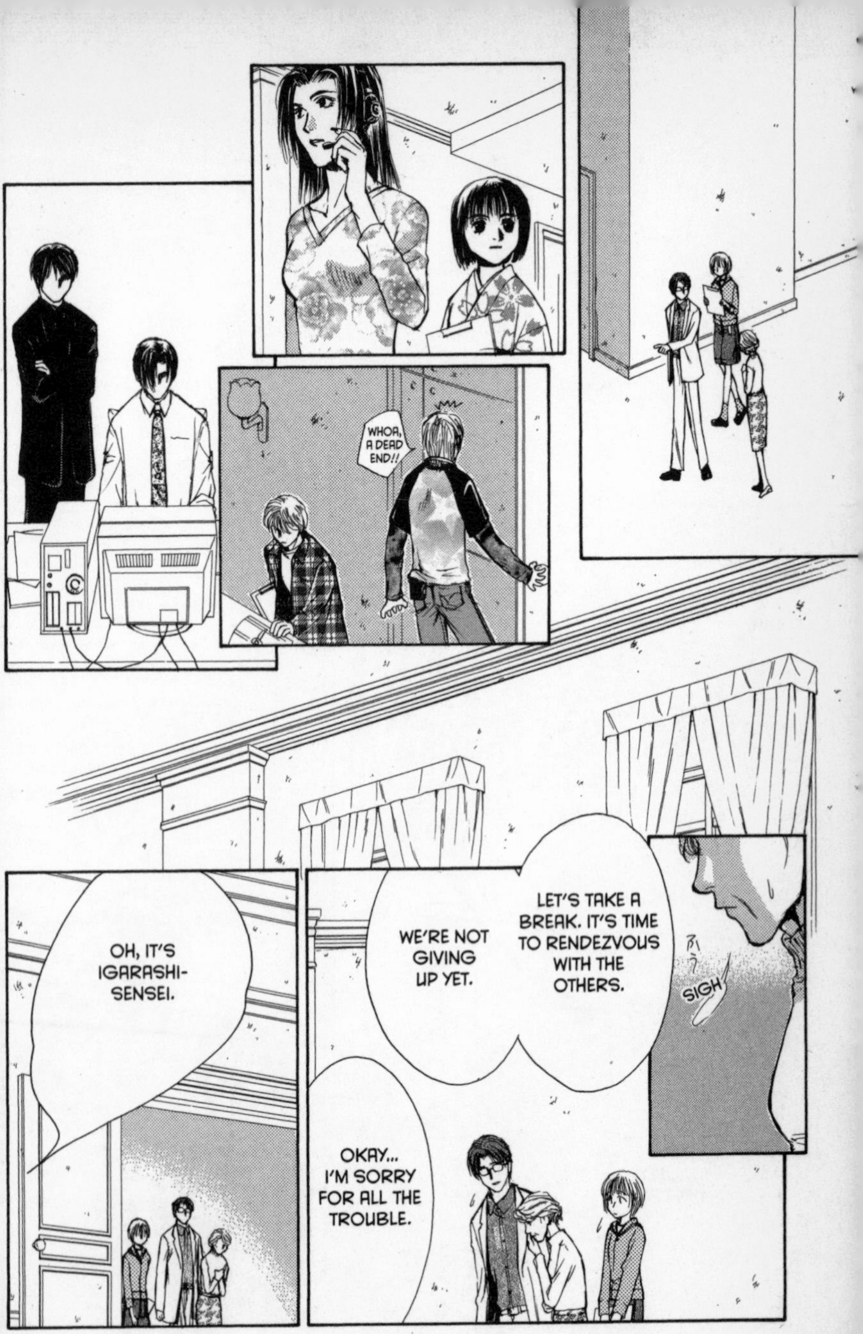
WHOA, A DEAD END!!
SIGH
LET'S TAKE A BREAK. IT'S TIME TO RENDEZVOUS WITH THE OTHERS.
WE'RE NOT GIVING UP YET.
OKAY... I'M SORRY FOR ALL THE TROUBLE.
OH, IT'S IGARASHI-SENSEI.

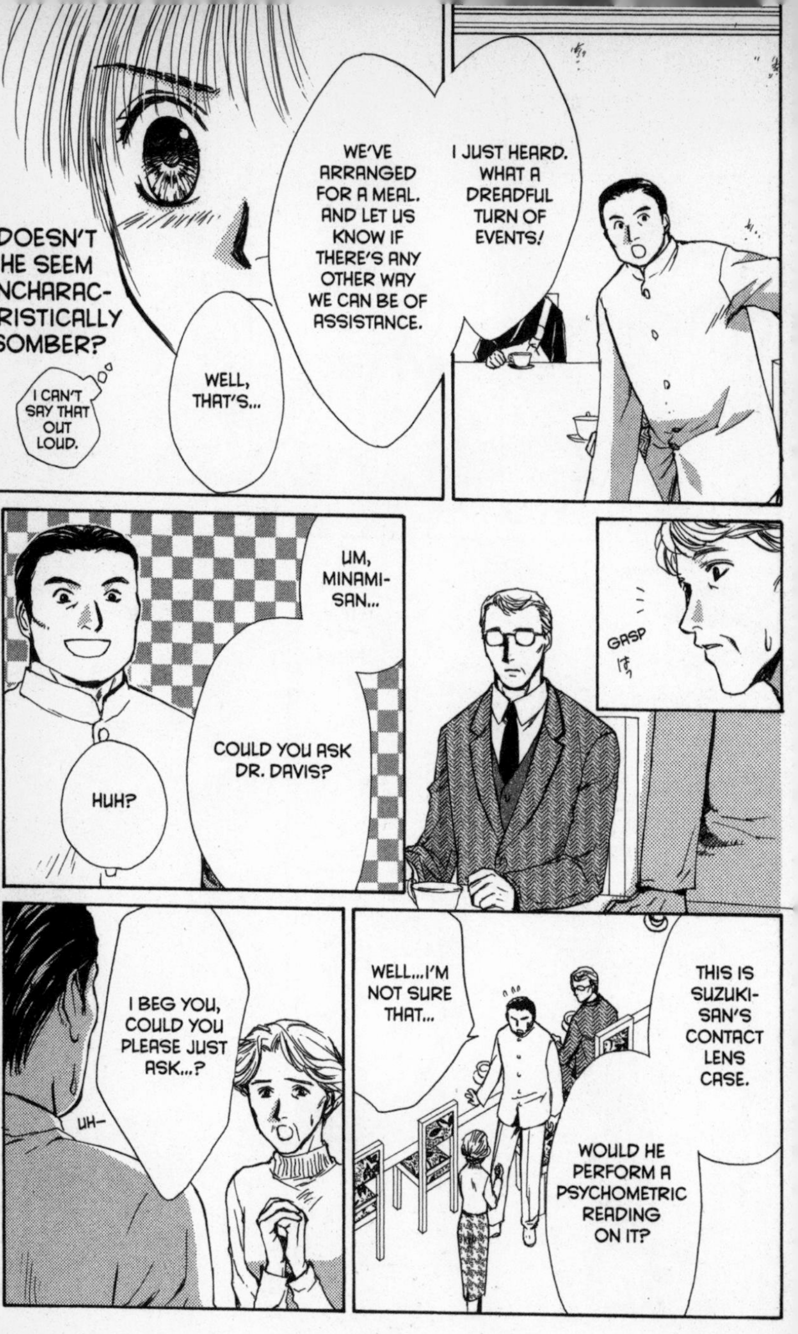
I JUST HEARD. WHAT A DREADFUL TURN OF EVENTS!
WE'VE ARRANGED FOR A MEAL. AND LET US KNOW IF THERE'S ANY OTHER WAY WE CAN BE OF ASSISTANCE.
WELL, THAT'S...
DOESN'T HE SEEM UNCHARACTERISTICALLY SOMBER?
I CAN'T SAY THAT OUT LOUD.
GASP
はっ
UM, MINAMI-SAN...
COULD YOU ASK DR. DAVIS?
HUH?
THIS IS SUZUKI-SAN'S CONTACT LENS CASE.
WOULD HE PERFORM A PSYCHOMETRIC READING ON IT?
WELL...I'M NOT SURE THAT...
I BEG YOU, COULD YOU PLEASE JUST ASK...?
UH-

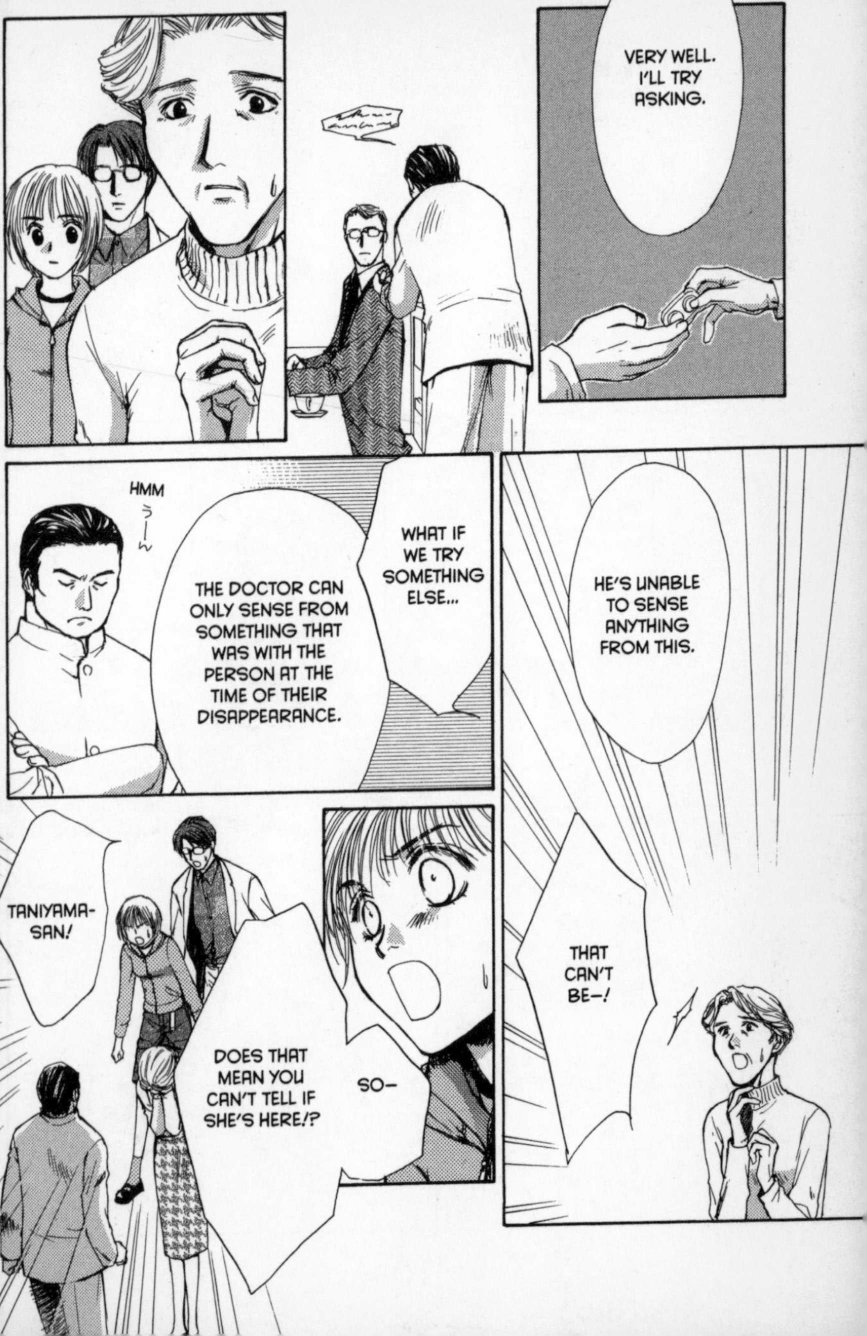
VERY WELL. I'LL TRY ASKING.
HE'S UNABLE TO SENSE ANYTHING FROM THIS.
THAT CAN'T BE—!
WHAT IF WE TRY SOMETHING ELSE...
THE DOCTOR CAN ONLY SENSE FROM SOMETHING THAT WAS WITH THE PERSON AT THE TIME OF THEIR DISAPPEARANCE.
HMM
うーん
SO—
DOES THAT MEAN YOU CAN'T TELL IF SHE'S HERE!?
TANIYAMA-SAN!

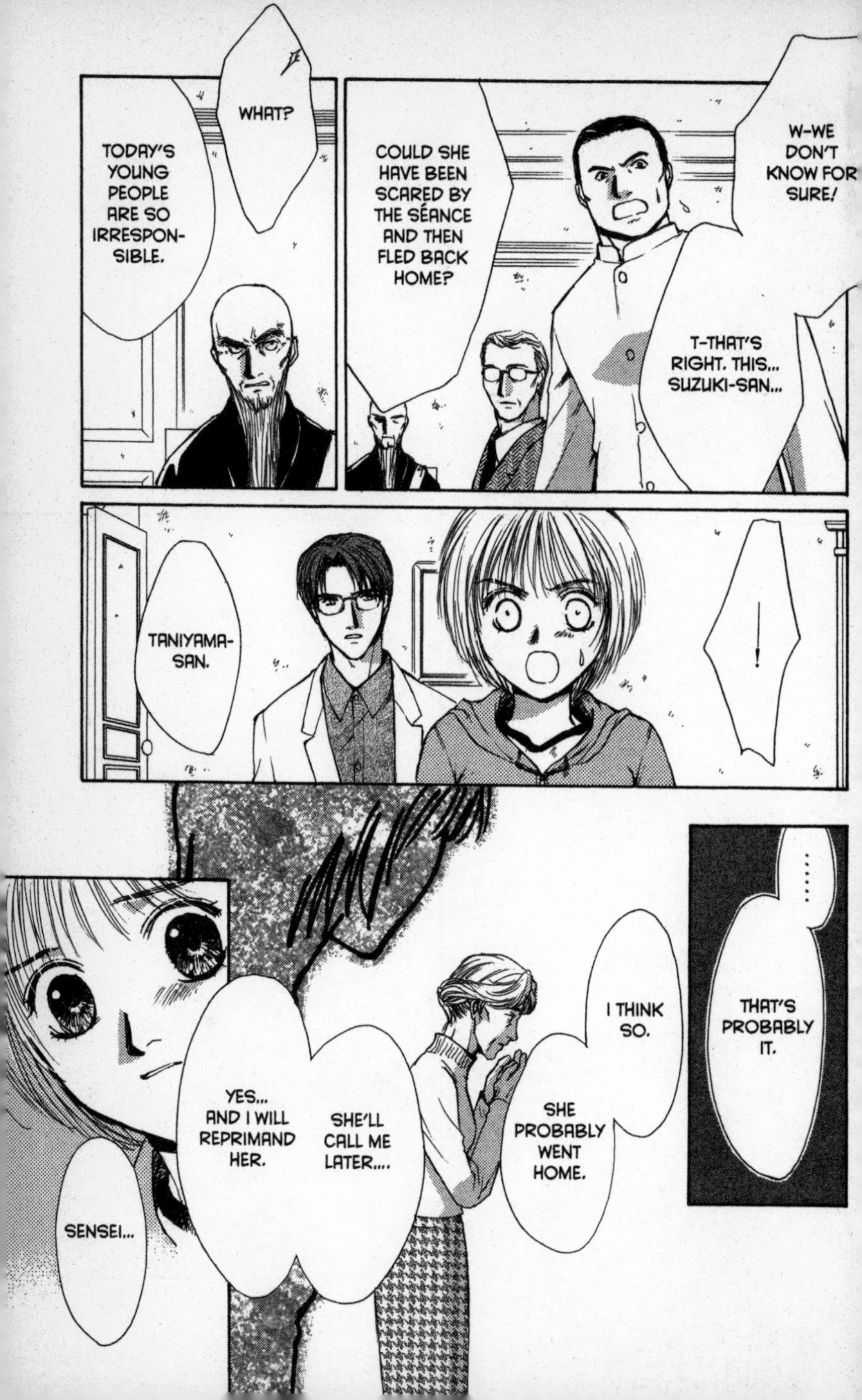
W-WE DON'T KNOW FOR SURE!
COULD SHE HAVE BEEN SCARED BY THE SÉANCE AND THEN FLED BACK HOME?
T-THAT'S RIGHT. THIS... SUZUKI-SAN...
WHAT?
TODAY'S YOUNG PEOPLE ARE SO IRRESPON-SIBLE.
!
TANIYAMA-SAN.
......
THAT'S PROBABLY IT.
I THINK SO.
SHE PROBABLY WENT HOME.
SHE'LL CALL ME LATER....
YES... AND I WILL REPRIMAND HER.
SENSEI...

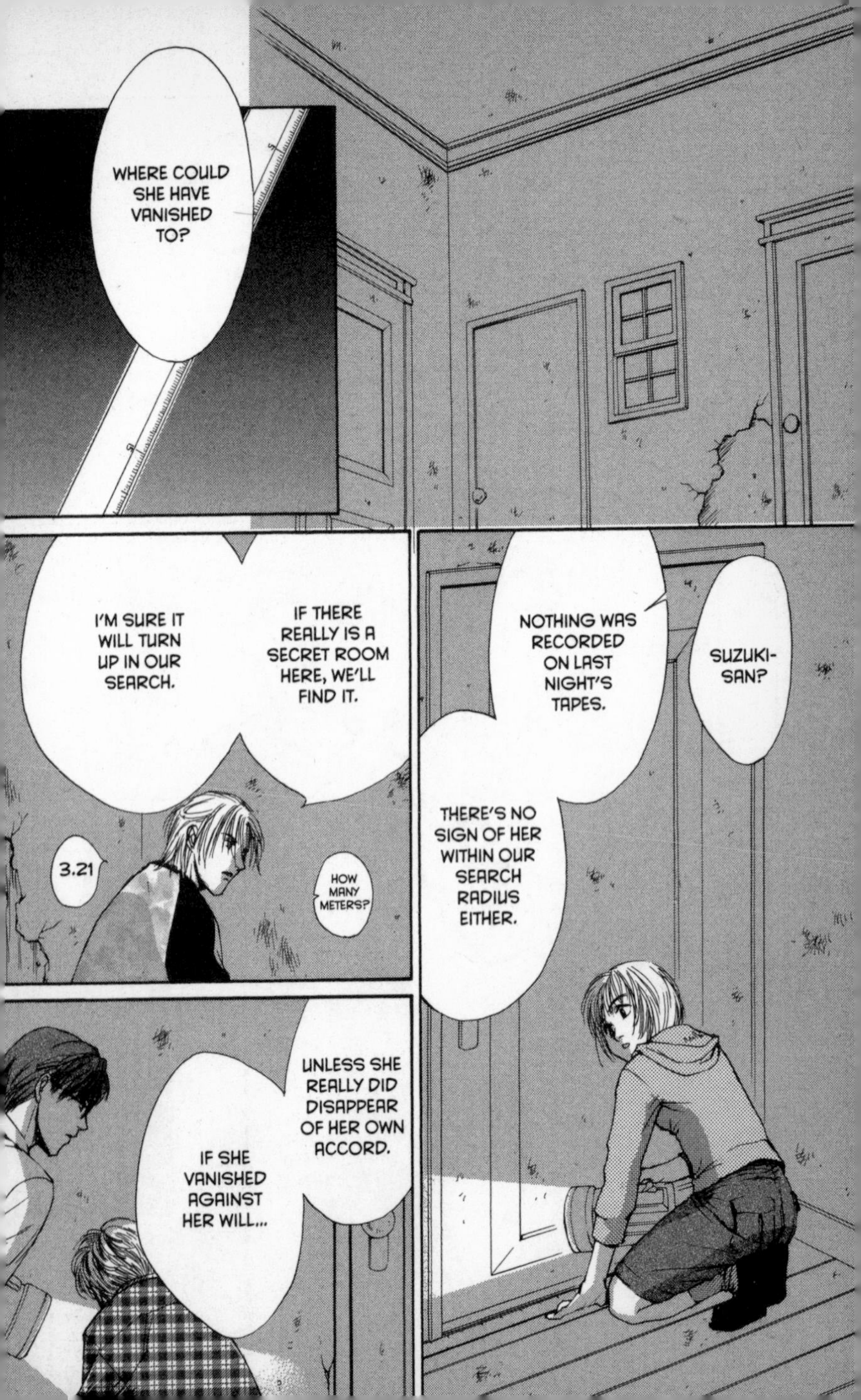
WHERE COULD SHE HAVE VANISHED TO?
SUZUKI-SAN?
NOTHING WAS RECORDED ON LAST NIGHT'S TAPES.
THERE'S NO SIGN OF HER WITHIN OUR SEARCH RADIUS EITHER.
IF THERE REALLY IS A SECRET ROOM HERE, WE'LL FIND IT.
I'M SURE IT WILL TURN UP IN OUR SEARCH.
HOW MANY METERS?
3.21
UNLESS SHE REALLY DID DISAPPEAR OF HER OWN ACCORD.
IF SHE VANISHED AGAINST HER WILL...

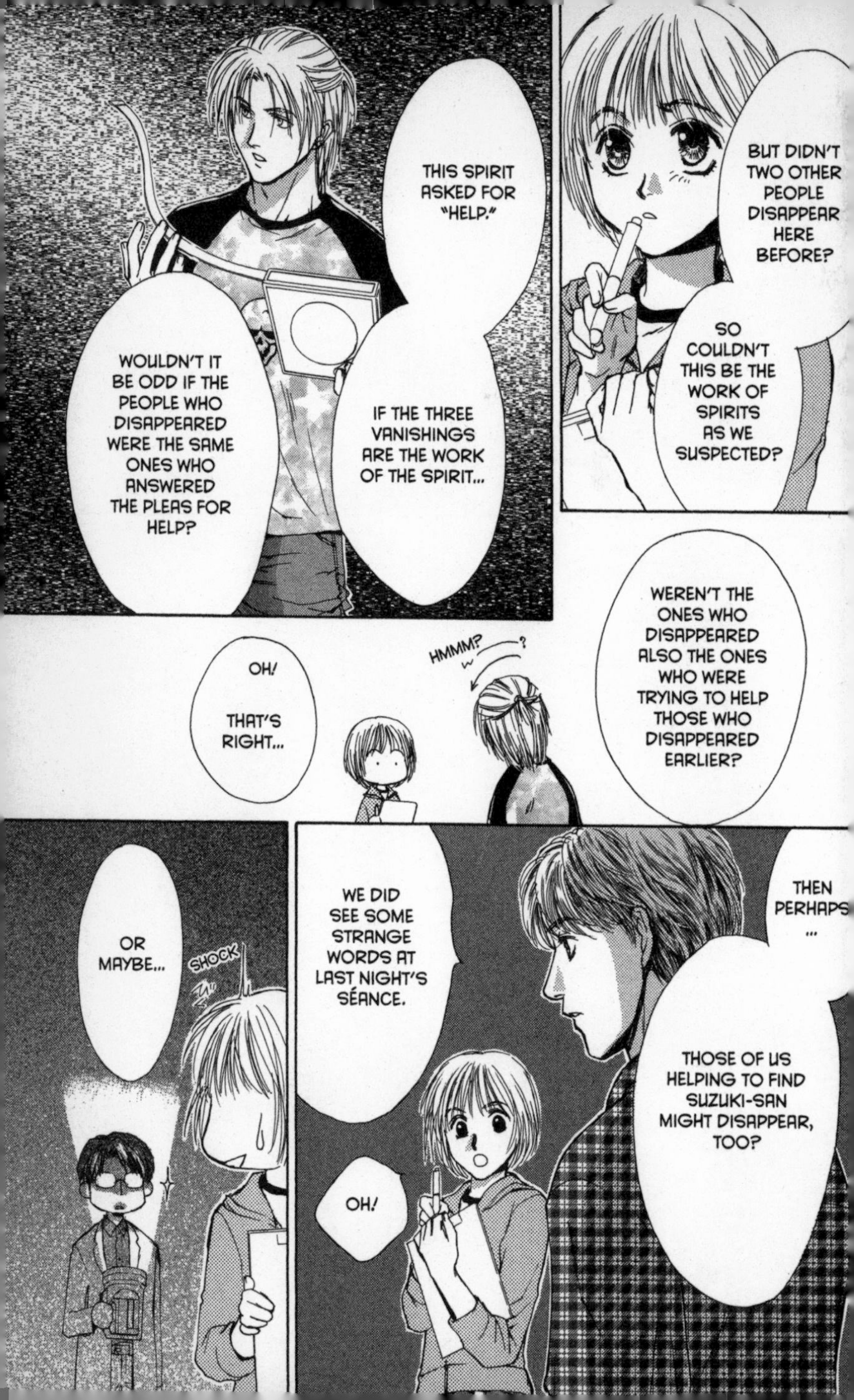
BUT DIDN'T TWO OTHER PEOPLE DISAPPEAR HERE BEFORE?
SO COULDN'T THIS BE THE WORK OF SPIRITS AS WE SUSPECTED?
THIS SPIRIT ASKED FOR "HELP."
IF THE THREE VANISHINGS ARE THE WORK OF THE SPIRIT...
WOULDN'T IT BE ODD IF THE PEOPLE WHO DISAPPEARED WERE THE SAME ONES WHO ANSWERED THE PLEAS FOR HELP?
WEREN'T THE ONES WHO DISAPPEARED ALSO THE ONES WHO WERE TRYING TO HELP THOSE WHO DISAPPEARED EARLIER?
HMMM?
?
OH!
THAT'S RIGHT...
THEN PERHAPS...
THOSE OF US HELPING TO FIND SUZUKI-SAN MIGHT DISAPPEAR, TOO?
WE DID SEE SOME STRANGE WORDS AT LAST NIGHT'S SÉANCE.
OH!
OR MAYBE...
SHOCK

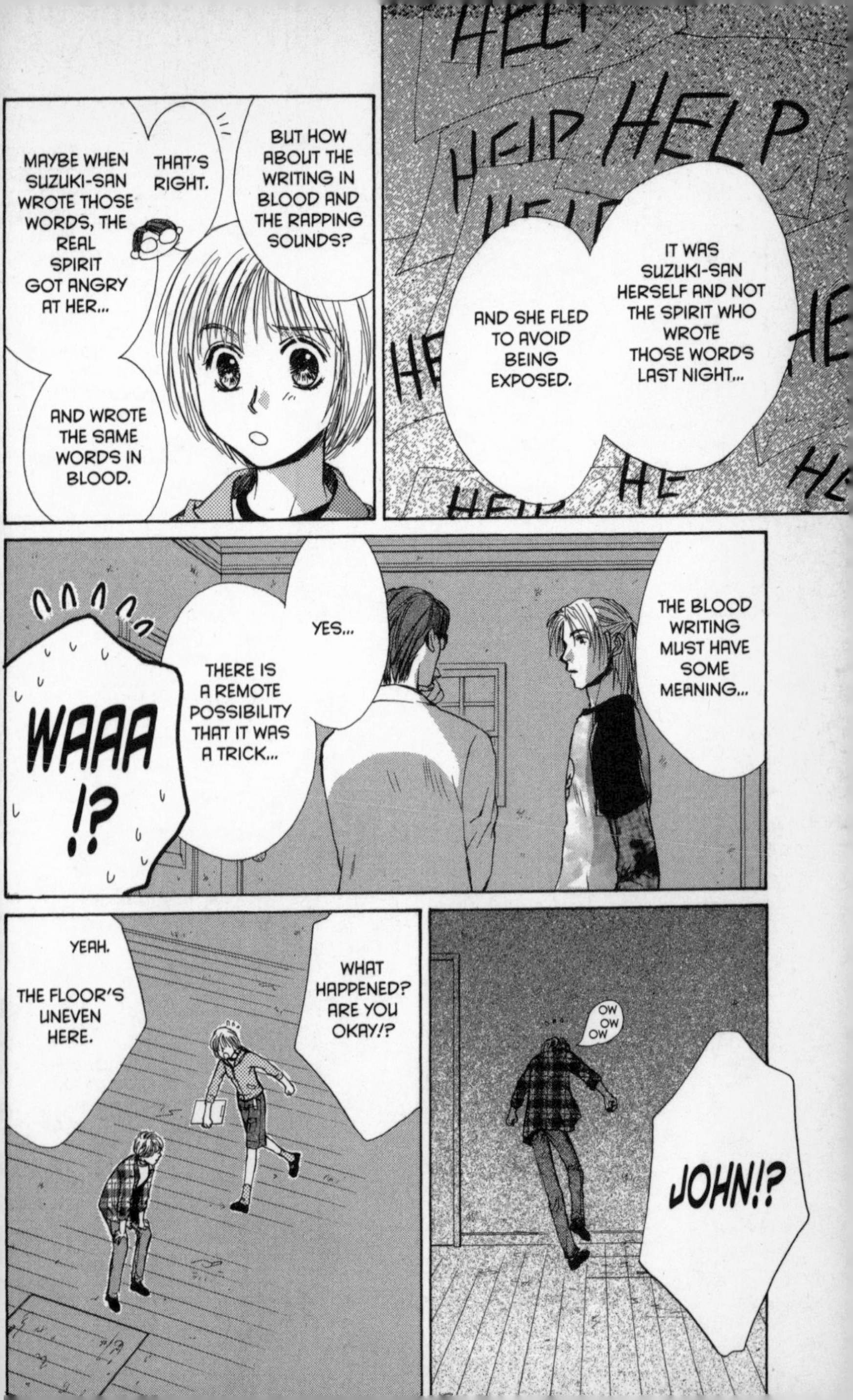
HELP HELP
IT WAS SUZUKI-SAN HERSELF AND NOT THE SPIRIT WHO WROTE THOSE WORDS LAST NIGHT...
AND SHE FLED TO AVOID BEING EXPOSED.
BUT HOW ABOUT THE WRITING IN BLOOD AND THE RAPPING SOUNDS?
THAT'S RIGHT.
MAYBE WHEN SUZUKI-SAN WROTE THOSE WORDS, THE REAL SPIRIT GOT ANGRY AT HER...
AND WROTE THE SAME WORDS IN BLOOD.
THE BLOOD WRITING MUST HAVE SOME MEANING...
YES...
THERE IS A REMOTE POSSIBILITY THAT IT WAS A TRICK...
WAAA!?
JOHN!?
OW OW OW
WHAT HAPPENED? ARE YOU OKAY!?
YEAH.
THE FLOOR'S UNEVEN HERE.

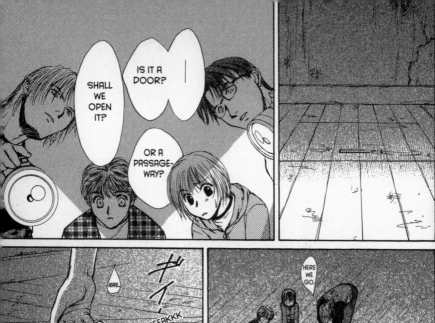

IS IT A DOOR?
OR A PASSAGE-WAY?
SHALL WE OPEN IT?
HERE WE GO.
HEAVE...
ギイー
CREEAKKK
もんわ~
WHOOSH
WHOA!?
THAT'S MUSTY!
HEY...
HMM?

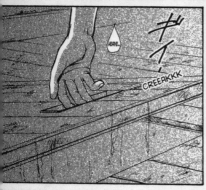

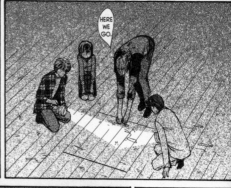

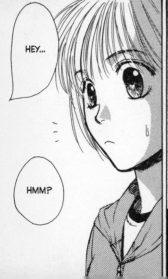

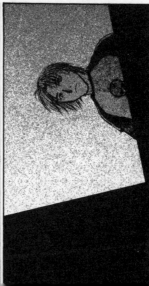

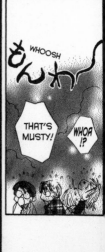

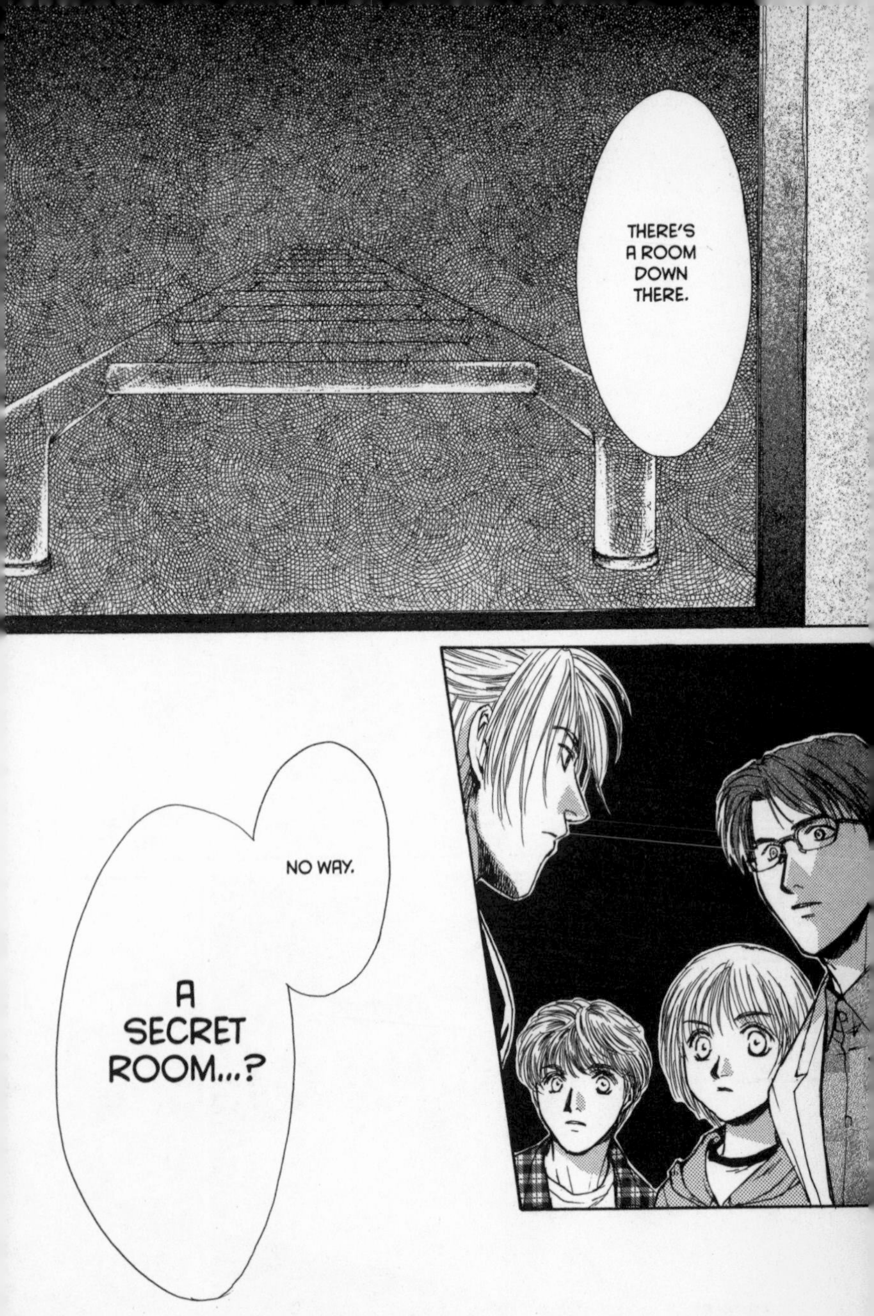
THERE'S A ROOM DOWN THERE.
NO WAY.
A SECRET ROOM...?

GHOST HUNT

— THE BLOODSTAINED LABYRINTH —

FILE 4

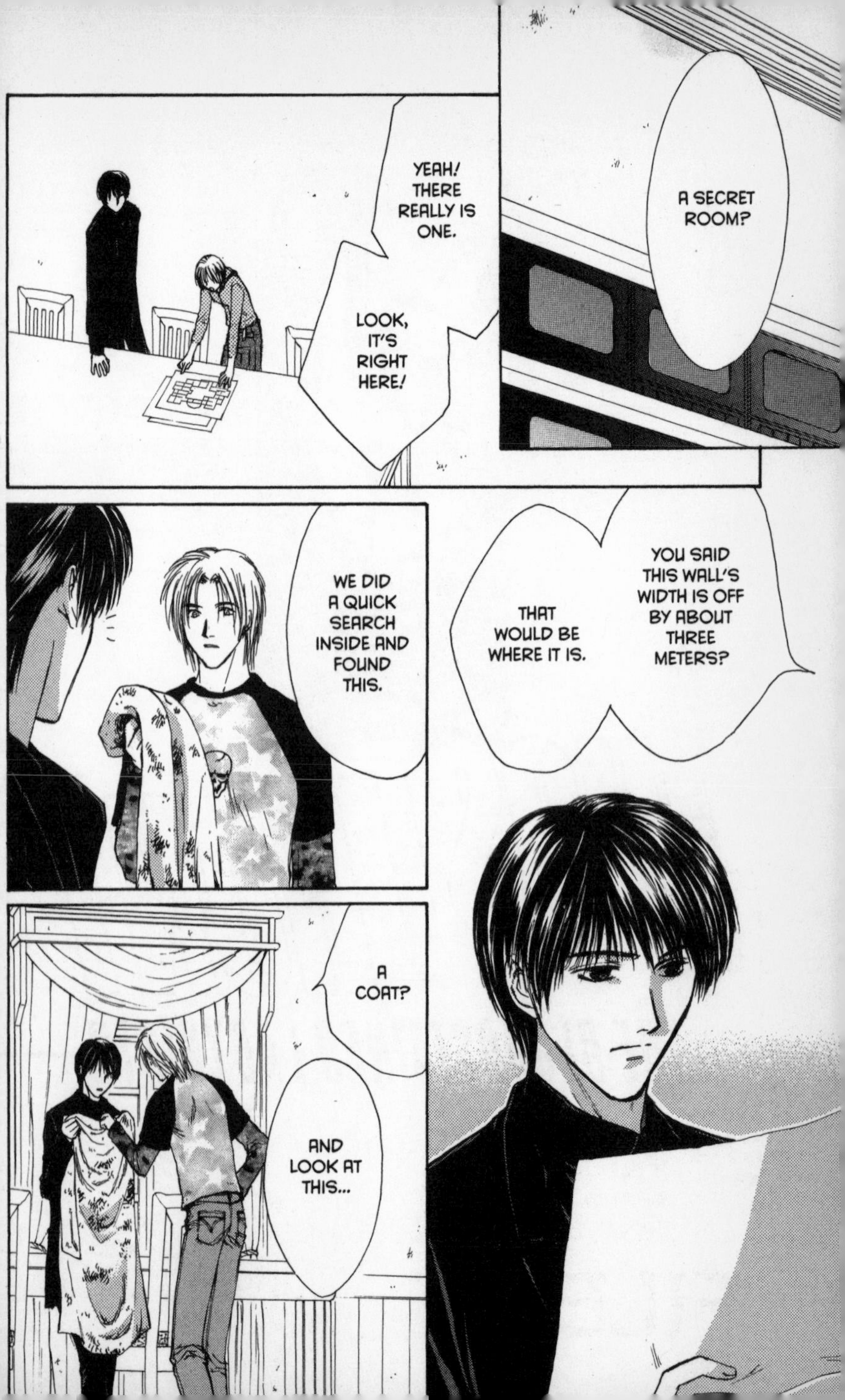
A SECRET ROOM?
YEAH! THERE REALLY IS ONE.
LOOK, IT'S RIGHT HERE!
YOU SAID THIS WALL'S WIDTH IS OFF BY ABOUT THREE METERS?
THAT WOULD BE WHERE IT IS.
WE DID A QUICK SEARCH INSIDE AND FOUND THIS.
A COAT?
AND LOOK AT THIS...

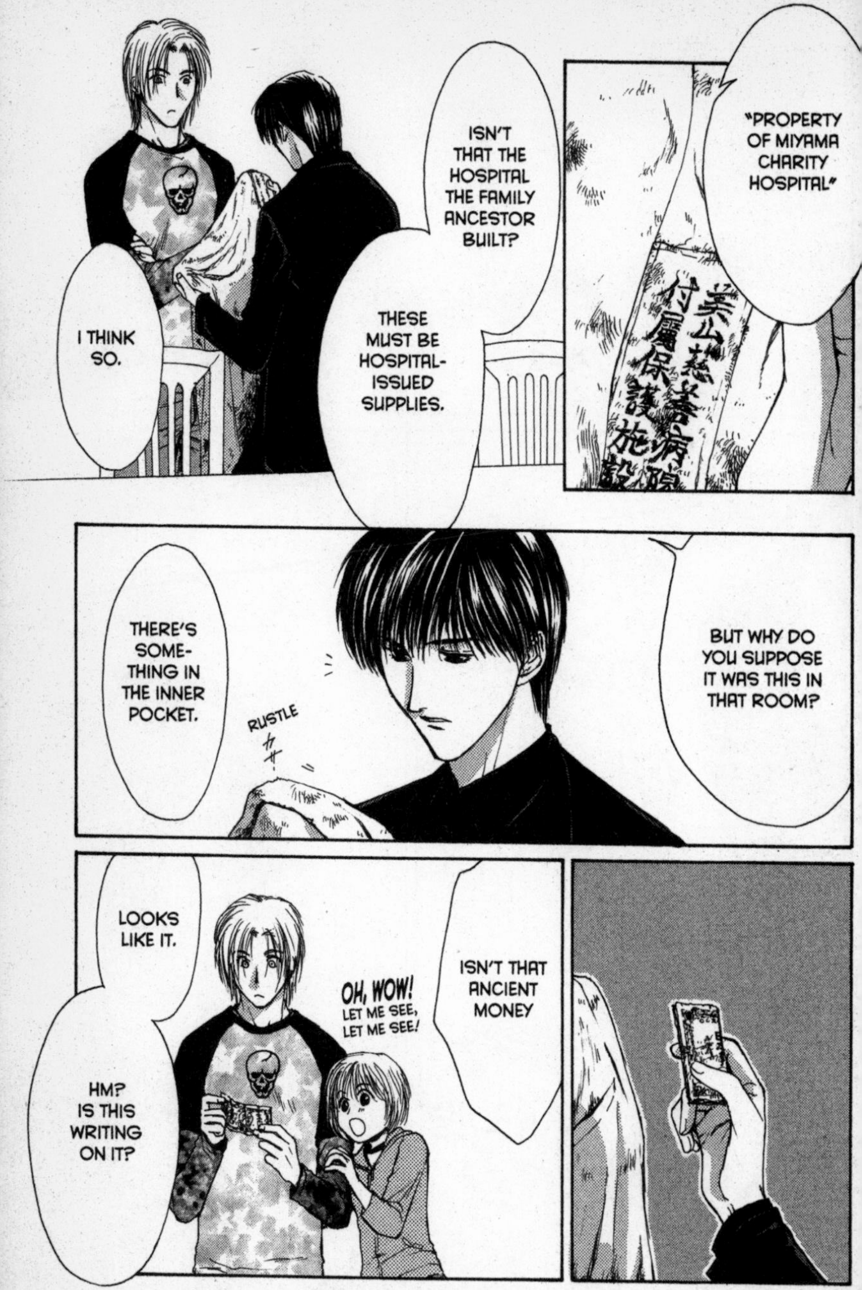
"PROPERTY OF MIYAMA CHARITY HOSPITAL"
美山慈善病院
付屬保護施設
ISN'T THAT THE HOSPITAL THE FAMILY ANCESTOR BUILT?
THESE MUST BE HOSPITAL-ISSUED SUPPLIES.
I THINK SO.
BUT WHY DO YOU SUPPOSE IT WAS THIS IN THAT ROOM?
RUSTLE
THERE'S SOME-THING IN THE INNER POCKET.
ISN'T THAT ANCIENT MONEY
OH, WOW! LET ME SEE, LET ME SEE!
LOOKS LIKE IT.
HM? IS THIS WRITING ON IT?

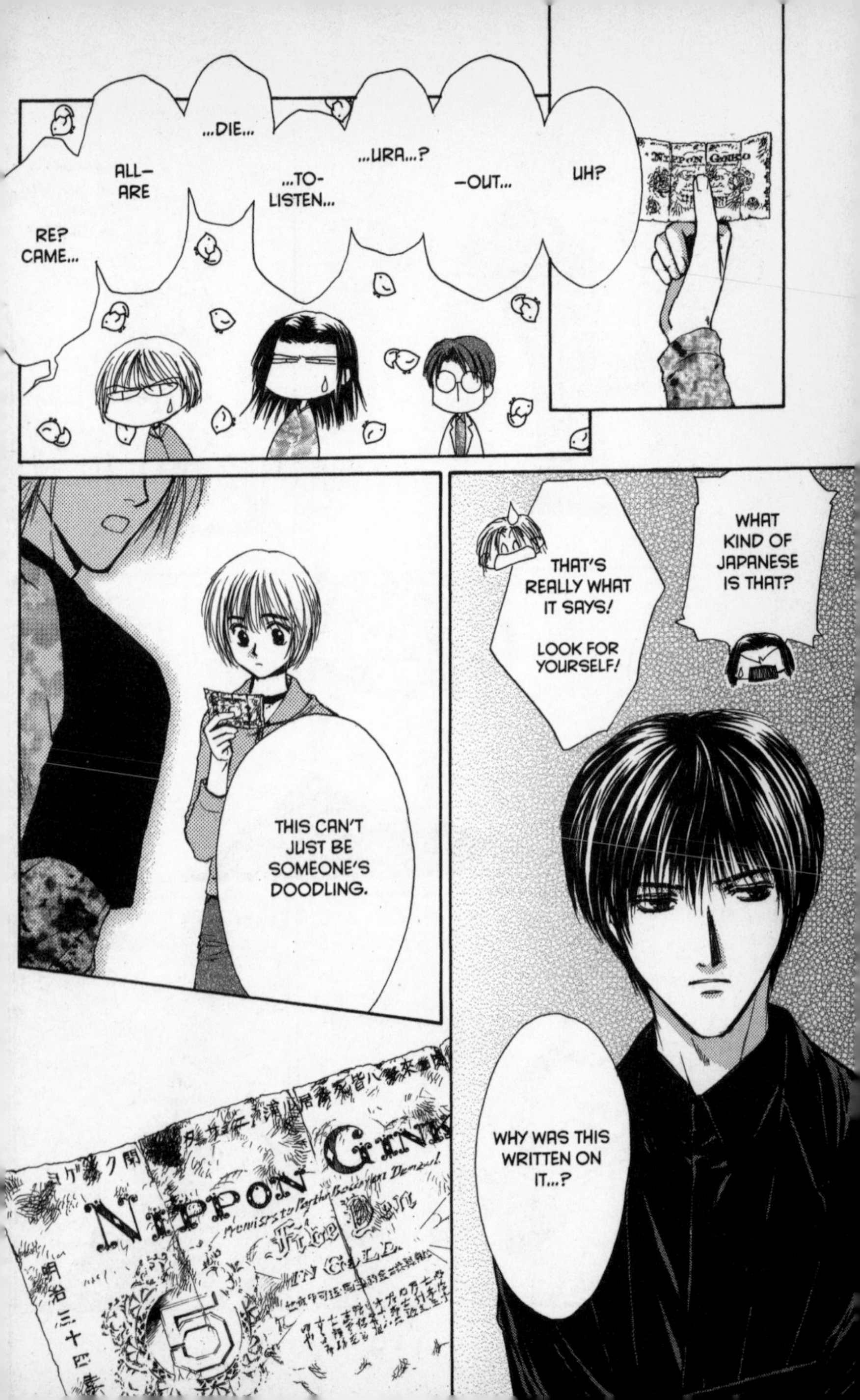
UH?
-OUT...
...URA...?
...TO- LISTEN...
...DIE...
ALL- ARE
RE? CAME...
WHAT KIND OF JAPANESE IS THAT?
THAT'S REALLY WHAT IT SAYS!
LOOK FOR YOURSELF!
WHY WAS THIS WRITTEN ON IT...?
THIS CAN'T JUST BE SOMEONE'S DOODLING.
NIPPON

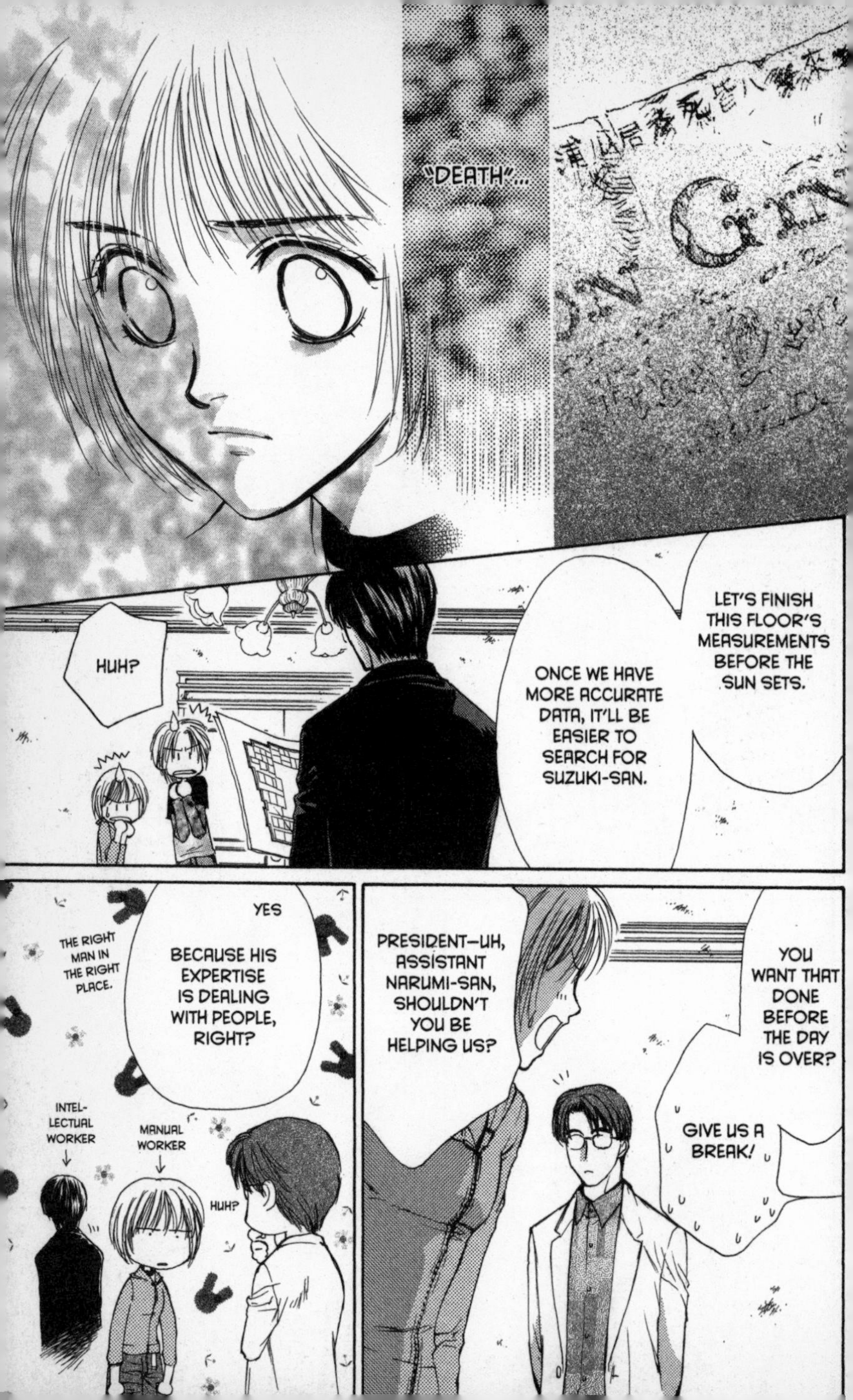
"DEATH"...
LET'S FINISH THIS FLOOR'S MEASUREMENTS BEFORE THE SUN SETS.
ONCE WE HAVE MORE ACCURATE DATA, IT'LL BE EASIER TO SEARCH FOR SUZUKI-SAN.
HUH?
YOU WANT THAT DONE BEFORE THE DAY IS OVER?
GIVE US A BREAK!
PRESIDENT—UH, ASSISTANT NARUMI-SAN, SHOULDN'T YOU BE HELPING US?
YES
BECAUSE HIS EXPERTISE IS DEALING WITH PEOPLE, RIGHT?
THE RIGHT MAN IN THE RIGHT PLACE.
INTEL-LECTUAL WORKER
MANUAL WORKER
HUH?

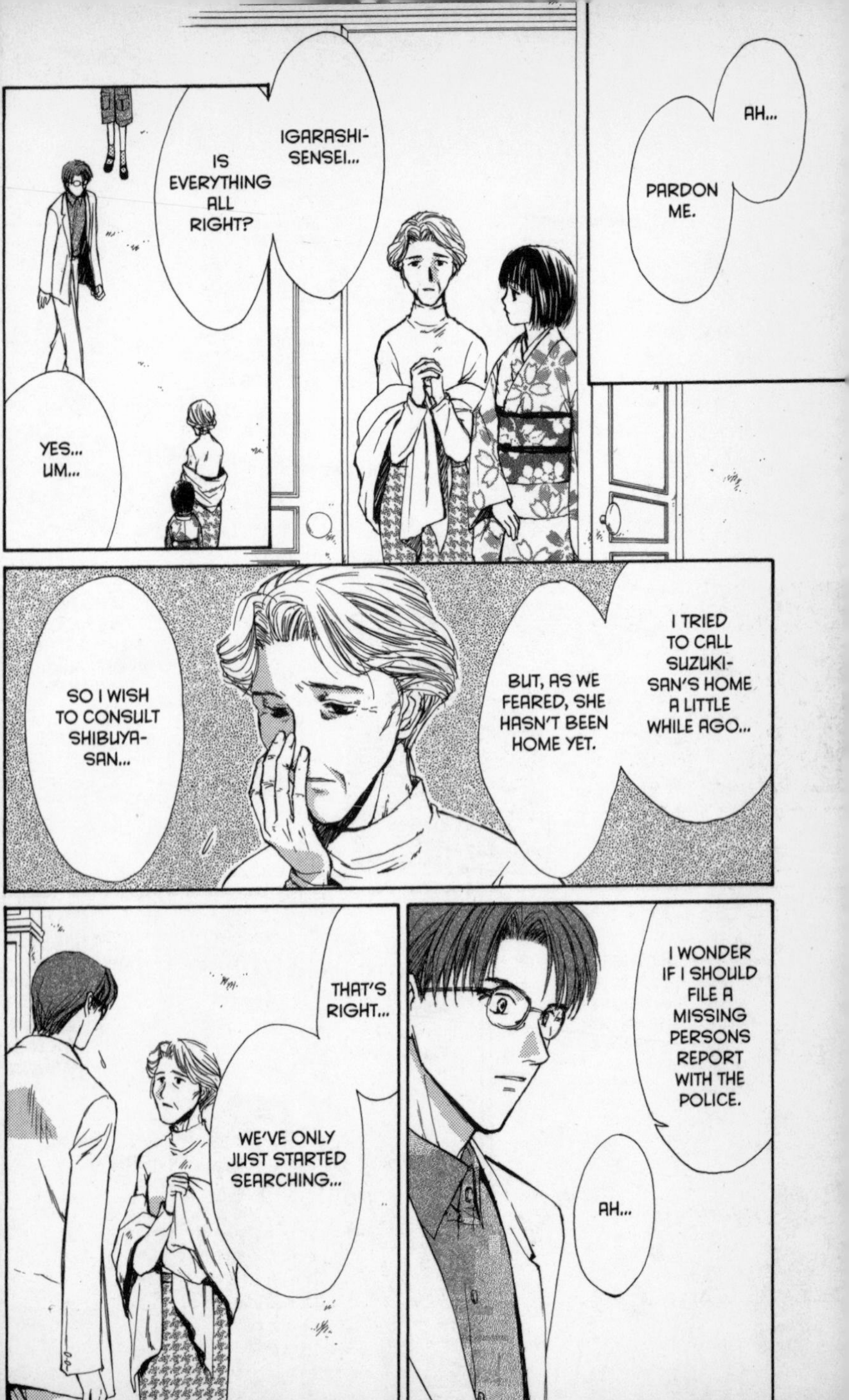
AH...
PARDON ME.
IGARASHI-SENSEI...
IS EVERYTHING ALL RIGHT?
YES... UM...
I TRIED TO CALL SUZUKI-SAN'S HOME A LITTLE WHILE AGO...
BUT, AS WE FEARED, SHE HASN'T BEEN HOME YET.
SO I WISH TO CONSULT SHIBUYA-SAN...
I WONDER IF I SHOULD FILE A MISSING PERSONS REPORT WITH THE POLICE.
AH...
THAT'S RIGHT...
WE'VE ONLY JUST STARTED SEARCHING...

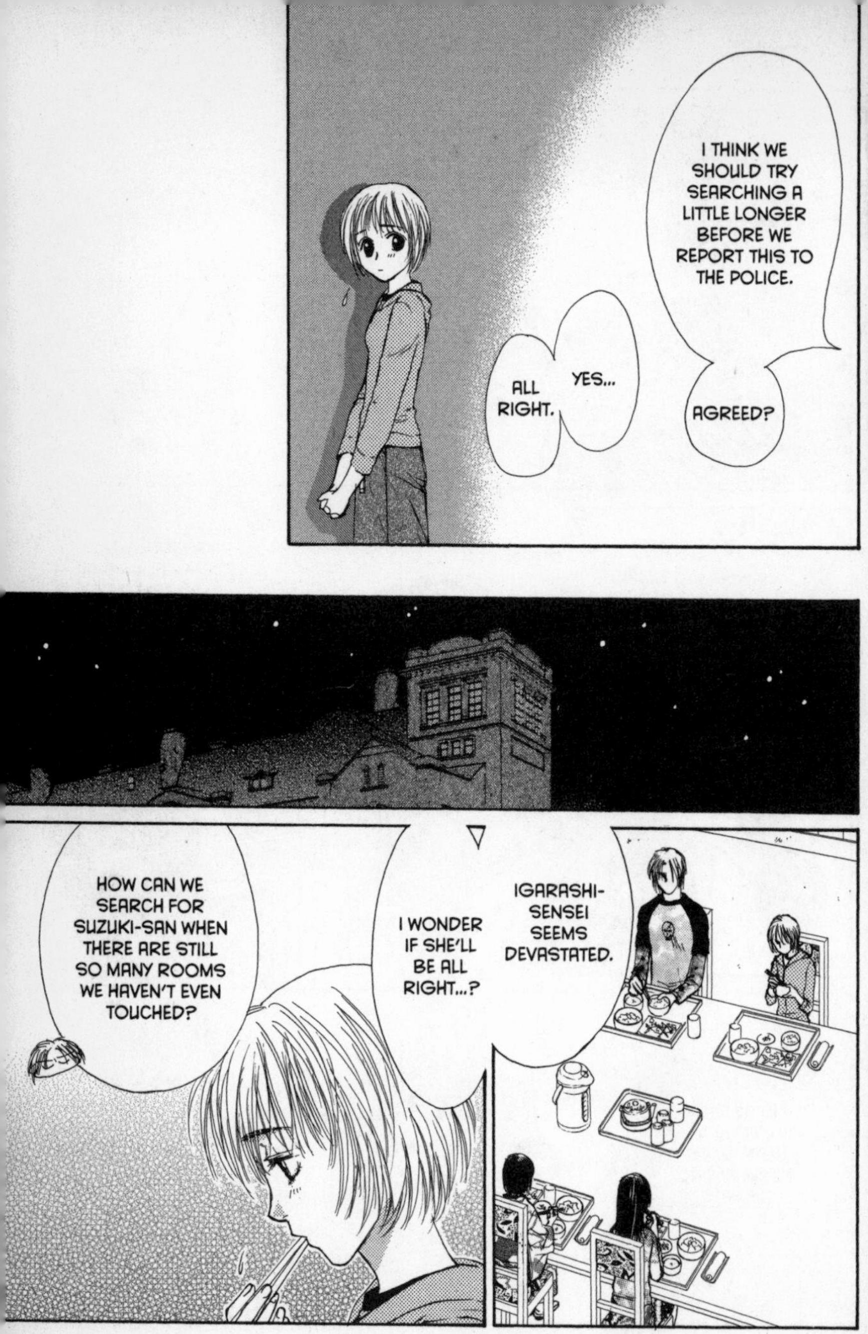
I THINK WE SHOULD TRY SEARCHING A LITTLE LONGER BEFORE WE REPORT THIS TO THE POLICE.
AGREED?
YES...
ALL RIGHT.
IGARASHI-SENSEI SEEMS DEVASTATED.
I WONDER IF SHE'LL BE ALL RIGHT...?
HOW CAN WE SEARCH FOR SUZUKI-SAN WHEN THERE ARE STILL SO MANY ROOMS WE HAVEN'T EVEN TOUCHED?

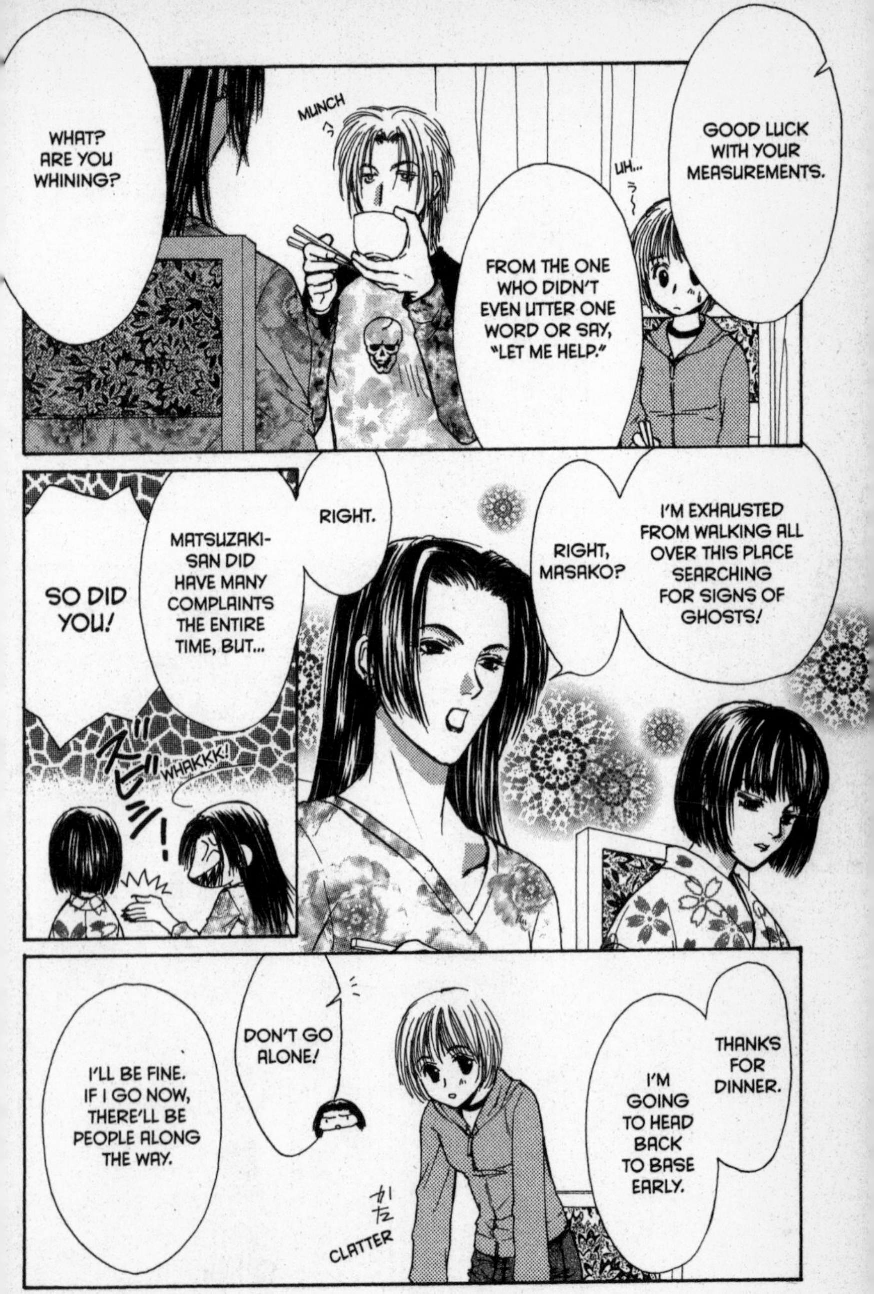
GOOD LUCK WITH YOUR MEASUREMENTS.
UH...
FROM THE ONE WHO DIDN'T EVEN UTTER ONE WORD OR SAY, "LET ME HELP."
MUNCH
WHAT? ARE YOU WHINING?
I'M EXHAUSTED FROM WALKING ALL OVER THIS PLACE SEARCHING FOR SIGNS OF GHOSTS!
RIGHT, MASAKO?
RIGHT.
MATSUZAKI-SAN DID HAVE MANY COMPLAINTS THE ENTIRE TIME, BUT...
SO DID YOU!
WHAKKK!
THANKS FOR DINNER.
I'M GOING TO HEAD BACK TO BASE EARLY.
CLATTER
DON'T GO ALONE!
I'LL BE FINE. IF I GO NOW, THERE'LL BE PEOPLE ALONG THE WAY.

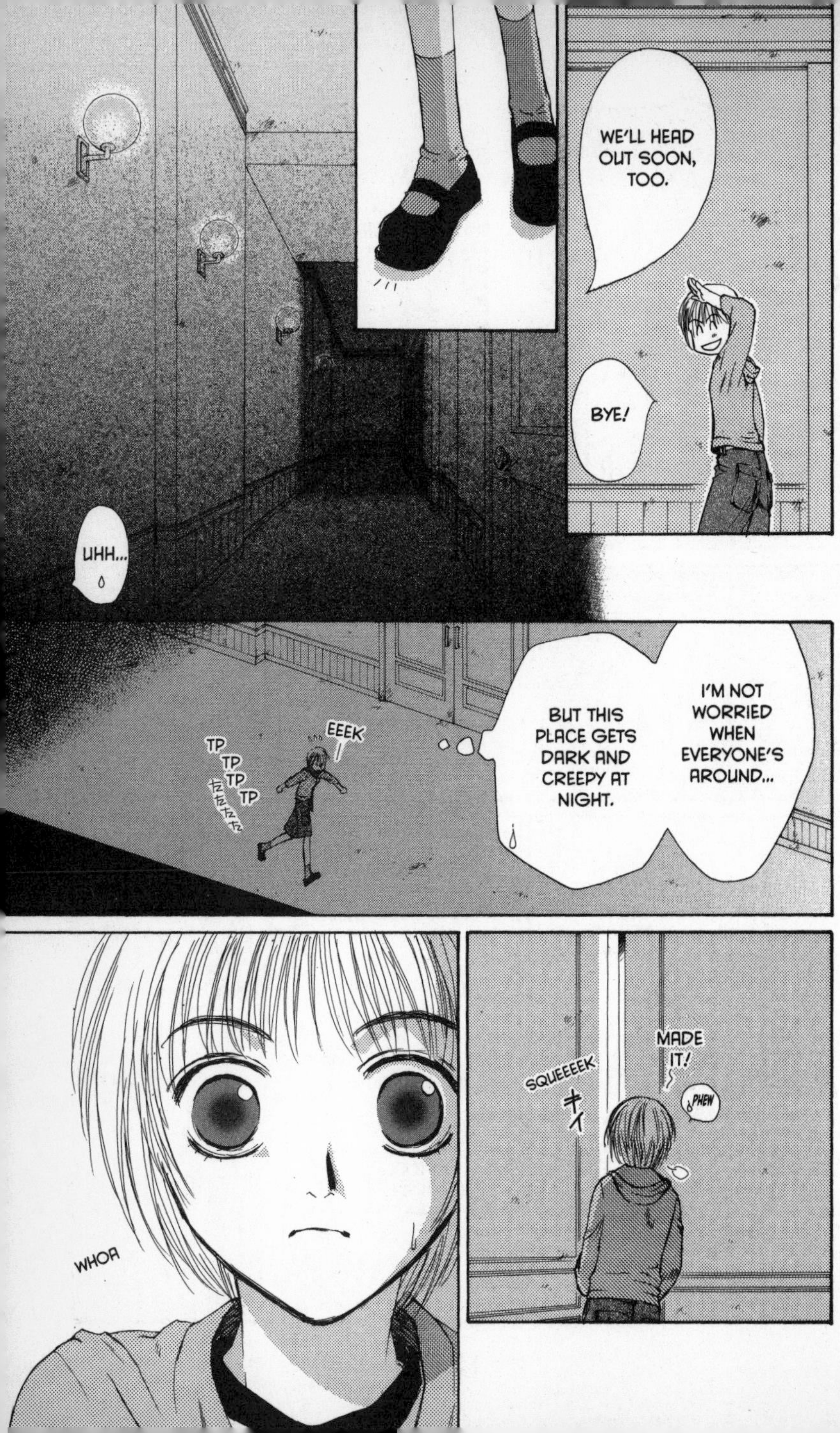
WE'LL HEAD OUT SOON, TOO.
BYE!
UHH...
I'M NOT WORRIED WHEN EVERYONE'S AROUND...
BUT THIS PLACE GETS DARK AND CREEPY AT NIGHT.
EEEK
TP TP TP TP
たたたた
MADE IT!
PHEW
SQUEEEEK
キイ
WHOA

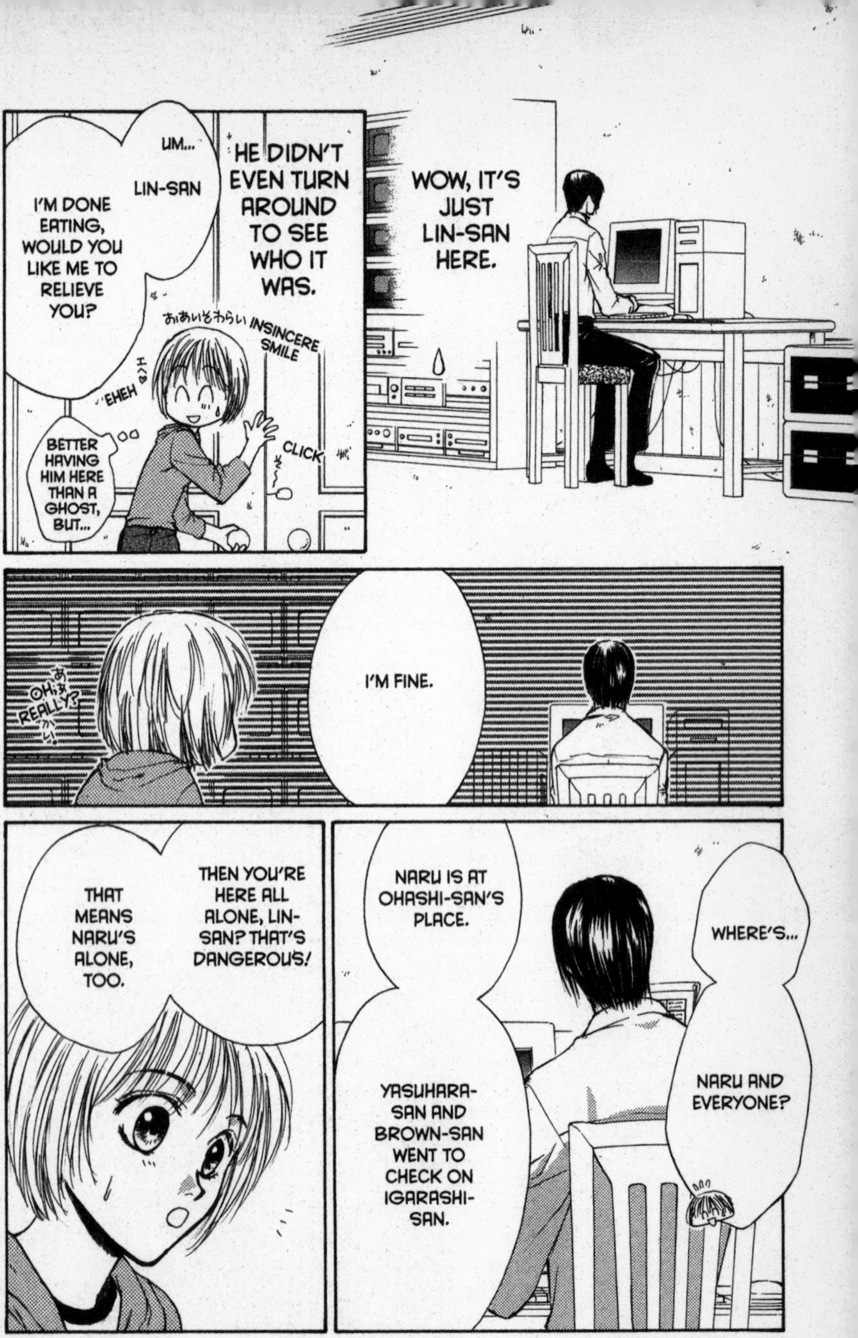
WOW, IT'S JUST LIN-SAN HERE.
HE DIDN'T EVEN TURN AROUND TO SEE WHO IT WAS.
UM... LIN-SAN
I'M DONE EATING, WOULD YOU LIKE ME TO RELIEVE YOU?
おあいそわらい INSINCERE SMILE
EHEH
CLICK
BETTER HAVING HIM HERE THAN A GHOST, BUT...
I'M FINE.
OH, REALLY?
WHERE'S...
NARU AND EVERYONE?
NARU IS AT OHASHI-SAN'S PLACE.
YASUHARA-SAN AND BROWN-SAN WENT TO CHECK ON IGARASHI-SAN.
THEN YOU'RE HERE ALL ALONE, LIN-SAN? THAT'S DANGEROUS!
THAT MEANS NARU'S ALONE, TOO.

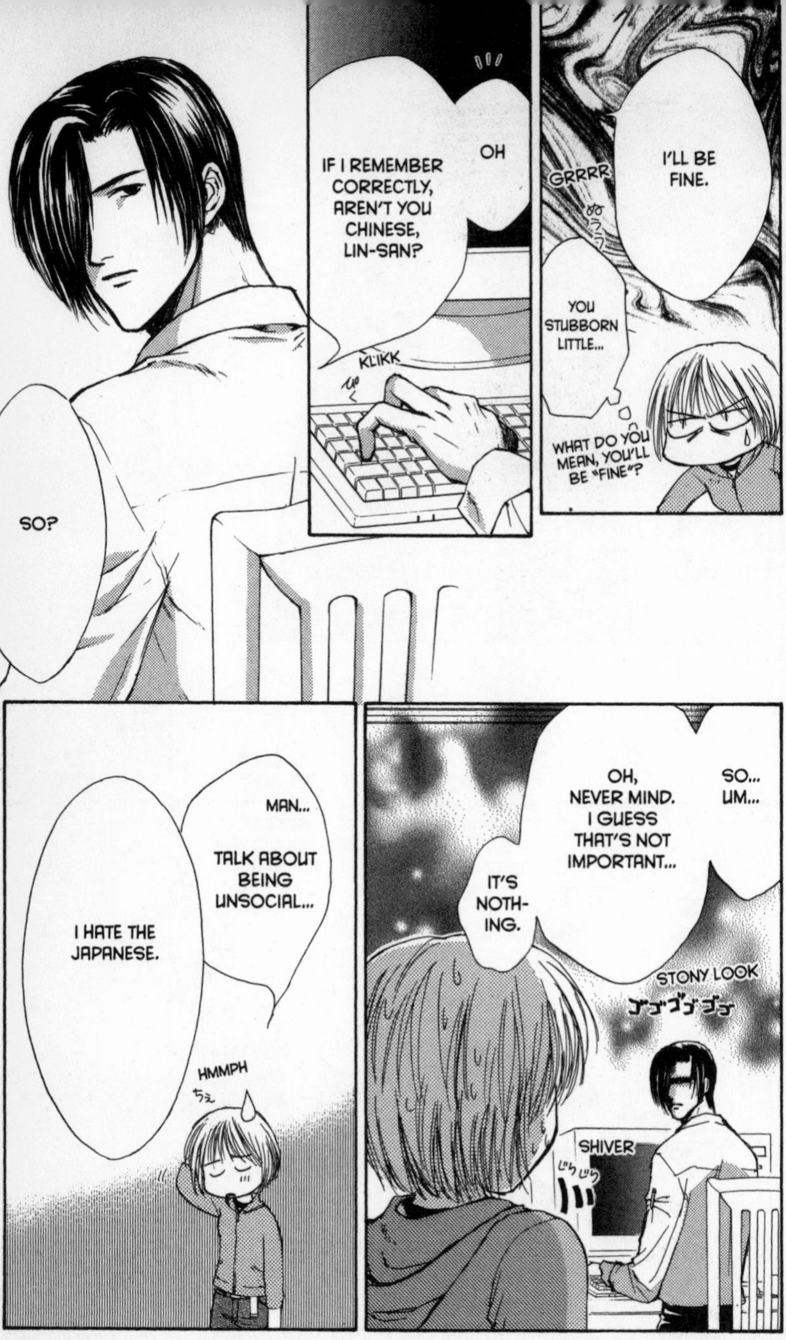
I'LL BE FINE.
GRRRR
YOU STUBBORN LITTLE...
WHAT DO YOU MEAN, YOU'LL BE "FINE"?
OH
IF I REMEMBER CORRECTLY, AREN'T YOU CHINESE, LIN-SAN?
KLIKK
SO?
SO... UM...
OH, NEVER MIND. I GUESS THAT'S NOT IMPORTANT...
IT'S NOTH-ING.
STONY LOOK
SHIVER
I HATE THE JAPANESE.
MAN...
TALK ABOUT BEING UNSOCIAL...
HMMPH

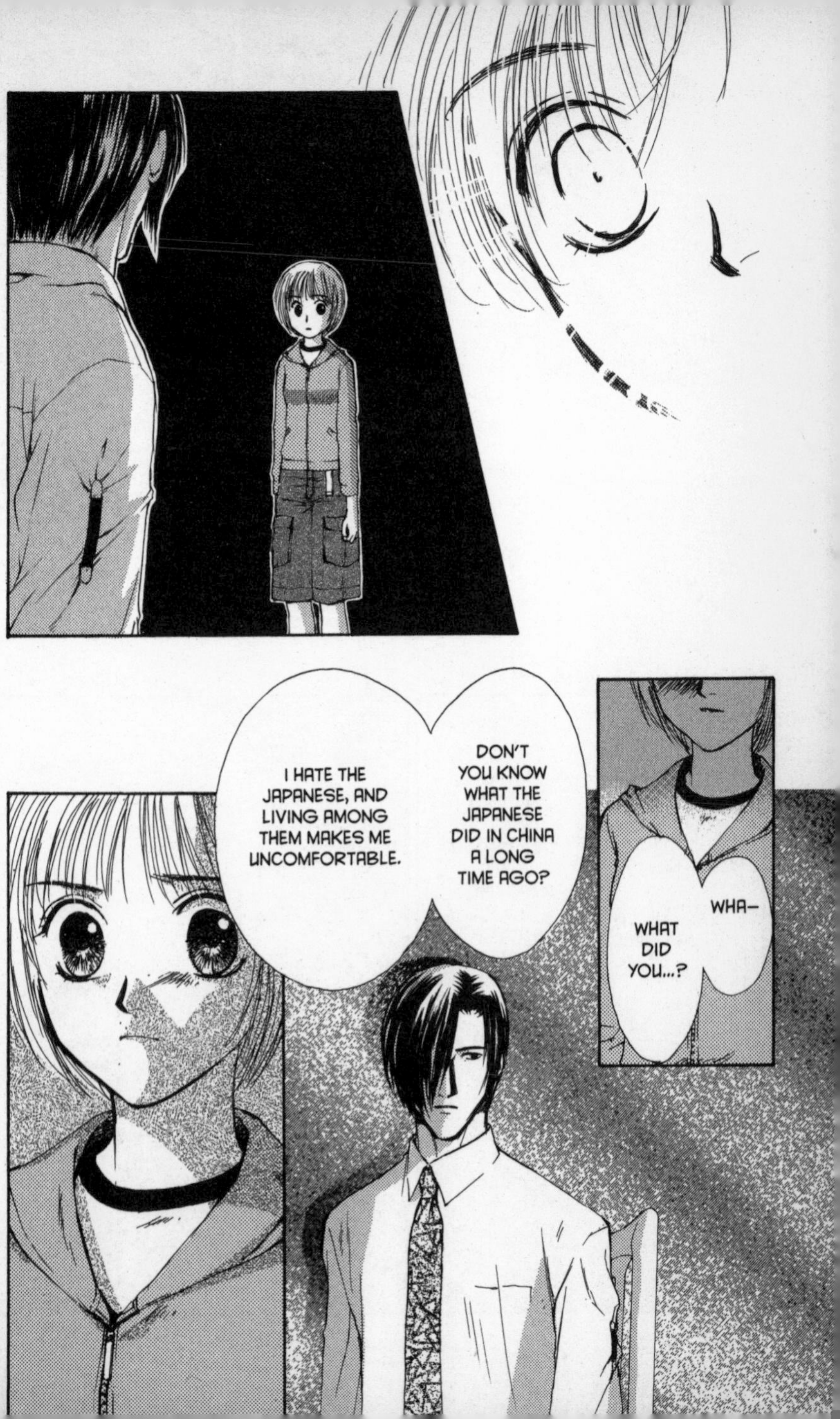
WHA—
WHAT DID YOU...?
DON'T YOU KNOW WHAT THE JAPANESE DID IN CHINA A LONG TIME AGO?
I HATE THE JAPANESE, AND LIVING AMONG THEM MAKES ME UNCOMFORTABLE.

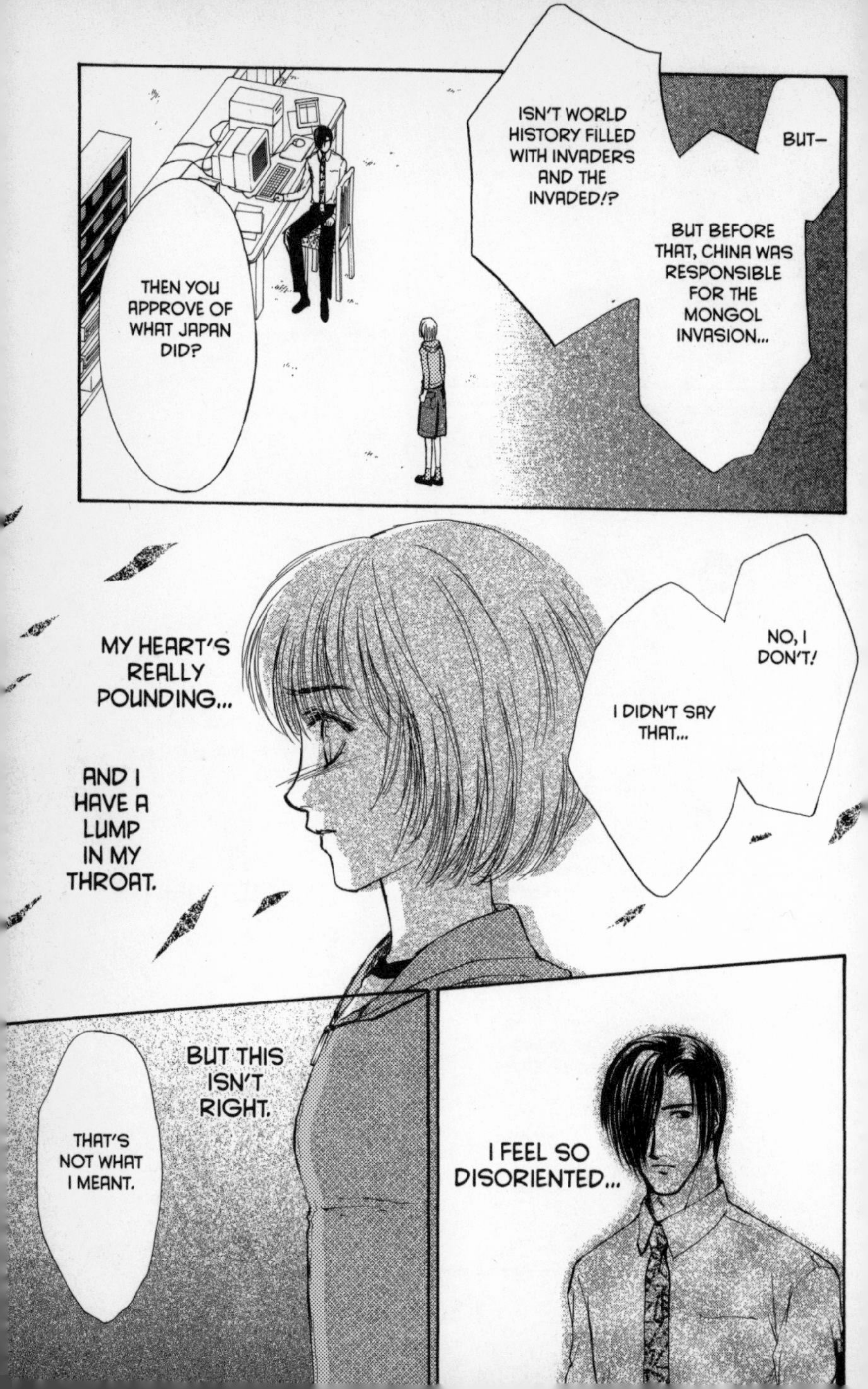
BUT—
BUT BEFORE THAT, CHINA WAS RESPONSIBLE FOR THE MONGOL INVASION...
ISN'T WORLD HISTORY FILLED WITH INVADERS AND THE INVADED!?
THEN YOU APPROVE OF WHAT JAPAN DID?
NO, I DON'T!
I DIDN'T SAY THAT...
MY HEART'S REALLY POUNDING...
AND I HAVE A LUMP IN MY THROAT.
I FEEL SO DISORIENTED...
BUT THIS ISN'T RIGHT.
THAT'S NOT WHAT I MEANT.

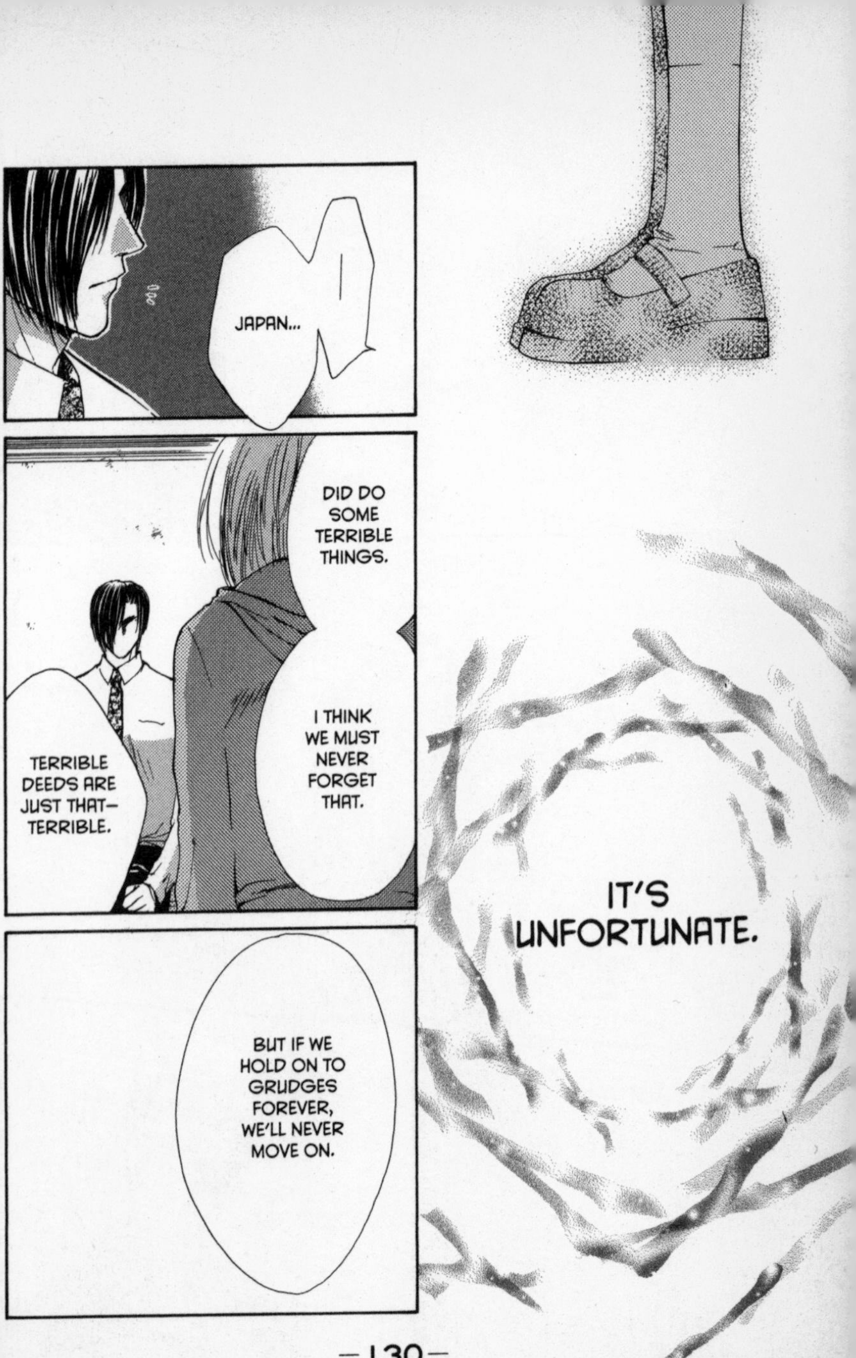
IT'S UNFORTUNATE.
JAPAN...
DID DO SOME TERRIBLE THINGS.
I THINK WE MUST NEVER FORGET THAT.
TERRIBLE DEEDS ARE JUST THAT—TERRIBLE.
BUT IF WE HOLD ON TO GRUDGES FOREVER, WE'LL NEVER MOVE ON.

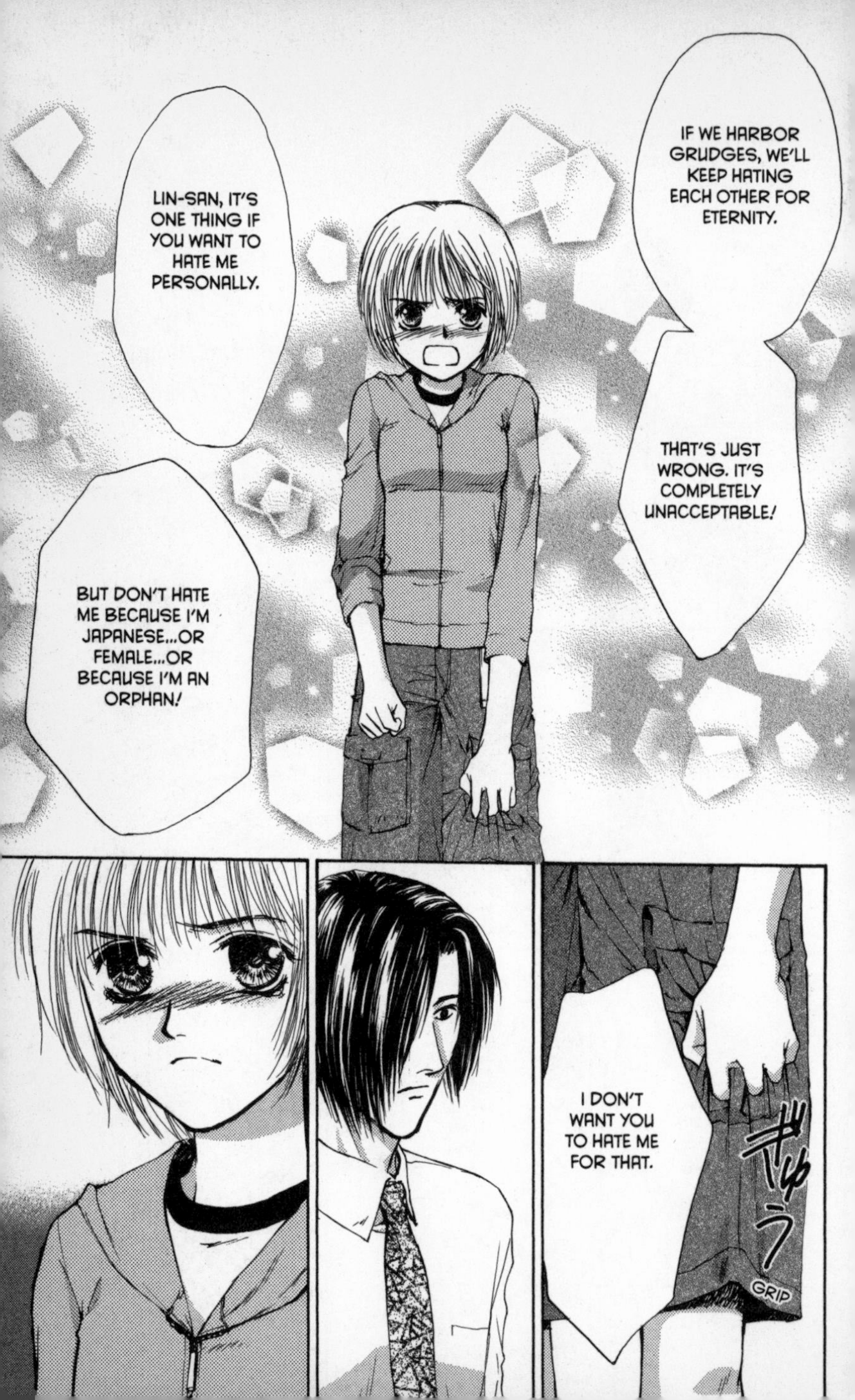
IF WE HARBOR GRUDGES, WE'LL KEEP HATING EACH OTHER FOR ETERNITY.
LIN-SAN, IT'S ONE THING IF YOU WANT TO HATE ME PERSONALLY.
THAT'S JUST WRONG. IT'S COMPLETELY UNACCEPTABLE!
BUT DON'T HATE ME BECAUSE I'M JAPANESE...OR FEMALE...OR BECAUSE I'M AN ORPHAN!
I DON'T WANT YOU TO HATE ME FOR THAT.
ぎゅう
GRIP

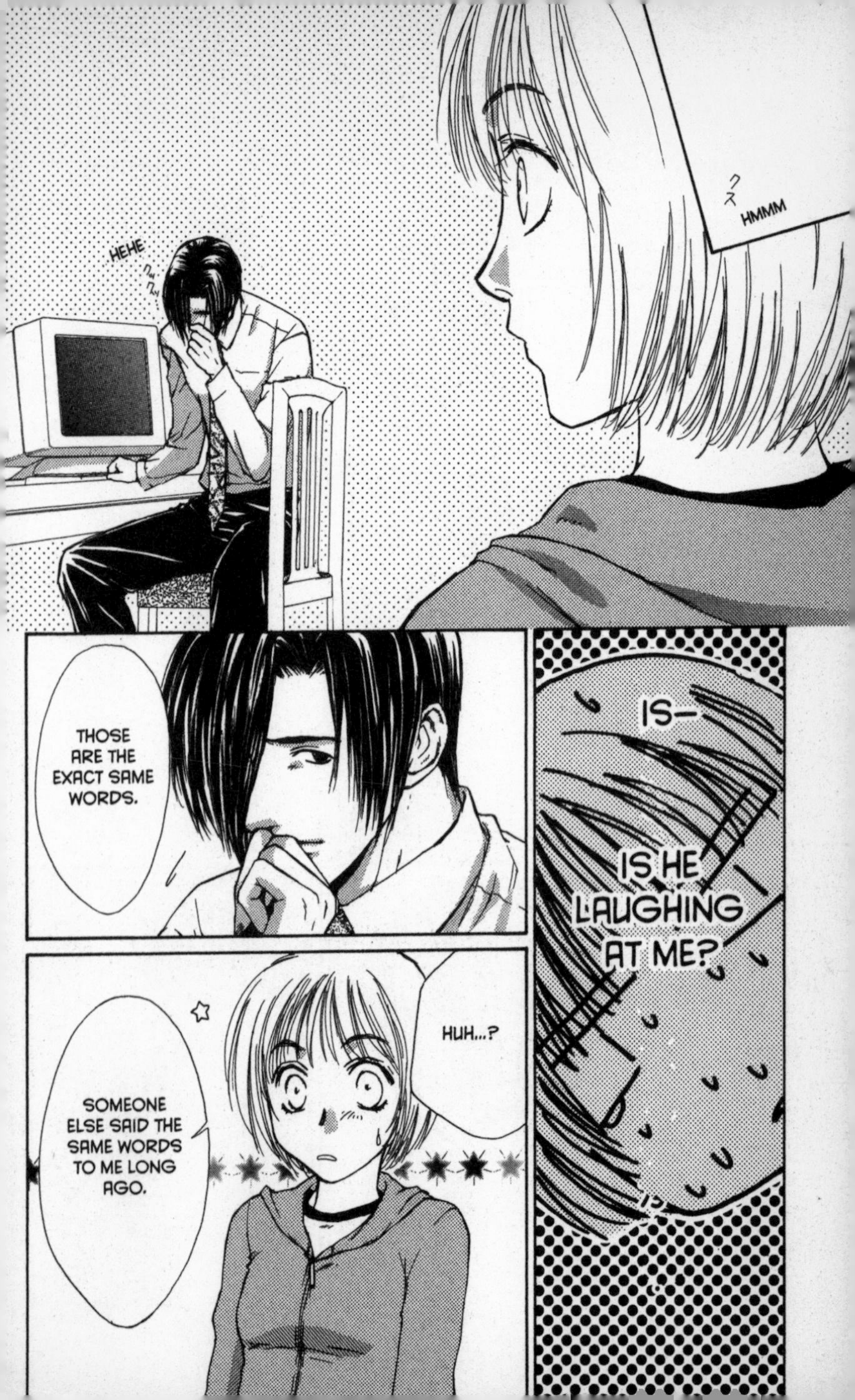

クス
HMMM
HEHE
IS—
IS HE LAUGHING AT ME?
THOSE ARE THE EXACT SAME WORDS.
HUH...?
SOMEONE ELSE SAID THE SAME WORDS TO ME LONG AGO.

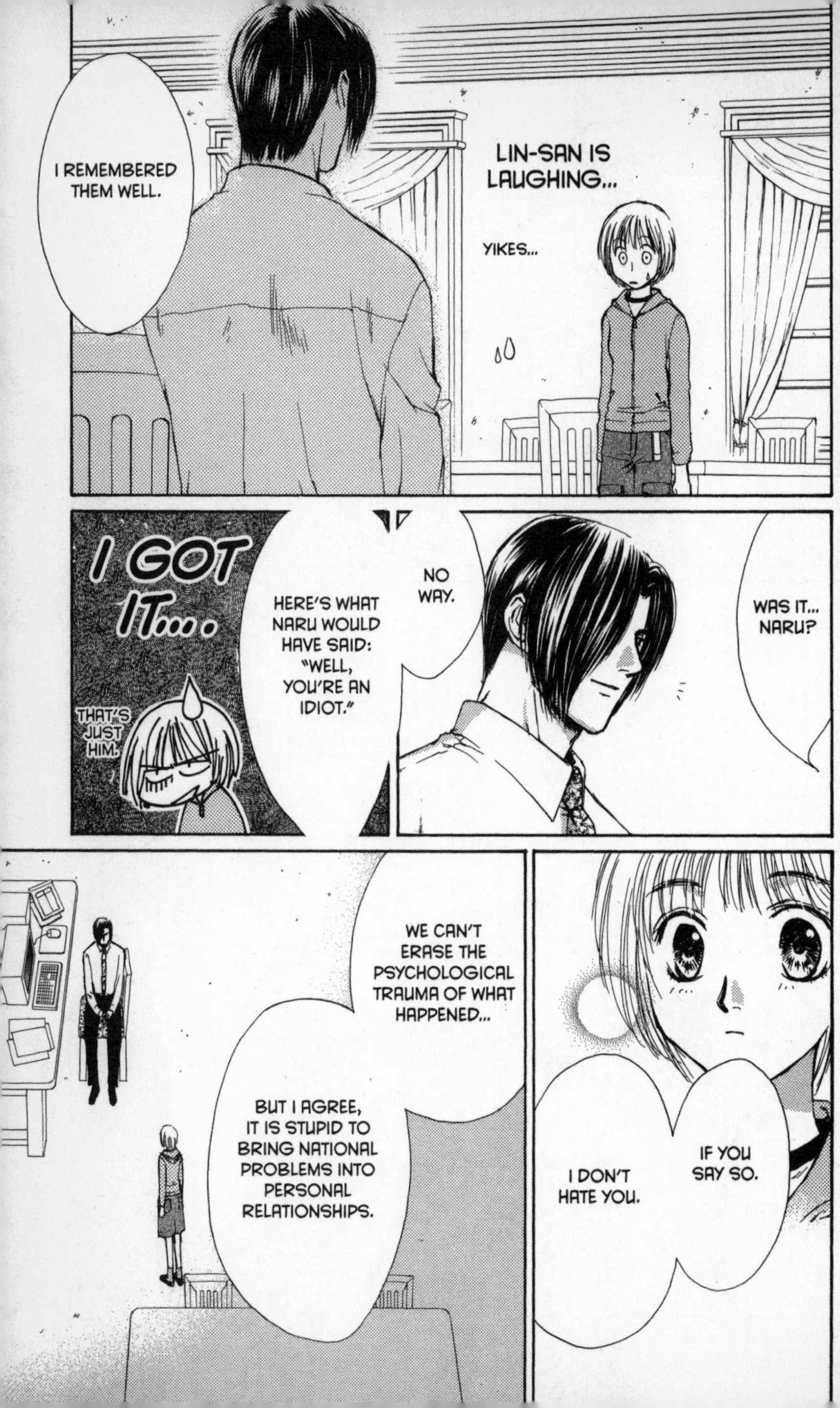
LIN-SAN IS LAUGHING...
YIKES...
I REMEMBERED THEM WELL.
WAS IT... NARU?
NO WAY.
HERE'S WHAT NARU WOULD HAVE SAID: "WELL, YOU'RE AN IDIOT."
I GOT IT....
THAT'S JUST HIM.
IF YOU SAY SO.
I DON'T HATE YOU.
WE CAN'T ERASE THE PSYCHOLOGICAL TRAUMA OF WHAT HAPPENED...
BUT I AGREE, IT IS STUPID TO BRING NATIONAL PROBLEMS INTO PERSONAL RELATIONSHIPS.

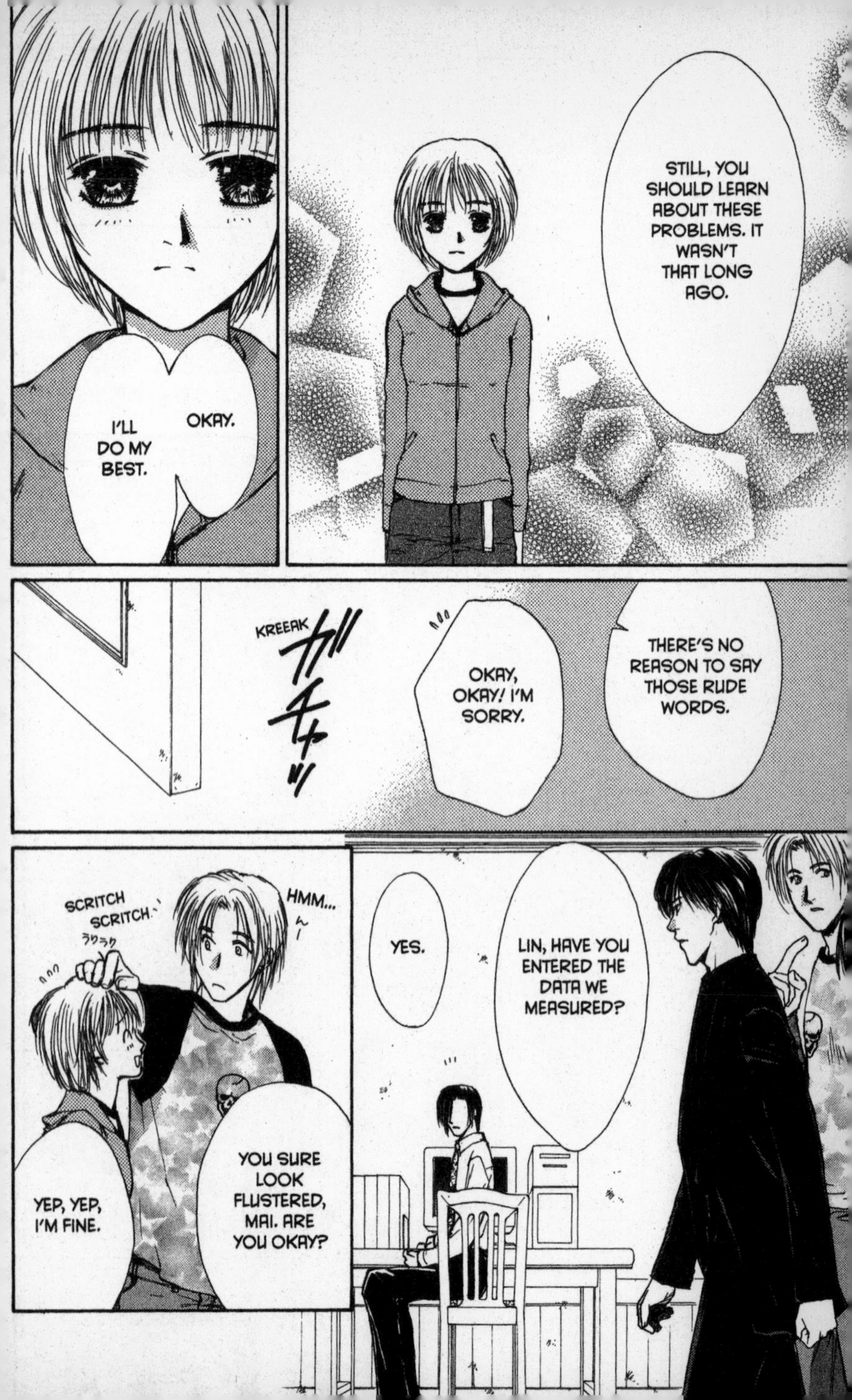
STILL, YOU SHOULD LEARN ABOUT THESE PROBLEMS. IT WASN'T THAT LONG AGO.
OKAY.
I'LL DO MY BEST.
THERE'S NO REASON TO SAY THOSE RUDE WORDS.
OKAY, OKAY! I'M SORRY.
KREEAK
LIN, HAVE YOU ENTERED THE DATA WE MEASURED?
YES.
HMM...
SCRITCH SCRITCH
YOU SURE LOOK FLUSTERED, MAI. ARE YOU OKAY?
YEP, YEP, I'M FINE.

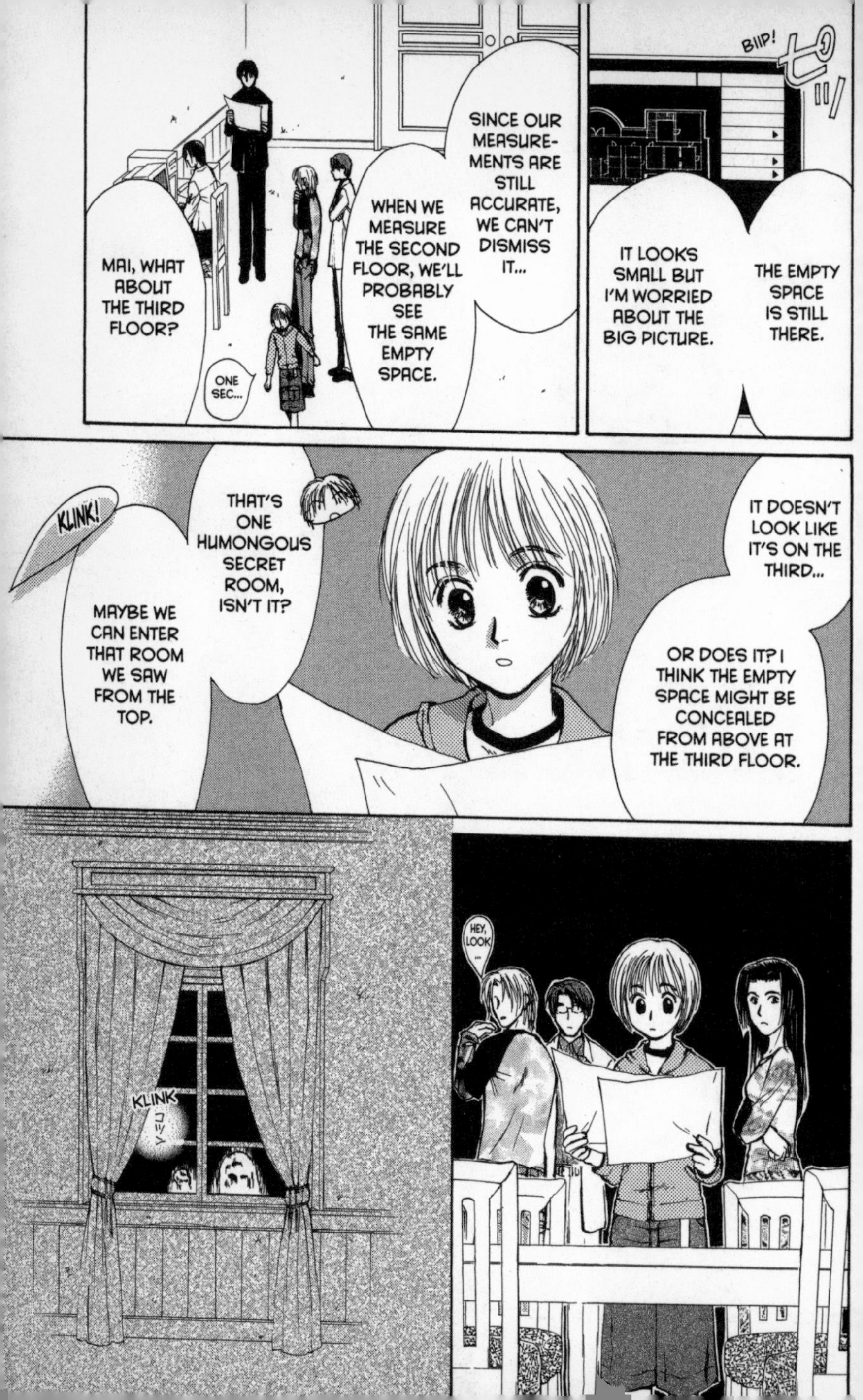
BIIP!
THE EMPTY SPACE IS STILL THERE.
IT LOOKS SMALL BUT I'M WORRIED ABOUT THE BIG PICTURE.
SINCE OUR MEASUREMENTS ARE STILL ACCURATE, WE CAN'T DISMISS IT...
WHEN WE MEASURE THE SECOND FLOOR, WE'LL PROBABLY SEE THE SAME EMPTY SPACE.
MAI, WHAT ABOUT THE THIRD FLOOR?
ONE SEC...
IT DOESN'T LOOK LIKE IT'S ON THE THIRD...
OR DOES IT? I THINK THE EMPTY SPACE MIGHT BE CONCEALED FROM ABOVE AT THE THIRD FLOOR.
THAT'S ONE HUMONGOUS SECRET ROOM, ISN'T IT?
MAYBE WE CAN ENTER THAT ROOM WE SAW FROM THE TOP.
KLINK!
HEY, LOOK...
KLINK

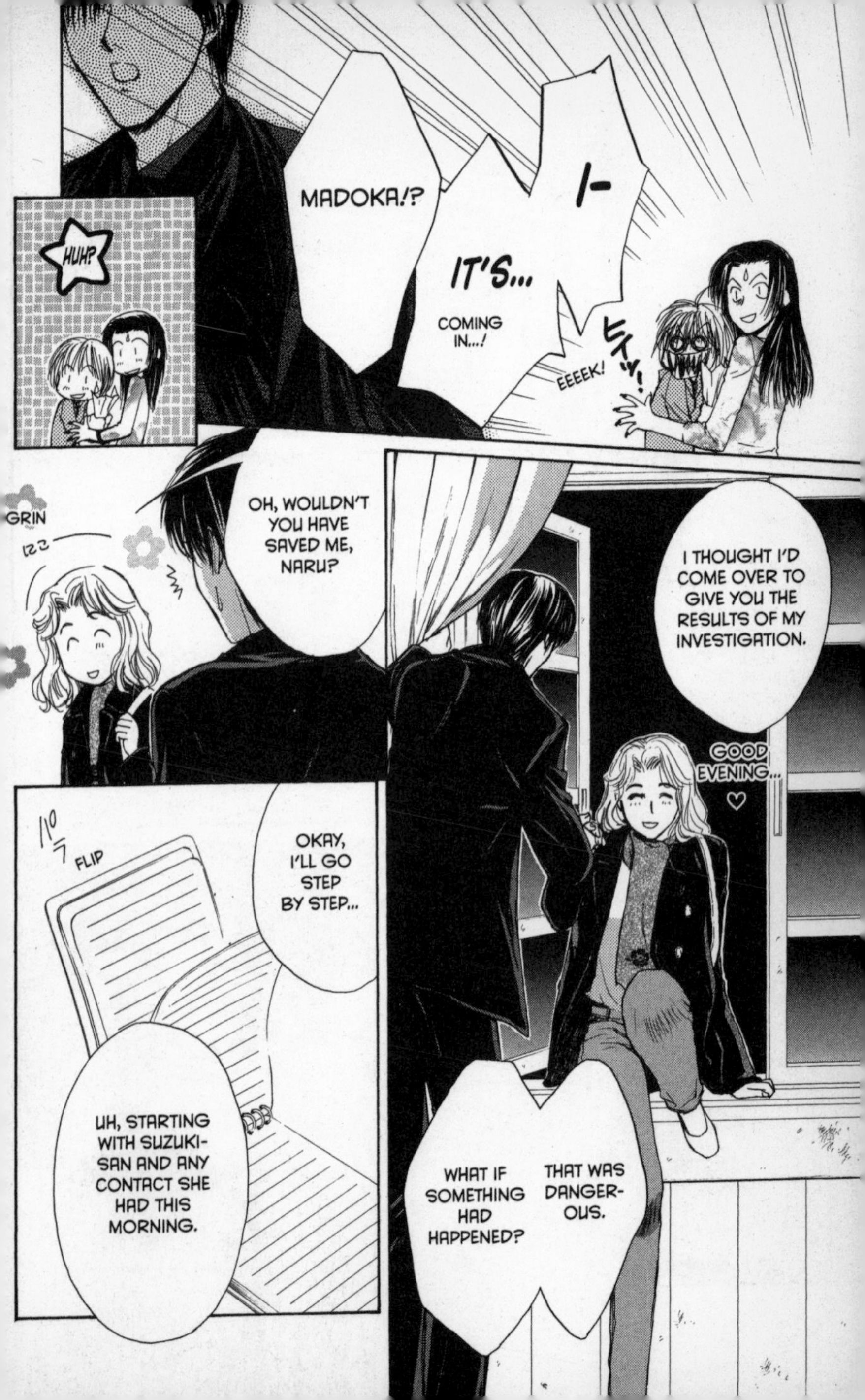
I-
IT'S...
COMING IN...!
ヒイッ!
EEEEK!
MADOKA!?
HUH?
I THOUGHT I'D COME OVER TO GIVE YOU THE RESULTS OF MY INVESTIGATION.
GOOD EVENING...♥
OH, WOULDN'T YOU HAVE SAVED ME, NARU?
にこ
GRIN
THAT WAS DANGER-OUS.
WHAT IF SOMETHING HAD HAPPENED?
OKAY, I'LL GO STEP BY STEP...
パラ
FLIP
UH, STARTING WITH SUZUKI-SAN AND ANY CONTACT SHE HAD THIS MORNING.

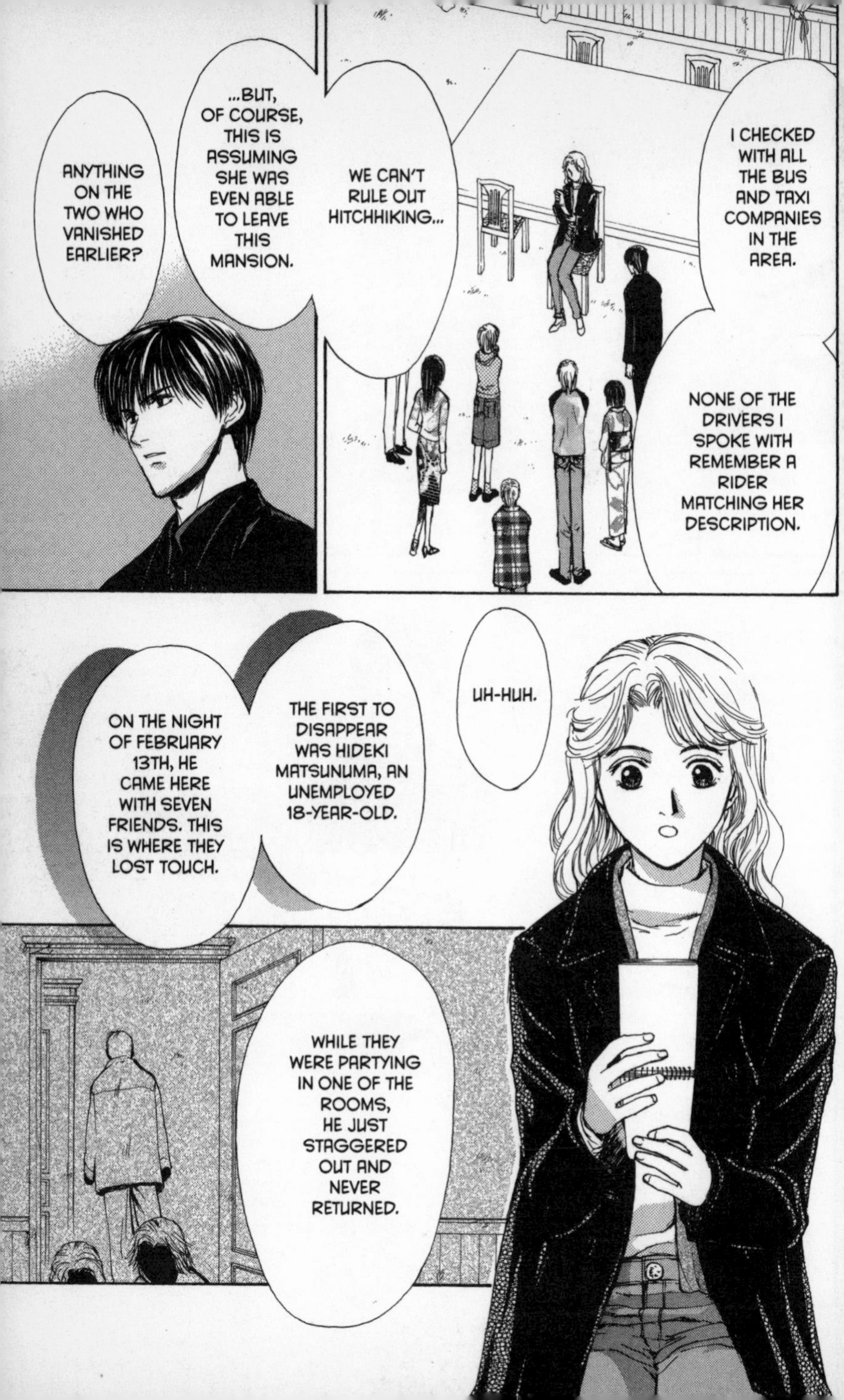
I CHECKED WITH ALL THE BUS AND TAXI COMPANIES IN THE AREA.
NONE OF THE DRIVERS I SPOKE WITH REMEMBER A RIDER MATCHING HER DESCRIPTION.
WE CAN'T RULE OUT HITCHHIKING...
...BUT, OF COURSE, THIS IS ASSUMING SHE WAS EVEN ABLE TO LEAVE THIS MANSION.
ANYTHING ON THE TWO WHO VANISHED EARLIER?
UH-HUH.
THE FIRST TO DISAPPEAR WAS HIDEKI MATSUNUMA, AN UNEMPLOYED 18-YEAR-OLD.
ON THE NIGHT OF FEBRUARY 13TH, HE CAME HERE WITH SEVEN FRIENDS. THIS IS WHERE THEY LOST TOUCH.
WHILE THEY WERE PARTYING IN ONE OF THE ROOMS, HE JUST STAGGERED OUT AND NEVER RETURNED.

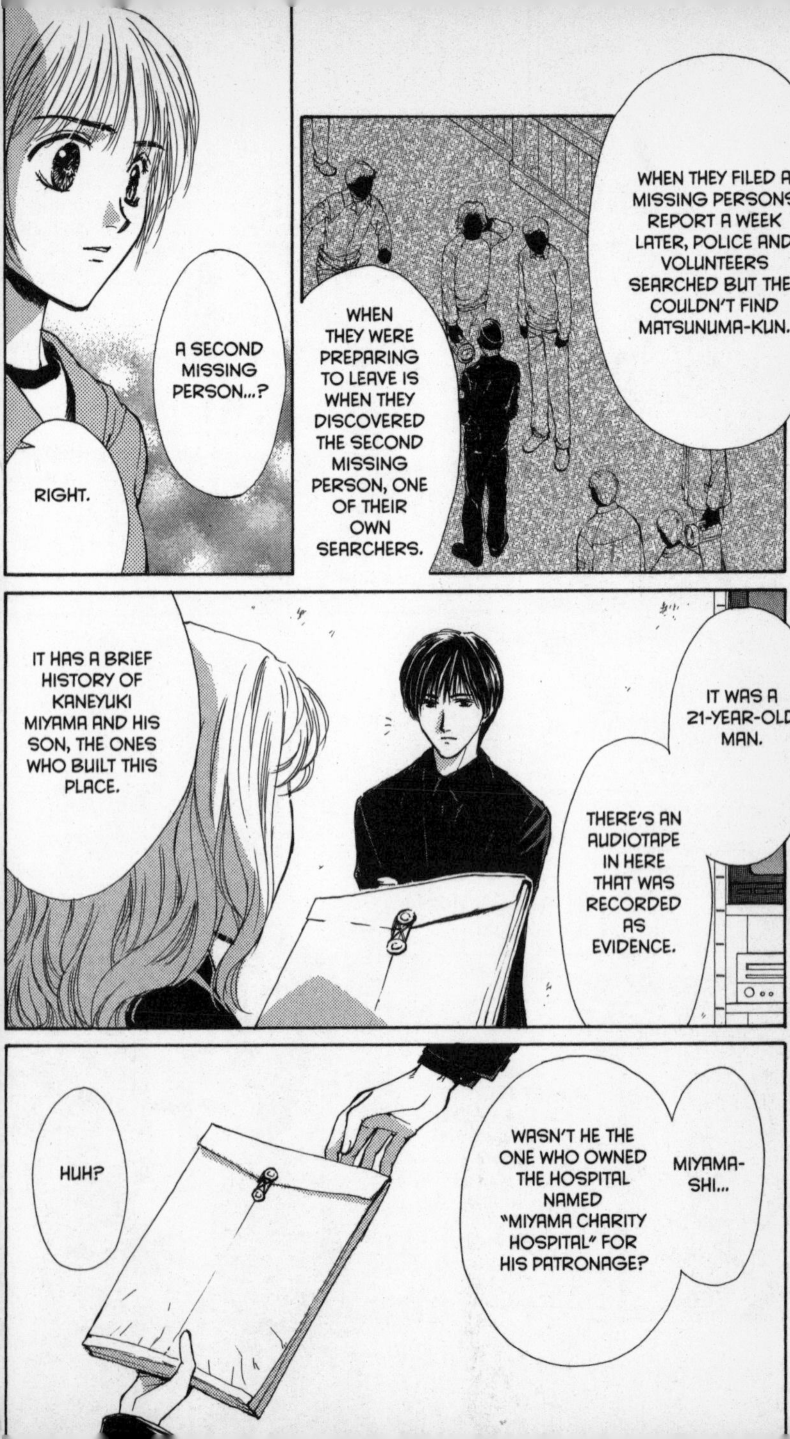
WHEN THEY FILED A MISSING PERSONS REPORT A WEEK LATER, POLICE AND VOLUNTEERS SEARCHED BUT THEY COULDN'T FIND MATSUNUMA-KUN.
WHEN THEY WERE PREPARING TO LEAVE IS WHEN THEY DISCOVERED THE SECOND MISSING PERSON, ONE OF THEIR OWN SEARCHERS.
A SECOND MISSING PERSON...?
RIGHT.
IT WAS A 21-YEAR-OLD MAN.
THERE'S AN AUDIOTAPE IN HERE THAT WAS RECORDED AS EVIDENCE.
IT HAS A BRIEF HISTORY OF KANEYUKI MIYAMA AND HIS SON, THE ONES WHO BUILT THIS PLACE.
MIYAMA-SHI...
WASN'T HE THE ONE WHO OWNED THE HOSPITAL NAMED "MIYAMA CHARITY HOSPITAL" FOR HIS PATRONAGE?
HUH?

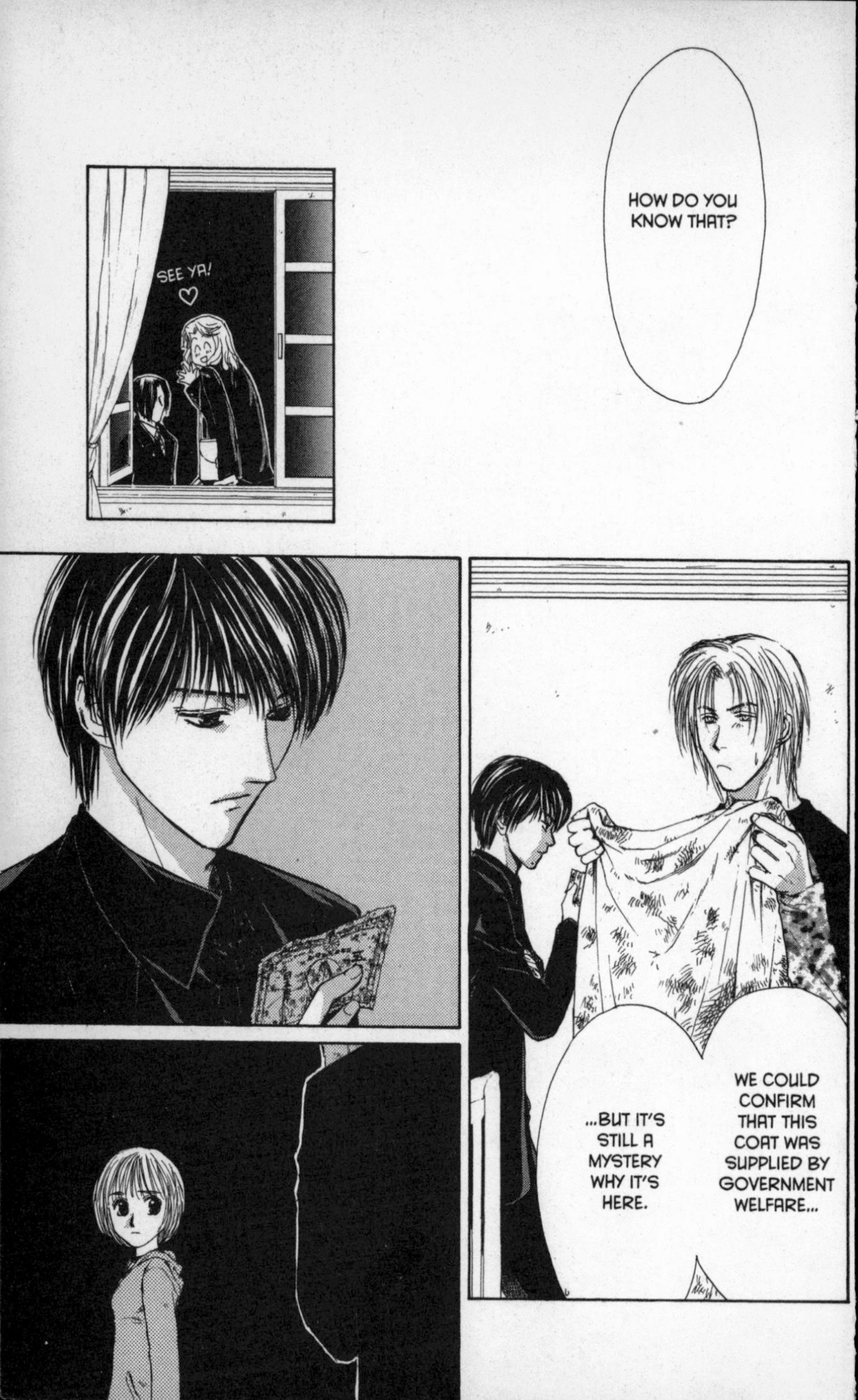
HOW DO YOU KNOW THAT?
SEE YA!
WE COULD CONFIRM THAT THIS COAT WAS SUPPLIED BY GOVERNMENT WELFARE...
...BUT IT'S STILL A MYSTERY WHY IT'S HERE.

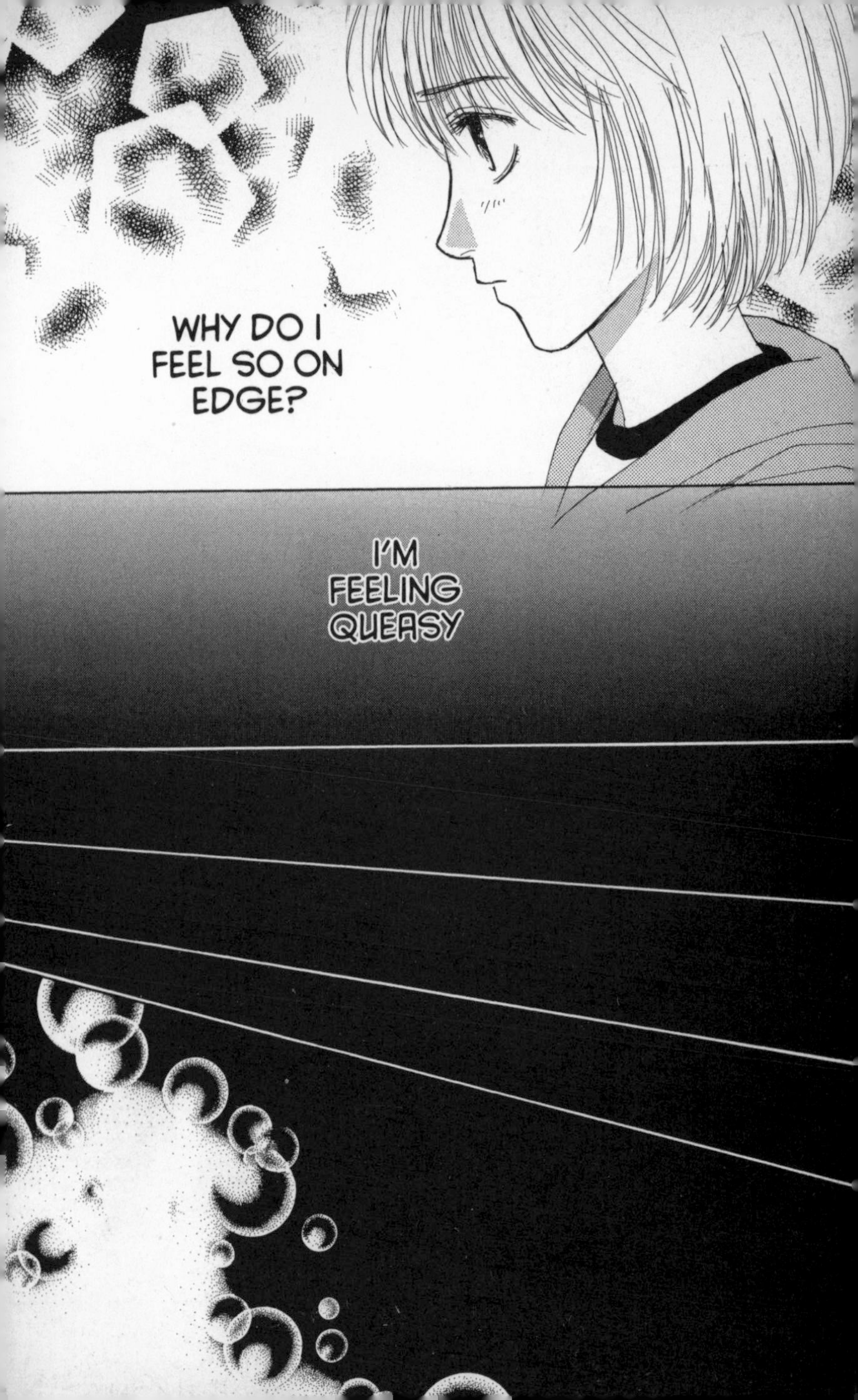
WHY DO I
FEEL SO ON
EDGE?
I'M
FEELING
QUEASY

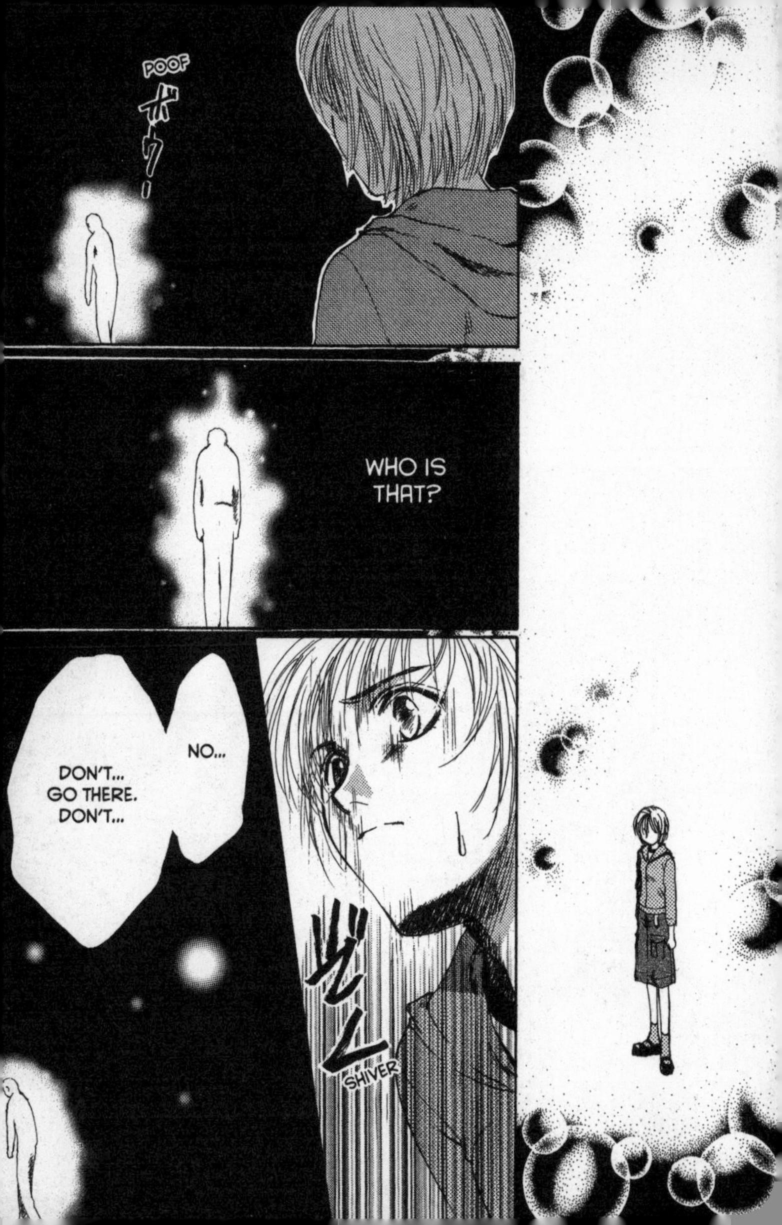
POOF
WHO IS THAT?
NO...
DON'T... GO THERE. DON'T...
SHIVER

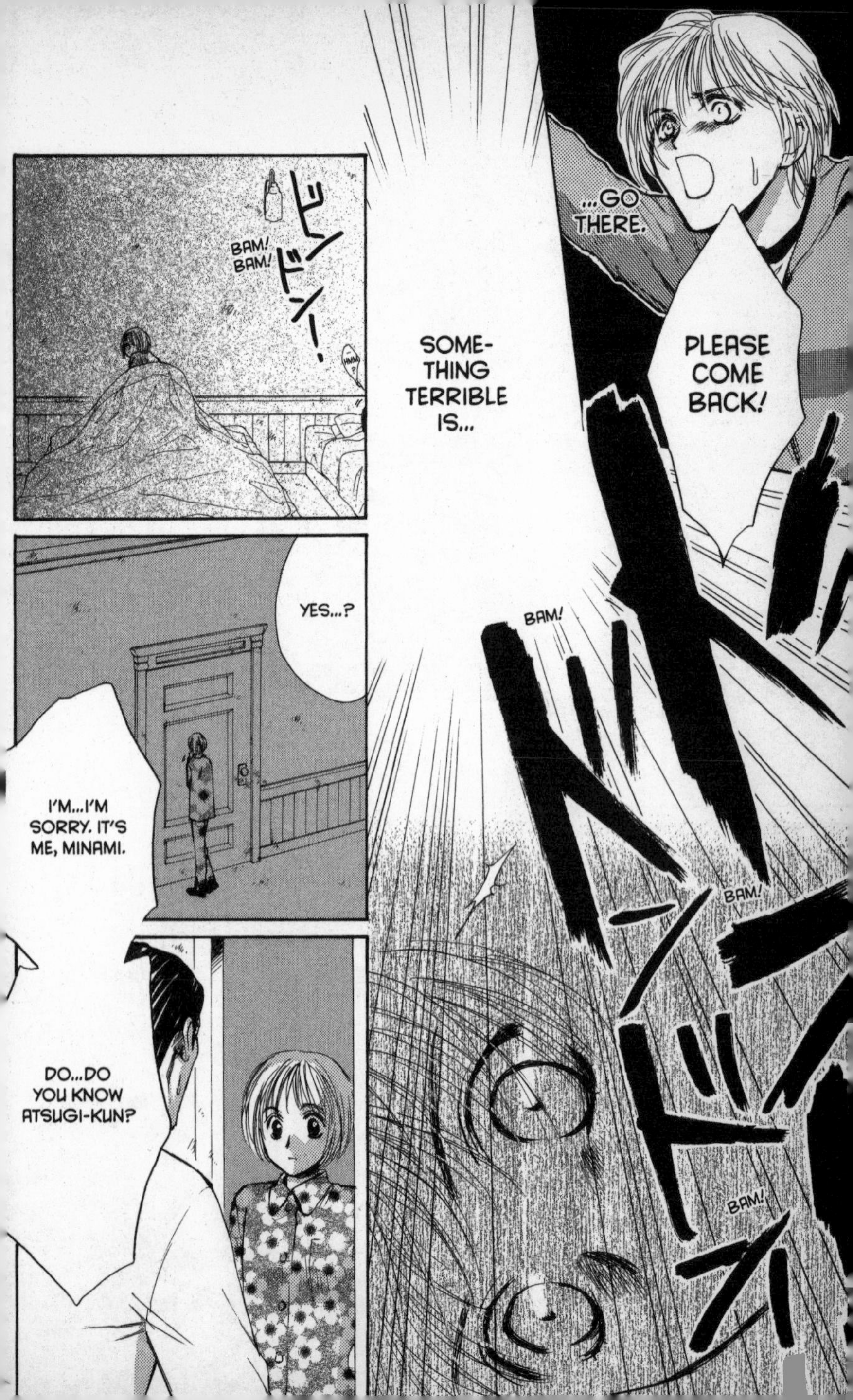
...GO THERE.
PLEASE COME BACK!
SOME-THING TERRIBLE IS...
BAM!
BAM!
BAM!
BAM! BAM!
HMM?
YES...?
I'M...I'M SORRY. IT'S ME, MINAMI.
DO...DO YOU KNOW ATSUGI-KUN?

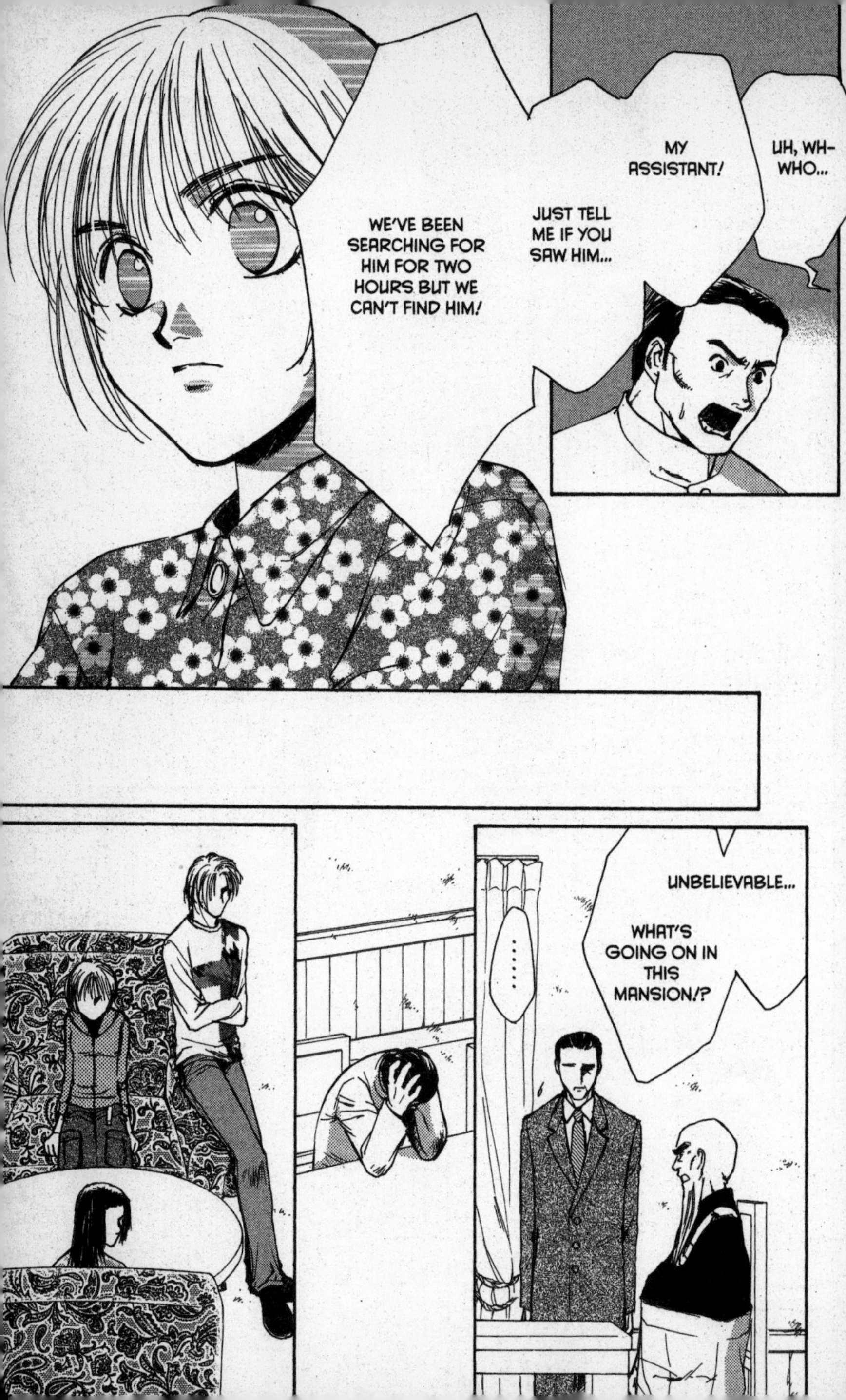
UH, WH-WHO...
MY ASSISTANT!
JUST TELL ME IF YOU SAW HIM...
WE'VE BEEN SEARCHING FOR HIM FOR TWO HOURS BUT WE CAN'T FIND HIM!
UNBELIEVABLE...
WHAT'S GOING ON IN THIS MANSION!?
......

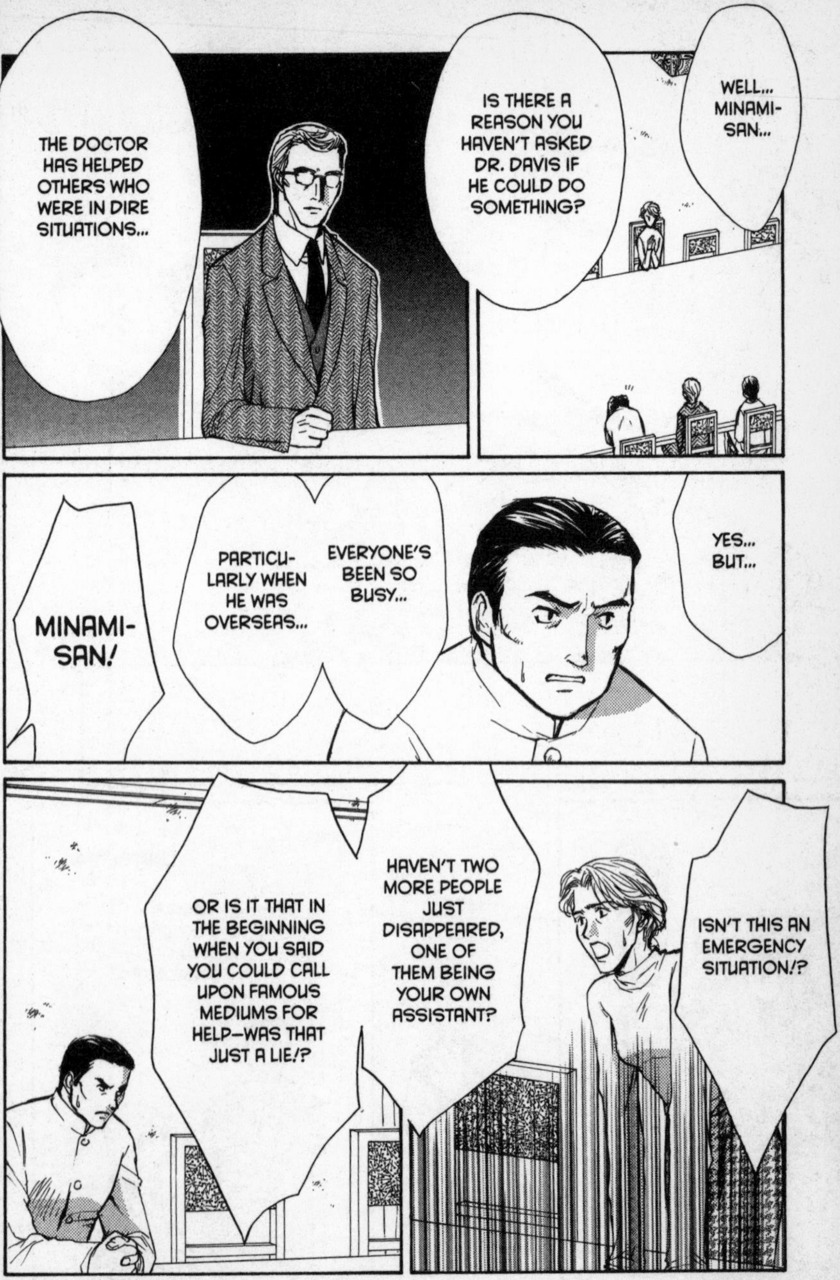
WELL... MINAMI-SAN...
IS THERE A REASON YOU HAVEN'T ASKED DR. DAVIS IF HE COULD DO SOMETHING?
THE DOCTOR HAS HELPED OTHERS WHO WERE IN DIRE SITUATIONS...
YES... BUT...
EVERYONE'S BEEN SO BUSY...
PARTICULARLY WHEN HE WAS OVERSEAS...
MINAMI-SAN!
ISN'T THIS AN EMERGENCY SITUATION!?
HAVEN'T TWO MORE PEOPLE JUST DISAPPEARED, ONE OF THEM BEING YOUR OWN ASSISTANT?
OR IS IT THAT IN THE BEGINNING WHEN YOU SAID YOU COULD CALL UPON FAMOUS MEDIUMS FOR HELP—WAS THAT JUST A LIE!?

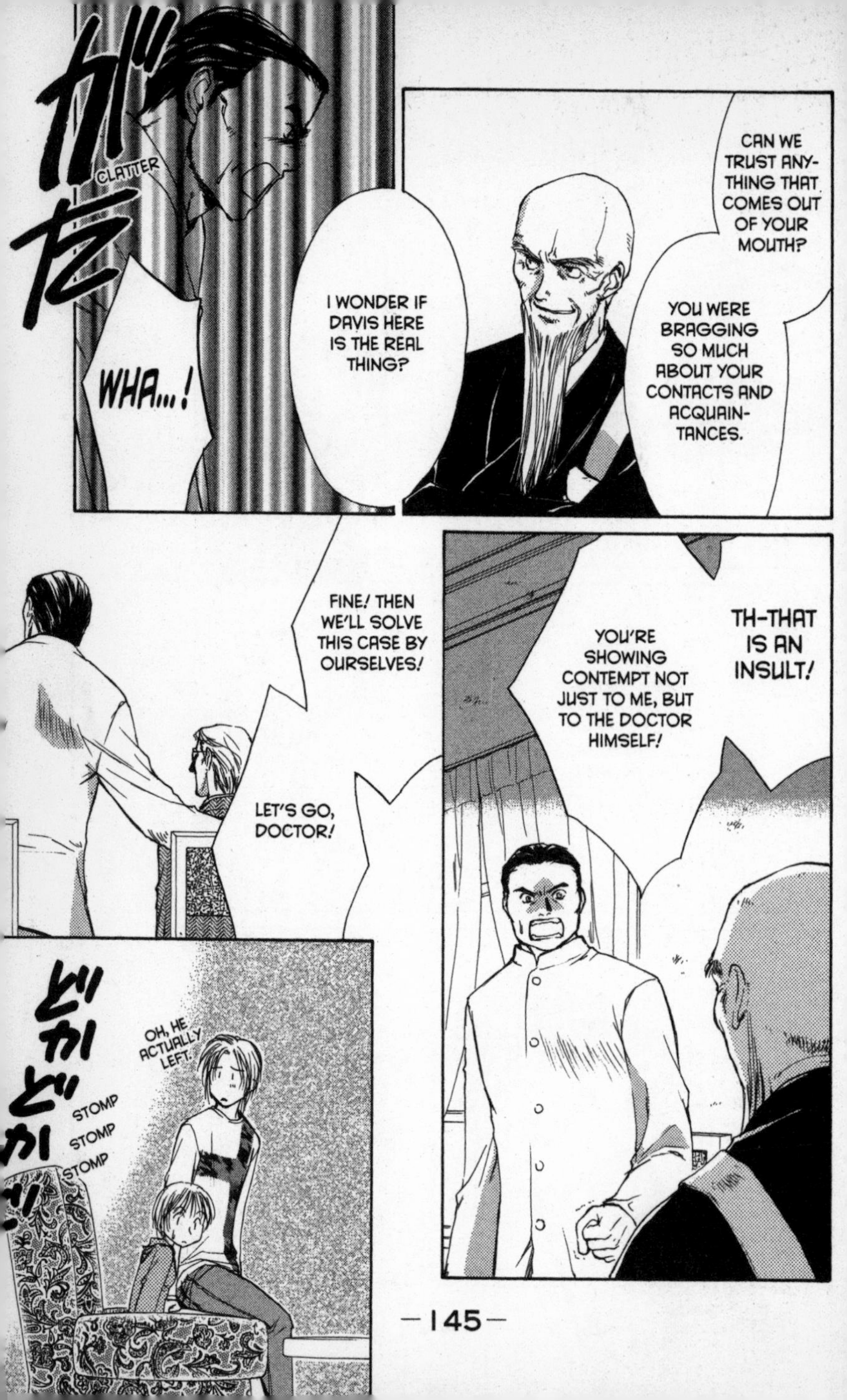
CAN WE TRUST ANY-THING THAT COMES OUT OF YOUR MOUTH?
YOU WERE BRAGGING SO MUCH ABOUT YOUR CONTACTS AND ACQUAIN-TANCES.
I WONDER IF DAVIS HERE IS THE REAL THING?
ガた
CLATTER
WHA...!
TH-THAT IS AN INSULT!
YOU'RE SHOWING CONTEMPT NOT JUST TO ME, BUT TO THE DOCTOR HIMSELF!
FINE! THEN WE'LL SOLVE THIS CASE BY OURSELVES!
LET'S GO, DOCTOR!
どかどか
STOMP
STOMP
STOMP
OH, HE ACTUALLY LEFT.

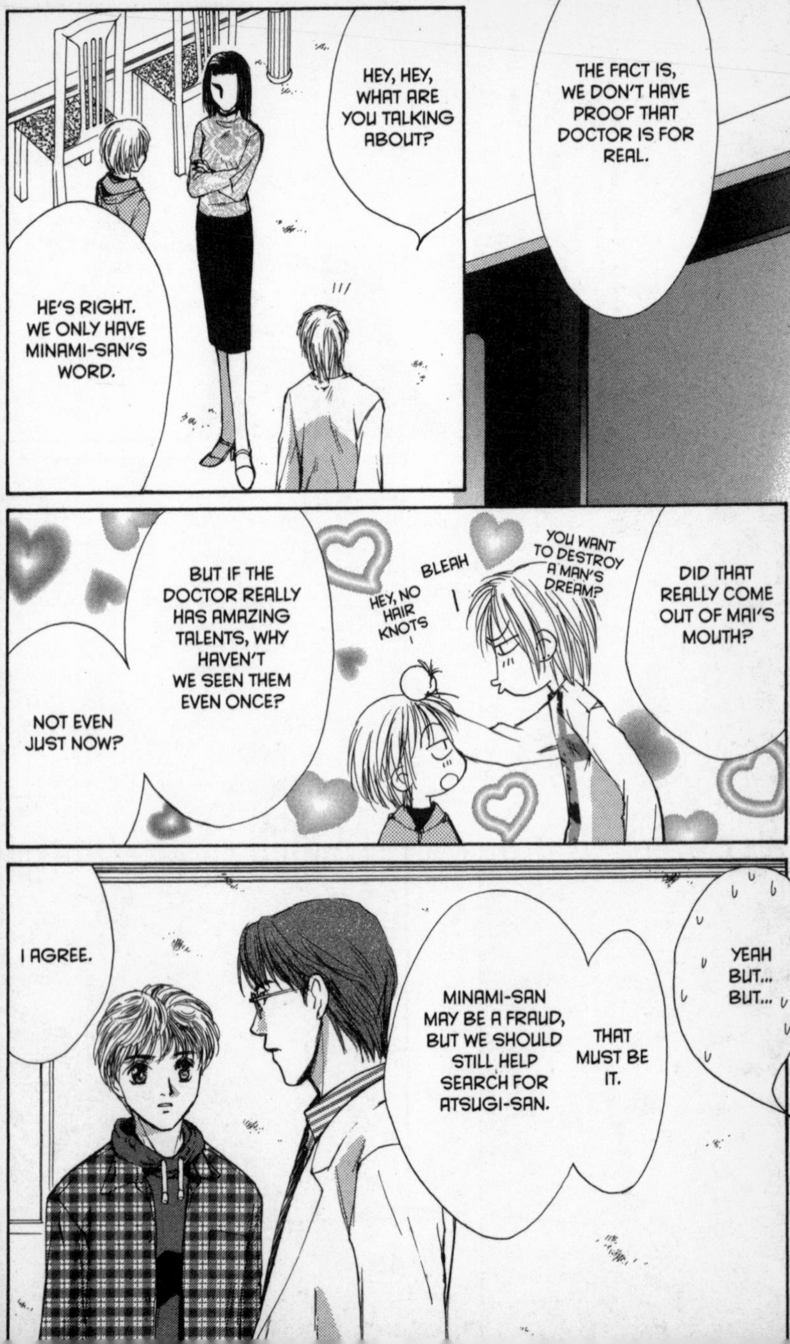
THE FACT IS, WE DON'T HAVE PROOF THAT DOCTOR IS FOR REAL.
HEY, HEY, WHAT ARE YOU TALKING ABOUT?
HE'S RIGHT. WE ONLY HAVE MINAMI-SAN'S WORD.
DID THAT REALLY COME OUT OF MAI'S MOUTH?
YOU WANT TO DESTROY A MAN'S DREAM?
BLEAH
HEY, NO HAIR KNOTS
BUT IF THE DOCTOR REALLY HAS AMAZING TALENTS, WHY HAVEN'T WE SEEN THEM EVEN ONCE?
NOT EVEN JUST NOW?
YEAH BUT... BUT...
THAT MUST BE IT.
MINAMI-SAN MAY BE A FRAUD, BUT WE SHOULD STILL HELP SEARCH FOR ATSUGI-SAN.
I AGREE.

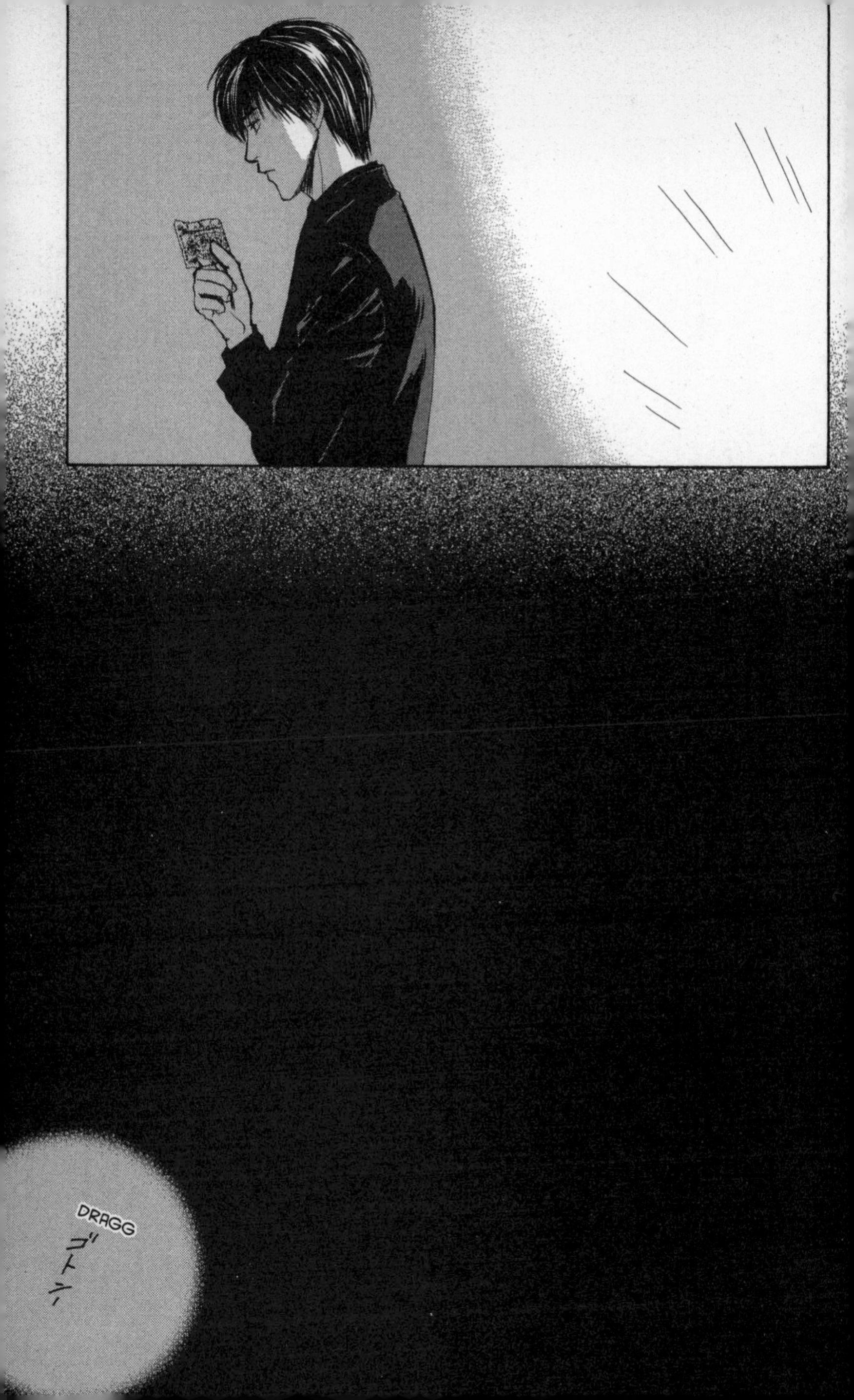
DRAGG
ゴトン

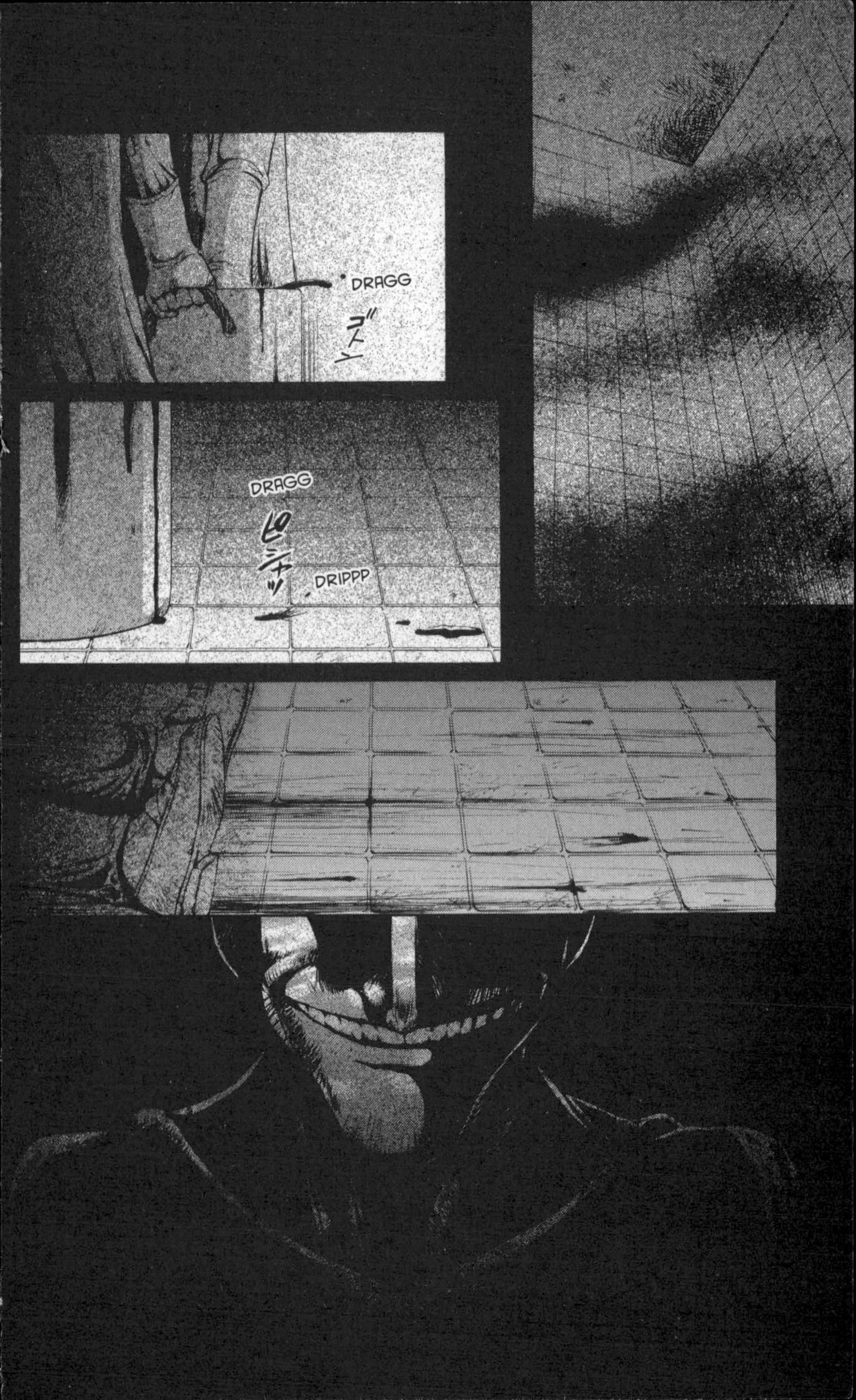
DRAGG
DRAGG
DRIPPP

GHOST HUNT

— **THE BLOODSTAINED LABYRINTH** —

FILE 5

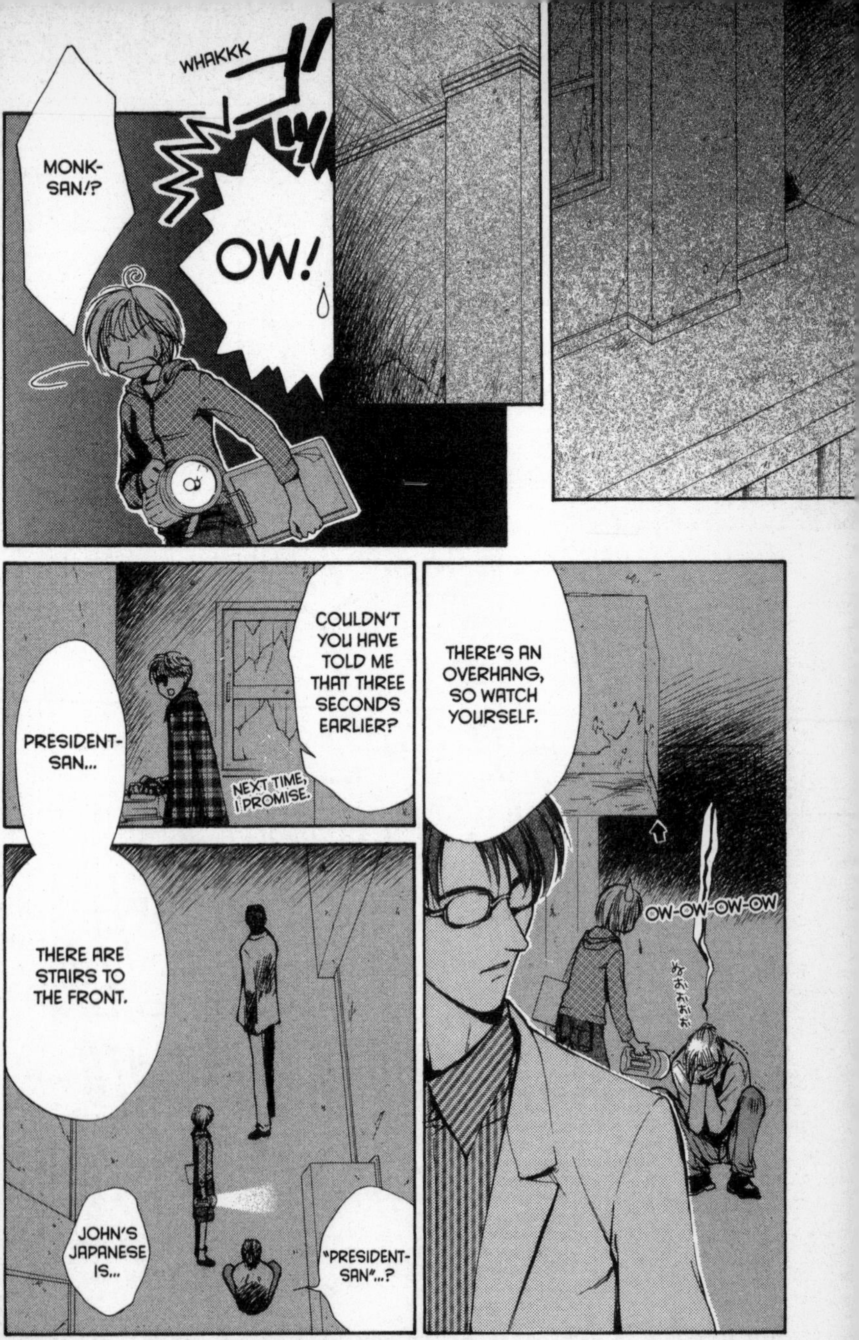
WHAKKK
OW!
MONK-SAN!?
THERE'S AN OVERHANG, SO WATCH YOURSELF.
OW-OW-OW-OW
ぬおおおお
COULDN'T YOU HAVE TOLD ME THAT THREE SECONDS EARLIER?
NEXT TIME, I PROMISE.
PRESIDENT-SAN...
THERE ARE STAIRS TO THE FRONT.
"PRESIDENT-SAN"...?
JOHN'S JAPANESE IS...

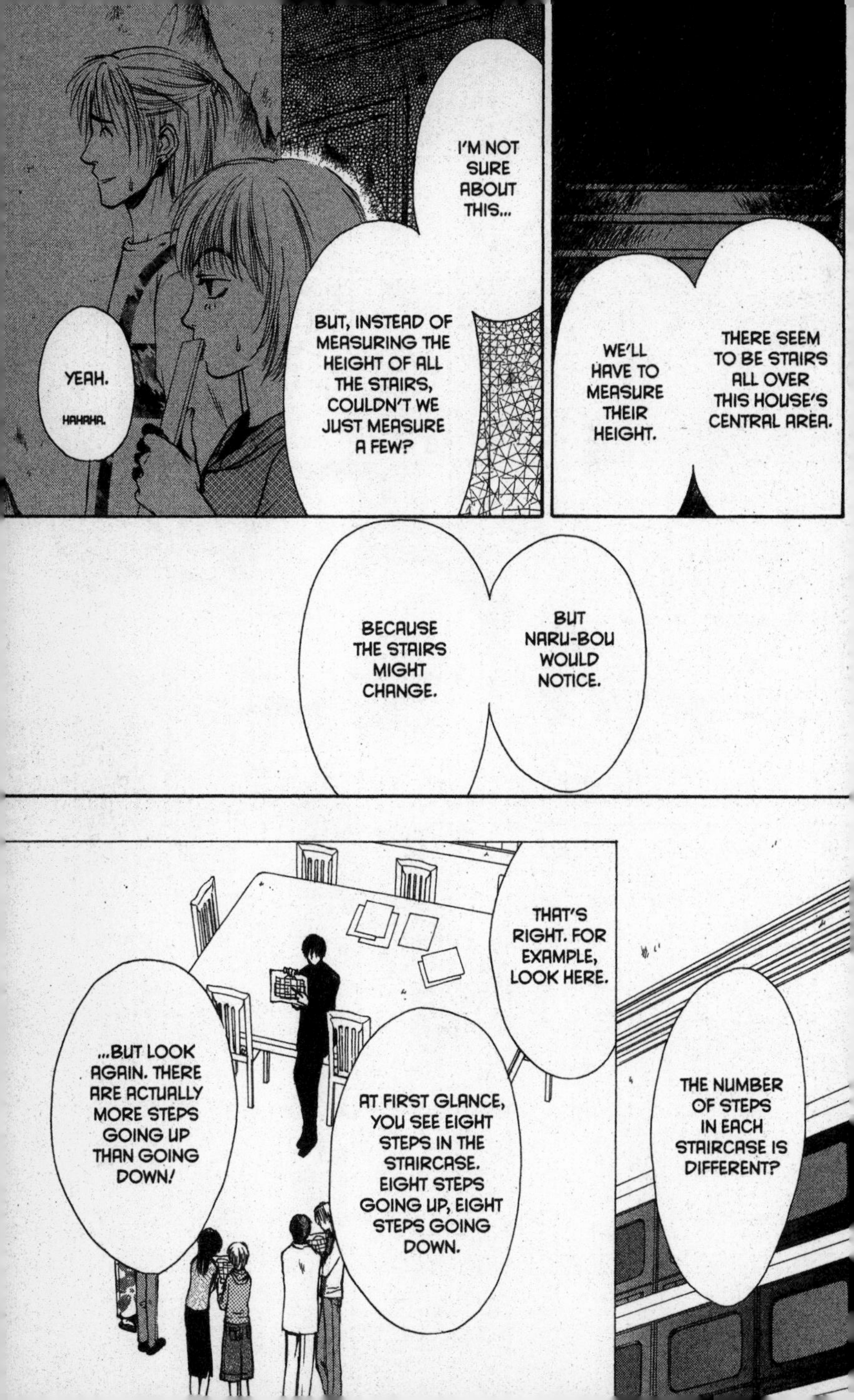
THERE SEEM TO BE STAIRS ALL OVER THIS HOUSE'S CENTRAL AREA.
WE'LL HAVE TO MEASURE THEIR HEIGHT.
I'M NOT SURE ABOUT THIS...
BUT, INSTEAD OF MEASURING THE HEIGHT OF ALL THE STAIRS, COULDN'T WE JUST MEASURE A FEW?
YEAH.
HAHAHA.
BUT NARU-BOU WOULD NOTICE.
BECAUSE THE STAIRS MIGHT CHANGE.
THE NUMBER OF STEPS IN EACH STAIRCASE IS DIFFERENT?
THAT'S RIGHT. FOR EXAMPLE, LOOK HERE.
AT FIRST GLANCE, YOU SEE EIGHT STEPS IN THE STAIRCASE. EIGHT STEPS GOING UP, EIGHT STEPS GOING DOWN.
...BUT LOOK AGAIN. THERE ARE ACTUALLY MORE STEPS GOING UP THAN GOING DOWN!

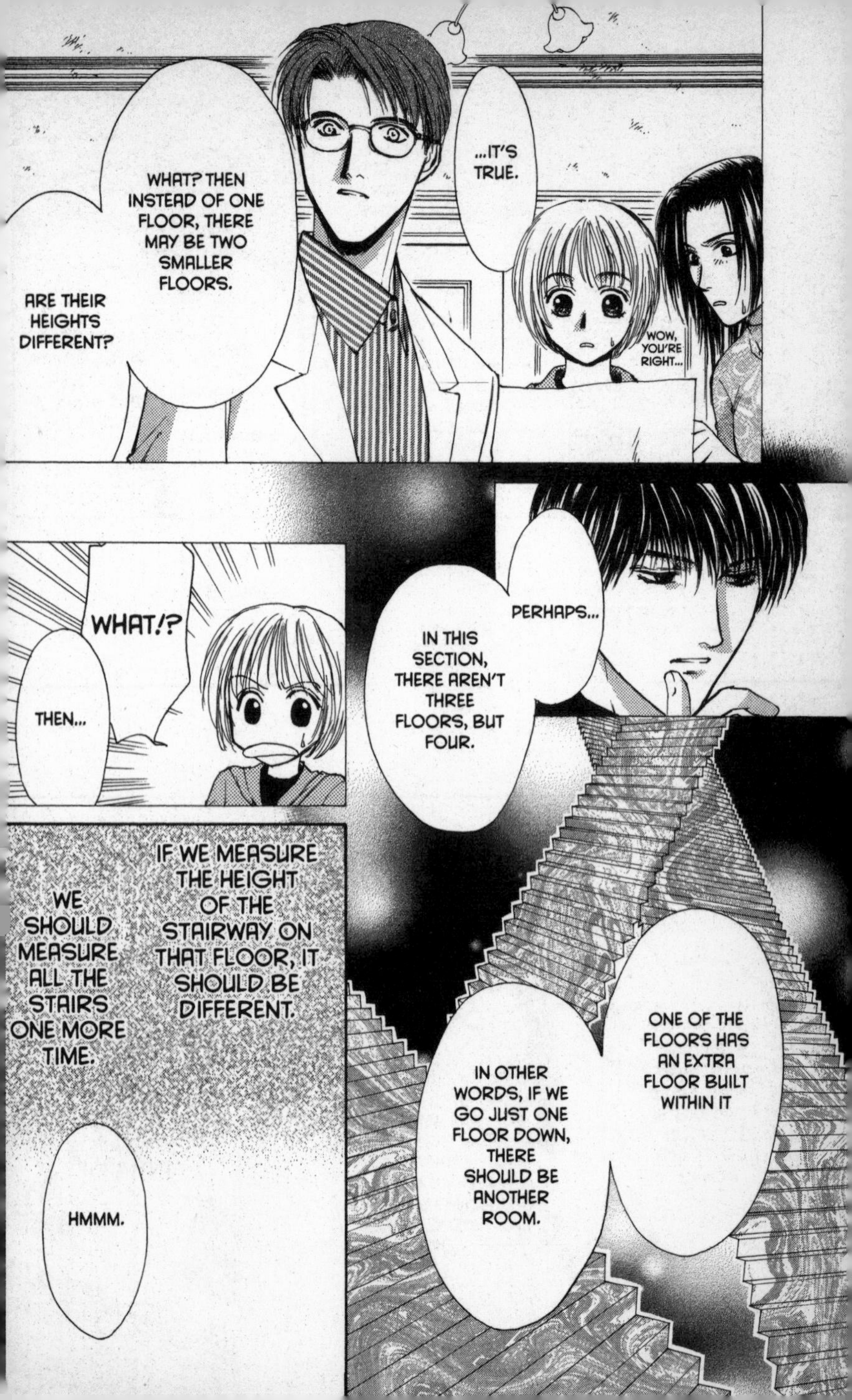
...IT'S TRUE.
WOW, YOU'RE RIGHT...
WHAT? THEN INSTEAD OF ONE FLOOR, THERE MAY BE TWO SMALLER FLOORS.
ARE THEIR HEIGHTS DIFFERENT?
PERHAPS...
IN THIS SECTION, THERE AREN'T THREE FLOORS, BUT FOUR.
WHAT!?
THEN...
ONE OF THE FLOORS HAS AN EXTRA FLOOR BUILT WITHIN IT
IN OTHER WORDS, IF WE GO JUST ONE FLOOR DOWN, THERE SHOULD BE ANOTHER ROOM.
IF WE MEASURE THE HEIGHT OF THE STAIRWAY ON THAT FLOOR, IT SHOULD BE DIFFERENT.
WE SHOULD MEASURE ALL THE STAIRS ONE MORE TIME.
HMMM.

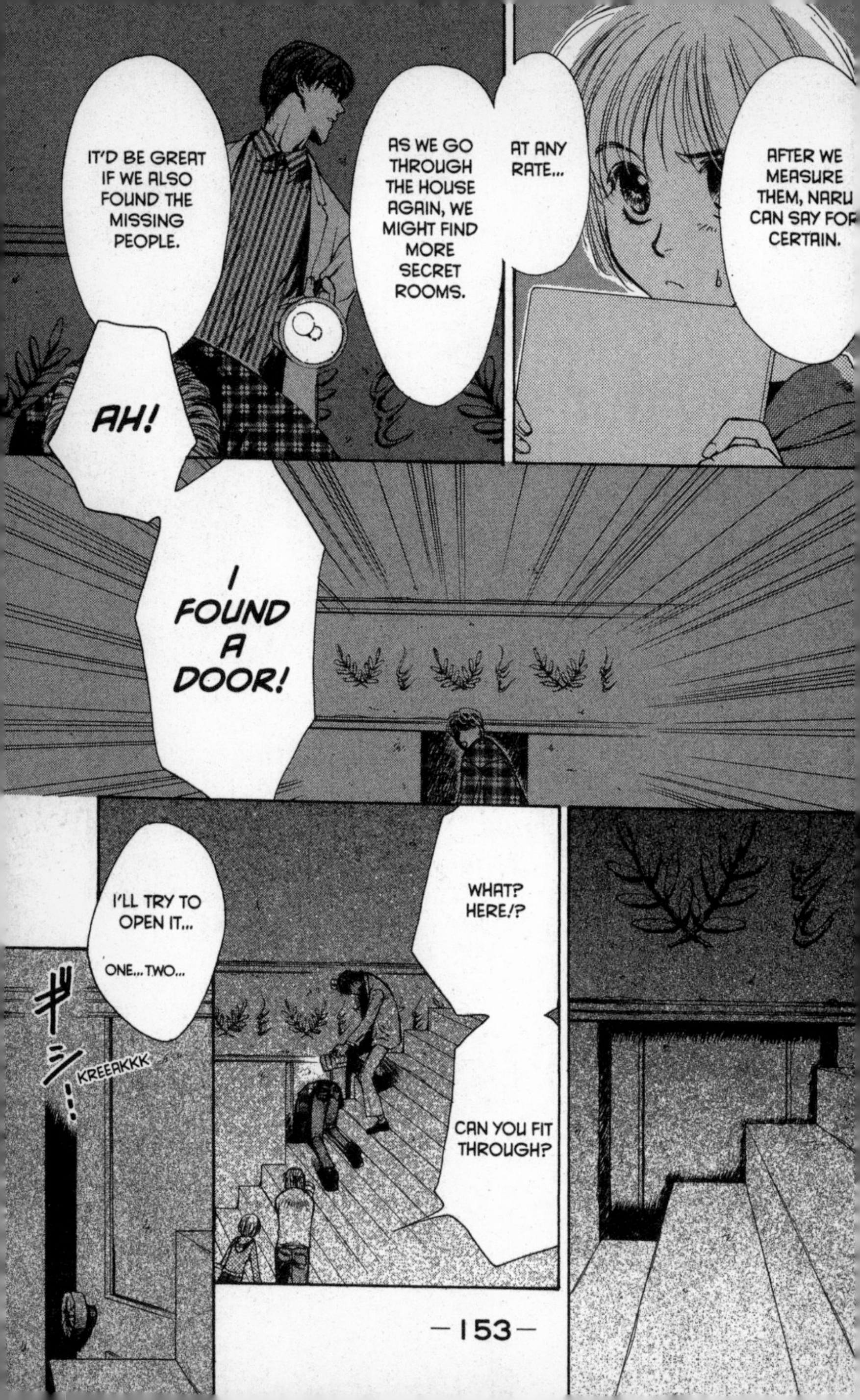
AFTER WE MEASURE THEM, NARU CAN SAY FOR CERTAIN.
AT ANY RATE...
AS WE GO THROUGH THE HOUSE AGAIN, WE MIGHT FIND MORE SECRET ROOMS.
IT'D BE GREAT IF WE ALSO FOUND THE MISSING PEOPLE.
AH!
I FOUND A DOOR!
WHAT? HERE!?
CAN YOU FIT THROUGH?
I'LL TRY TO OPEN IT...
ONE... TWO...
KREEAKKK

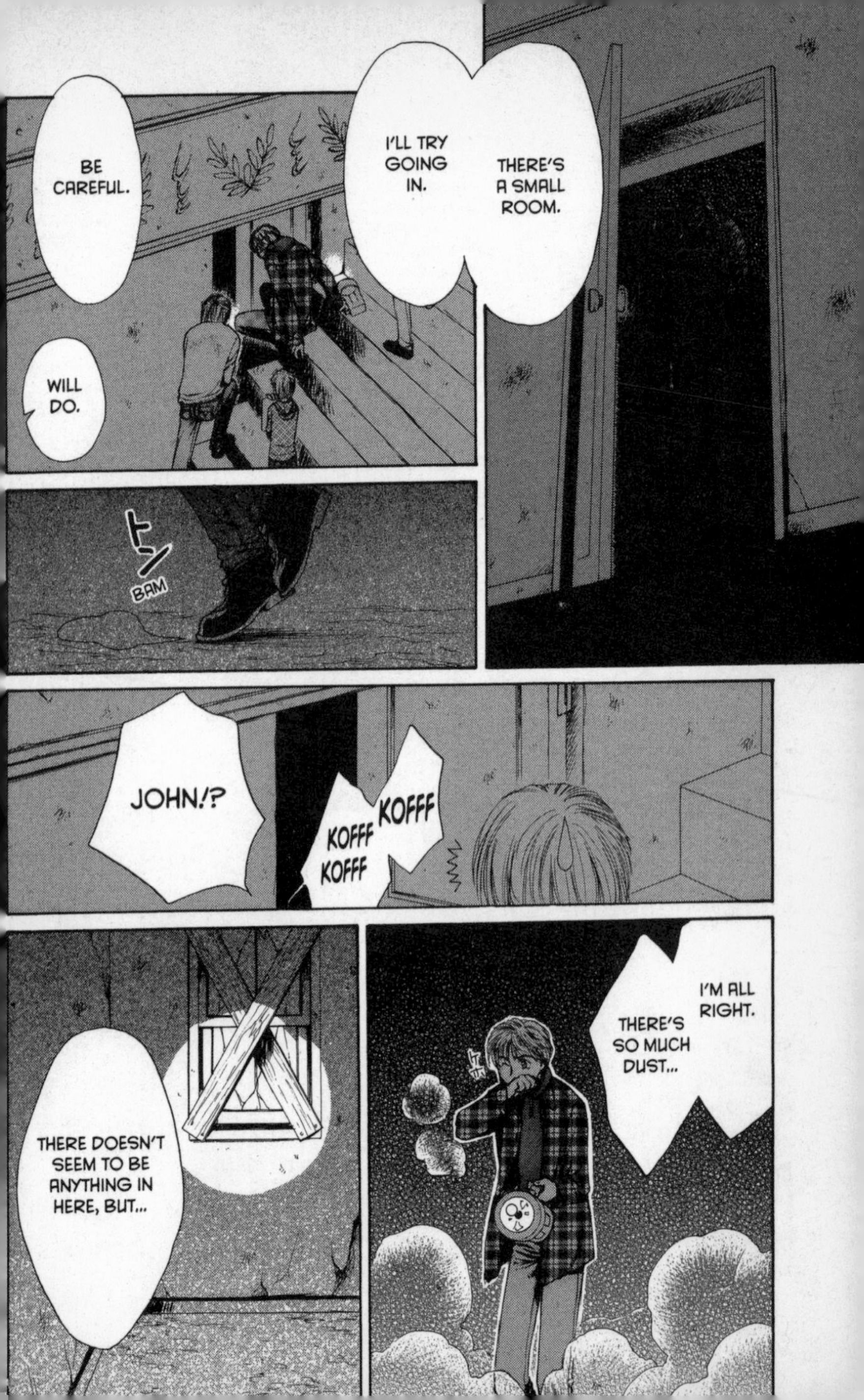
THERE'S A SMALL ROOM.
I'LL TRY GOING IN.
BE CAREFUL.
WILL DO.
BAM
KOFFF
KOFFF KOFFF
JOHN!?
I'M ALL RIGHT.
THERE'S SO MUCH DUST...
THERE DOESN'T SEEM TO BE ANYTHING IN HERE, BUT...

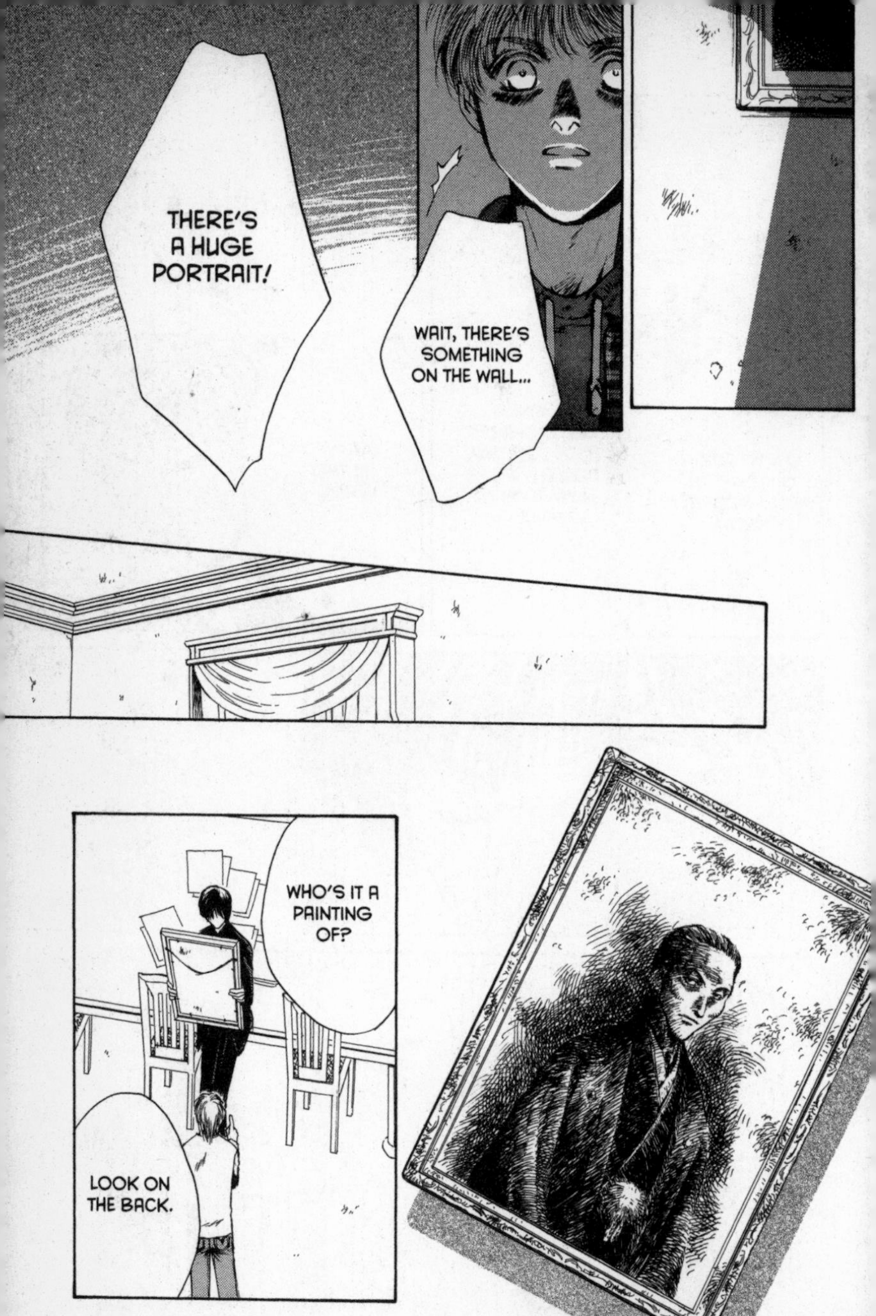
WAIT, THERE'S SOMETHING ON THE WALL...
THERE'S A HUGE PORTRAIT!
WHO'S IT A PAINTING OF?
LOOK ON THE BACK.

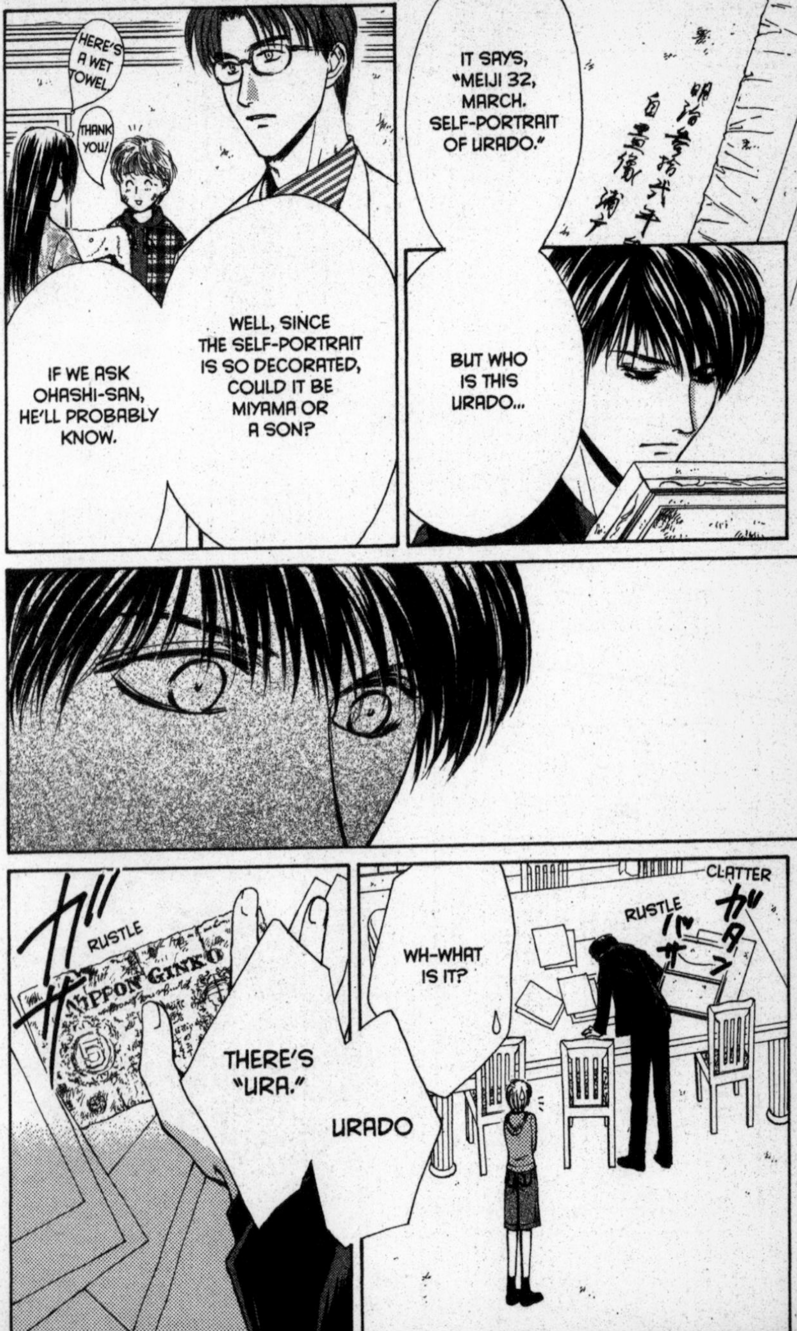
IT SAYS, "MEIJI 32, MARCH. SELF-PORTRAIT OF URADO."
BUT WHO IS THIS URADO...
HERE'S A WET TOWEL.
THANK YOU!
WELL, SINCE THE SELF-PORTRAIT IS SO DECORATED, COULD IT BE MIYAMA OR A SON?
IF WE ASK OHASHI-SAN, HE'LL PROBABLY KNOW.
CLATTER
ガタン
RUSTLE
バサ
WH-WHAT IS IT?
THERE'S "URA."
URADO
RUSTLE
NIPPON GINKO

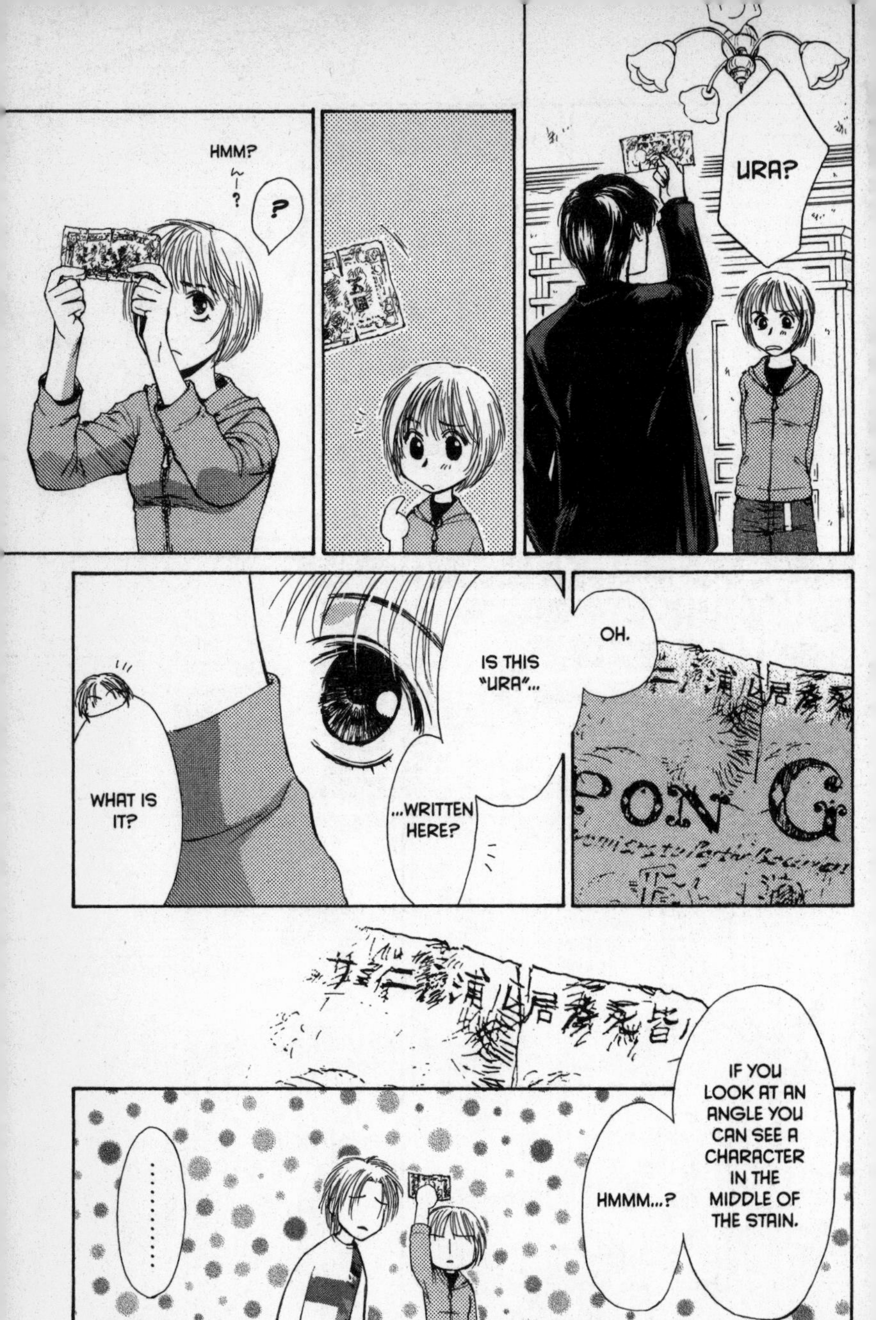
URA?
HMM?
ん～?
?
OH.
IS THIS "URA"...
...WRITTEN HERE?
WHAT IS IT?
PON G
IF YOU LOOK AT AN ANGLE YOU CAN SEE A CHARACTER IN THE MIDDLE OF THE STAIN.
HMMM...?
......

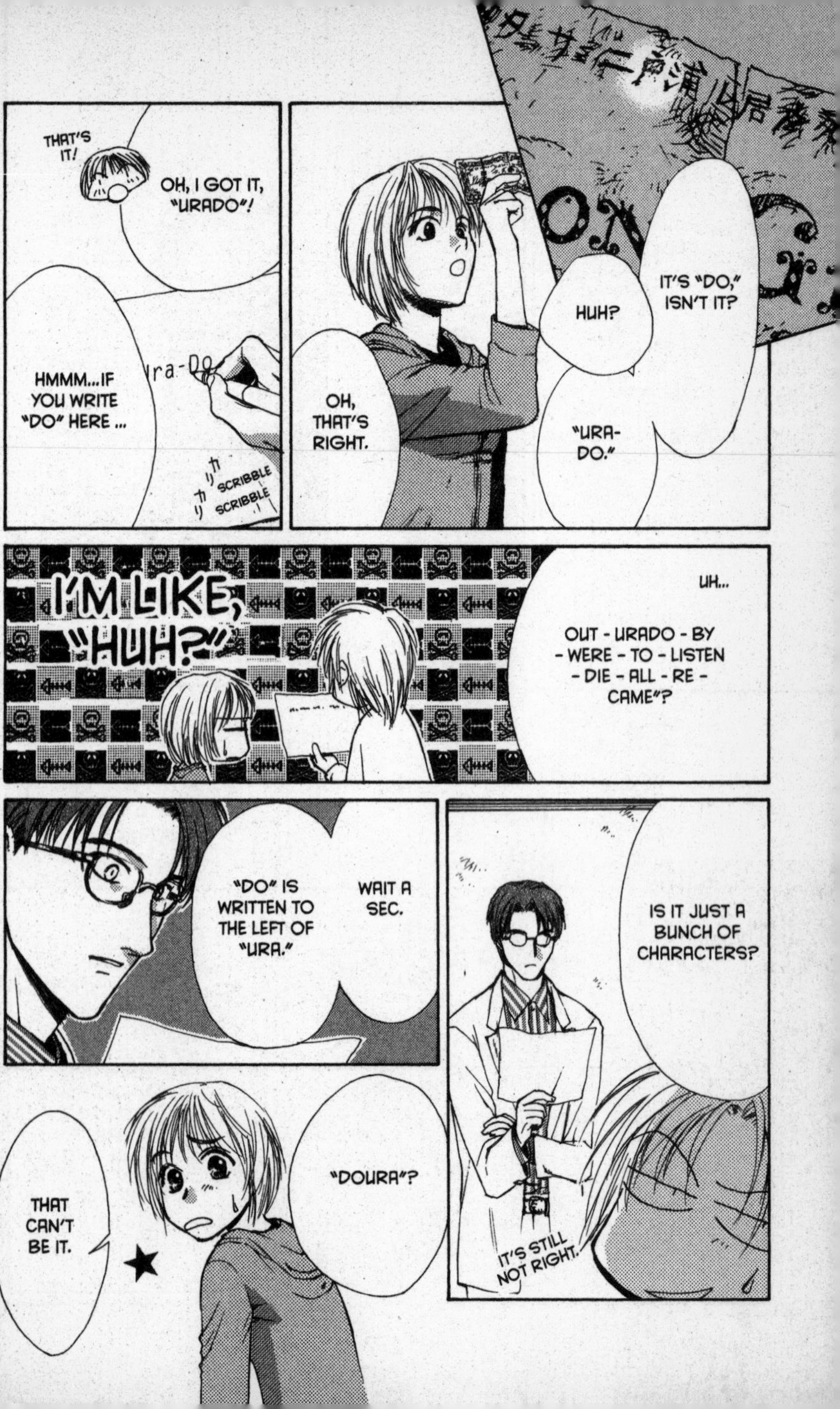
IT'S "DO," ISN'T IT?
HUH?
"URA-DO."
OH, THAT'S RIGHT.
THAT'S IT!
OH, I GOT IT, "URADO"!
HMMM...IF YOU WRITE "DO" HERE ...
Ura-Do
SCRIBBLE SCRIBBLE
UH...
OUT - URADO - BY - WERE - TO - LISTEN - DIE - ALL - RE - CAME"?
I'M LIKE, "HUH?"
IS IT JUST A BUNCH OF CHARACTERS?
IT'S STILL NOT RIGHT.
WAIT A SEC.
"DO" IS WRITTEN TO THE LEFT OF "URA."
"DOURA"?
THAT CAN'T BE IT.

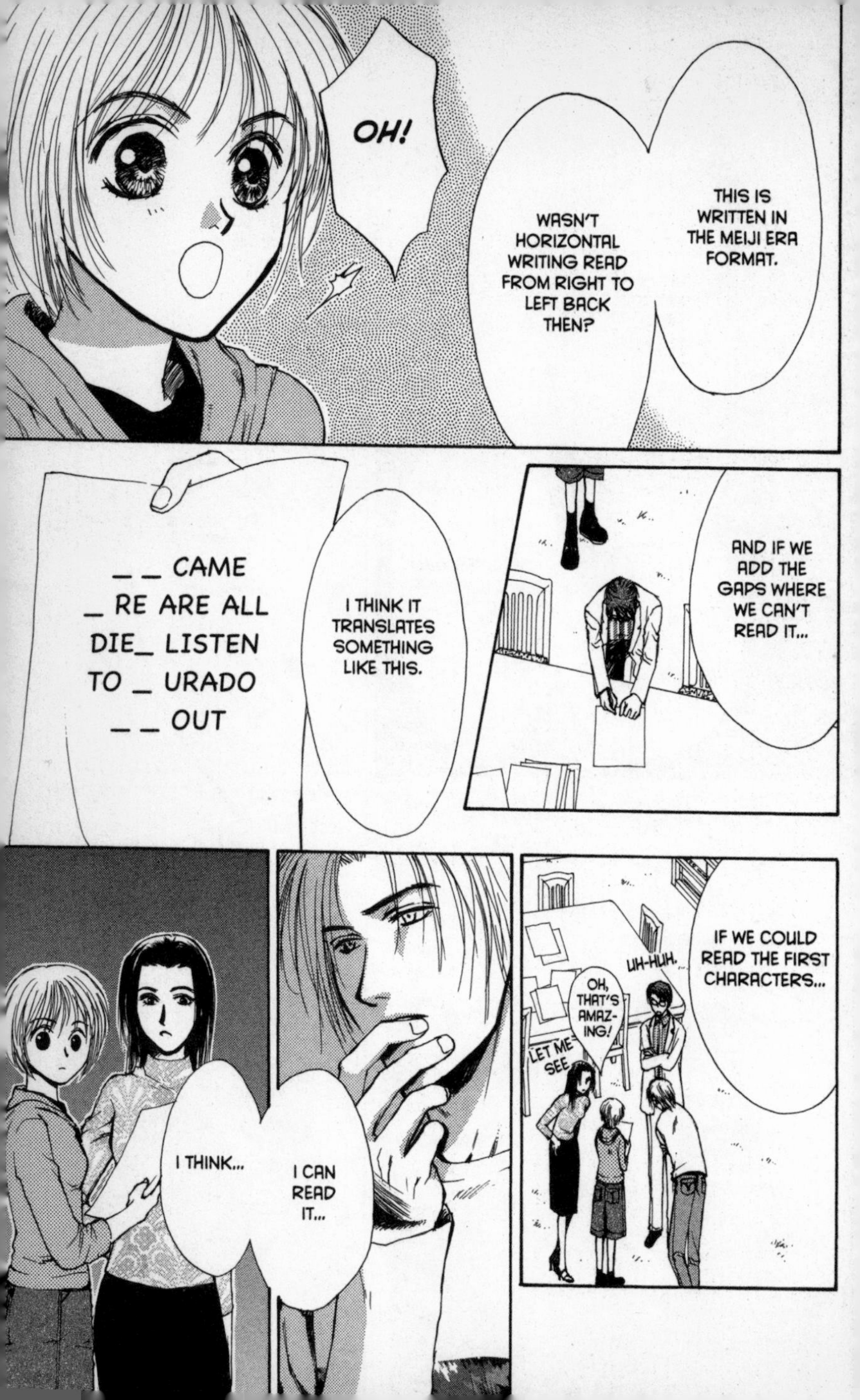
THIS IS WRITTEN IN THE MEIJI ERA FORMAT.
WASN'T HORIZONTAL WRITING READ FROM RIGHT TO LEFT BACK THEN?
OH!
AND IF WE ADD THE GAPS WHERE WE CAN'T READ IT...
I THINK IT TRANSLATES SOMETHING LIKE THIS.
_ _ CAME
_ RE ARE ALL
DIE_ LISTEN
TO _ URADO
_ _ OUT
IF WE COULD READ THE FIRST CHARACTERS...
UH-HUH.
OH, THAT'S AMAZ-ING!
LET ME SEE
I THINK...
I CAN READ IT...

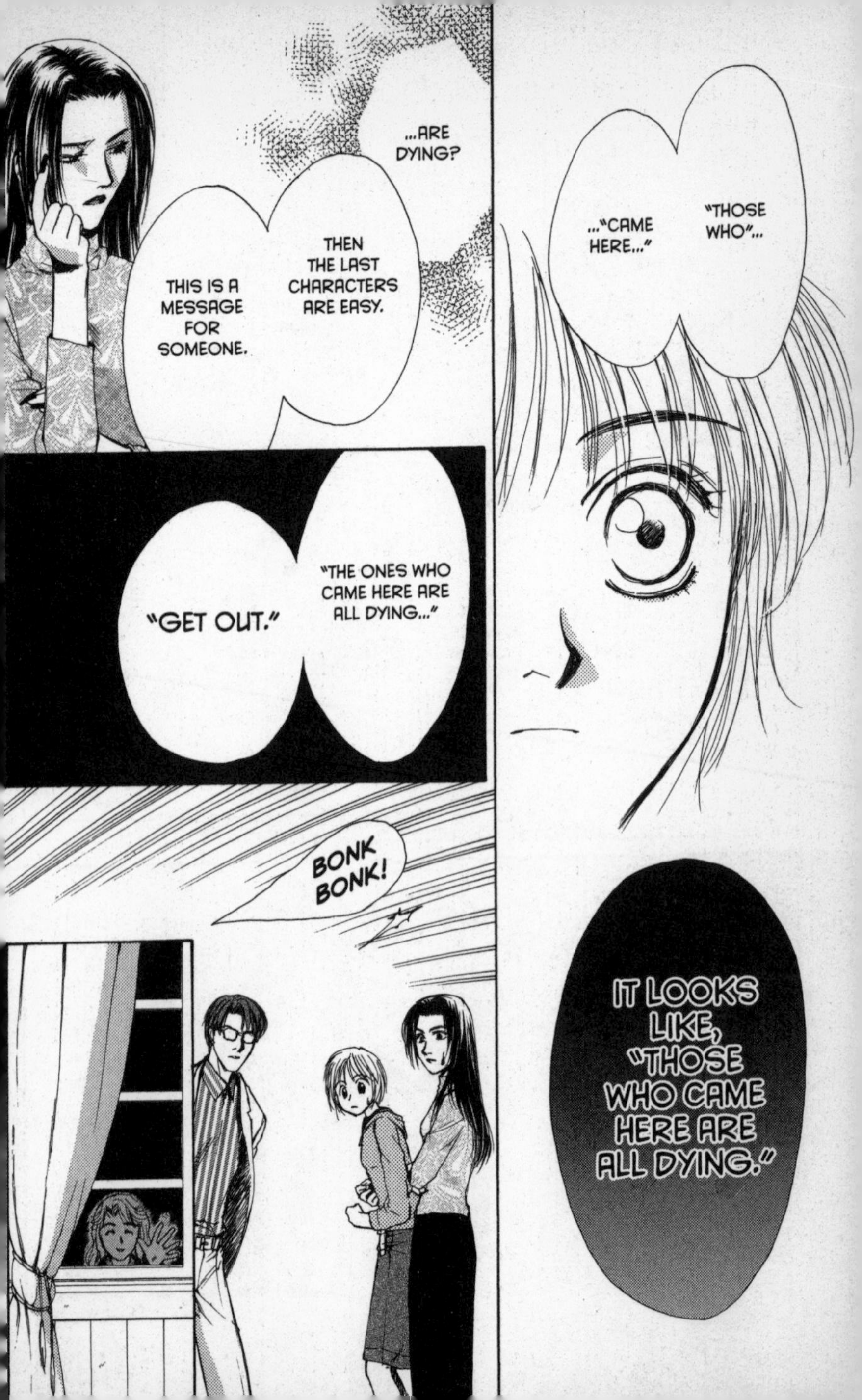
"THOSE WHO"...
..."CAME HERE..."
IT LOOKS LIKE, "THOSE WHO CAME HERE ARE ALL DYING."
...ARE DYING?
THEN THE LAST CHARACTERS ARE EASY.
THIS IS A MESSAGE FOR SOMEONE.
"THE ONES WHO CAME HERE ARE ALL DYING..."
"GET OUT."
BONK BONK!

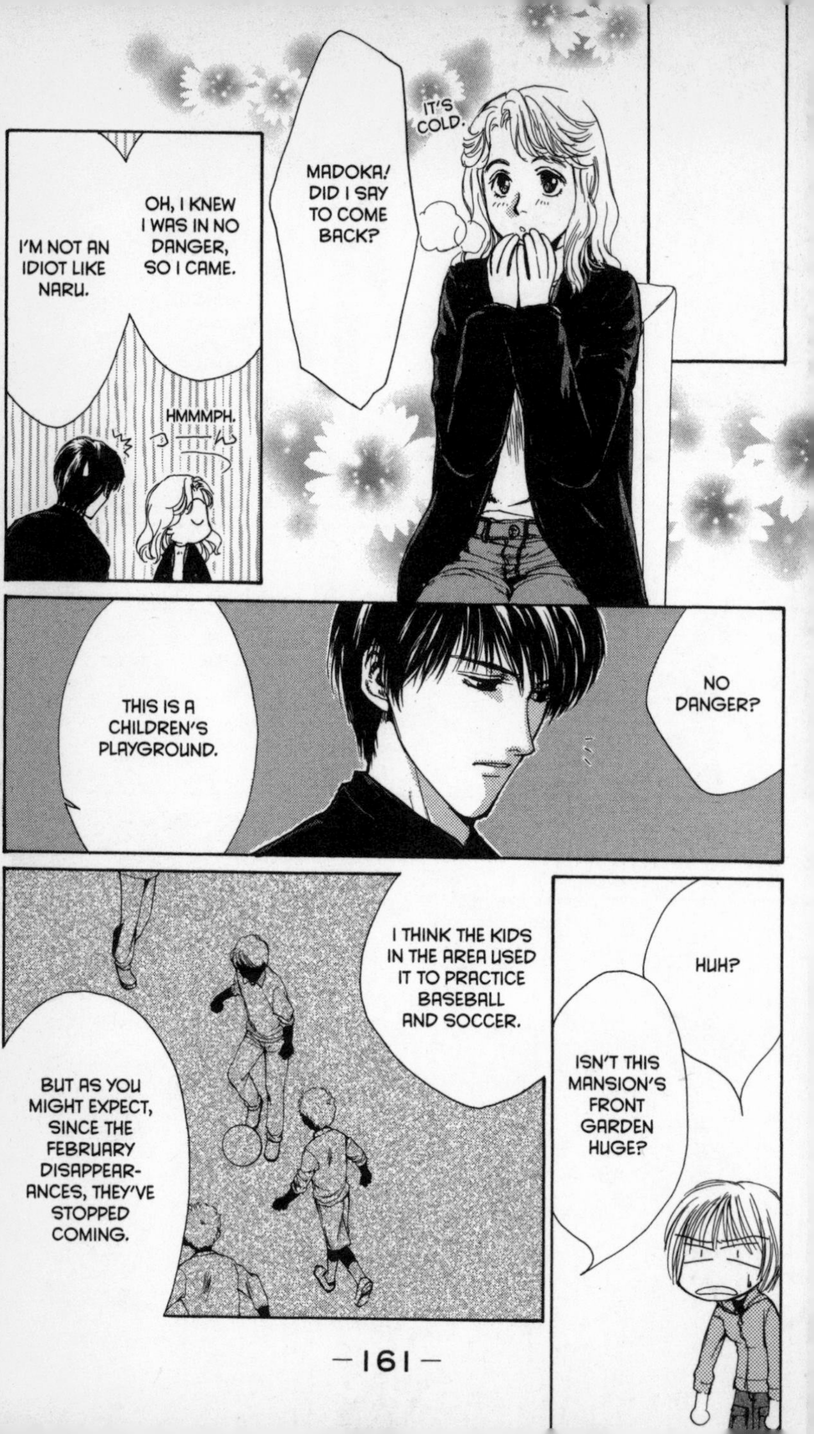
IT'S COLD.
MADOKA! DID I SAY TO COME BACK?
OH, I KNEW I WAS IN NO DANGER, SO I CAME.
I'M NOT AN IDIOT LIKE NARU.
HMMMPH.
NO DANGER?
THIS IS A CHILDREN'S PLAYGROUND.
HUH?
ISN'T THIS MANSION'S FRONT GARDEN HUGE?
I THINK THE KIDS IN THE AREA USED IT TO PRACTICE BASEBALL AND SOCCER.
BUT AS YOU MIGHT EXPECT, SINCE THE FEBRUARY DISAPPEAR-ANCES, THEY'VE STOPPED COMING.

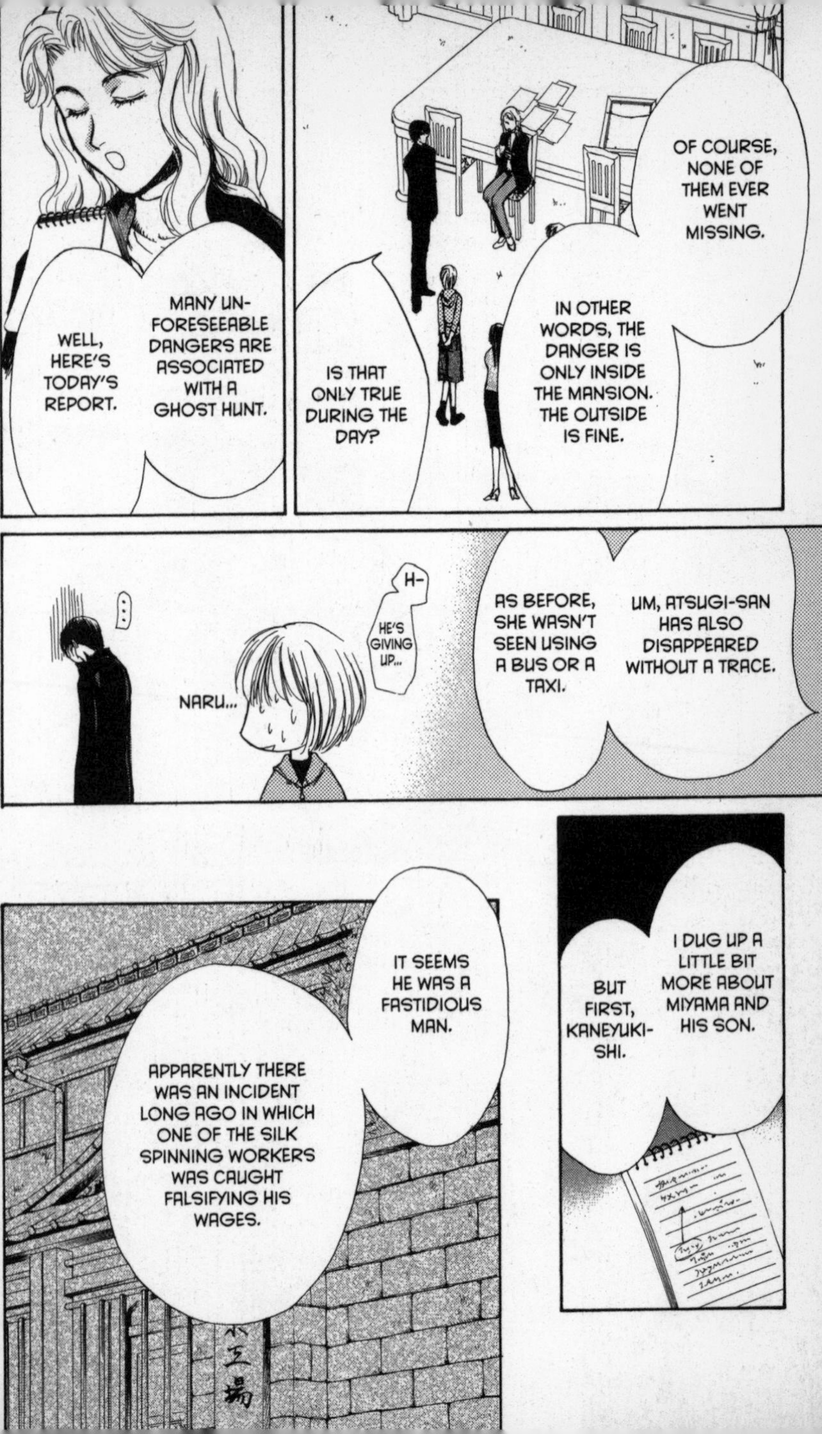
OF COURSE, NONE OF THEM EVER WENT MISSING.
IN OTHER WORDS, THE DANGER IS ONLY INSIDE THE MANSION. THE OUTSIDE IS FINE.
IS THAT ONLY TRUE DURING THE DAY?
MANY UN-FORESEEABLE DANGERS ARE ASSOCIATED WITH A GHOST HUNT.
WELL, HERE'S TODAY'S REPORT.
UM, ATSUGI-SAN HAS ALSO DISAPPEARED WITHOUT A TRACE.
AS BEFORE, SHE WASN'T SEEN USING A BUS OR A TAXI.
H-
HE'S GIVING UP...
NARU...
...
I DUG UP A LITTLE BIT MORE ABOUT MIYAMA AND HIS SON.
BUT FIRST, KANEYUKI-SHI.
IT SEEMS HE WAS A FASTIDIOUS MAN.
APPARENTLY THERE WAS AN INCIDENT LONG AGO IN WHICH ONE OF THE SILK SPINNING WORKERS WAS CAUGHT FALSIFYING HIS WAGES.

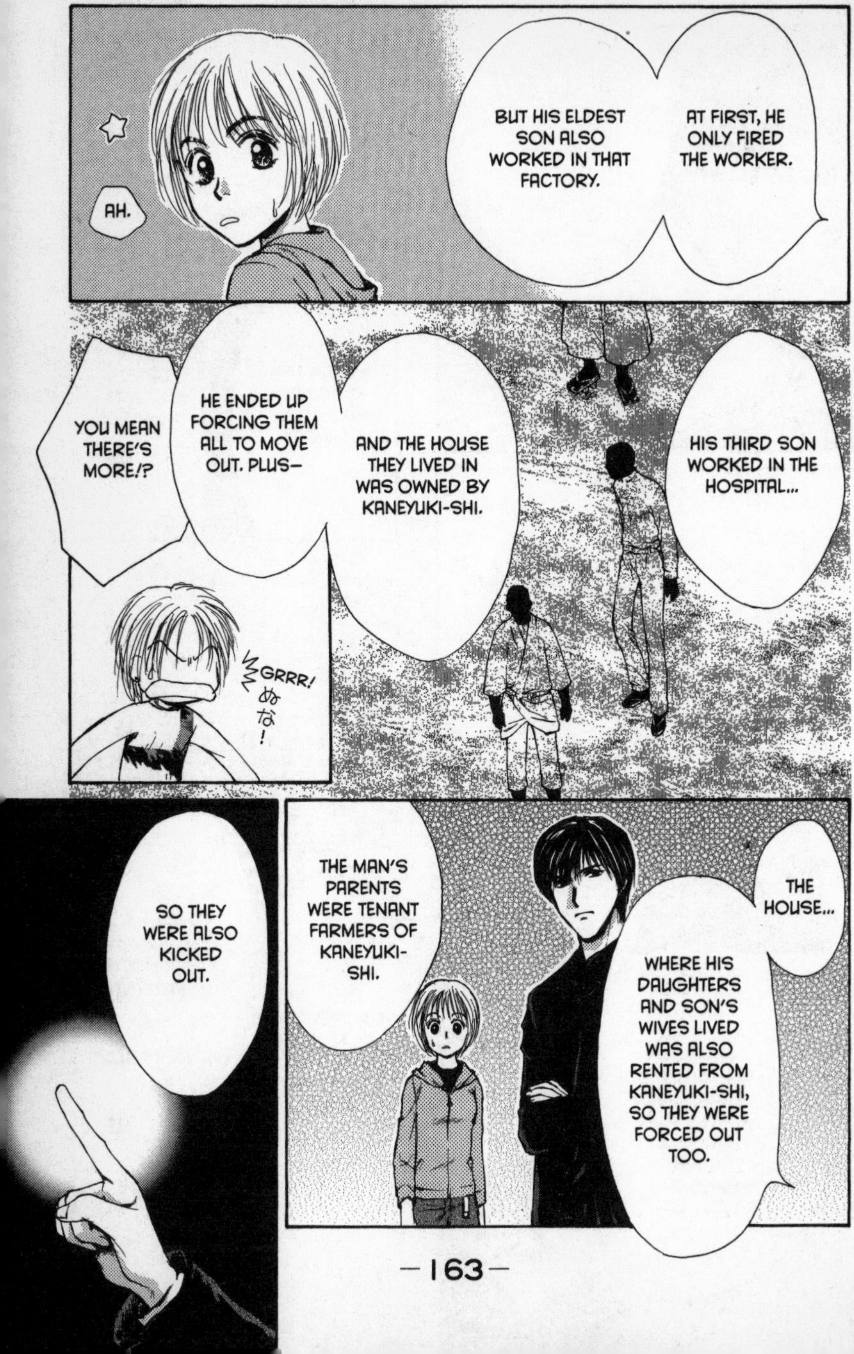
AT FIRST, HE ONLY FIRED THE WORKER.
BUT HIS ELDEST SON ALSO WORKED IN THAT FACTORY.
AH.
HIS THIRD SON WORKED IN THE HOSPITAL...
AND THE HOUSE THEY LIVED IN WAS OWNED BY KANEYUKI-SHI.
HE ENDED UP FORCING THEM ALL TO MOVE OUT. PLUS—
YOU MEAN THERE'S MORE!?
GRRR!
ぬな!
THE HOUSE...
WHERE HIS DAUGHTERS AND SON'S WIVES LIVED WAS ALSO RENTED FROM KANEYUKI-SHI, SO THEY WERE FORCED OUT TOO.
THE MAN'S PARENTS WERE TENANT FARMERS OF KANEYUKI-SHI.
SO THEY WERE ALSO KICKED OUT.

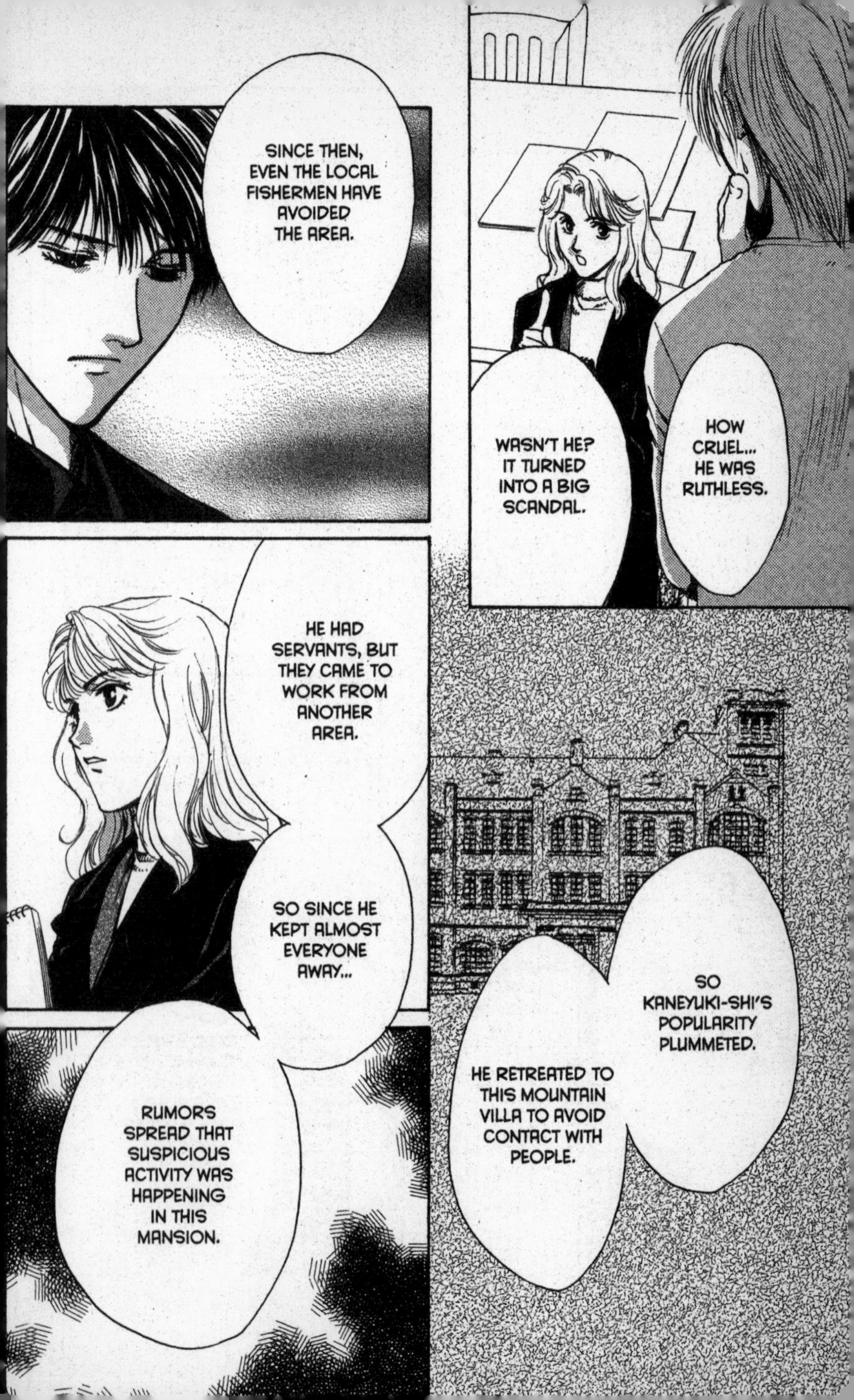
HOW CRUEL... HE WAS RUTHLESS.
WASN'T HE? IT TURNED INTO A BIG SCANDAL.
SO KANEYUKI-SHI'S POPULARITY PLUMMETED.
HE RETREATED TO THIS MOUNTAIN VILLA TO AVOID CONTACT WITH PEOPLE.
SINCE THEN, EVEN THE LOCAL FISHERMEN HAVE AVOIDED THE AREA.
HE HAD SERVANTS, BUT THEY CAME TO WORK FROM ANOTHER AREA.
SO SINCE HE KEPT ALMOST EVERYONE AWAY...
RUMORS SPREAD THAT SUSPICIOUS ACTIVITY WAS HAPPENING IN THIS MANSION.

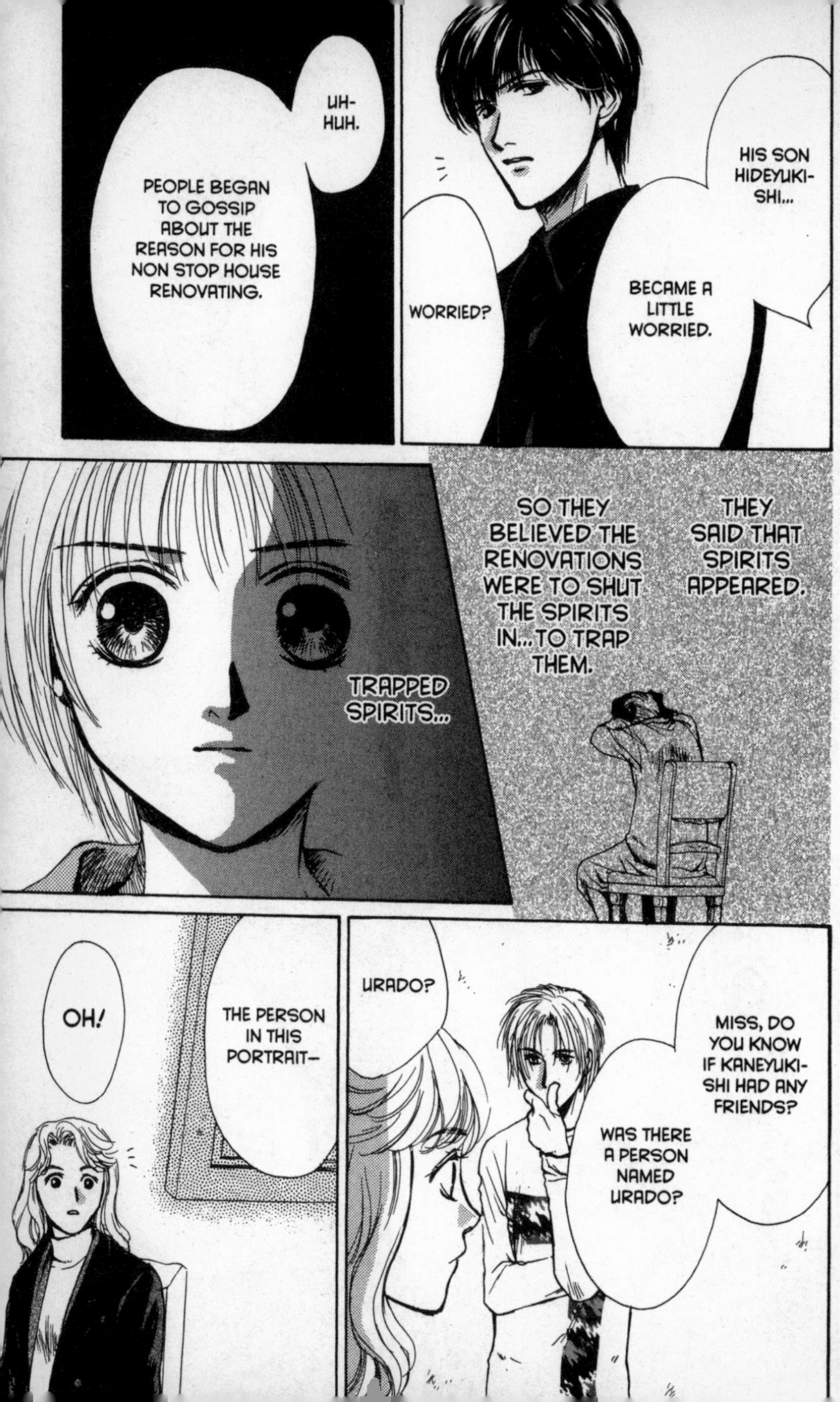
HIS SON HIDEYUKI-SHI...
BECAME A LITTLE WORRIED.
WORRIED?
UH-HUH.
PEOPLE BEGAN TO GOSSIP ABOUT THE REASON FOR HIS NON STOP HOUSE RENOVATING.
THEY SAID THAT SPIRITS APPEARED.
SO THEY BELIEVED THE RENOVATIONS WERE TO SHUT THE SPIRITS IN... TO TRAP THEM.
TRAPPED SPIRITS...
MISS, DO YOU KNOW IF KANEYUKI-SHI HAD ANY FRIENDS?
WAS THERE A PERSON NAMED URADO?
URADO?
THE PERSON IN THIS PORTRAIT—
OH!

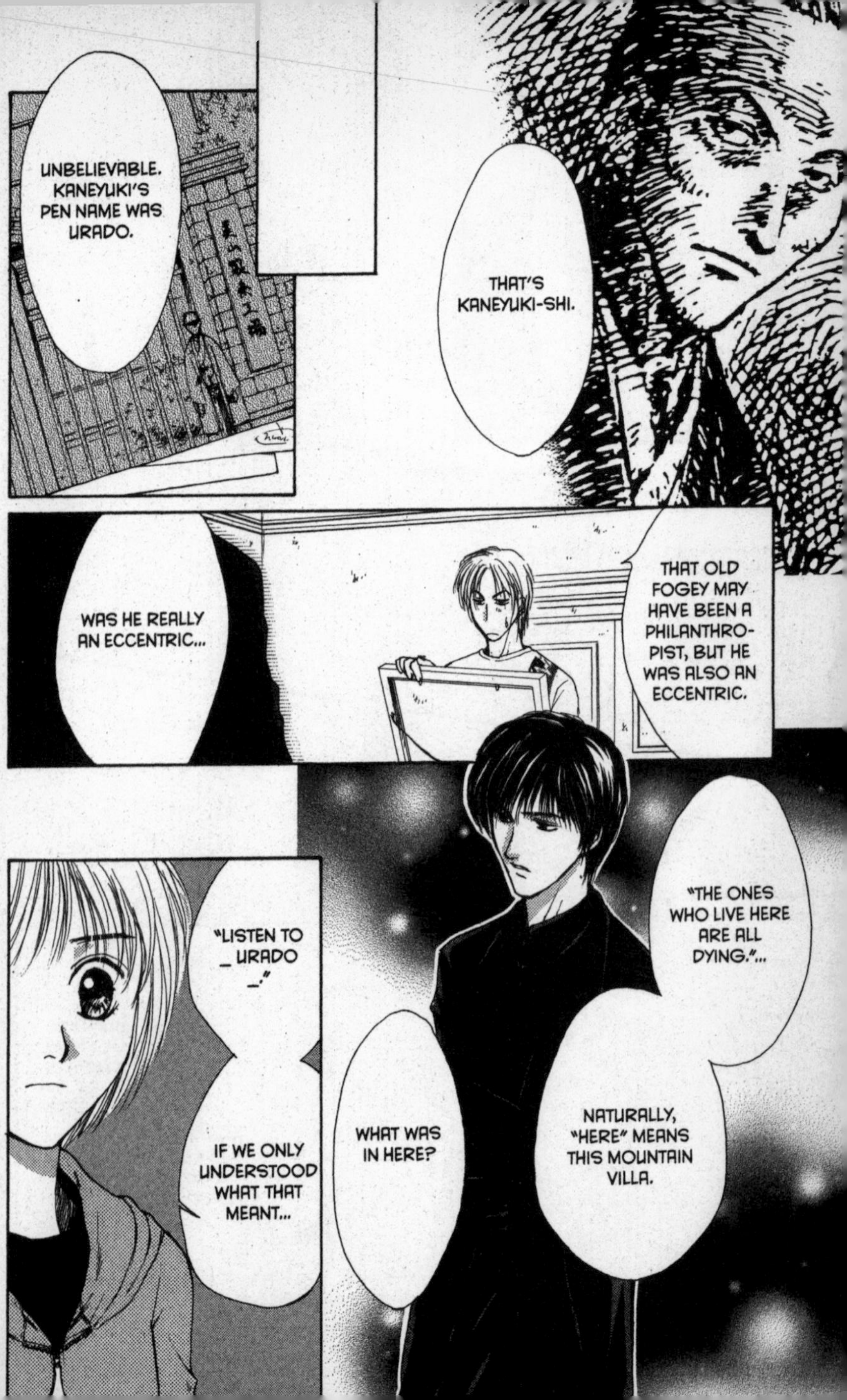
THAT'S KANEYUKI-SHI.
UNBELIEVABLE. KANEYUKI'S PEN NAME WAS URADO.
THAT OLD FOGEY MAY HAVE BEEN A PHILANTHRO-PIST, BUT HE WAS ALSO AN ECCENTRIC.
WAS HE REALLY AN ECCENTRIC...
"THE ONES WHO LIVE HERE ARE ALL DYING."...
NATURALLY, "HERE" MEANS THIS MOUNTAIN VILLA.
WHAT WAS IN HERE?
"LISTEN TO _ URADO _."
IF WE ONLY UNDERSTOOD WHAT THAT MEANT...

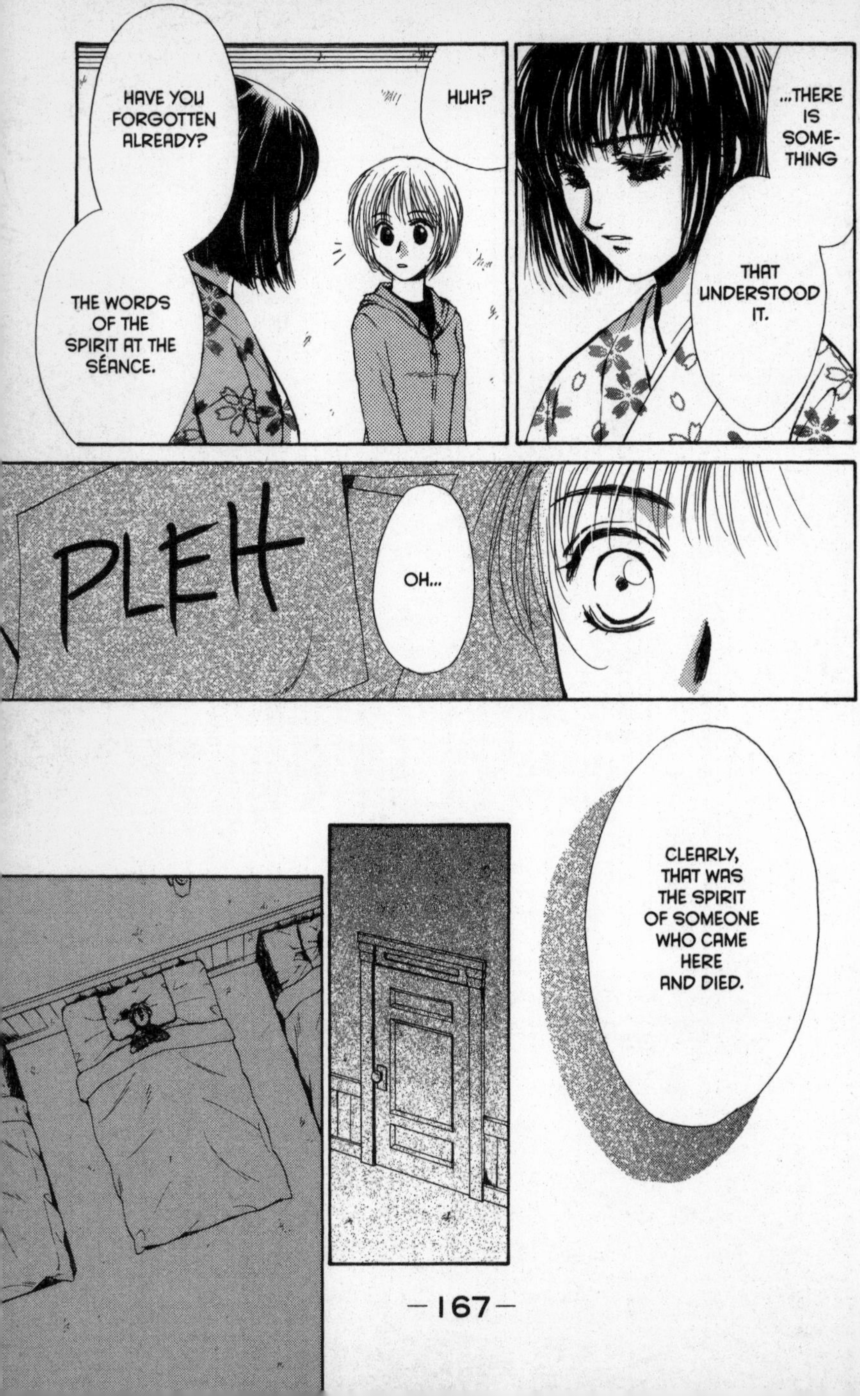
...THERE IS SOME-THING
THAT UNDERSTOOD IT.
HAVE YOU FORGOTTEN ALREADY?
HUH?
THE WORDS OF THE SPIRIT AT THE SÉANCE.
OH...
PLEH
CLEARLY, THAT WAS THE SPIRIT OF SOMEONE WHO CAME HERE AND DIED.

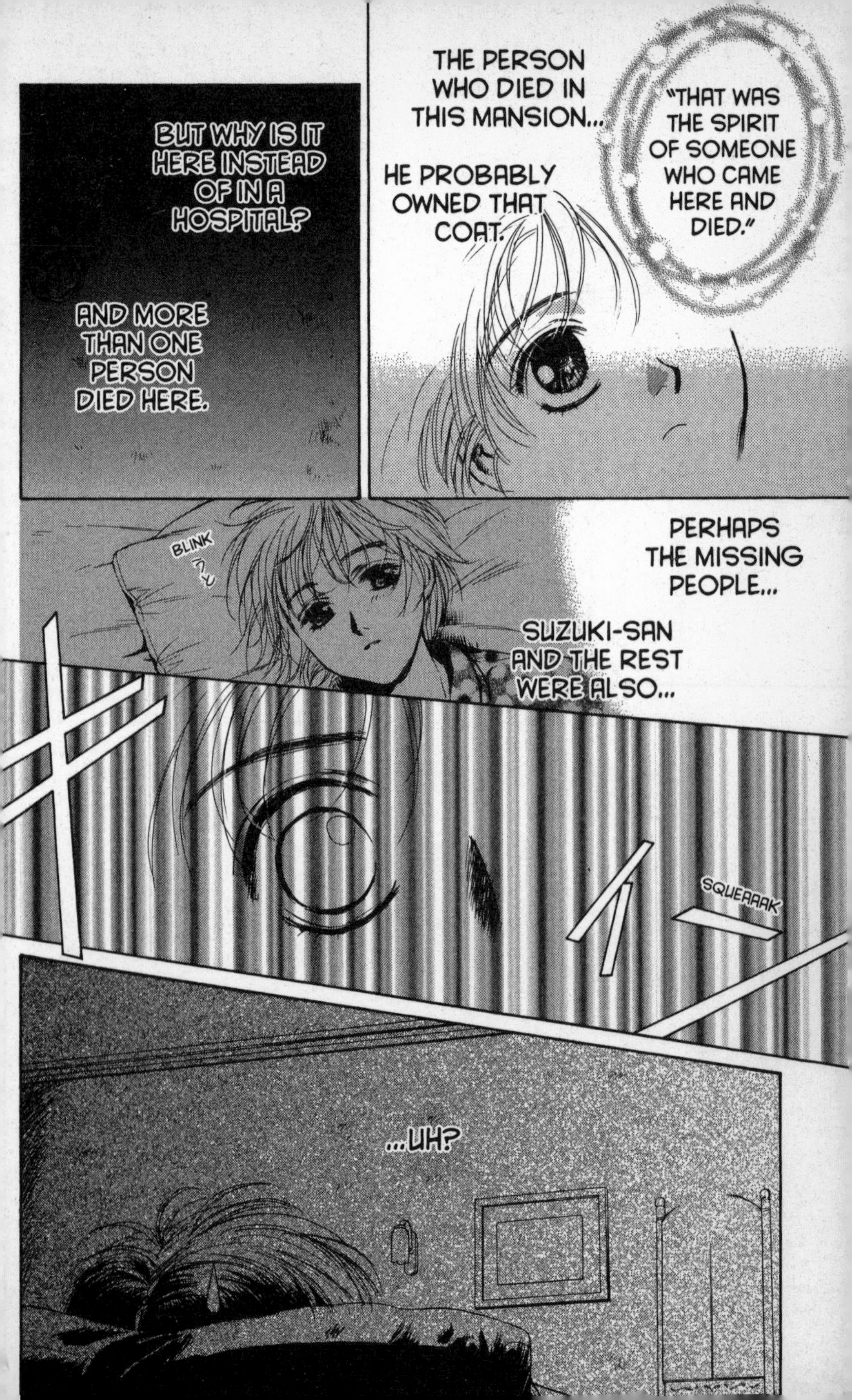
"THAT WAS THE SPIRIT OF SOMEONE WHO CAME HERE AND DIED."
THE PERSON WHO DIED IN THIS MANSION...
HE PROBABLY OWNED THAT COAT.
BUT WHY IS IT HERE INSTEAD OF IN A HOSPITAL?
AND MORE THAN ONE PERSON DIED HERE.
PERHAPS THE MISSING PEOPLE...
SUZUKI-SAN AND THE REST WERE ALSO...
BLINK
SQUEAAAK
...UH?

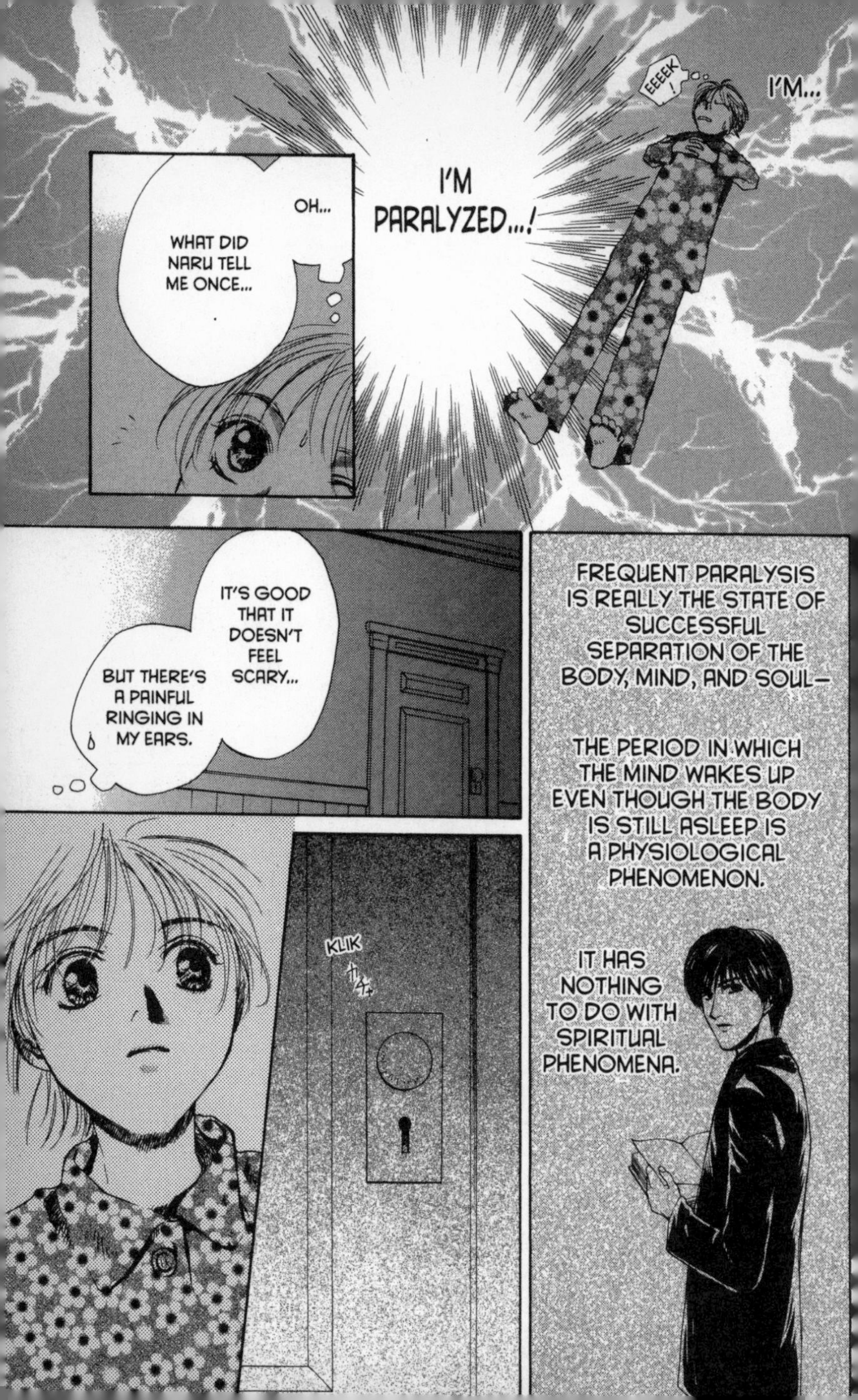
I'M...
EEEEK!
I'M PARALYZED...!
OH...
WHAT DID NARU TELL ME ONCE...
FREQUENT PARALYSIS IS REALLY THE STATE OF SUCCESSFUL SEPARATION OF THE BODY, MIND, AND SOUL—
THE PERIOD IN WHICH THE MIND WAKES UP EVEN THOUGH THE BODY IS STILL ASLEEP IS A PHYSIOLOGICAL PHENOMENON.
IT HAS NOTHING TO DO WITH SPIRITUAL PHENOMENA.
IT'S GOOD THAT IT DOESN'T FEEL SCARY...
BUT THERE'S A PAINFUL RINGING IN MY EARS.
KLIK

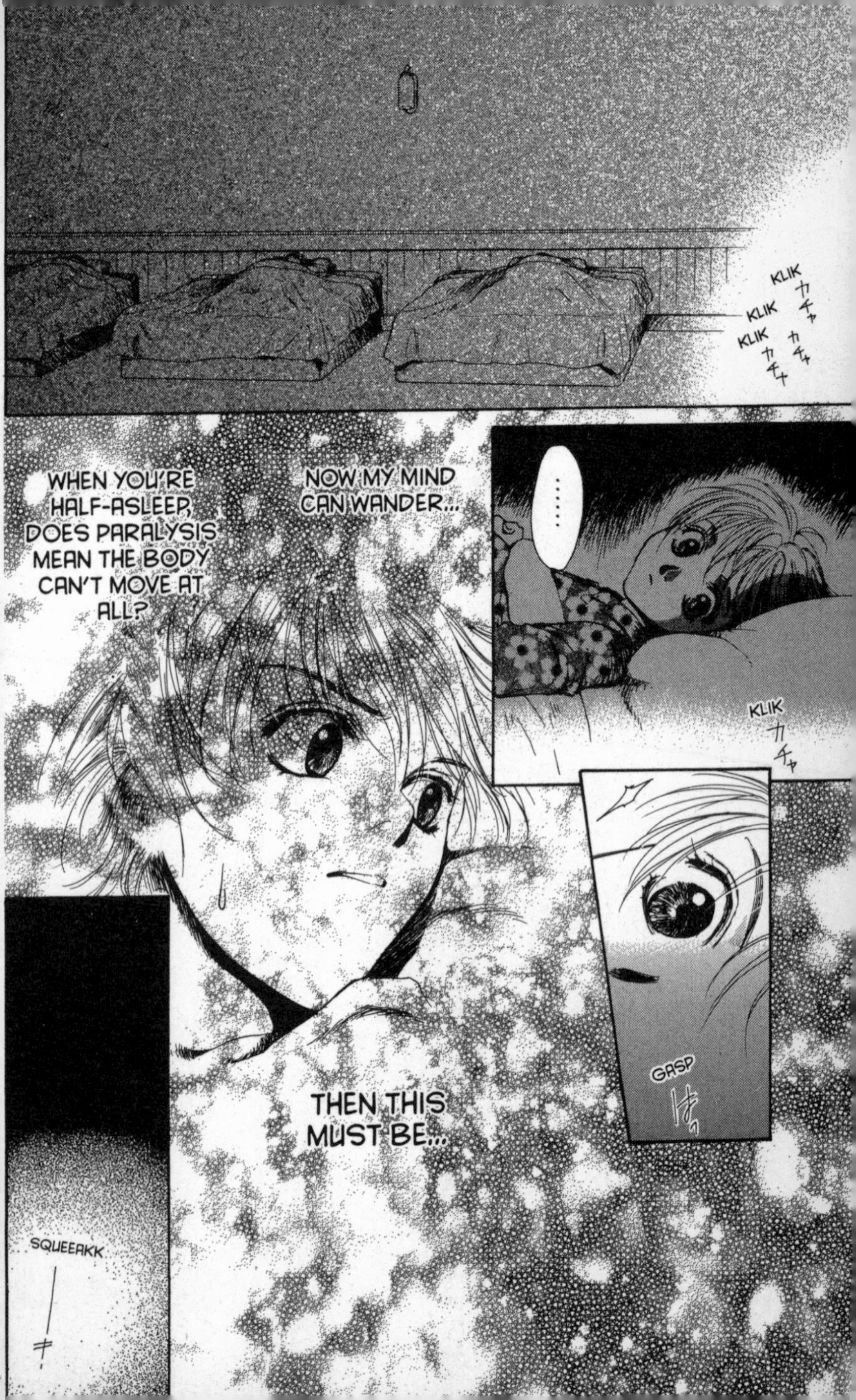
KLIK カチャ
KLIK カチャ
KLIK カチャ
......
KLIK カチャ
NOW MY MIND CAN WANDER...
WHEN YOU'RE HALF-ASLEEP, DOES PARALYSIS MEAN THE BODY CAN'T MOVE AT ALL?
GASP はっ
THEN THIS MUST BE...
SQUEEAKK キー

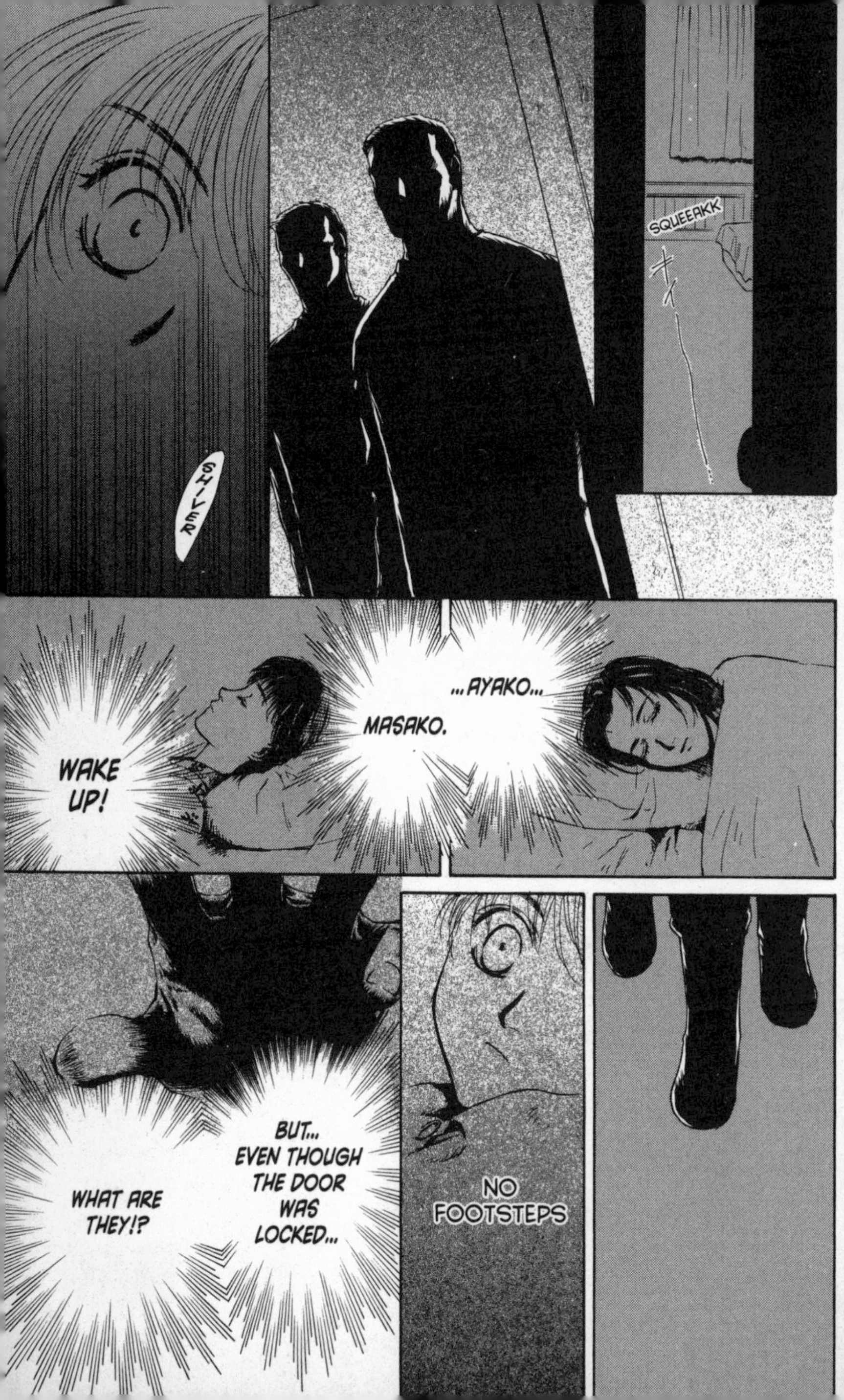
SQUEEAKK
SHIVER
...AYAKO...
MASAKO.
WAKE UP!
NO FOOTSTEPS
BUT... EVEN THOUGH THE DOOR WAS LOCKED...
WHAT ARE THEY!?

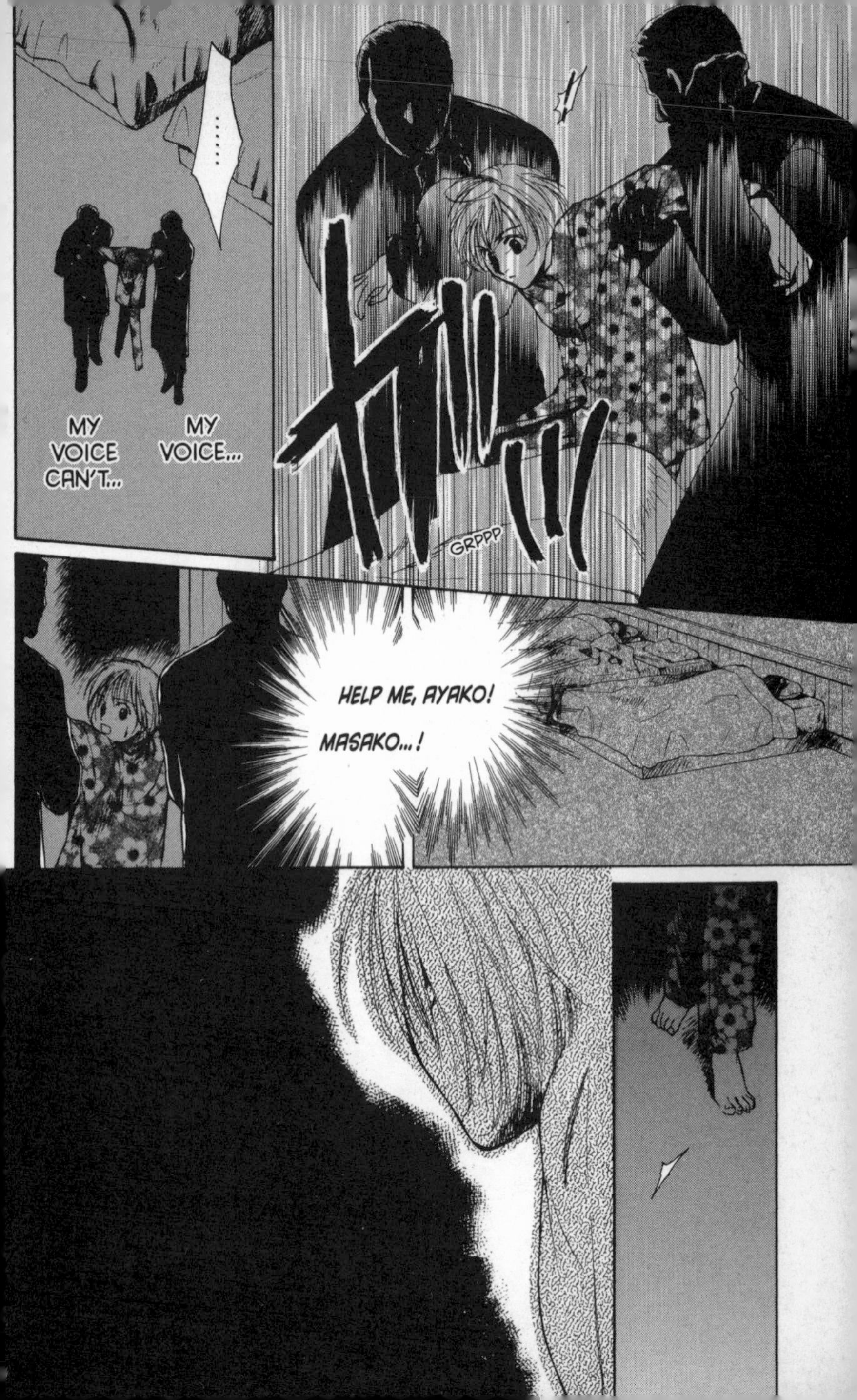
GRPPP
......
MY VOICE...
MY VOICE CAN'T...
HELP ME, AYAKO!
MASAKO...!

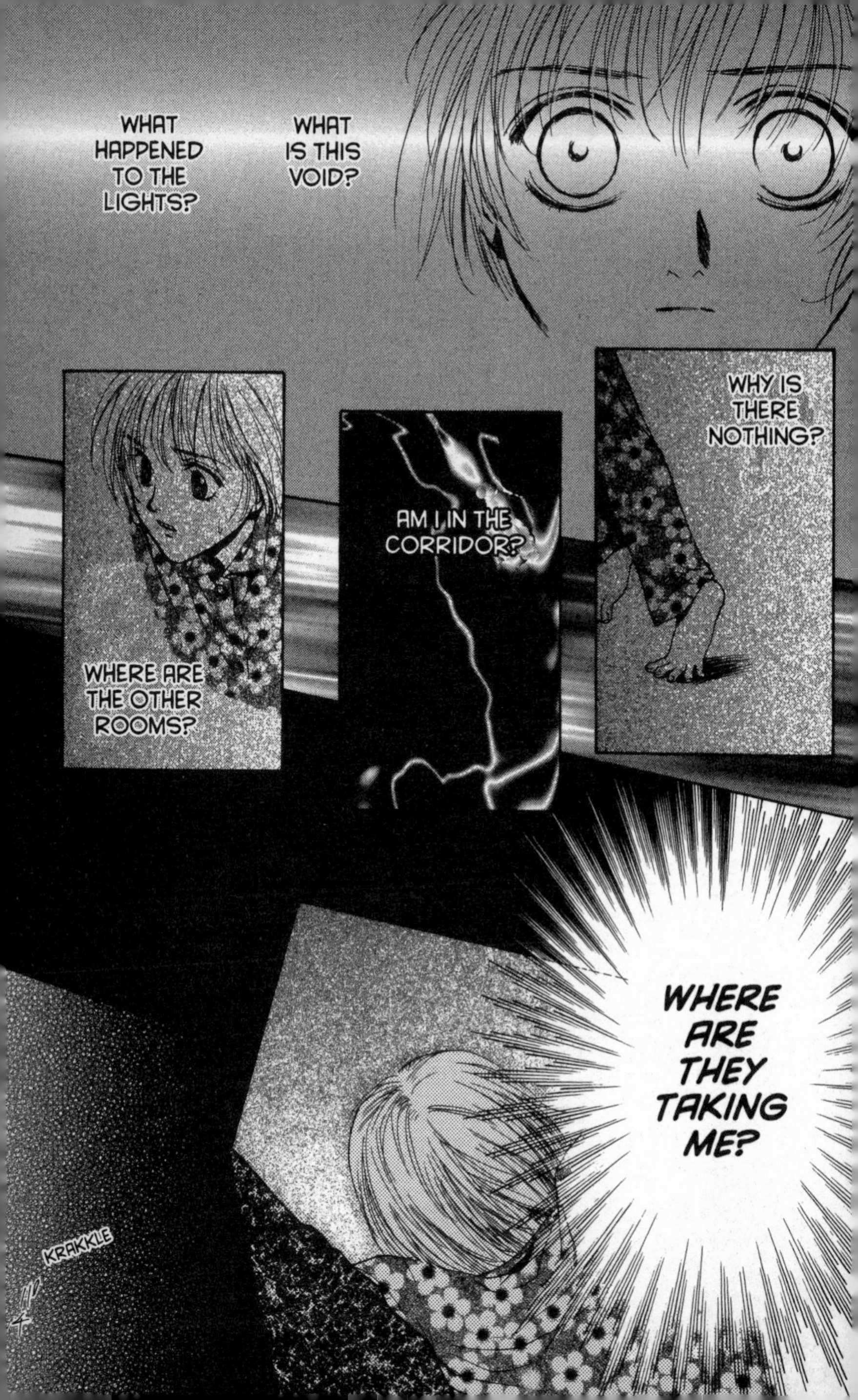
WHAT IS THIS VOID?
WHAT HAPPENED TO THE LIGHTS?
WHY IS THERE NOTHING?
AM I IN THE CORRIDOR?
WHERE ARE THE OTHER ROOMS?
WHERE ARE THEY TAKING ME?
KRAKKLE

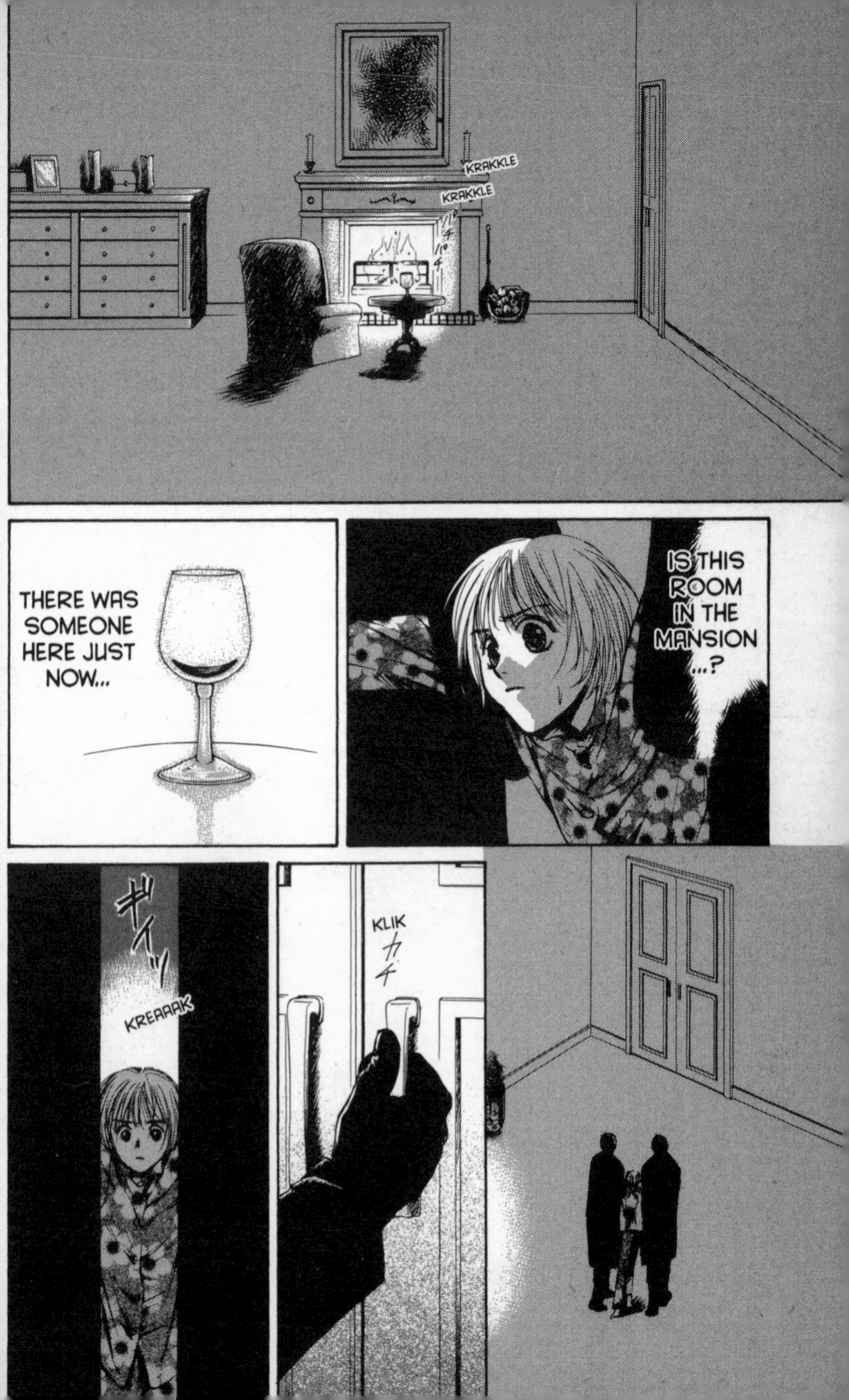
KRAKKLE
KRAKKLE
パチパチ
IS THIS ROOM IN THE MANSION ...?
THERE WAS SOMEONE HERE JUST NOW...
KLIK
カチ
ギイッ
KREAAAK

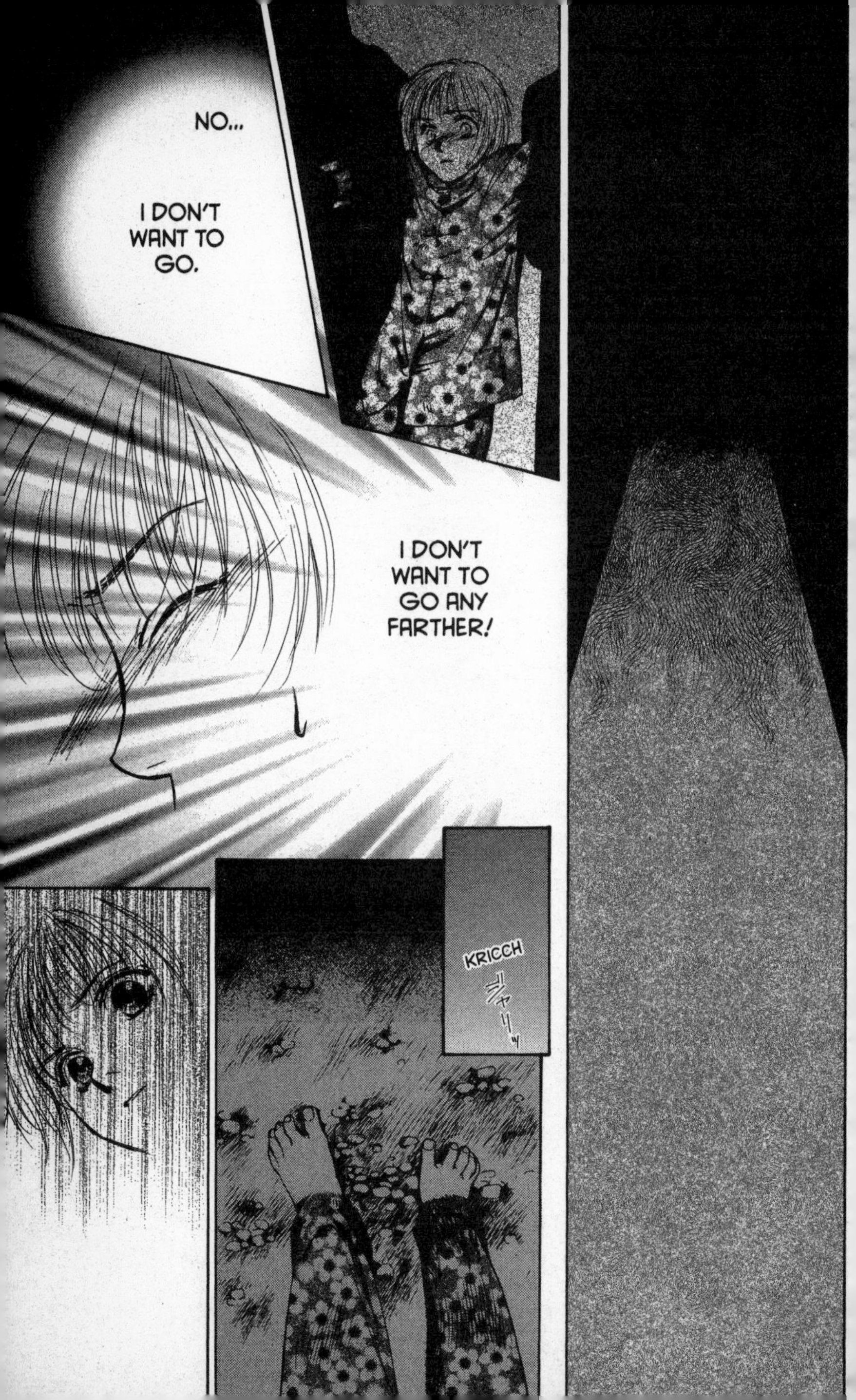
NO...
I DON'T WANT TO GO.
I DON'T WANT TO GO ANY FARTHER!
KRICCH
ジャリーッ

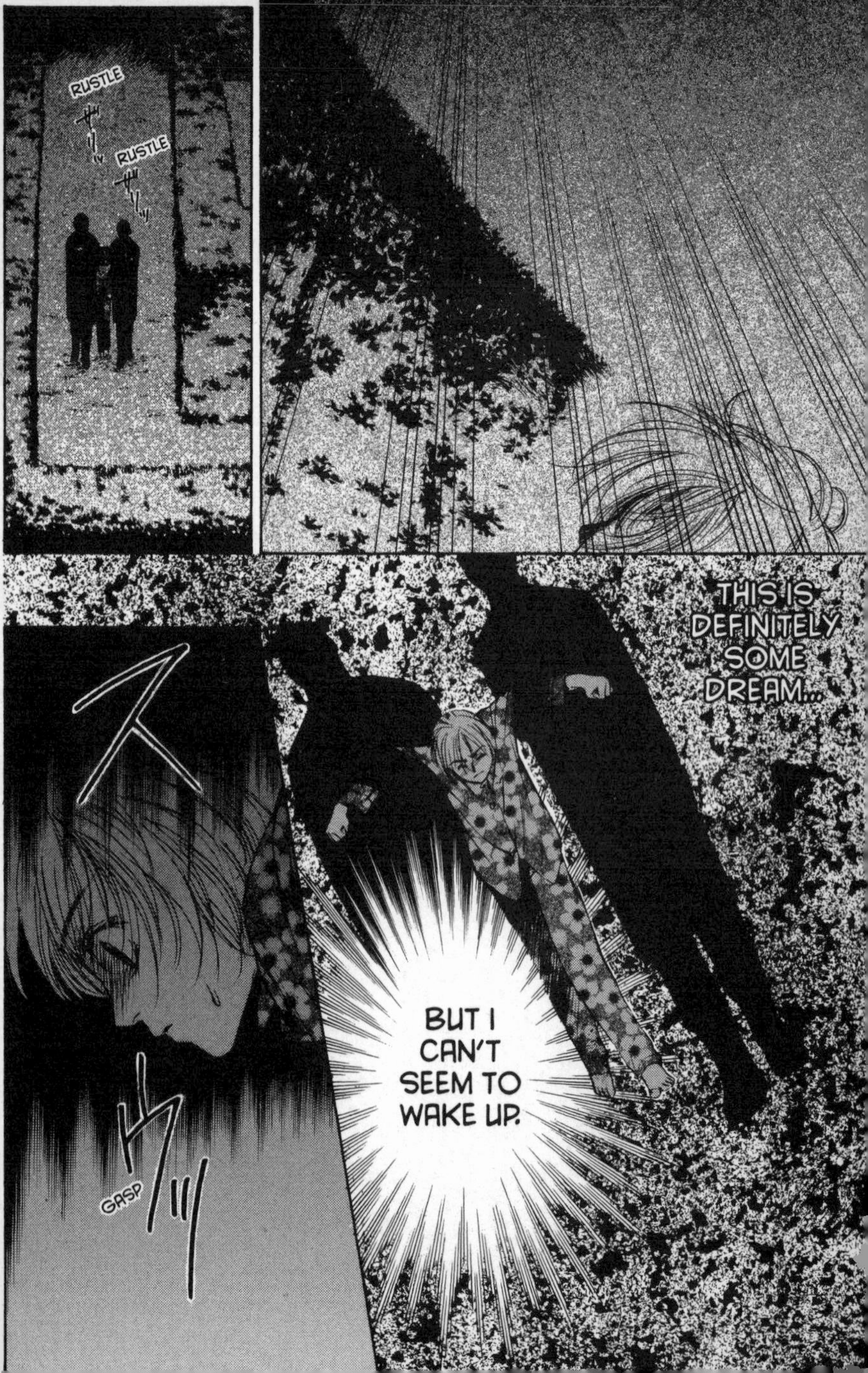
RUSTLE
RUSTLE
THIS IS DEFINITELY SOME DREAM...
BUT I CAN'T SEEM TO WAKE UP.
GASP

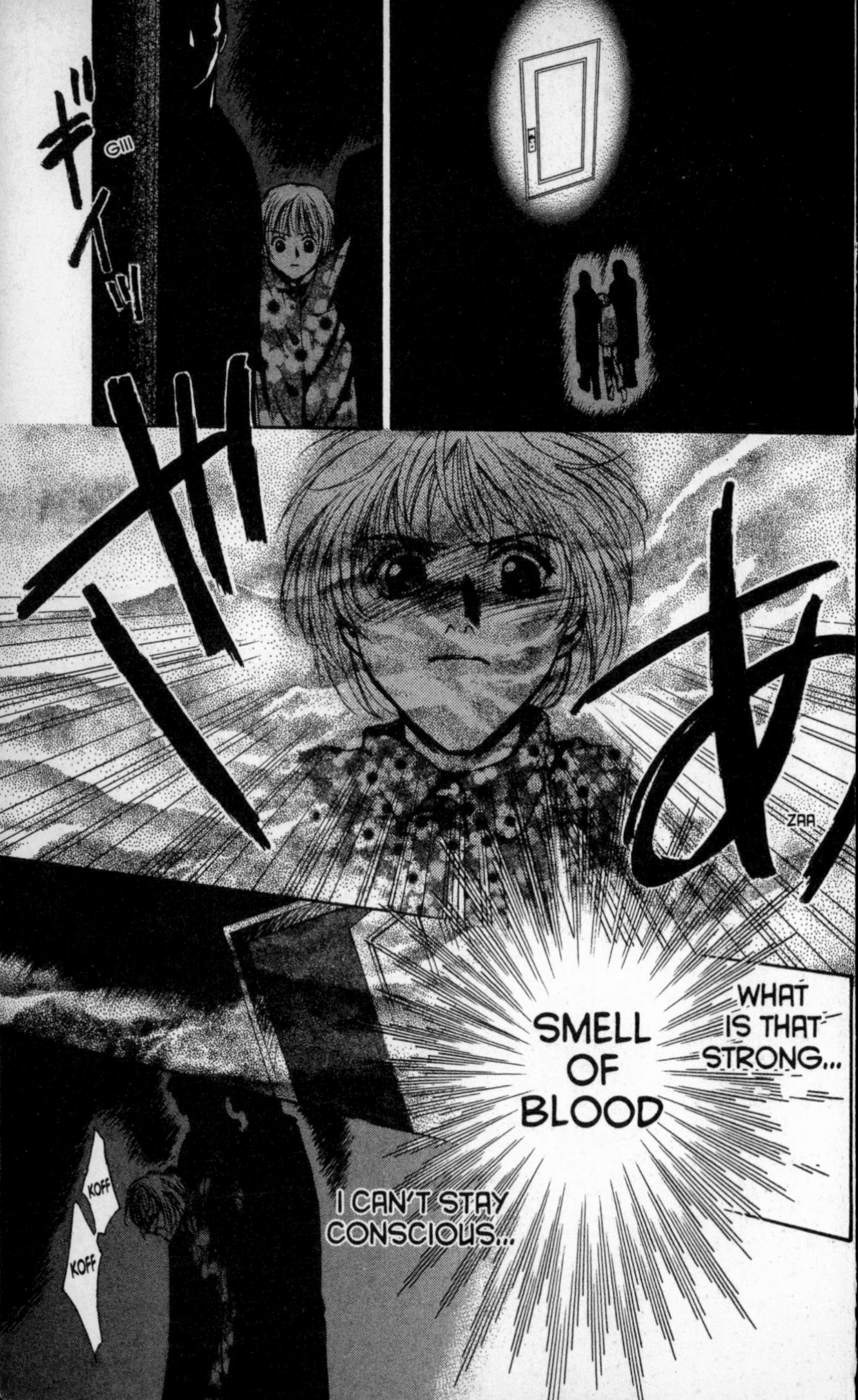
GIII
ZAA
WHAT IS THAT STRONG...
SMELL OF BLOOD
I CAN'T STAY CONSCIOUS...
KOFF
KOFF

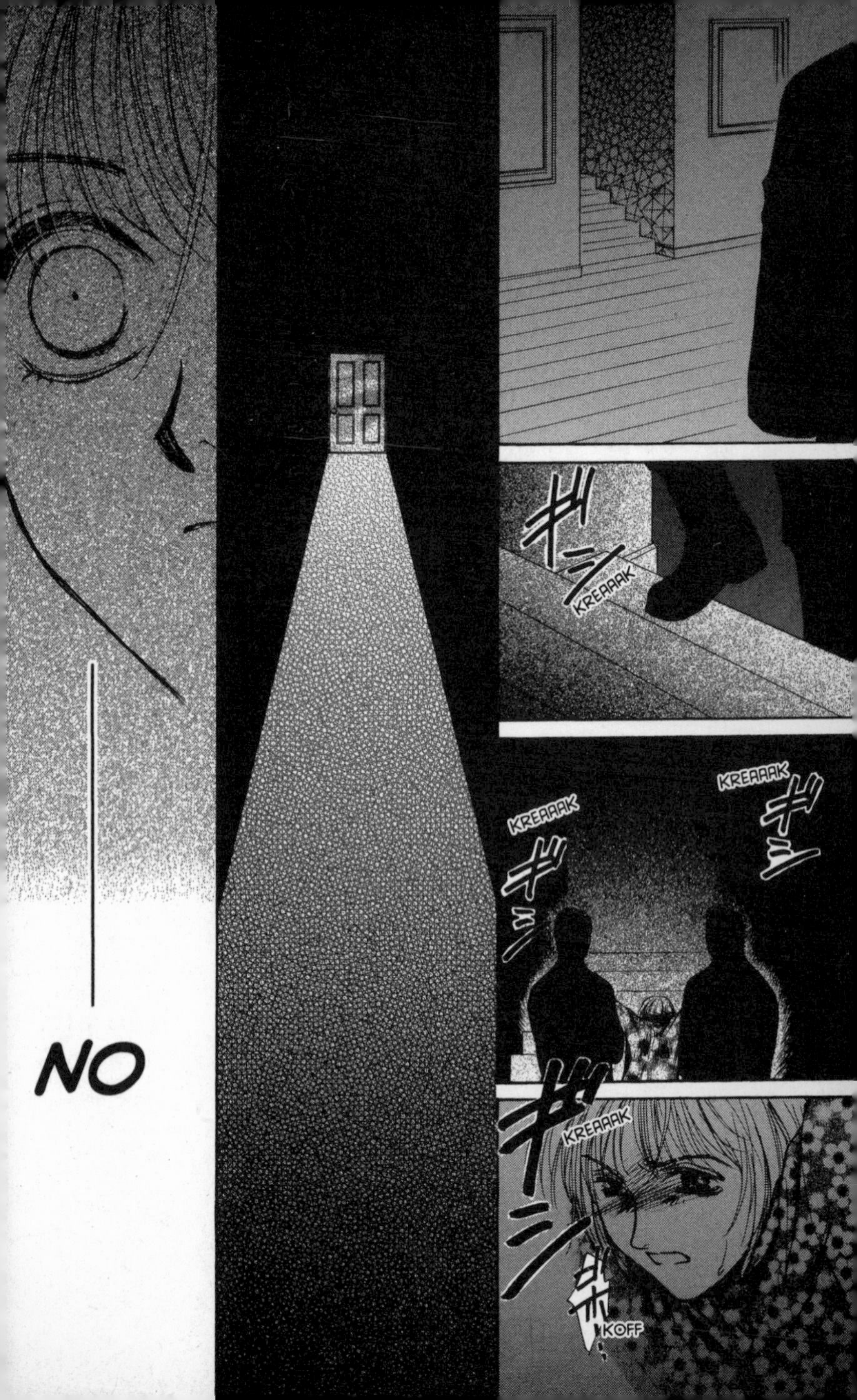
KREAAAK
KREAAAK
KREAAAK
KREAAAK
KOFF
NO

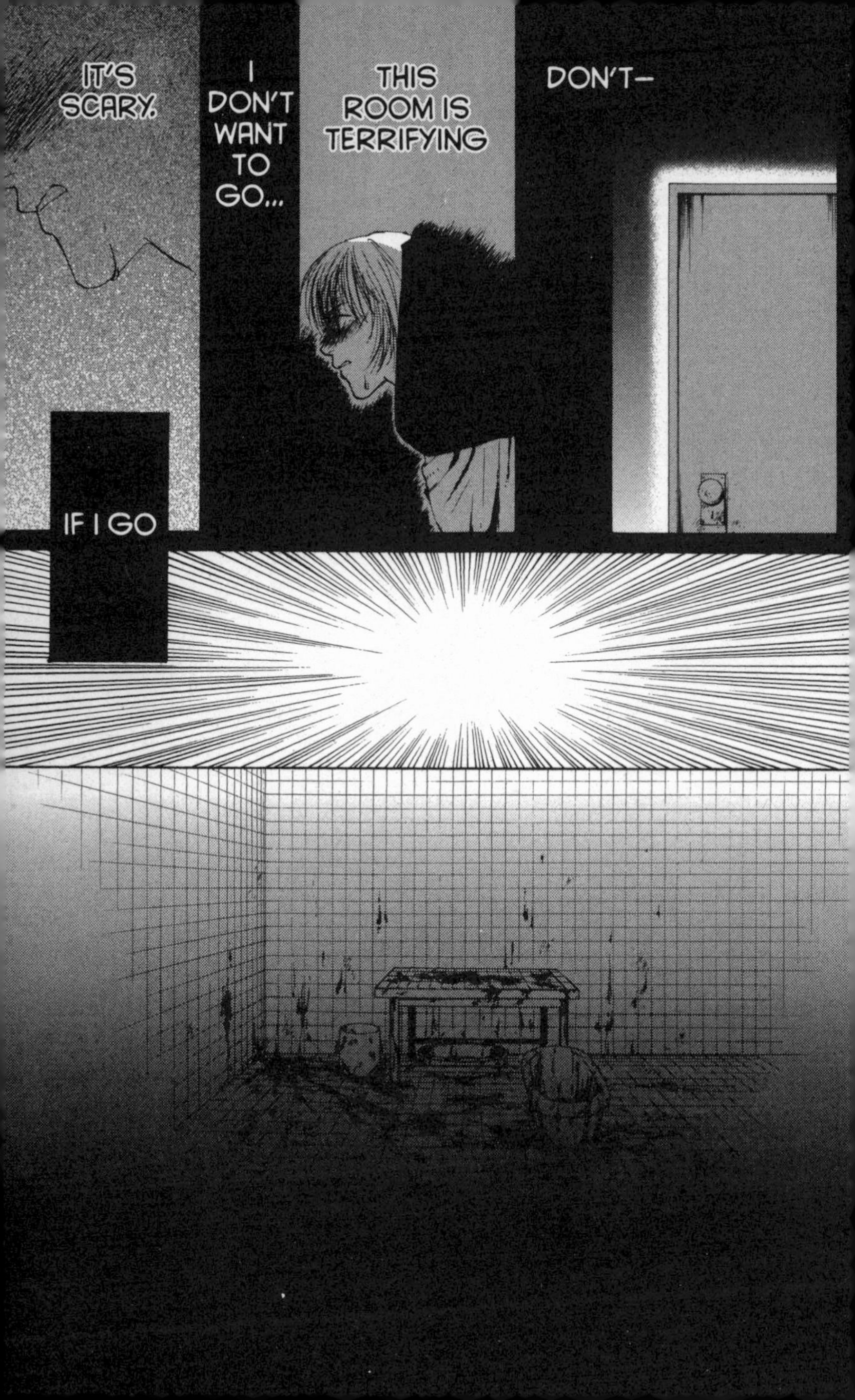
DON'T-
THIS ROOM IS TERRIFYING
I DON'T WANT TO GO...
IT'S SCARY.
IF I GO

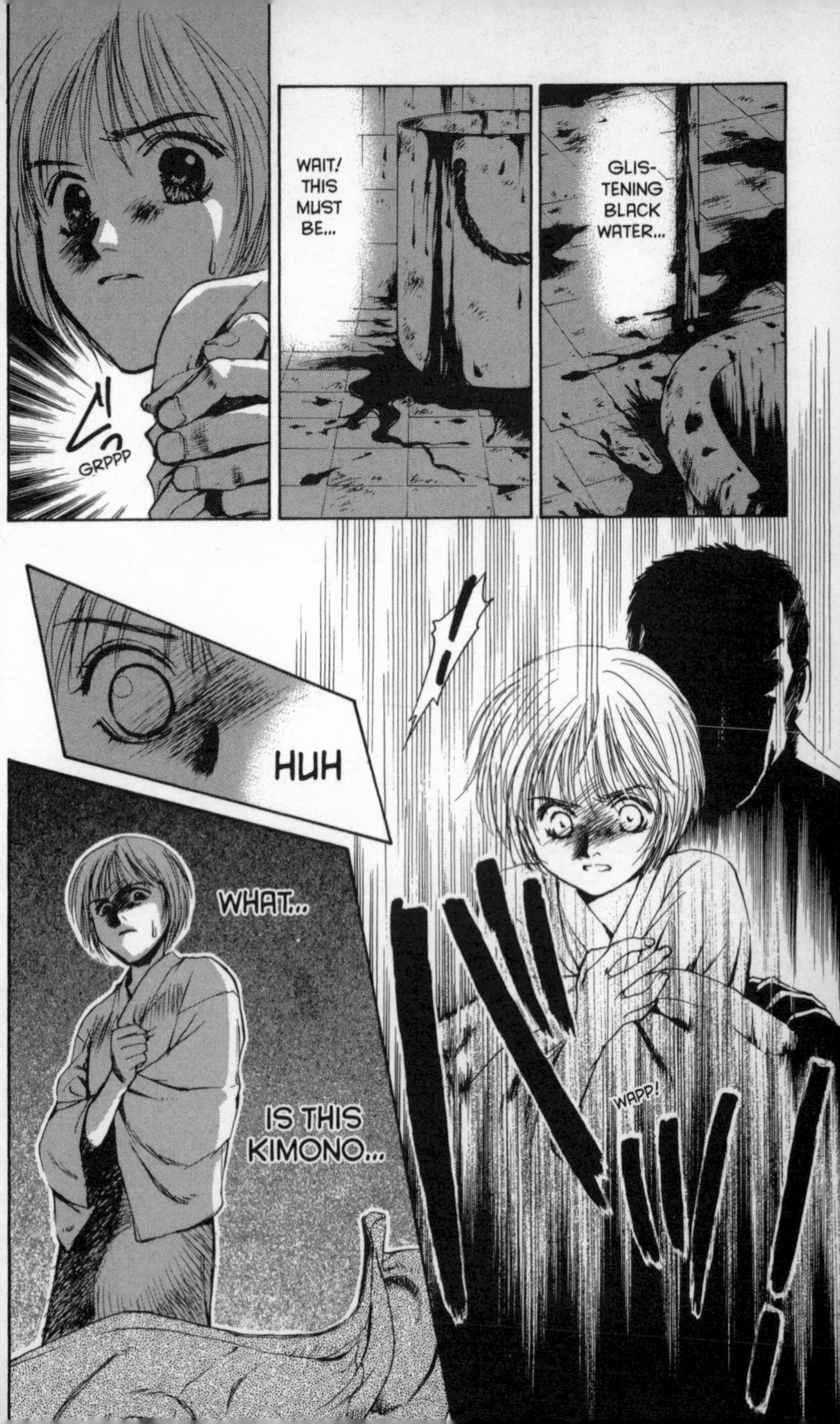
GLIS-TENING BLACK WATER...
WAIT! THIS MUST BE...
GRPPP
WAPP!
HUH
WHAT...
IS THIS KIMONO...

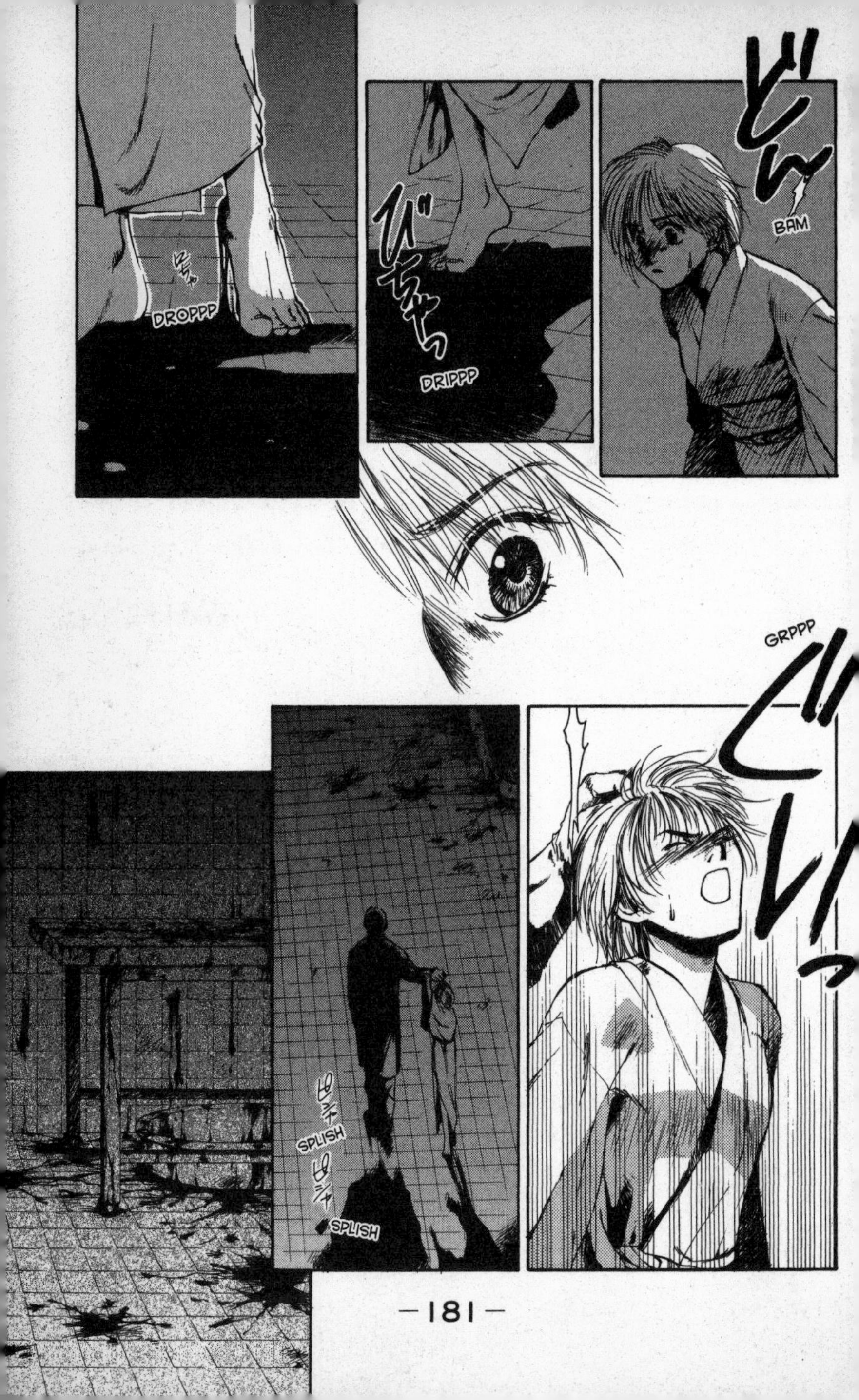
どん
BAM
びちゃっ
DRIPPP
DROPPP
GRPPP
ぐいっ
SPLISH
SPLISH

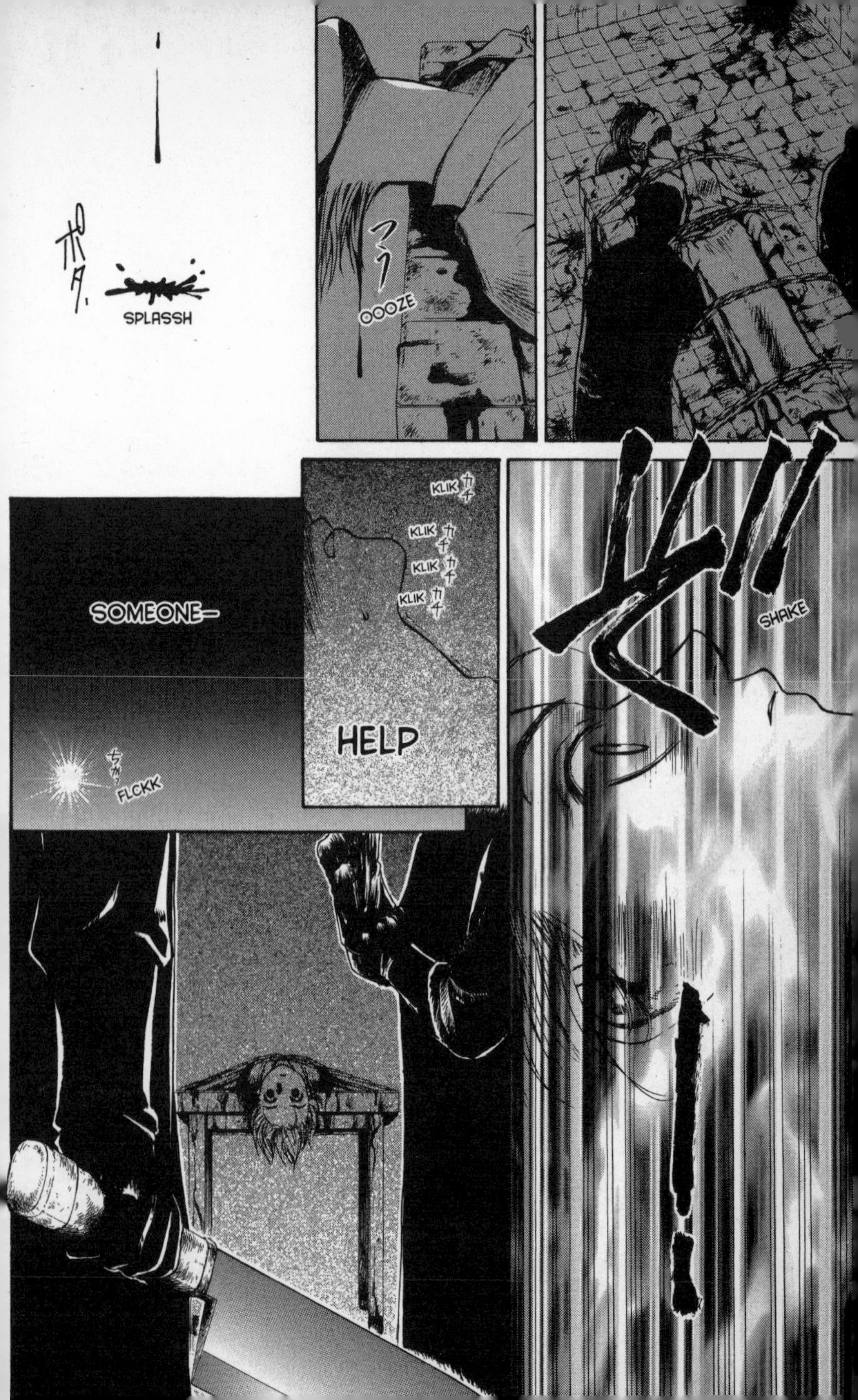

OOOZE
SPLASSH
SHAKE
KLIK
KLIK
KLIK
KLIK
HELP
SOMEONE—
FLCKK

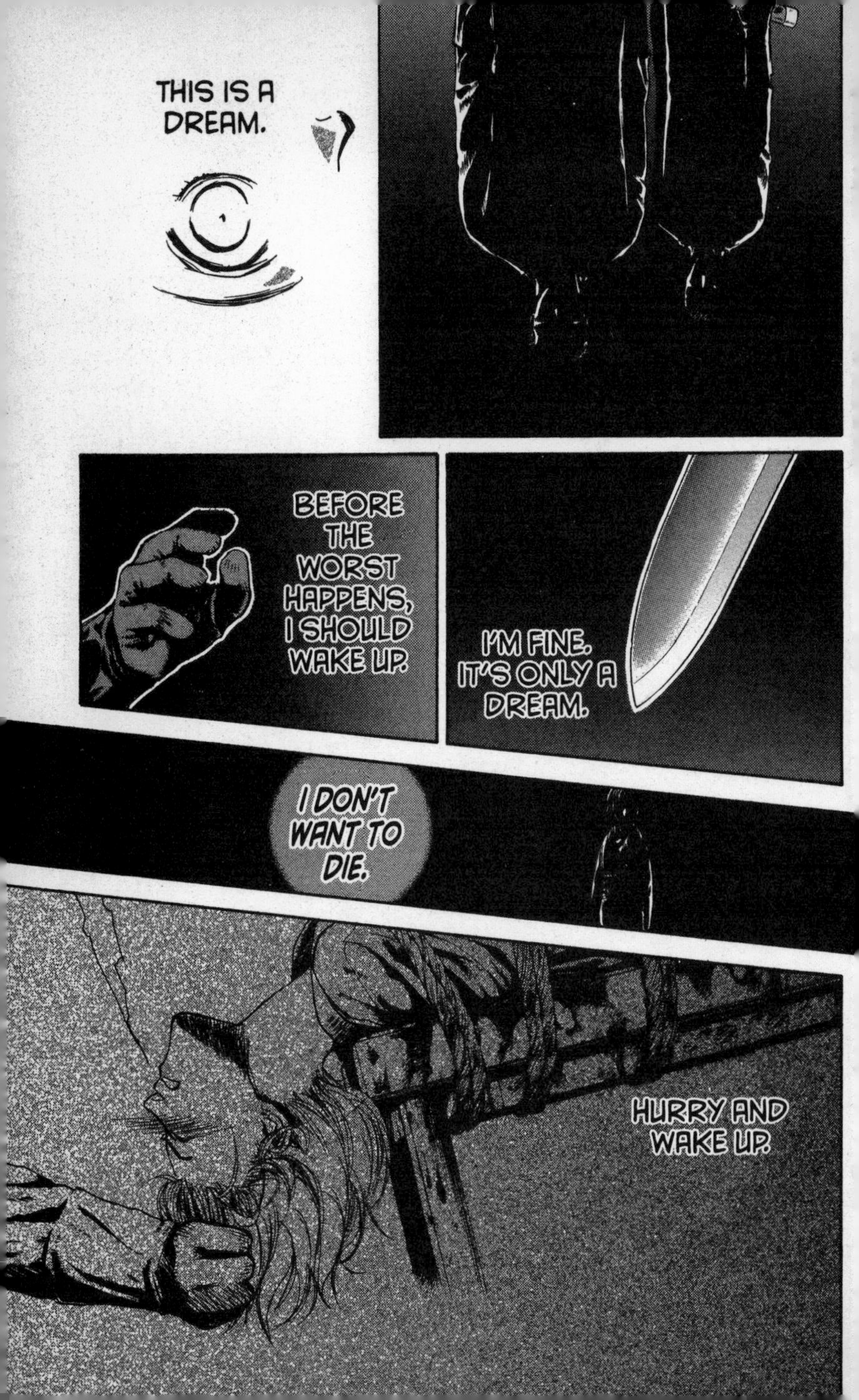
THIS IS A DREAM.
I'M FINE. IT'S ONLY A DREAM.
BEFORE THE WORST HAPPENS, I SHOULD WAKE UP.
I DON'T WANT TO DIE.
HURRY AND WAKE UP.

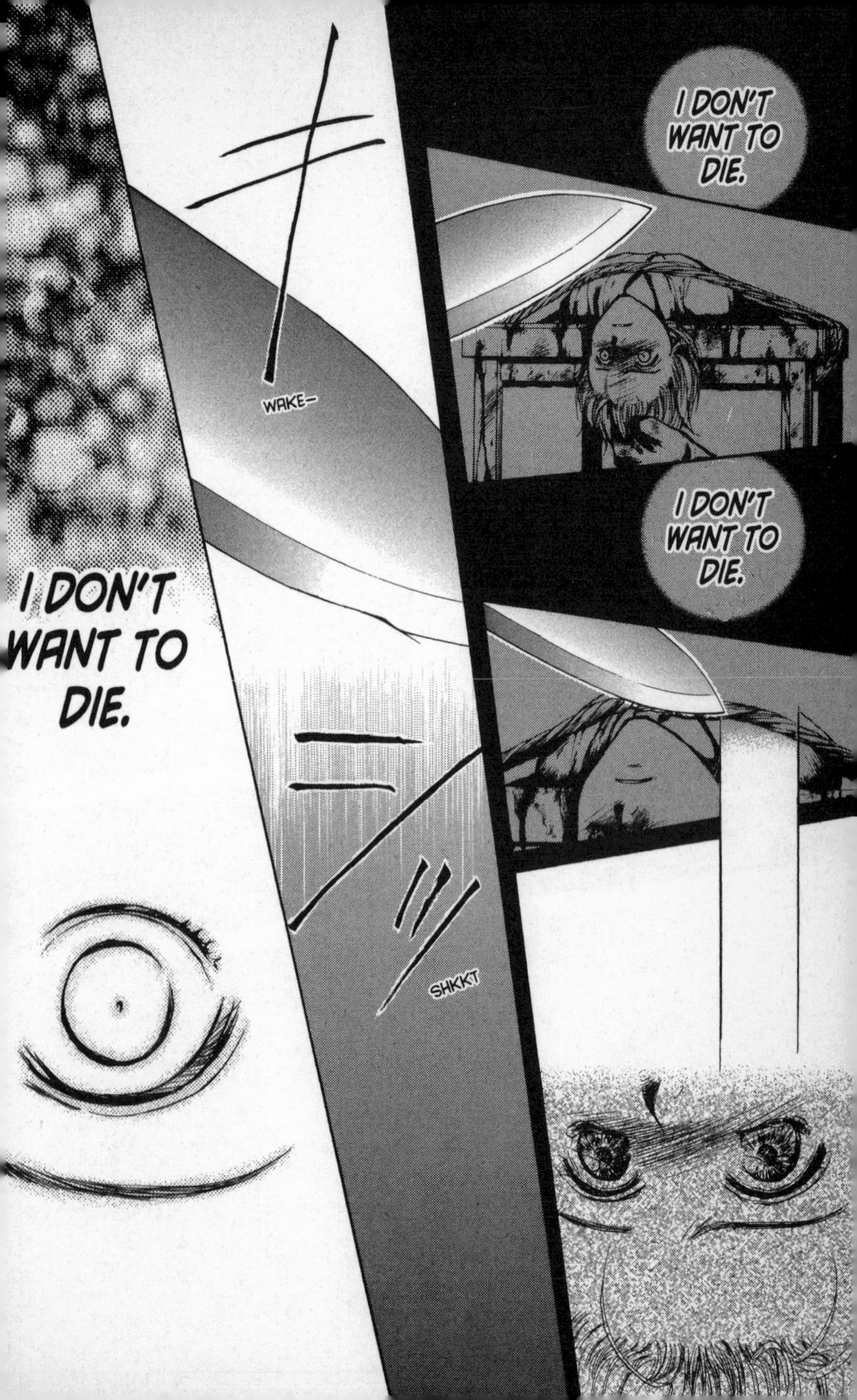
I DON'T WANT TO DIE.
I DON'T WANT TO DIE.
WAKE—
SHKKT
I DON'T WANT TO DIE.

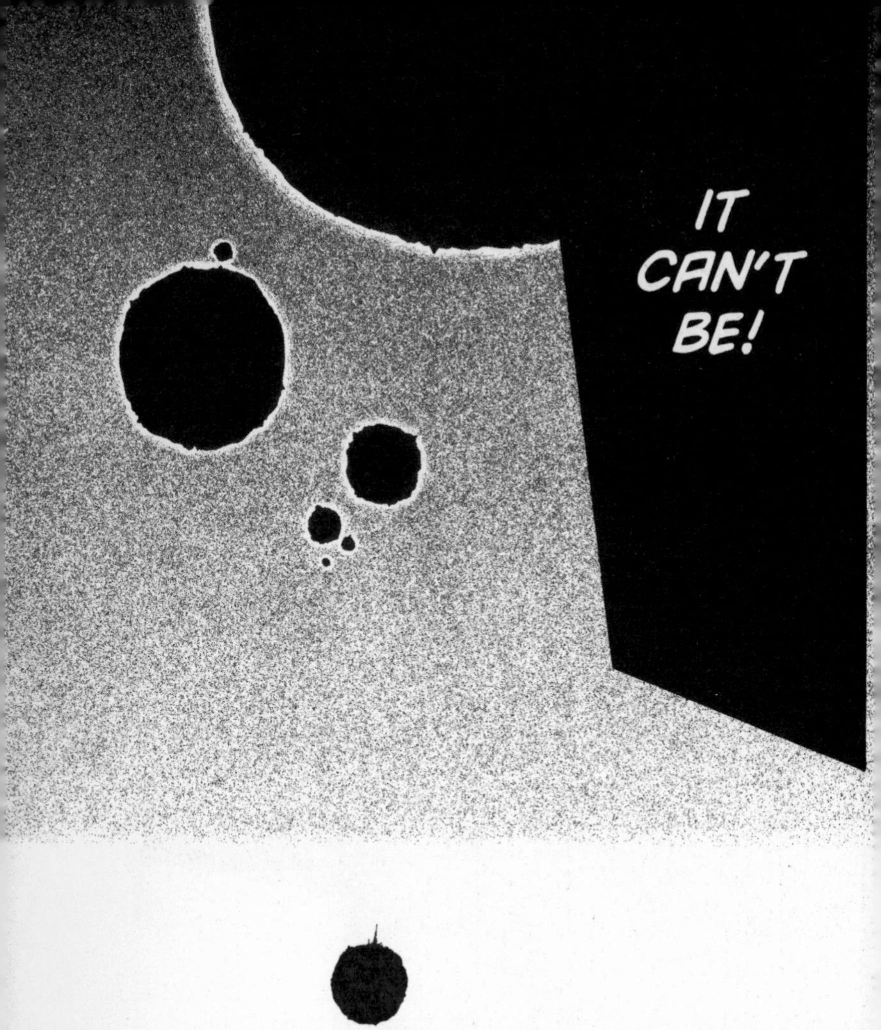
IT CAN'T BE!

— CONTINUED IN VOL. 7 —

HORROR STORIES 3

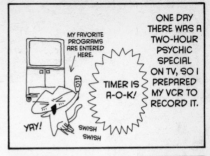

ONE DAY THERE WAS A TWO-HOUR PSYCHIC SPECIAL ON TV, SO I PREPARED MY VCR TO RECORD IT.
MY FAVORITE PROGRAMS ARE ENTERED HERE.
TIMER IS A-O-K!
SWISH SWISH
YAY!
WHEN THE APPOINTED TIME CAME AND I HIT THE BUTTON TO RECORD, I HEARD A "JIIIIII!" SOUND.
PANIC
WHAT'S GOING ON? I JUST WANT TO WATCH IT!
SWOOSH
JIII
WHAT THE—!
FOR SOME REASON, THE TAPE GOT STUCK AND WOULDN'T MOVE AT ALL.
WHAT THE HELL!
WHAT IS THAT "JIII" SOUND? THAT "JII" SOUND!
SO I COULDN'T RECORD IT....
EEEK!
WHAM
OUCH! WHAT DID I DO?
REMOTE
I TALKED WITH A FRIEND ABOUT IT.
YOU MUST HAVE THOUGHT AT THAT MOMENT "HAH, THIS MUST BE A PSYCHIC INCIDENT!?..."
OH.
OH, SEE YOU LATER!
THE THOUGHT NEVER OCCURRED TO ME UNTIL SHE SAID THAT.
I HAVE TO GO.

RECENTLY, I'VE BEEN THINKING TO MYSELF: "I'M GETTING MORE TALENTED. (FINALLY!)"

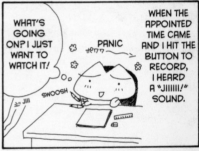

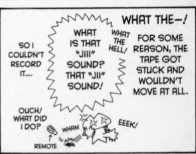

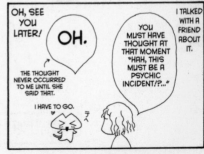

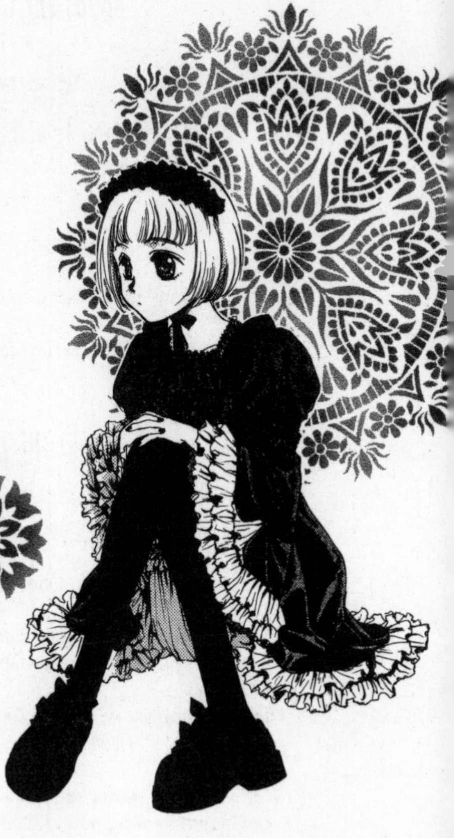

SPECIAL THANX

- A.SAKAMOTO
- M.HONMA
- C.INOUE
- T.WATANABE
- M.ŌKI
- H.SEKIYA
- Y.ARAI
- N.KAJIWARA
- F.ONO

editor T.KAMAGATA / K.KAWAMOTO

and YOU

LET'S MEET AGAIN IN VOL. 7.

S.INADA

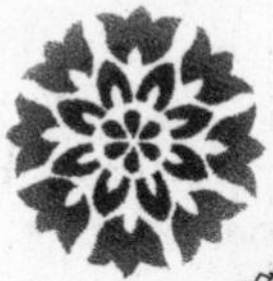

About the Creators of Ghost Hunt

ABOUT THE CREATOR

•

Shiho Inada

Born on October 17 in Kanagawa Prefecture.

Sign: Libra.

Blood type: B.

She made her debut with *Camouflage* in 1994.

Her best-known work is *Ghost Hunt*.

ABOUT THE WRITER

•

Fuyumi Ono

Born in Oita Prefecture.

She made her debut with *Teen's Heart*,
published on Kodansha X Library.

Her most popular works are the *Evil Spirit* series and the *Twelve Kingdom* series.

Her works are widely read, and although her novels are considered young adult fiction, her works are read by people from all walks of life.

Translation Notes

Japanese is a tricky language for most Westerners, and translation is often more art than science. For your edification and reading pleasure, here are notes on some of the places where we could have gone in a different direction in our translation of the work, or where a Japanese cultural reference is used.

PAGE 26, *RIN-CHAN*

If "Lin" was our tall, dark, and handsome stranger's first name (instead of his family name), then he would have been called "Rin-chan" as a baby in Japan. The SPR members are joking at his expense since "Rin-chan" just happens to be what the Japanese call the famous Hollywood dog hero Rin Tin Tin.

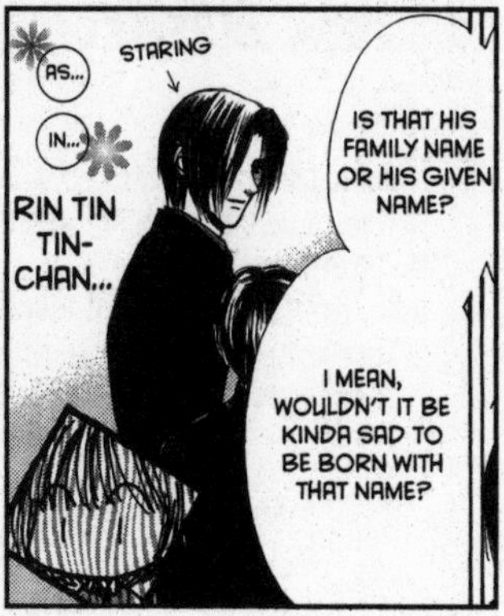
IS THAT HIS FAMILY NAME OR HIS GIVEN NAME?
I MEAN, WOULDN'T IT BE KINDA SAD TO BE BORN WITH THAT NAME?
STARING
AS...
IN...
RIN TIN TIN-CHAN...

PAGE 30, HOUSEN TEMPLE, DEFENSE ACADEMY, MINAMI PSYCHIC RESEARCH CENTER, BRITISH SOCIETY FOR PSYCHIC RESEARCH

Housen Temple and the National Defense Academy are actual cultural and governmental institutions in Japan, although neither would publicly admit to making psychic house calls. Like Shibuya Psychic Research, the Minami Psychic Research Center and British Society for Psychic Research are strictly fictional, although any similarities to the real Society for Psychical Research (founded by Cambridge University professors) in Great Britain are probably best left unexplained.

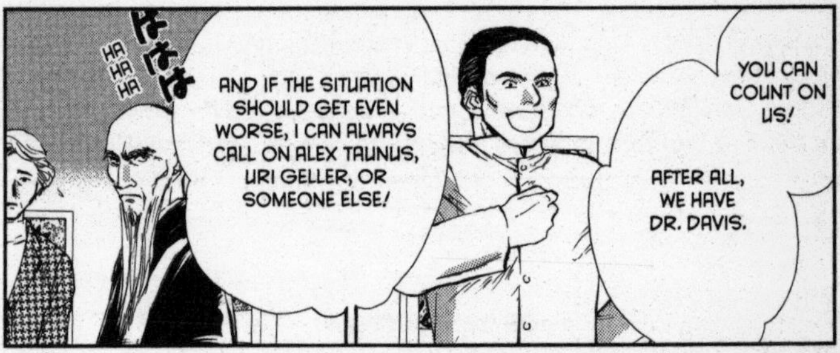
YOU CAN COUNT ON US!
AFTER ALL, WE HAVE DR. DAVIS.
AND IF THE SITUATION SHOULD GET EVEN WORSE, I CAN ALWAYS CALL ON ALEX TAUNUS, URI GELLER, OR SOMEONE ELSE!
ははは
HA HA HA

PAGE 31, ALEX "TAUNUS," URI GELLER

Alex *Tanous* and Uri Geller were internationally famous (and controversial) claimants of psychic abilities. Unfortunately, Alex Tanous passed away in 1990, before Ono-sensei wrote the 1991 novel (*I Don't Want to Become an Evil Spirit!*) that inspired this manga. It is no coincidence that in that novel and this manga, Minami mentions the famous psychic Alex *Taunus* instead. (Notice the spelling.) For his part, Uri Geller is most famous for claiming to bend spoons with his mind on live television.

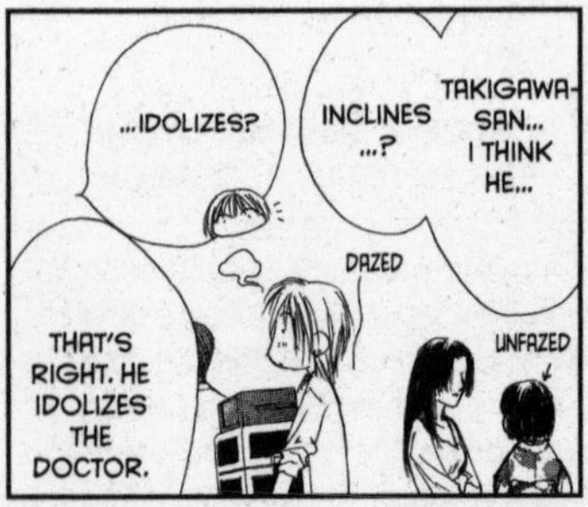
TAKIGAWA-SAN... I THINK HE...
INCLINES ...?
...IDOLIZES?
UNFAZED
DAZED
THAT'S RIGHT. HE IDOLIZES THE DOCTOR.

PAGE 32, "INCLINES" AND "IDOLIZES"

As a foreigner, John fumbles over the Japanese word for "inclines" *(keikou)* when he really means to say "idolizes" *(keitou).*

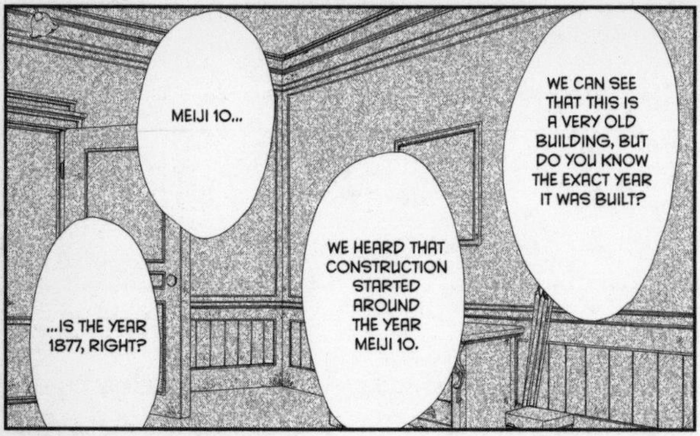
WE CAN SEE THAT THIS IS A VERY OLD BUILDING, BUT DO YOU KNOW THE EXACT YEAR IT WAS BUILT?
WE HEARD THAT CONSTRUCTION STARTED AROUND THE YEAR MEIJI 10.
MEIJI 10...
...IS THE YEAR 1877, RIGHT?

PAGE 36, MEIJI 10

The Japanese number years by the reign of their emperors. For example, Emperor Meiji (Mutsuhito) began his rule in AD 1868, so “Meiji 10” stands for the tenth year of Meiji’s reign, or AD 1877.

PAGE 37, SUWA REGION

The Suwa region used to be an old mountainous province in central Japan. It is now part of the modern-day province of Nagano, the home of the 1998 Winter Olympics.

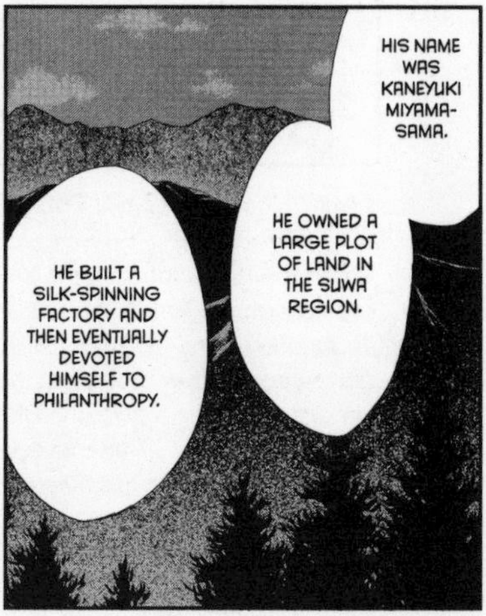
HIS NAME WAS KANEYUKI MIYAMA-SAMA.
HE OWNED A LARGE PLOT OF LAND IN THE SUWA REGION.
HE BUILT A SILK-SPINNING FACTORY AND THEN EVENTUALLY DEVOTED HIMSELF TO PHILANTHROPY.

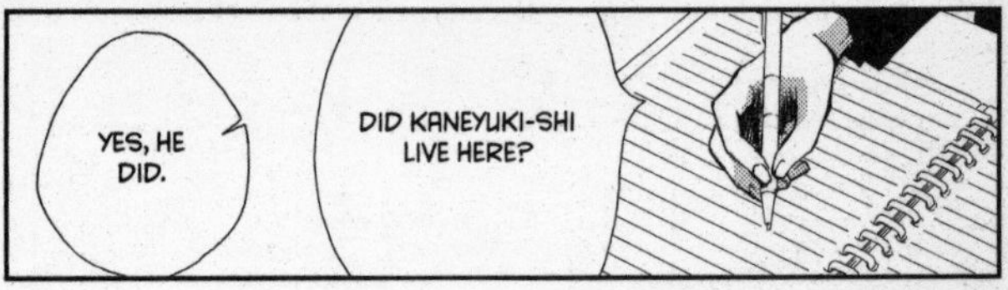
DID KANEYUKI-SHI LIVE HERE?
YES, HE DID.

PAGE 38, KANEYUKI-SHI

Japanese speakers use "-shi" instead of "-san" when speaking formally about people with whom they are personally unacquainted. For example, newspapers use "-shi" when mentioning a person's name, and textbooks add "-shi" to almost every historical figure's name. Here, Naru calls the mansion's former owner "Kaneyuki-shi" because Naru knows Kaneyuki only from books and historical records.

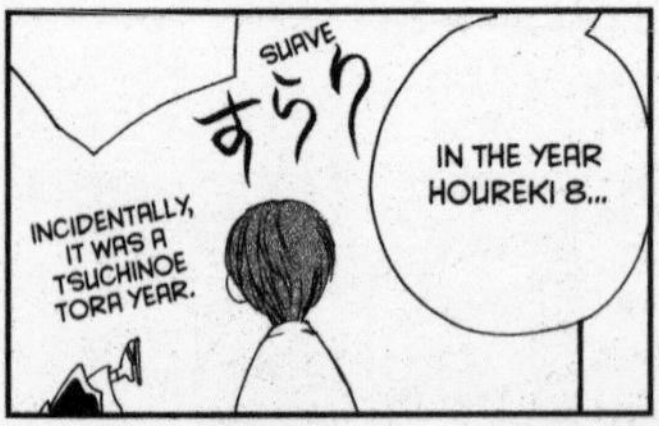
IN THE YEAR HOUREKI 8...
SUAVE
INCIDENTALLY, IT WAS A TSUCHINOE TORA YEAR.

PAGE 76, HOUREKI 8, TSUCHINOE TORA YEAR

When the monk Imura tests Yasuhara's cover story, Yasuhara claims he was born in the year Houreki 8, the ancient Japanese era name for 1758 AD. The ancient Japanese also borrowed another method of counting years from the Chinese via Korea. This method combined ten Chinese heavenly stems with the Chinese 12-animal zodiac. Tsuchinoe Tora (5th Sign, Year of the Tiger) is the fifteenth year of a sixty-year cycle.

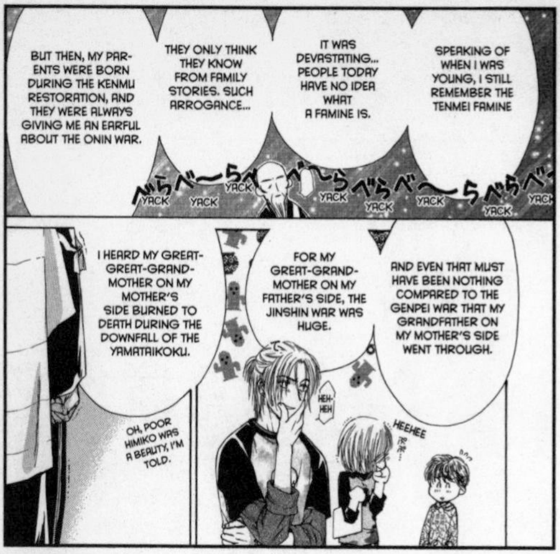
SPEAKING OF WHEN I WAS YOUNG, I STILL REMEMBER THE TENMEI FAMINE
IT WAS DEVASTATING... PEOPLE TODAY HAVE NO IDEA WHAT A FAMINE IS.
THEY ONLY THINK THEY KNOW FROM FAMILY STORIES. SUCH ARROGANCE...
BUT THEN, MY PAR-ENTS WERE BORN DURING THE KENMU RESTORATION, AND THEY WERE ALWAYS GIVING ME AN EARFUL ABOUT THE ONIN WAR.
YACK YACK YACK YACK YACK YACK YACK YACK
AND EVEN THAT MUST HAVE BEEN NOTHING COMPARED TO THE GENPEI WAR THAT MY GRANDFATHER ON MY MOTHER'S SIDE WENT THROUGH.
FOR MY GREAT-GRAND-MOTHER ON MY FATHER'S SIDE, THE JINSHIN WAR WAS HUGE.
I HEARD MY GREAT-GREAT-GRAND-MOTHER ON MY MOTHER'S SIDE BURNED TO DEATH DURING THE DOWNFALL OF THE YAMATAIKOKU.
HEH-HEH
HEEHEE
OH, POOR HIMIKO WAS A BEAUTY, I'M TOLD.

PAGE 76, TENMEI FAMINE

Yasuhara proceeds to rattle off historical events in Japan to impress Imura-san with his cover story's family "history." Those historical events include the Tenmei Famine (1783–90), the Onin War (1467–1477), the Kemnu Restoration (1333–36), the Gen-pei War (1180–1185), Jinshin War (672), and the mythical fall of Queen Himiko's Yamataikoku nation (date uncertain).

PAGE 86, PARDON US

Out of politeness, Japanese people will often say *o-jama shimasu* when entering someone's home. It literally means, "Pardon my intrusion," but guests say this even when the host invited them in the first place.

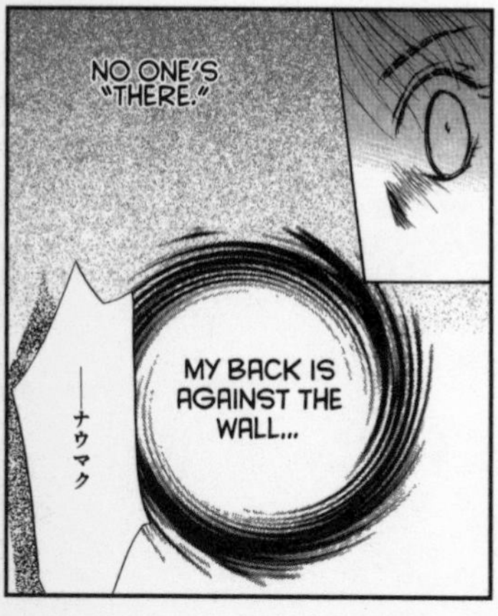
NO ONE'S "THERE."
MY BACK IS AGAINST THE WALL...
——ナウマク

PAGE 93, *NANMAKU*

The team is reusing the same *Tai-Mahou* (a type of Japanese counterspell) that it also used in volume 5. It is a Buddhist mantra *(Naumaku Sanmanda Bazaradan Kan)* dedicated to the deity Acala. It is difficult to give a literal translation in a foreign language; therefore, we have left it in Japanese to preserve its authenticity.

GHOST HUNT

7

MANGA BY SHIHO INADA

STORY BY FUYUMI ONO

We are pleased to present to you a preview
from the next volume of Ghost Hunt. *Volume
7 will be available in English on March 27,
2007, but for now, you'll have to make do
with Japanese!*

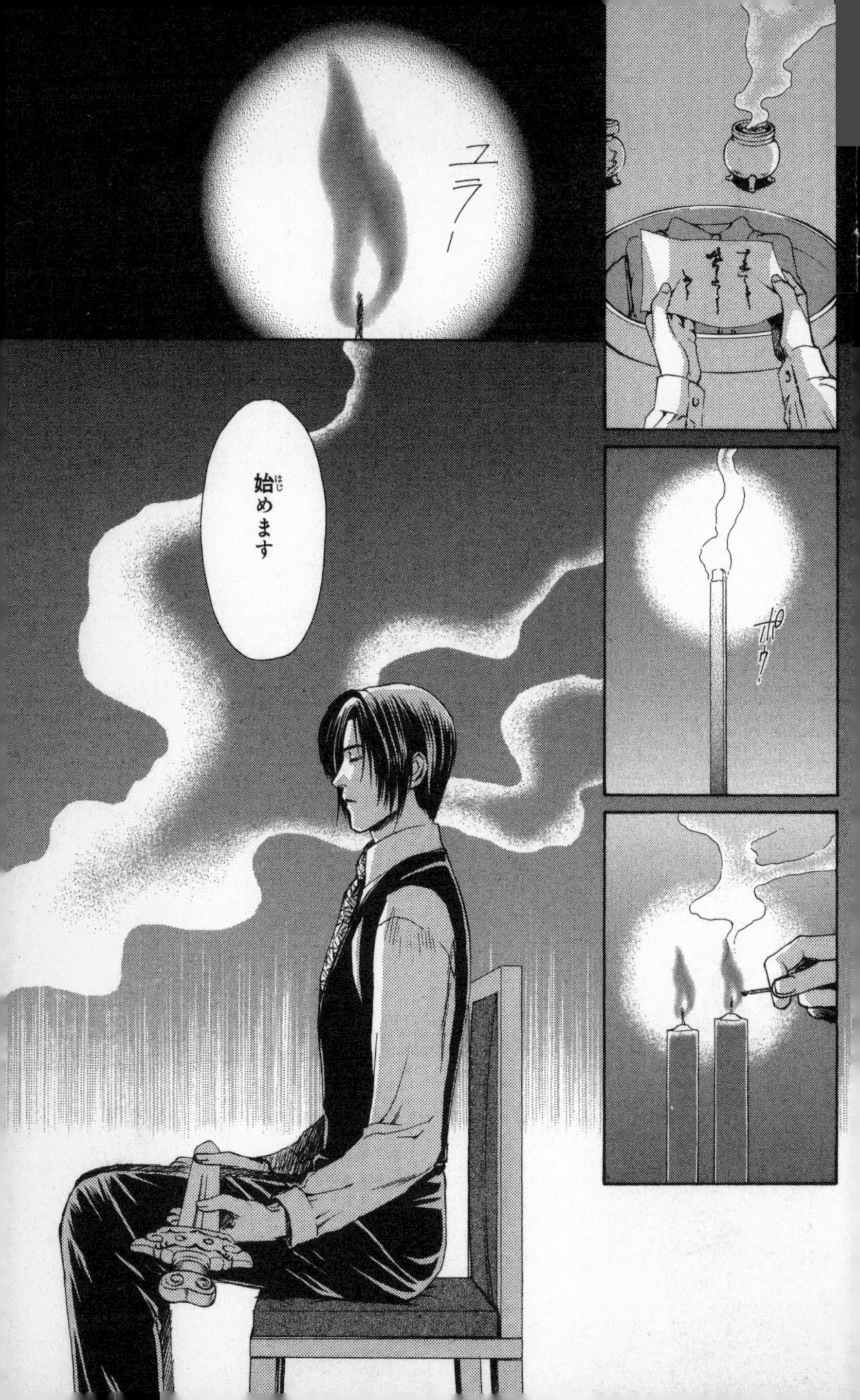
ポゥ!
ユラー
始めます

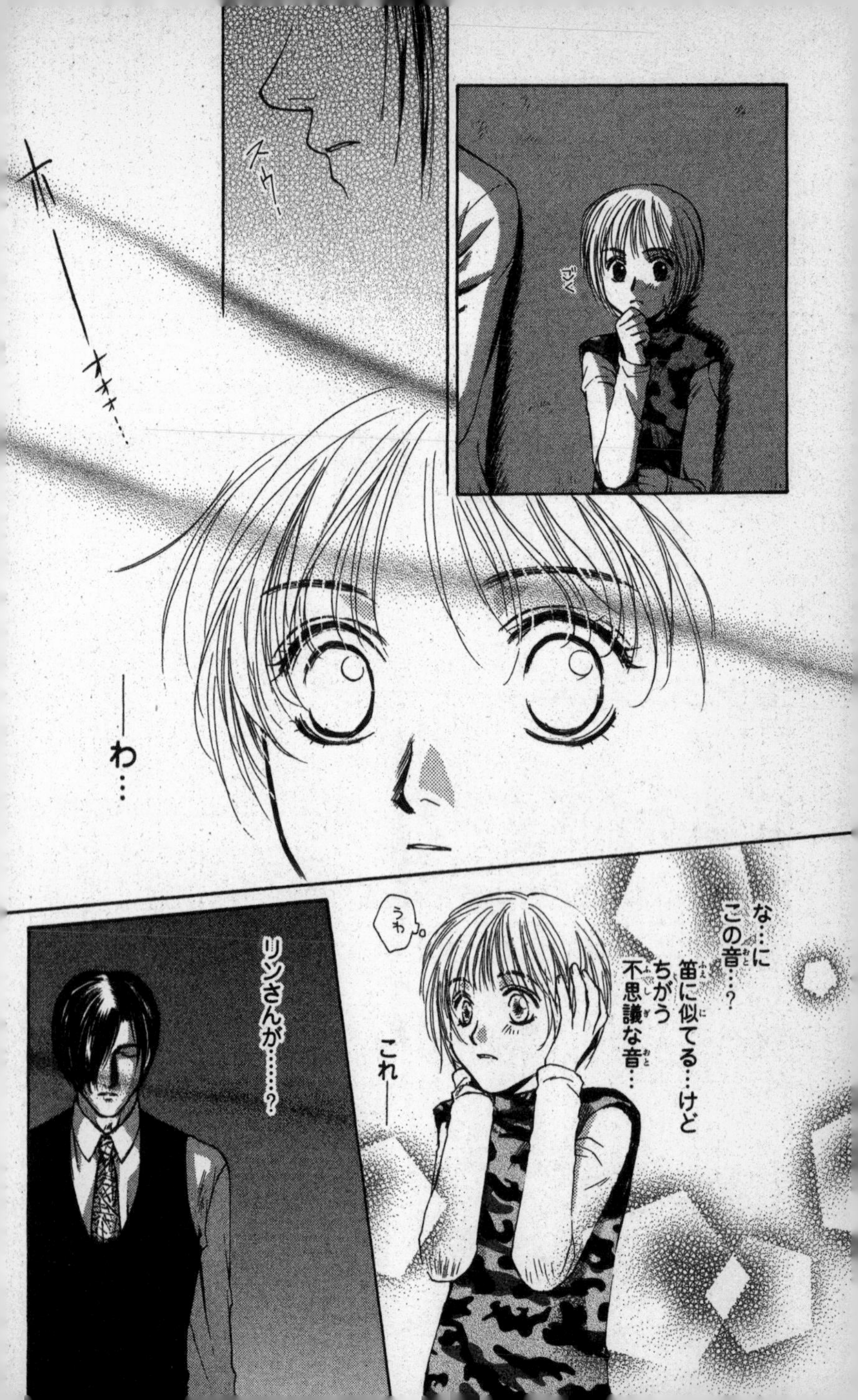
スウー…
ホーーーオオォ……
―わ…
な…に
この音…?
笛に似てる…けど
ちがう
不思議な音…
これ―
うわ
リンさんが……?

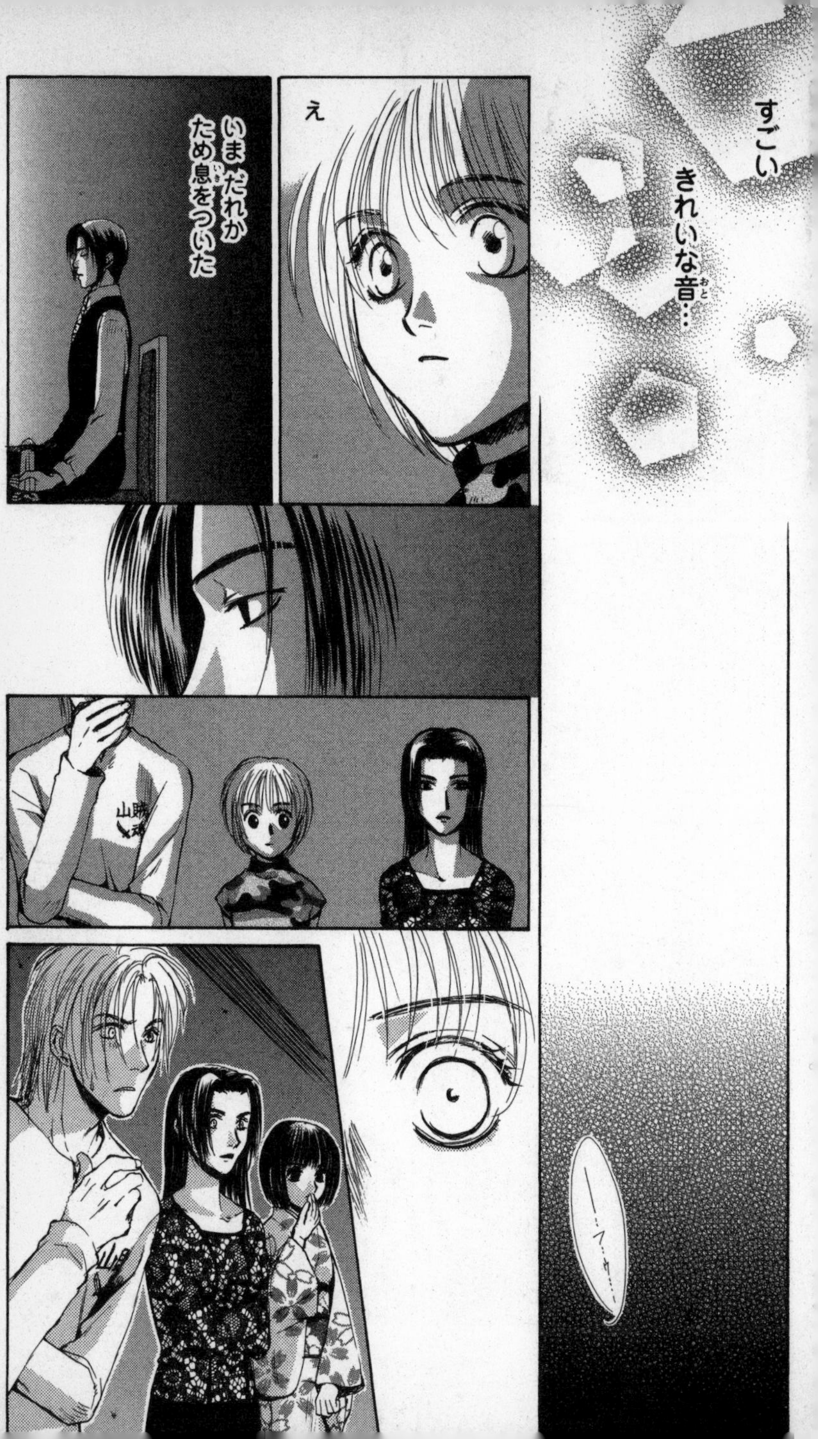
すごい
きれいな音(おと)…
ー…ハ…ゥ…ー
え
いま だれか
ため息(いき)をついた

ナル
日がよくない

しゃべらせることは
できないし
そんなに長くは
呼んでおけません

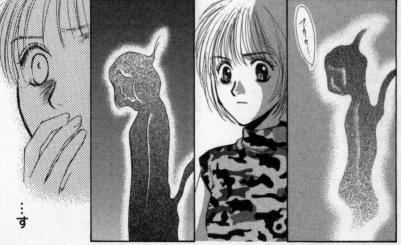

フカウ……

…す

RESERVoir CHRoNiCLE
TSUBASA
BY CLAMP

Sakura is the princess of Clow. Syaoran is her childhood friend, and leader of the archaeological dig that cost him his father. Fans of Cardcaptor Sakura will recognize the names and the faces, but these aren't the people you know. This is an alternate reality where everything is familiar and strange at the same time.

Sakura has a mysterious power, a power that no one understands, a power that can change the world. On the day she goes to the dig to declare her love for Syaoran, a mysterious symbol is uncovered that will have vast repercussions for Sakura and Syaoran. It marks the beginning of a quest that will take Syaoran and his friends

NEW FROM THE CREATORS OF *CHOBITS*!

Ages: 13 +

through worlds that will be familiar to any CLAMP fan, as our heroes encounter places and characters from X, Chobits, Magic Knight Rayearth, xxxHOLiC, and many more! But all that matters to Syaoran is his goal: saving Sakura.

Special extras in each volume! Read them all!

VISIT WWW.DELREYMANGA.COM TO:
• View release date calendars for upcoming volumes
• Sign up for Del Rey's free manga e-newsletter
• Find out the latest about new Del Rey Manga series

KURO GANE

BY KEI TOUME

AN EERIE, HAUNTING SAMURAI ADVENTURE

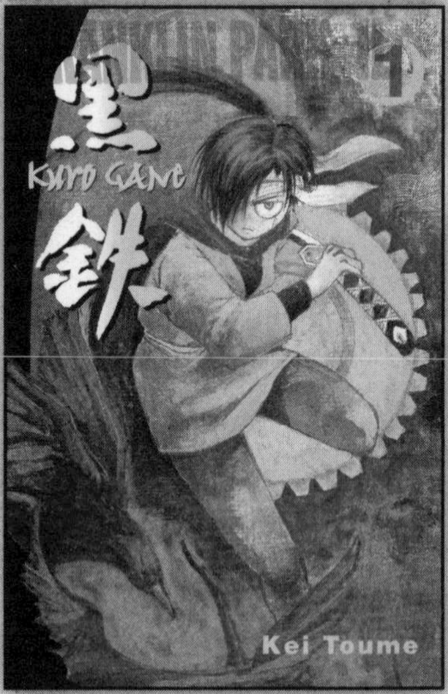
黒
KURO GANE
鉄
1
Kei Toume

Teen: Ages 13 +

Avenging his father's murder is a matter of honor for the young samurai Jintetsu. But it turns out that the killer is a corrupt government official—and now the powers that be are determined to hunt Jintetsu down. There's only one problem: Jintetsu is already dead.

Torn to pieces by a pack of dogs, Jintetsu's ravaged body has been found by Genkichi, outcast and master inventor. Genkichi gives the dead boy a new, indestructible steel body and a talking sword—just what he'll need to face down the gang that's terrorizing his hometown and the mobster who ordered his father's hit. But what about Otsuki, the beautiful girl he left behind? Steel armor is defense against any sword, but it can't save Jintetsu from the pain in his heart.

Special extras in each volume! Read them all!

DEL REY

VISIT WWW.DELREYMANGA.COM TO:

- Read sample pages
- View release date calendars for upcoming volumes
- Sign up for Del Rey's free manga e-newsletter
- Find out the latest about new Del Rey Manga series

School Rumble

BY JIN KOBAYASHI

SUBTLETY IS FOR WIMPS!

She . . . is a second-year high school student with a single all-consuming question: Will the boy she likes ever really notice her?

He . . . is the school's most notorious juvenile delinquent, and he's suddenly come to a shocking realization: He's got a huge crush, and now he must tell her how he feels.

Life-changing obsessions, colossal foul-ups, grand schemes, deep-seated anxieties, and raging hormones—School Rumble portrays high school as it really is: over-the-top comedy!

Ages: 16 +

Special extras in each volume! Read them all!

TOMARE!

STOP!

YOU'RE GOING THE WRONG WAY!

MANGA IS A COMPLETELY DIFFERENT TYPE OF READING EXPERIENCE.

TO START AT THE *BEGINNING*, GO TO THE *END*!

THAT'S RIGHT!

AUTHENTIC MANGA IS READ THE TRADITIONAL JAPANESE WAY— FROM RIGHT TO LEFT. EXACTLY THE **OPPOSITE** OF HOW AMERICAN BOOKS ARE READ. IT'S EASY TO FOLLOW: JUST GO TO THE OTHER END OF THE BOOK, AND READ EACH PAGE—AND EACH PANEL—FROM RIGHT SIDE TO LEFT SIDE, STARTING AT THE TOP RIGHT. NOW YOU'RE EXPERIENCING MANGA AS IT WAS MEANT TO BE.